* Johnson on Henry Thrale (1781) — in <u>Thraliana</u> —

'Mr Thrale eat voraciously — <u>so</u> voraciously — that encouraged by Jebb & Pepys who had charged me so to do — I checked him rather severely, & Mr Johnson added these remarkable Words. Sir — after the Denunciation of your Physicians this Morning, such eating is little better than Suicide.'

(4. p.61
in <u>Clanson</u>)

DYING TO BE ENGLISH: SUICIDE NARRATIVES AND NATIONAL IDENTITY, 1721–1814

Gender and Genre

Series Editor: Ann Heilmann
Editorial Board: Mark Llewellyn
                    Johanna M. Smith
                    Margaret Stetz

Titles in this Series

Forthcoming Titles

www.pickeringchatto.com/gender

DYING TO BE ENGLISH: SUICIDE NARRATIVES AND NATIONAL IDENTITY, 1721–1814

BY

Kelly McGuire

PICKERING & CHATTO
2012

Published by Pickering & Chatto (Publishers) Limited
21 Bloomsbury Way, London WC1A 2TH

2252 Ridge Road, Brookfield, Vermont 05036-9704, USA

www.pickeringchatto.com

BRITISH LIBRARY CATALOGUING IN PUBLICATION DATA

McGuire, Kelly.
Dying to be English: suicide narratives and national identity, 1721–1814. –
(Gender and Genre)
1. Suicide in literature. 2. Nationalism in literature. 3. Self-sacrifice in literature. 4. Women in literature. 5. English fiction – 18th century – History and
criticism. 6. Literature and society – Great Britain – History – 18th century. 7.
Women – Suicidal behavior – Great Britain – History – 18th century.
I. Title II. Series
823.5'09353–dc23

ISBN-13: 9781848931107
e: 9781848931114

Typeset by Pickering & Chatto (Publishers) Limited
Printed and bound in the United Kingdom by the MPG Books Group

CONTENTS

For Kyle

... atque in perpetuum, frater, ave atque vale.

ACKNOWLEDGEMENTS

This project was supported by SSHRC doctoral and postdoctoral fellowships, and the assistance of libraries at the University of Western Ontario, the University of British Columbia and the University of Toronto, as well as the Huntington Library and the Charles E. Young library at UCLA.

Earlier versions of Chapter 3 and a section of Chapter 4 first appeared in article form: Chapter 3 as 'Corruptible Bodies: Suicide and the Aesthetics of the English Malady in John Shebbeare's *Lydia; or, Filial Piety*', in G. Colburn (ed.), *The English Malady: Enabling and Disabling Fictions* (Newcastle upon Tyne: Cambridge Scholars Press, 2008), pp. 95–123, and a section of Chapter 4 as 'True Crime: Contagion, Print Culture, and Herbert Croft's *Love and Madness; or, A Story too True*', *Eighteenth-Century Fiction*, 24:1 (2011), pp. 55–75. I thank Cambridge Scholars Press and the editor of *Eighteenth-Century Fiction* for their permission to reproduce this material.

I am deeply fortunate in having had the opportunity to learn from the best of mentors, and most incisive of critics, Alison Conway, who has challenged me from the moment I met her, in more ways than one. I also owe debts of gratitude to Mary Helen McMurran for her lucid criticism of this work in its early stages, to Kristina Straub for her thoughtful comments and supportiveness, and to Mark McDayter for his encouragement and invaluable advice. I thank Felicity Nussbaum for recommending a 'fallow season'. Having benefited from the insight of exceptional scholars, I alone bear responsibility for the shortcomings of this book.

I have been fortunate to find in my colleagues at Trent University a warm and supportive family. I extend my thanks to the entire English department, and acknowledge the support particularly of Lorrie Clark, Kathryn Chittick, Charmaine Eddy, Sara Humphreys, Zailig Pollock and my past and present chairs, Suzanne Bailey, Elizabeth Popham and Margaret Steffler. Paulette Nichols has been a constant source of good cheer and encouragement. The dedicated students at Trent have deepened my understanding of and enthusiasm for this period immeasurably.

Lisa Zeitz has been a steadfast and stalwart friend. Her funds of generosity are boundless, and to her and the kindness of her spouse, Peter Thoms, I owe some of my fondest memories of eastern Ontario. Melina Baum Singer has also offered unwavering support, and has been the truest of friends in all the time I have known her, but most especially during the writing of this book. Anderson Araujo offered cogent criticism on early versions of several of my chapters and was a good friend besides. I am also fortunate to be able to count as a friend Suha Kudsieh, whose warmth and goodwill are unsurpassed. I am grateful to Sally Chivers, for her collegiality and for therapeutic dog walks, which sustained me in the darkest hours of revision. I also thank the entire Martin family for kindnesses I can never reciprocate but will always remember.

I offer my eternal thanks to my selfless and kind-hearted brother, Kyle, who inspired this work, and to whose memory it is dedicated. I also owe immense debts of gratitude to my parents who epitomize the meaning of 'sacrifice', and to my ever-supportive siblings and their spouses, Kari and Jeff, Kevin and Michele, and my nephews and niece, Liam, Sean, Declan, Fionn and Abi. I offer my warmest appreciation to Susan Canfield, Ann McGuire, Mary Rose McGuire, Cheryle Munn, Barbara Bell and all the other members of my immense extended family who are too many to name but all important in their own unique ways. My heartfelt thanks and love to Salma and Malachi, and to Aliya, who has taught me everything about life in her nineteen months of exuberant existence. Finally, my deepest appreciation goes to my brilliant reader, critic and love, Mohammad Salama, for keeping close amidst distance and seeing it all with an unsurpassed insight and clarity. My greatest debt is by far to him.

Finally, I offer my deep appreciation to Ann Heilmann, the Gender and Genre Series Editor, and to Mark Pollard and the editors and anonymous readers at Pickering & Chatto, for their astute comments and general helpfulness.

PREFACE

In the *Space of Literature*, the French literary theorist and philosopher Maurice Blanchot poses a series of questions that many eighteenth-century novels sought to answer: 'Is suicide always the act of a man whose thought is already obscured, whose will is sick? Is it always an involuntary act?'[1] With the cultivation of the human sciences, suicide and the series of vexing questions it provokes came under particular scrutiny. Whereas early in the eighteenth century suicide was ascribed to demonic temptation, by the end of the Enlightenment this attitude had, in the view of the historian Georges Minois, 'given way to a secularized view' that suicide was 'a problem that lay somewhere between society and individual psychology. Individual responsibility was diluted to become part of a complex whole in which the criminal was transformed into a victim – the victim of his own cerebral physiology'.[2] This rhetoric of victimhood served the ends of both church and state, since it precluded the possibility of active choice in the disposal of one's life, which in theory continued to belong to the higher institutions. Thus various forms of determinism in this period all reinforce the notion that suicide never represents a completely voluntary or rational act.

Undertaking a genealogy of suicide in the eighteenth-century novel, this study attempts to elucidate how eighteenth-century suicide narratives are shaped by and in turn participate in the period's production of discourses of gender and national identity. The eighteenth century presents a particularly rich field of inquiry for suicide research; the expansion of print culture established a veritable industry of sermon literature, medical literature and prose fiction, among other forms, none of which was held distinct from the other in the sense that disciplines are carefully divided today. Today's 'interdisciplinary movement' itself speaks to the extent to which we rigorously section off areas of inquiry, and in fact looks back to the eighteenth century for a model of the blending of fields of research and critical engagement. This confluence of genres makes available and in turn promotes discussion of suicide, an act that emerges as a crucial subject of interest in the so-called Age of Enlightenment, when emphasis on individual autonomy and self-determination become more pronounced than ever before.

As the period in which suicide gradually came to be viewed less as a sin than a product of insanity, the 'long eighteenth century' offers a particularly rich albeit understudied landscape for this study. This process is not as straightforward as relatively recent histories of suicide, including Michael MacDonald and Terency Murphy's *Sleepless Souls: Suicide in Early Modern England* (1990) and Minois's *History of Suicide: Voluntary Death in Western Culture* (1999) would have us believe. Both studies trace a narrative of secularization, relying heavily on the decisions of coroner's juries that increasingly delivered the *non compos mentis* ('not of sound mind') as opposed to the *felo de se* (literally, 'felon of oneself') verdict as the century progressed.[3] However, more recent work has met these claims with suspicion, pointing to the preponderance of evidence drawn from records of popular opinion and the press suggesting that 'leniency' did not necessarily characterize reactions to and ways of dealing with voluntary death in this period.

Paradoxically, we see this 'reality' reflected most vividly in the fictional space of the novel. The confluence of discourses of suicide and martyrdom suggests that even as the representation of suicide becomes more acceptable in the novel, it remains inflected by residual moralistic tendencies. On the surface of things, it might appear that the picture of suicide in the eighteenth century is quite different from how we view it today, but is this in fact the case? Do suicide and sacrifice remain related terms in contemporary discourse? To what extent have we abandoned this identification of suicide and sacrifice, and is it possible that our treatment of suicide today could tell us something about our 'secularist' assumptions and perhaps even expose the tenacity of the moral imperatives that managed to survive the Age of Enlightenment?

More recent work on the modern history of suicide sheds some illumination on these questions. For instance, John Weaver relates in *A Sadly Troubled History: The Meanings of Suicide in the Modern Age* (2009) that the suicide notes of women – specifically, older women – present 'ideas of self-sacrifice' that often function to strengthen resolve and intent.[4] However, as Weaver explains, men also 'deflect an anticipated charge of cowardice by pointing to altruism or chivalry in their self-destruction'. Sacrifice could be coupled with the idea of the breadwinner' in their final notes.[5] The picture of suicide in Weaver's meticulous and sensitive reading of suicide notes and case studies in Australia and New Zealand suggests that the language of sacrifice is often invoked in at least a rhetorical sense in the last communications of individuals who have accomplished their aim of self-destruction. Sacrifice, then, might be seen as a significant component of intentionality in the structure of modern suicide. But how does it figure in the reception of the act? Which is to say, are 'survivors' of suicide, and even society in a more general sense, likely to look for sacrificial motives as they respond to cases of self-inflicted death? This is a difficult question to answer given the emotionally charged nature of the inquiry: survivors might react to suicide with anger at the deceased for leaving them behind or not permitting them to offer more assistance, or with extreme dismay and incomprehension that renders objective analysis nearly impossible. Meanwhile, survivors might be inclined through sheer affection to see their loved ones as victims and hence martyrs of a social system that has failed them, or to assign them basically altruistic motives so as to preserve the exalted image of the deceased beyond the point of death. The social tendency to judge those who have ended their lives presents a further impediment to 'reading' suicide.

We no longer punish the bodies of those who have taken their lives by symbolically executing them for an unlawful act and burying them at a crossroads with a stake through their hearts, but the attitudes informing this brutal reaction to suicide still persist, albeit in a more diluted form. The residue of judgement lingers almost adhesively, confused as it can often be with sympathetic and well-meaning but misdirected indignation on behalf of 'those left behind'. Stigma is a loaded term, but in the case of suicide, it is seemingly insurmountable. One might lament openly a friend whose life has been claimed by a terminal disease, but it is with more muted tones or perhaps not even at all that we articulate our feelings about dear ones who have claimed their own lives. There is no public space for suicide, it seems, although in some ways, it is the most public of acts. Even when carried out in private, suicide thrusts the cast-off body into the realm of forensic pathology and the criminal justice system, not to mention the courthouse of public opinion, where endless speculation regarding the motives, psychology, and even morals of the deceased ensure that nothing private whatsoever regarding the life and the death of that individual might remain. Yet, the mourning of suicide remains a deeply private act, which serves as a further impediment to understanding or even coming to terms with this most elusive and distressing of deaths.

What I am arguing in part is that empirical evidence largely discounts the claims of the 'medicalization thesis', summed up so evocatively by Zohyreh Bayatrizi in her recent sociology of mortality: 'The modern Western imperative to subject suicide to scientific objectification stripped the self-killer of any claim to subjective meanings and intentions: if he killed himself, he was merely driven by social or psychological forces'.[6] In support of her argument regarding the pervasiveness of our tendency to pathologize suicide, Bayatrizi observes that even the 'actions of suicide bombers are sometimes explained in terms of underlying psychopathological factors'.[7] Hence, even in the presence of strongly compelling causes for which one might die – religiosity, patriotism – we cannot resist the pathological turn. As Bayatrizi argues, this pathologization of suicide divests the individual of any degree of agency in his or her death. While she is correct in her assessment of the effect of the 'compulsory ontology of pathology', she and most other theorists exaggerate the extent to which medicalization intervenes in the reception of suicide to prevent the deceased from carrying responsibility for her death. The inevitability of judgement that I referred to earlier suggests rather that the project of pathologization is neither complete nor wholly successful. In popular opinion, the suicide retains a degree of agency and hence responsibility for the wilful abrogation of life. In this regard, the medicalization thesis is persuasive but totalizing, and hence must be qualified to take into account the strongly moralistic terms in which the non-medical community (which is not to suggest that doctors are exempt from these attitudes) evaluates suicide today. In this sense, in our popular attitudes we have more in common with the eighteenth than the nineteenth century. Just because suicide falls under the purview of medicine does not mean that compassion necessarily follows from seeing it as the result of mental illness.[8] A more compassionate response to suicide would require attitudes towards mental illness to change fundamentally; too often, we respond to mental illness with the same attitudes levelled at suicide: dismissing both as the signs of failure, weakness, irresponsibility, etc. Furthermore, even if we acknowledge a degree of agency in suicide, or even venture so far as to see suicide as a kind of agency, does moral judgement necessarily have to follow from the refusal to read every suicide as a symptom, expression, or result of mental illness?

Perhaps owing to the 'climate of discomfort' that dominates discussion of a topic that remains largely unmentionable,[9] and 'the powerful residual traces of suicide's history of shame' that impose strictures upon the discourse of suicide,[10] we do not always pause to consider carefully our critical responses to suicide, especially those that pertain to gender. Do we respond differently to female than to male suicide? Which is to say, are we more likely to judge a man as 'weak' for having taken his own life? Do we react to reports of a woman's suicide with more surprise, as if one sex is more naturally 'immune' to suicide than the other? Do we see suicide as a masculine or a feminine act? The public health specialist Howard Kushner provides a useful entry point into the debate with his work on the history of suicide in the west. According to Kushner's reading, historically 'Suicide among women was portrayed as an individual emotional act, and thus inconsequential, while male suicide was seen as a barometer of national economic and social well-being'.[11] However, in eighteenth-century Britain, when suicide becomes tied to an understanding of national identity, female self-destruction acquires a wider significance, especially as represented in literary narratives, as I show in this study.

More particularly, this study argues that the novel participates in the construction of a national consciousness through its deployment of a particularly gendered form of suicide reconstituted as sacrifice. Although I agree with the argument that the novel as a cultural instrument works to forge identities, this study contends that this genre produces a sense of national identity and authority consolidated not so much through the loss as through the voluntary forfeiture of one kind of identity in exchange for another. The concept of the nation as founded upon a notion of sacrifice is central to these texts' understanding of female suicide; in eighteenth-century novels, this concern with sacrifice is linked with self-destruction, which becomes both an indicator of the pathology of Englishness and a measure of personal autonomy. This study thus connects women's self-accomplished death with an idea of Englishness, and more broadly, with concerns of the British nation, which in many standard accounts, represents a fictive community that cannot accommodate suicide, or even women, as Partha Chatterjee suggests (albeit in relation to racial as opposed to gender identity) in his seminal essay 'Whose Imagined Community?'.[12] I also consider how women participate in the formation of a national subject: do women as 'boundary subjects'[13] participate simply through their evacuation from the entire system? This investigation offers a corrective to the notion that women participate in national affairs in an exclusively metaphorical way, where men's relations to national identity are by contrast metonymic and contiguous.[14] My book accordingly interrogates what happens when the sign of femininity strays beyond the strictly symbolic realm and ceases to be metaphorical. I argue that novels highlight suicide in a manner that ties the act to national concerns and allows it to venture beyond the realm of the symbolic. As suicide 'goes public' the act acquires increasing social and transformative relevance to women's status as private beings.

The increased prominence of the novel as a product of and as *producing* cultural discourse intersects neatly not only with the development of a national 'idea' but also with the imagination of the English nation as the bastion of an inordinately suicidal culture. Suicide and the English become synonymous over the course of the century, an identification that the novel thematizes recurrently, from Eliza Haywood's amatory fiction of the 1720s to Frances Burney's domestic novels both before and after the French Revolution. This study spans that period from 1721 to 1814, taking as its point of departure Haywood's early writings that come on the heels of the 'birth of Britain', and concluding with Burney's last novel, which examines a quite different but no less vexed nation, beset with paranoia and fears fuelled by events across the English Channel. Yet, I would like to clarify that I am not arguing that the novel actively constructs the nation, but rather that it serves as a precondition for the sensibility that comes to be identified with an emergent national consciousness in this period.[15] The title of this book – *Dying to be English* – suggests that suicide was England's malady, rather than a problem associated specifically with Britain. This identification has much to do with the fact that 'Britain' as a 'nation' was a work in progress in the eighteenth century (and arguably continues to be). There were many different 'Britains', and many subjects of Britain – particularly the Scots – preferred to see the malady as a specifically English problem with which they did not identify. As I discuss in Chapter 1, writers like Eliza Haywood employ the term 'British' with a specific understanding, which is by no means consistent or coherent across the period. Except where otherwise indicated, 'Englishness' more than 'Britishness' is my concern in this study, although the practical interchangeability of the descriptors, both in the period under discussion and in the present, confirms Kathleen Wilson's claim that national identities in eighteenth-century Britain were inherently 'episodic and unstable'.[16] As Wilson argues, 'Britishness and Englishness were not immutable and eternal formations, but sites of struggle whose tropes of representation are specific to particular periods'.[17] Suicide, as both a challenge to collective stability and a mode of defining the nation's character, demonstrates just how precarious the idea of 'belonging' at the heart of national identity formation can actually be.

In the so-called 'grand narrative' of the history of ideas, suicide emerges as a set of multiple discourses, nebulously defined and produced within discussions of the English Malady, the so-called 'Werther effect' and questions of national identity, which are central to the novel's engagement with the problem of suicide. The interrelatedness of writings of all disciplines in the period renders a straightforward history of suicide impossible and necessitates a genealogy of subjugated knowledge and overlooked experience, one that looks to both so-called 'classic' novels such as Samuel Richardson's *Clarissa* and less recognized works like Herbert Croft's *Love and Madness* for clues to untangling the cultural web of the 'secret history' of suicide. My introductory chapter offers a genealogy of suicide in the period, positioning this act as a contingent phenomenon shaped by the discourses of natural law, commodity culture, Protestantism, emergent ideas of nationhood and gendered notions of sacrifice. As suicide becomes a phenomenon to be managed, studied and ultimately contained in this period, print culture is both implicated in this project and stands apart from it in conceptualizing, often through the language of sacrifice, various ways in which suicide (either the act or the contemplation thereof) might function as an expression of individual autonomy.

Chapter 1, 'Suicide and Spectrality in Eliza Haywood's Amatory Fiction', explores how self-destruction consolidates a sense of community set against an English elite society but nonetheless associated with an emergent sense of Britishness. One of the earliest female social critics to comment on the problem of the English Malady, Haywood represents self-inflicted death less as a part of the 'human condition' than as specific to the newly constructed British nation and its culture. Suicide authenticates female desire in Haywood's early fiction, even as it works to establish female sacrifice as the precondition for the integrity of the larger community, in itself inextricably bound up in an emergent idea of the nation. A narrative that at first glance appears to advocate the disciplining of a recalcitrant female body, Haywood's *The British Recluse* ultimately recuperates a suicidal subjectivity as the foundation for an alternative community of British subjects. In her early work, suicide is a spectral figure that in turn exposes the spectral aspect of the nation and, specifically, women's places within it. Spectrality functions as a trope suggestive of women's intermediary positions, revealing the extent to which suicide itself lacks the ontological finality of death and the material reality of existence. Ultimately, Haywood advocates a Mary Astell-like plan of female retirement as an alternative mode of agency that does not, however, fall under the rubric of 'domestic ideology'.

In Chapter 2, '*Mors Voluntaria*: Clarissa and the Agency of Martyrdom', I examine Samuel Richardson's construction of Clarissa as a modern-day Lucretia integral to the development of a larger sense of Englishness and community predicated on a 'republic of letters'. *Clarissa* is central to the novel tradition of the eighteenth century, as evidenced by the tendency of later novels to return to the problems broached by Richardson, particularly in relation to female sacrifice, martyrdom and mourning, themes that are deeply implicated in a development of national consciousness. In its treatment of voluntary death, *Clarissa* affords a glimpse of an alternative conception of agency that, though far from empowering, nonetheless allows for some limited degree of self-determination on the part of a character circumscribed on every side by social and familial constraints. It is precisely in his construction of Clarissa as a 'new Lucretia' that Richardson accords to her a source of agency that renders her suicide foundational to a larger sense of community and nationhood. Whereas in his preoccupation with her 'chastity suicide' Augustine overlooks the national resonance of Lucretia's final act, Richardson foregrounds this aspect of her story by representing suicide as a locus of power in Clarissa rather than simply a capitulation to extant social codes. Clarissa's suicide is an intersubjective act, predicated on a notion of a 'social self' and an epistolary form defined more by the communal than the individual. Paradoxically, Clarissa realizes a form of discursive agency precisely by locating its source in the larger community, and this is the very act that imparts to her death the structure of martyrdom. Ultimately, Richardson vexes the boundary between suicide and self-sacrifice by drawing upon heterodox religious discourses and by elaborating an atavistic form of selfless suicide in Clarissa.

Chapter 3, 'English Maladies and Material Culture at Mid-Century', engages directly with the role of the English Malady in formulating a sense of pathological Englishness intimately connected to the monument culture of the period and its aestheticizing of sacrifice. The symbolic repositories of commemoration in John Shebbeare's *Lydia* (1751) stage a peculiar form of mourning that is intimately tied to sacrifice and suicide. The novel carves out alternative meanings of suicide and in some instances, as seen in this section, explores the possibilities of a 'feminine' basis for national identification through a retrieval of a melancholic sensibility of commemoration. Shebbeare's project involves rehabilitating the material bases of national identity by grounding it in a culture of 'authenticity' that serves as a corrective to an English taste for the very luxury items that, for Shebbeare, are both causes and symptoms of the English Malady.

Chapter 4, 'The Pathology of Sentiment: Politics, Sacrifice and Wertherism in the English Novel of Sensibility', reveals that canonicity is not a prominent concern in this book, which considers so-called 'potboilers' like *Love and Madness,* Herbert Croft's redaction of James Hackman's notorious murder of Martha Ray and subsequent suicide attempt, to be just as relevant as more canonical works to an understanding of the construction of suicide in relation to the popular culture of the day. This chapter narrows the discussion of material culture to a focus on print culture and its dissemination of emotional and social 'contagion' through the so-called 'Werther effect'. This chapter also engages with the notion of a cultural death drive deployed through the spectre of revolution and in turn contained by the assertion of the principles of a providential poetic justice at work in the novel of this period. In Croft's *Love and Madness* and Charlotte Smith's *Desmond,* a concern with intertextual contagion specifically concentrated on the figure of 'young Werther' places suicide squarely at the centre of 'Jacobin' and revolutionary discourse. This chapter broadens the 'gender debate' by considering in more depth the issue of male suicide in relation to the cult of sensibility that flourished during this period. The reduplication of a Werther, who briefly inhabits James Hackman's body in *Love and Madness* and then proceeds to infiltrate Smith's Jacobin novel (a form in which both male Werthers and female Rousseauian Julies proliferate), speaks not so much to a lack of originality or a susceptibility to textual contagion on the part of English authors, as to the dynamic appeal asserted by this intertext. As Werther's textual body organizes the discourse of suicide in this novel, his suicidal subjectivity brings to the foreground of national debate the reality of suicide, which subsequently produces the idea of a transnational community that was inimical to British conservatism.

Chapter Five, '"The Death of Reason": Vitalism, Transnational Identity and Frances Burney', returns to the revolutionary evocations of suicide, examining the impact that a transition from a mechanist to a vitalist outlook at the end of the eighteenth century asserts on Frances Burney's representation of suicide in her final two novels, *Camilla* (1796) and *The Wanderer, or Female Difficulties* (1814). Vitalist views, translated into practice by transnational organizations like the Humane Society (originally founded in Amsterdam as the 'Institution for Affording Relief to Individuals Apparently Dead from Drowning'), appear to destabilize the 'nationalization' of suicide, but, as *Camilla*'s suicide narrative demonstrates, actually work to consolidate a notion of voluntary death as a distinctly British phenomenon. In arguing that Burney's representation of the suicidal body ultimately becomes a larger metaphor for a vitalist conception of the nation in *The Wanderer*, I explore how Frances Burney's ambivalence to an idea of the nation is figured through her representation of suicide.

The political possibilities of discourses of voluntary death become heightened rather than diminished by events of the late eighteenth century, and for this reason, the final two chapters of this book are devoted to tracing and uncovering the interpenetration of discourses of sacrifice and suicide in novels of the latter part of the eighteenth century. In this sense, the 'funereal and thanophilic character' that is central to official Western national culture[18] asserts no less of a presence in the English novel, which continually represents suicide yet deflects its usual associations with 'deviant' and 'unpatriotic' behaviour. In all of its chapters, this book focuses fundamentally on the connection between the nation and death, a link that had been firmly established long before Benedict Anderson began his study of the socially constructed nation in *Imagined Communities* (1983) with this premise. Despite Anderson's insistence that mortality organizes the nation, his account lacks the pathological component that most contemporary discussions attribute to the nation as a result of its exclusive, alienating and hegemonic contours.[19] The English Malady and the concomitant notion of an English affinity for suicide were more instrumental in shaping a pathological sense of Englishness than is often acknowledged. In the eighteenth century, the nation itself was seen as a malady, the product of luxury, civilization and nerves, but above all, was defined by *voluntary* death. Yet, in these constructions, contagion functions as a unifying force, engendering the ability to overcome difference in the act of sympathy and commiseration. Hence we find that the experience of acute physical suffering, as delineated intimately and exhaustively by George Cheyne's confessional 'Case of the Author' in *The English Malady* (1733), is at once profoundly individualistic and strikingly communal, constitutive of basic affective relations between one afflicted subject and another, between an imaginary ward of patients and the space of a nation. This masochistic model of national commiseration becomes slowly but inexorably translated into the novel in its simulation of character subjectivity. The eighteenth-century novel thus highlights the intersubjective aspect of suicide rather than the individualism typically associated with the act. Suicide becomes a national and increasingly a transnational concern given that the English Malady and the corresponding myth of the suicidal English suggest an identity forged within a larger European context.

Notes
1. Blanchot, *The Space of Literature*, trans. A. Smock (Lincoln: University of Nebraska Press, 1982), p. 99
2. G. Minois, *History of Suicide: Voluntary Death in Western Culture*, trans. L. G. Cochrane (Baltimore: Johns Hopkins Press, 1999), p. 301.

3. As the historian, Donna Andrew, observes, 'a variety of possible verdicts could be found for someone who had died by their own hand. "Accident" or "visitation of God" were two possible judgements, but most commonly the verdicts were *"felo de se"* (that is, self-murder, premeditated and done in a rational state of mind) or "lunacy"'. Andrew, 'The Suicide of Sir Samuel Romilly', p. 174.

4. J. C. Weaver, *A Sadly Troubled History: The Meanings of Suicide in the Modern Age* (Montreal and Kingston: McGill-Queen's Press, 2009), p. 277.

5. Weaver, *A Sadly Troubled History*, p. 272.

6. Z. Bayatrizi, *Life Sentences: The Ordering of Mortality* (Toronto: University of Toronto Press, 2010), p. 93.

7. Ibid., p. 94.

8. In this respect, I agree with Susan Morrissey, who claims that the moral explanation of suicide did not simply disappear with the emergence of a medical model. S. Morrissey, 'Drinking to death: vodka, suicide, and religious burial in Russia', *Past and Present*, 186 (2005), pp. 117 – 146, on p. 145.

9. Minois, *History of Suicide*, p. 1.

10. L. Woodstock, 'Hide and Seek: The Paradox of Documenting a Suicide', *Text and Performance Quarterly* 21:4 (2001), pp. 247-260, on p. 255.

11. Kushner, 'Women and Suicidal Behaviour: Epidemiology, Gender and Lethality in Historical Perspective' in S. S. Canetto and D. Lester (eds), *Women and Suicidal Behaviour* (New York: Springer Press, 1995), pp. 11-35, on p. 29.

12. Chatterjee, 'Whose Imagined Community?', *Millennium - Journal of International Studies* 20:3 (1991), pp. 521-525.

13. Kristeva, *Nations without Nationalism,* trans. L. S. Roudiez (New York: Columbia University Press, 1990), p. 35.

14. McClintock, '"No Longer in a Future Heaven": Nationalism, Gender, and Race' in G. Eley and R. G. Suny (eds), *Becoming National. A Reader* (New York: Oxford University Press, 1996), pp. 260-283, on p. 262.

15. In this respect I follow Jonathan Culler's cautionary advice in 'Anderson and the Novel' in *Diacritics* 29:4 (1999), pp. 20-39, on p. 23.

16. K. Wilson, *The Island Race: Englishness, Empire and Gender in the Eighteenth Century* (London: Routledge, 2003), p. 4.

17. Ibid., p. 4.

18. M. Redfield, *The Politics of Aesthetics: Nationalism, Gender, Romanticism* (Stanford, CA: Stanford University Press, 2003), p. 59.

19. Our contemporary view of nationalism is somewhat indebted to Hannah Arendt's insistence that 'nationalism is a pathology of citizenship that, having subordinated the state to the idea of the nation, generates a further pathology in a more expansionary notion of nationhood surpassing the boundaries (and therefore the moral limits) of the state'. As paraphrased in R. Beiner, 'Arendt and Nationalism' in D. Villa (ed.), *The Cambridge Companion to Hannah Arendt* (New York: Cambridge University Press, 2000), pp., 44-64. According to the historian, Krishan Kumar, 'The idea that nationalism is something pathological, something at the same time deeply foreign, is part of an English understanding of it. Hence the unwillingness to accept that there is or can be such a thing as English nationalism'. K. Kumar, *The Making of English National Identity* (Cambridge: Cambridge University Press, 2003), on p. 20.

INTRODUCTION: A GENEALOGY OF SUICIDE

I

In a satirical piece entitled 'A Receptacle for Suicides', a contributor to Adam
Fitz-Adam's periodical *The World* (1756) outlines his scheme to 'sanitize' the
experience of 'self-killing' by supplying not only the venue for individuals seeking to end their lives, but also the means by which they might achieve their goal.[1]
Remarking on 'the number of sudden deaths that abound in this island',[2] 'John
Anthony Tristman' invokes England's eighteenth-century reputation as a suicidal nation afflicted by a kind of cultural death drive. The aptly named Tristman
helpfully proposes to 'remedy th[e] inconveniencies' encountered by 'all such of
the nobility, gentry and others as are tired of life' by providing 'convenient apart-
ments' and expeditious methods of self-disposal less shocking to the 'delicacy' of
such individuals than popular means of suicide.[3] The author concludes his maca-
bre, semi-Swiftian excursus by claiming only the heads of suicides as his 'constant
fee, that by frequent dissections and examinations into the several brains, [he]
may at least discover the cause of so unnatural a propensity'.[4] Paradoxically, the
contributor suggests a biological cause for suicide even while identifying the act
as unnatural, thereby reinforcing the divide between the body and nature that
was already conceptualized in the mechanistic philosophy of the period.

In this satire, suicide is denoted by the euphemism 'sudden death', reflecting the Christian concern with the abridgement of and interference with time
that the individual's act of 'rushing into eternity' ostensibly involved. In this
period, the term 'suicide' itself was a neologism arguably indicative of the alteration of attitudes towards voluntary death in the eighteenth century.[5] Walter
Charleton is commonly credited with coining the term in his translation of the
Ephesian and Cimmerian Matrons (1652)[6], although others argue that it was
originally introduced into the English language in the early seventeenth century
by Thomas Browne and adopted decades later by Robert Burton. Regardless of
its origin, the word entered the vocabulary of the novel at roughly the mid-eighteenth century mark. Samuel Richardson's second work, *Clarissa*, is commonly
viewed as the first English novel to employ the term, since it is cited by Johnson's

Dictionary under the entry for suicide, but one can find numerous examples of early novelistic experiments that liberally employ the term.[7] Scholarly opinion holds that the word 'suicide' afforded a more objective, less judgemental alternative to 'self-murder', the term that was still very much in usage at this time, but there is little consensus on this point. The word itself, which constitutes 'bad Latin' in its unorthodox use of a pronoun as a prefix, was probably avoided by philologists and students of the 'Ancients' as a debasement of the Latin language. Hence, the history of the term itself is a vexed one; the invention of the word possibly precipitated the adjustment of attitudes towards the deed it describes, but it is equally conceivable that changing beliefs necessitated a term that was simultaneously technical abstraction and euphemism. Whatever the case may be, by the mid-eighteenth century the word had infiltrated the English vocabulary sufficiently that Richardson could employ the term in *Clarissa* and expect to be understood. With the coining of the word 'suicide', a comprehensive category was introduced that arguably allowed for the progressive narrowing of the understanding of diverse modes of self-destruction available to the human. The invention of the term also brought suicide under the scrutiny of institutional authority and thus rendered it a new object of power.

The satire's concern with the containment and disposal of the suicidal body reflects the medicalization of suicide that gradually took place over the course of the eighteenth century. The projector's scheme and expressed desire to 'open up a few corpses' (to borrow Foucault's catch-phrase) satirically anticipates the quest of scientific research from the nineteenth century to the present day to isolate an organic cause for suicide.[8] The eighteenth-century 'clinic' and organizations devoted to resuscitation like the Royal Humane Society in part initiated these investigations when they vexed the boundary between life and death, and intervened in the efforts of those determined to die. Whereas the satirical persona 'Tristman' devotes his attention to facilitating suicide, the mainstream medical establishment sought out ways to keep the body alive.

This concern with the administration of life denotes a form of 'biopower', according to Michel Foucault, who chronicles the emergence of disciplinary techniques and invisible, increasingly incorporated apparatuses of control, which inaugurated a shift away from the sovereign 'right of power over death' amid the burgeoning of liberal capitalism in the late eighteenth and early nineteenth centuries.[9] The birth of 'biopolitics', however, does not ratify a 'social contract of mutual self-interest and cooperation among free and equal natural persons', as Bruce Jennings emphasizes, but rather erects 'a structure of protection designed to preserve the life of functional, productive, and efficient bodies'.[10] Integral to this renovated approach to death was an altered outlook on suicide for, as Foucault observes, the 'determination to die ... was one of the first astonishments of a society in which political power had assigned itself the task of administering life'.[11] Under this rubric, suicide emerged as a troubling assertion of individual rights, becoming, as Ian Marsh notes, less a 'transgression to be punished, [than] a problem to be managed' in this period.[12] The appearance of this form of internally regulating power has considerable repercussions for any sustained consideration of suicide, an act that, according to Foucault, demonstrates that 'life has [not] been totally integrated into the techniques that govern and administer it; it constantly escapes them'.[13] Although the era of biopower (which for Foucault marks the threshold of modernity[14]) ushers in the privatization of death, suicide stands out as a singularity, at once subjected to and resisting the operations of power.

As the eighteenth century progresses, suicide acquires an increasingly public dimension, originating present-day notions that it is 'an account of a death made warrantable and recorded in the work of a state agency'. As the sociologist Dorothy Smith insists,

> Suicide is not and cannot be simply a characterization of a death. Rather, it ... expresses a relation between state interests, the established frame of reference in which those interests are realized as an array of legally warranted categories, and an event that is constituted as such by practical activities of agents of the state.[15]

As Smith goes on to explain, suicide generates medical records and death certificates and becomes the concern of 'coroners' courts, police work, and the legislative and administrative processes that maintain, articulate, and regulate these'.[16] As such, government and social institutions interrogate all of the particulars of self-inflicted death in a way that posthumously brings the individual back into the biopolitical fold.

The public scrutiny to which cases of suicide have been subjected historically became more focused in the eighteenth century, owing to medical intervention and the proliferation of forms of print media dedicated to scrutinizing the minutiae of everyday life. Indeed, both suicide and martyrdom are often viewed as 'anarchic or rogue manifestations of mortality' that, according to Zohreh Bayatrizi, 'need to be brought under a regime of ordering or given an appearance of orderliness within the institutionally authorized frameworks of public health, penal law, epidemiology and medicine'.[17] The novel as an interactive participant in the public sphere through print culture must be considered another disciplinary framework that exposes suicide to scrutiny, analysis and even, in certain instances, containment. This is not to say that the novel passively reflects ideology; as a genre of the intelligentsia, the novel may even, in the words of Dominick LaCapra, work through ideological 'forces in critical and at times potentially transformative fashion' and 'contain programmatic elements in outlining desirable alternatives'.[18] However, even LaCapra concedes that this is 'not a prominent feature' in many novels, including those that are central to his study, for in crude terms, there is no 'outside' ideology. As a form of meta-politics, the novel may be considered one of many 'literary-aesthetic apparatuses' that, as Tony Bennett notes in his consideration of the 'sociology of literature', belong to 'a broader field of liberal technologies bringing social conduct under the influence of specific regimes of truth and authority'.[19] This study postulates that novelistic works navigate a middle course between passive reflection of and active opposition to ideology, particularly in reference to representations of suicide in eighteenth-century British narrative.

This study's consideration of the novel's representation of self-accomplished death in relation to eighteenth-century conceptions of power and knowledge seeks to recover and historicize gendered meanings of suicide in this period, meanings that Foucault's understanding of the act as a political relation largely overlooks. Foucault's disregard for gender difference stems from the fact that the neutral body he theorizes is persistently masculine, which to a large extent is owing to the fact that he works within the philosophical tradition of Western liberalism.[20] In many of the novels examined in this study, suicide accords agency to novelistic characters typically denied any measure of personal autonomy as a result of their social status. However, since these texts seldom allow suicide to figure as an individual act – which is ironic given the emphasis on the individual in Enlightenment discourse – the agency suicide confers is constantly deferred or displaced onto a higher level of signification or purposiveness through the construction of suicidal sacrifice as a national affair. This is the chief thrust of my argument in this book.

The perception of suicide as a mode of resistance to social control in the eighteenth century was mediated through and obfuscated by the discourse of property rights, which John Locke developed almost in opposition to theories of natural law and their tacit endorsement of instinctual drives. In his *Second Treatise of Government*, Locke maintains that the individual 'has an uncontrollable liberty to dispose of his person or possessions, yet he has not liberty to destroy himself, or so much as any creature in his possession, but where some nobler use than its bare preservation calls for it'.[21] In the late seventeenth century, Locke thus constitutes the body as property of a divine authority, viewing suicide as an appropriation of property to which the individual has no legitimate claim. Over the course of the next century, however, this very attempt to locate the suicidal body within the discursive network of property rights results in precisely the inverse effect of the intended repression; survivors of the deceased (particularly among the upper classes) increasingly resisted the forfeiture of their inheritances to the Crown. The historian Donna Andrew has argued persuasively that the jury decisions regarding suicide cases brought before the Crown 'reflected as much a growing concern with the sanctity of property inheritance as with the secularization of society'.[22] According to this argument, attitudes towards voluntary death changed not because of increasing 'enlightenment' on the part of civil structures of government, but rather owing to emergent notions of property rights.[23] During this period, institutions of power sensed their hold on the body slowly slipping away and consequently rechannelled their energies into other networks of sociological systemization. One of the techniques, as it were, of explaining away the aberration of suicide involved subjecting it to the array of systematizing and normalizing apparatuses that helped construct it as an irrational act. The notion that, as the philosopher Ian Hacking observes, 'one can improve – control – a deviant subpopulation by enumeration and classification,'[24] accounts for the fact that suicide has historically been the subject of sociological statistical analysis. Inevitably, the unexamined notion that suicide constitutes 'deviant' or pathological behaviour distorts statistics and the organization of knowledge from the outset of the formal study of this phenomenon, which consistently grapples with the view that suicide may vex but need not necessarily violate reason.

Given the permeation and institutionalization of this ideological apparatus, this study situates the eighteenth-century novel's treatment of suicide within the discursive categories of the 'natural' and 'unnatural', with closer attention to the form's mediation of the notion of a 'death principle', which logically emerged as a counterpart to the 'life principle' promoted by moralists, members of the clergy and political thinkers. According to Thomas Hobbes,

> A Law of Nature (*lex naturalis*) is a Precept or a General rule, found out by Reason, by which a Man is forbidden to do that, which is destructive of his Life, or taketh away the Means of preserving the same; and to omit that, by which he thinketh it may be best preserved.[25]

This denial of the right to death is essential to the smooth operation of Hobbes's Leviathan state, in which we find precisely this sovereign hold over the life of the subject steadily tightening. Suicide, according to this perspective, co-opts the power of the state over the life of the subject, and constitutes a political act rather than a mortal sin. The state, as Hobbes reads it, depends upon the prohibition of suicide for, if self-preservation ceases to be an issue, then the social contract loses its potency and the 'Leviathan' diminishes into a feeble creature. A suicide, in this sense, can veritably be called a 'crime' against the state and humankind itself. For all intents and purposes, Hobbes politicizes the religious principle that self-love constitutes the most primal human instinct.

Early Christian theologians such as Thomas Aquinas condemned suicide on the grounds that it violated the tenets of natural law. Eighteenth-century moralists also affirm the notion that suicide contravenes the law of nature as they echo Aquinas's insistence that 'everything naturally loves itself' and 'naturally keeps itself in being' in accordance with a built-in divine decree.[26] A 1791 essay in the *Literary Magazine and British Review* offers the opinion that 'self-murder is always an act highly unnatural, and men who do not live in a state of civil society, will never be guilty of it'.[27] The notion that suicide is foreign to a 'state of nature' was consistently reiterated over the course of the century, and often refuted in novels such as John Shebbeare's *Lydia* (1753), when contact with aboriginal cultures disproved the idea that suicide was exclusively a phenomenon of metropolitan consumer culture. The fact that 'nature' was often invoked to illuminate the principles of natural law resulted in considerable slippage between the latter concept and the state of nature in this period.[28] Moreover, critics of the theory of natural law appealed to empirical evidence attesting that inveterate self-loathing might in fact appear to some individuals just as 'natural', or at least that the 'instinct' for self-preservation might be overcome under sufficiently dire circumstances. John Donne's assertion that 'man has a natural desire of dying' clings to the rhetoric of the 'natural' but turns it decisively on its head.[29] Although his thesis might appear to anticipate Freud's controversial 'death instinct', closer examination reveals that the desire for death acknowledged by Donne lacks the destructive component often associated with the Freudian drive, since it rather seeks to translate the individual from body into pure spirit.[30] Suicide, or *biathanatos* (to borrow Donne's coinage), becomes not so much a self-destructive gesture as a self-affirming act that registers one's belief in the afterlife. This much is affirmed in Richardson's *Clarissa*, where the degree to which a character anticipates death becomes a measure of the character's entitlement to a reward in the afterlife.

Not surprisingly, the political economist and philosopher Bernard Mandeville also voices his objection to the notion of an all-conquering instinct of self-preservation. Repudiating the social contract theory, Mandeville observes that 'there are things that a man may have a stronger aversion to than suicide', and 'he that makes death his choice must look upon it as less terrible than what he shuns by it'.[31] This notion of 'the natural', especially as encoded in natural law, drew the criticism of thinkers such as David Hume and Jeremy Bentham, as it came to be conceived that a rational individual might actually choose death over an undesirable life.[32] Hume's controversial essay 'On Suicide' (1783), published during his lifetime only in unauthorized editions, justifies voluntary death on the basis of the resilience of the natural world and its ability to adapt to unforeseeable circumstances and 'accidental occurrences'. According to this reasoning, suicide assumes the status of an accident that lacks the capacity to affect the 'laws of matter and motion' that govern the Newtonian universe. Forcefully arguing that suicide does not compromise the laws of motion, Hume substitutes an understanding of the laws of physical nature for the older rubric of natural law. His argument is predicated on the negative notion that the impact of suicide differs negligibly from that of involuntary death, which is intrinsic to the natural

order. If, in the grand scheme of things, a human being 'is of no greater importance than an oyster', the voluntary death of that individual can scarcely lay claim
to any greater significance.[33] Although Humean scepticism was not particularly
palatable to novelists like Richardson, who would likely have accused the philosopher of 'devaluing' life, the destabilization of categories of 'the natural' that
'the suicide debate' produced inevitably fostered an intellectual climate in which
the status of voluntary death itself was called into question.[34]

From some eighteenth-century perspectives, natural law emerges in this
treatment of suicide as an ideological construct elaborated in order to contain
the 'epidemic' of early Christian suicides. This ideology draws upon the discourse of nature in order to produce itself as natural in turn and thus assume
the backing of divine authority. While eighteenth-century thinkers increasingly
challenged this idea, the novel engaged more generally and perhaps obliquely
with the notion of the natural, and in particular with the persistent treatment of
suicide as an extension of sacrifice that is germane to the discourse of martyrology, which I will revisit in more detail later. For now, it is interesting to observe
that paradoxically, while the 'criminal' or transgressive aspect of suicide could
be mitigated through association with sacrifice, this very sacrifice was ostensibly forbidden by natural law and other forms of ideological management, which
insisted that the body was not one's to sacrifice.

Detractors of suicide apart from Locke uniformly rejected the notion that
the body, be it male or female, was the property of the person inhabiting it. In *A
Discourse of Self-Murder* (1716), John Cockburn insists that 'birth or habitation
makes us subject, and being subjects, we are under laws and government, and
so have no absolute power over our bodies and lives: that is the property and
prerogative of the sovereign'.[35] For writers like Cockburn, suicide constituted a
'double crime', as an offense against both God and the state. Similarly, a tract also
bearing the seemingly ubiquitous title *A Discourse on Self-Murder* (1732) and
tentatively ascribed to Peniston Booth, avers that 'a man's body is not absolutely
his own'.[36] This view would persist into the next century with Immanuel Kant's
emphatic pronouncement that 'Man cannot dispose of himself because he is not
a thing; he is not his own property ... He is not entitled to sell a limb, not even
one of his own teeth'.[37] Kant's mercantile statement conflates the sale of the body
with suicide, a tendency that became common as suicide was increasingly associated with the marketplace. This deontological conception of the body as leased
to the subject on the condition that it remain intact and inviolable unto death
was rejected by sceptics like Hume who, without necessarily advocating the open
sale of body parts, would not have questioned the right of the individual to dispose of his or her members. Indeed, one extrapolation of Hume's contrasting
belief in 'corporeal violability' holds that the human body 'as with any property
has a price'.[38] Hume's implicit approbation of slavery confirms this interpretation

of his attitude towards the body, although he would have assigned a degree of sanctity to the human body contingent upon discriminatory considerations of race. The slavery and suicide debates are highly contiguous not only in their contemplation of the body as a commodity, but also owing to the fact that suicide often afforded a source of agency to the enslaved as a mode of resistance to a corporeal techne of power. These considerations render suicide less a question of individual autonomy than a matter of property rights.

Eighteenth-century debates thus incorporated suicide into the economic context that resulted generally in the commodification of the body. In these deliberations, suicide represented both a political infraction and an economic transgression. In his *Elements of the History of England* (1770), Abbé Millot (Claude François Xavier) comments that

> [C]ommerce levels the distinction of wealth, and every Englishman is a free being, and feels his own importance. Humour, caprice, and whim, are the natural consequences of national liberty .... From the disdain and disgust that everything brings along with it, they will be unhappy ... Hence, undoubtedly, that rage of suicide, whereof England affords so many examples. An Englishman, upon principle, grows weary of living, and quietly says to himself, 'I will live no longer'.[39]

The Abbé's assessment of the English culture of suicide merely reiterates popular continental opinion of the country's melancholic cultivation of voluntary death. This so-called 'character flaw' was excused both internally and externally on the grounds that high suicide rates were a necessary corollary of the civil liberty on which England prided itself, and even rendered a condition of British virtue in popular medical works like George Cheyne's *The English Malady* (1733).[40] According to this standard Whig 'functionalist' position, their relative degree of autonomy empowered the English both to act as free agents and to commit suicide, an action that was typically seen as uncommon in nations where individual rights were relatively restricted. Hence, as literary critic Eric Gidal observes, European accounts situate England's 'civic melancholy' somewhere 'between enlightenment and pathology'.[41] As a result of this peculiar correlation of liberty with voluntary death, a paradox resides at the heart of English character that is never wholly resolved in either foreign or domestic discussions of the matter. This constructed sense of 'cultural difference' allocates to England a distinctive identity, albeit one contoured around negativity and a social stigma.

Beginning in the eighteenth century, the publicization of suicide rendered the phenomenon an index of the social health of the nation. This study explores the implications of the fact that the English were perceived in popular and elite thought as being more suicidal than their European counterparts, that on an individual level they were casualties of the judicial, civil and religious institutions presumably securing them the ability to take their own lives in the first place.

More significantly, in the eyes of social theorists the consolation that this suicide-mania was a by-product of British advancement as a 'civilization' overshadowed the social import of the supposedly high suicide rate. In this sense, suicide was merely annexed to luxury and effeminacy as the supposed after-effects of civilization. In order for one to live well, this logic argued, one must be prepared to die unwell, or at the very least prematurely. An early consumer-culture mentality presupposed that even death was a commodity that was available for the purchasing, as the satirical business venture discussed at the commencement of this introduction suggests. Further, the association of suicide with incipient consumerism heightened the sense that it was an unnatural act, a mere product of the artifice of civilization and a source of the pathological nature of the concept of the nation. The literary critic Margaret Higonnet has accurately described suicide as historically occupying 'the site of the Other, as both a feminine gesture and a sign of cultural alterity',[42] but the English fall outside of this paradigm, to a certain extent embracing and perpetuating the notion of their 'eternal disposition ... to suicide'[43] in at least the first half of the eighteenth century.

Prior to the rise of print media and as early as the seventeenth century, the London Bills of Mortality promoted the notion of a nationwide suicide pandemic. The figures tabulated in these bills supplied material evidence to authors of treatises against suicide like John Prince who in 1709 reported that 'there have been no less than thirty eight persons that destroyed themselves the last year in and about London only, as appears by the last Bill of Mortality'.[44] The reliability of the Bills as an accurate source of information concerning the higher rates of voluntary mortality in London as opposed to other European urban centres was frequently challenged on the basis of flawed methodology and the absence of a comparable source of statistics outside the country. My goal, however, is not to afford empirical evidence for eighteenth-century national stereotypes, but rather to begin to answer the questions posed so cogently by literary critic Max Novak in the closing remarks of his review of Georges Minois's *History of Voluntary Death*: 'If ... there was no English Malady, why was the idea embraced so eagerly by both the English and foreigners? What did it mean for the English to think of themselves as prone to suicide in both their literature and in the way they lived?'[45] This study locates the answer to this problem in the eighteenth-century English novel's negotiation of national and gendered identities.

II

In the preface to *The Deist's Manual: Or, A Rational Enquiry into the Christian Religion* (1705), Charles Gildon retracts an earlier defence of suicide offered on behalf of his (unlawfully) deceased friend, Charles Blount, and declares himself 'perfectly convinc'd, that Suicide is not lawful'.[46] However, notwithstanding his recantation, Gildon allows that 'it is sometimes a Virtue to Destroy our selves, or Voluntarily to Sacrifice our Lives for the Good of our Country, from this Maxim, That this Publick Good should be Prefer'd to any Particular'.[47] This qualification depends upon a clear distinction between suicide and self-sacrifice: 'the Principle of Self-Preservation ought never to be broke, but for the Preservation of that, which secures that of every Individual, that is, by promoting, and defending, the Preservation of the whole Community, to which each Particular owes his own Preservation'.[48] Yet Gildon still considers self-sacrifice a violation of the principle of self-preservation, even as his statement antedates Cèsare de Beccaria's more developed argument that exile does more harm to the national community than suicide.[49] While Gildon does not dispute that 'every Man has a Right of removing himself from one Government, or Nation, to another',[50] he insists that an emigrant remains still 'a Member of Humane Society' and as such, must 'do his Part to contribute to the Good of Mankind some where or other, whereas by destroying himself, he takes himself from all'.[51] Gildon's universalist argument evidently lacks the nationalist thrust of the more specified treatments of suicide in relation to Englishness (and Britishness) that increasingly surface in the ensuing decades of the eighteenth century. In this sense, Gildon lends support to Nicholas Hudson's argument that in the views of many eighteenth-century individuals, 'To sacrifice oneself for the nation or the public was, in an important sense, to embody eternal *human* values – an attitude captured with evidently resonant force by Addison's *Cato* (1713)'.[52] As Hudson argues, the notion of cultural particularity was not yet fully developed in the eighteenth century, although I contend that the novel sows the seeds of precisely such an understanding that would align voluntary death with a nationalist ethos.

Just as Gildon places voluntary death in a transnational context, his 'apology' similarly 'universalizes' gender, ignoring difference and positing a solitary male suicidal subject. In this respect, his work reflects the tendency of many of the suicide-constitutive discourses in the eighteenth century to elide the problem of female suicide. In the satire discussed at the opening of this introduction, the author laments 'the disgraceful methods that persons of both sexes in this metropolis are almost daily taking to get rid of their being'.[53] The obliging and enterprising 'Tristman' subsequently outlines his designs for 'a commodious bath for disappointed ladies, paved with marble ... where the patient may drown with the utmost privacy and elegance',[54] suggesting that the feminization of suicide demands the development of an aesthetics of the act. Women's contribution to the nation's reputation for suicide is acknowledged in this tract, but often overlooked in many of the moral and religious treatises published on the subject of 'self-murder' during this century, culminating with Charles Moore's sweeping dissertation on suicide in 1790, which deviates only negligibly from earlier studies such as John Jeffery's strongly titled, *Felo de se: Or, A Warning against the Most Horrid and Unnatural Sin of Self-Murder* (1702). Although these treatises persistently feminize voluntary death, they typically represent the agents of suicide as male.[55] Some might argue that these pamphlets merely posit a universal subject, although this argument obscures the fact that a neutral subject typically presupposes a masculine one, for as theorist Elizabeth Grosz states, 'the neuter can only be filled in by the male body and men's pleasures'.[56] While non-fiction writings posit a general, albeit highly masculinized (if unmarked) human subject, the subjects of novelistic treatments of suicide are either women, or 'effeminate' men. This book recovers a sense of gendered experience in eighteenth-century representations of and engagements with voluntary death, without subscribing to an essentialist sense of difference, but rather complicating an issue – the gender paradox of suicide – that is too often disregarded entirely in considerations of the subject. Despite the fact that this study deals with gender as opposed to women's experience exclusively, the first two chapters explore how representations of women lay the groundwork for the later novel's treatment of voluntary death. While novels in the first part of the century generally dwell upon the suicidal woman, after the 1750s, they increasingly devote attention to the suicidal male, the victim not only of the gambling hall but also of unrequited love.

The anthropologist, Mary Douglas, observes in *Purity and Danger* (1965) that 'the meanings of male suicides and of female suicides are different in Western societies'.[57] The eighteenth-century novel assumes this very distinction in dwelling on a specifically female form of voluntary death. However, the first well-recognized sociologist of suicide, Emile Durkheim, claimed that women lacked the intellectual development requisite to end their lives; in his view, women were more governed by instinct than men and accordingly more disposed to adhere to a principle of self-preservation.[58] According to this construction, suicide was a male behaviour and a mark of the superiority of the sex. Twentieth-century studies of suicide, such as Henry Romilly Fedden's *Suicide: A Social and Historical Study* (1972), reinforce the notion that women are less inclined to commit suicide than men, arguing that owing to limits imposed on their education, women were less disturbed by 'the unsettling influence of independence of thought, the weight of abstract problems of life and death'.[59] This mindset was pervasive in the eighteenth century, which, outside the literary record, consistently disputed women's capacity for voluntary death. In his historiography of suicide, Howard Kushner addresses this historical tendency to tie 'the disparity between female and male suicide rates to a set of gendered distinctions that conflated physical differences with what was metaphorically feminine'.[60] In his view, 'Social constructions ... as opposed to biological distinctions ... became the operative metaphors used to explain the alleged immunity of women to suicide'.[61] According to this model, women's suicide defies metaphysical social assumptions and is comprehensible only as deviation from traditional gender roles, while male suicide stems from the pressures of everyday responsibilities.

Eighteenth-century responses to literary or actual cases of female suicide were frequently complicated by the fact that under the law and in popular opinion women were denied the degree of agency deemed necessary to take their own lives. In her address to the English Legislature on the subject of *The Hardships of the English Laws in Relation to Wives* (1735), Sarah Chapone raised precisely this point, challenging the legal position that women cannot act as 'free agents' in their own deaths, as indicated by the verdict delivered by the coroner's jury in a case of a 1732 double suicide (ostensibly but never explicitly identified as that of Richard and Bridget Smith), which found the husband guilty of suicide and punished his corpse accordingly, yet purportedly excused the wife on the supposition that she hanged herself 'at the command of her husband'.[62] Chapone took issue with the notion that the law offers exemption from punishment as 'a favour to the weakness of the sex' and construes it rather as a 'fine compliment to the authority of our domestick lords and masters'.[63] The view that a woman possesses insufficient autonomy to take her own life was enshrined at the level of law, as Chapone's address makes clear, in a position that seems to contradict the clear movement towards an association of suicide with all things feminine. Many of the novels considered in this study appear to bolster this position, even while they assign a central position to female suicide. The very conditions that would render women's suicide possible are denied by the cultural codes that limit female agency, and this study suggests that the eighteenth-century English novel restores the historical reality of women's suicide by affording a space for the representation of the phenomenon.

The growing centrality of suicide to the eighteenth-century English novel might be considered the product of a 'feminization' of culture in the eighteenth century, a trend that social and cultural historians argue extended even to religious institutions.[64] In the medical discourse of the day, suicide represents a feminine condition, a sign of a weakened mind or body, while religious discourse similarly attributes the act to a lack of spiritual fortitude, or a feminine openness to temptation or an external tempter. However, in a political sense, suicide might yet denote a heroic and therefore masculine act, albeit one that undermined the authority of the state, while in an economic context, suicide was subsumed into the 'effeminate' continuum of luxury and consumption. Thus, although dominant discourses of the period mostly insist upon an a-suicidal female body, they simultaneously construct suicide as a typically feminine behaviour, suggesting that an understanding of voluntary death is both contingent on and limited by the indeterminate nature of gender itself.

Unlike most suicide historiography that evacuates gender, in *The Art of Suicide* (2001) Ron Brown acknowledges the centrality of gender to these investigations, arguing that 'in the late eighteenth and early nineteenth century new ascriptions arose of suicidal behaviour that were linked to tainted femininity'.[65] To a large extent this consideration is indebted to Elisabeth Bronfen's psycho-analytic work on the subject of the intimate relationship between femininity and death in addition to the implications of the aestheticized sacrifice. In addi-tion to Bronfen and Brown, Silvia Sara Canetto, Howard Kushner and Margaret Higonnet represent a minority of scholars who address the gendering of suicide. Canetto uncovers the 'gender scripts' that inform life-threatening behaviour, while Higonnet's work goes far towards explaining the dominant paradigm in Western culture which affords 'a mythic vision of suicide as feminine',[66] but does not specifically address suicide's bearing on the English novel. Although Hig-onnet historicizes suicide primarily in relation to the nineteenth century, her suggestive essays on this subject formulate their central theses at the expense of the eighteenth century.[67] Accordingly, the details rather than the larger argu-ments of her work are invaluable to this study. Whereas Higonnet locates the feminization of suicide in the nineteenth century, my study argues that suicide as a discourse is already feminized in eighteenth-century contexts, owing partially to the abandonment of the heroic paradigms of the classical tradition borrowed from Greece and Rome.

The fact that suicide as a phenomenon was gender marked during this period renders questions of gender highly relevant to considerations of the subject in relation to the novel. Female characters in these works contemplate suicide repeatedly, and even when their male counterparts commit suicide, they typi-cally do so only by sacrificing their masculinity. This study explores the process whereby suicide produces a gendered body, questioning whether suicide within this context becomes, in effect, to borrow Amanda Gilroy's term, 'a historically specific technology of gender'.[68] In a slight departure from contemporary theo-ry's concern with the 'lived body', my project concerns itself with the 'unlivable body', the body that wants to die.[69] This approach does not, however, advocate a return to the focus on the 'dead body' so central to the mechanistic, Cartesian legacy that some theorists believe still persists today in the assumptions of mod-ern medicine.[70] Instead, the suicidal body situates itself between the moribund and the animate, representing a particularly complex site of gender, unlike other related instances, in which gender ostensibly ceases to signify at the point of death. In its attempt to read suicide as part of a 'cultural politics of the body', this project's approach to gender draws partially upon Judith Butler's discursive understanding of the subject, albeit with an attempt to consider the relevance of the body as a material entity that subsequent feminist constructivist investiga-tions have sought to restore.[71] Just as the body can never entirely divorce itself from discourse, in the eighteenth-century novel the suicidal body stands behind and inhabits the discourse of voluntary death.

Although women's voluntary deaths contributed to the overall 'statistics' that offered empirical corroboration of the English Malady, accounts often overlook the relevance of women's experience to the linking of suicide with the 'nation's business'. While economic discourse constructs woman as the ideal consuming subject, it yet ascribes to her only a limited degree of liberty or self-determination, thereby corroborating Claudia Johnson's proviso that a 'woman's presence in a ... public sphere is not to be confused with her empowerment there'.[72] Literature of the period frequently attributes male suicide to financial ruin incurred by bad investments or dissipated lifestyle: the incapacity to lead a 'good' life impels men to choose a 'bad' death. The same literature presents women as somehow unaffected by and indifferent to material circumstances: their suicide attempts spring not from impoverishment or indigence, but rather from passions unfulfilled and unrequited. Women exist outside and beyond the economic systems of society according to this model, which, as feminist critic Genevieve Vaughn observes, dictates that they 'are brought up with the values that will allow them to do unilateral caregiving, often maintaining both paradigms internally, validating the exchange paradigm even while acting according to the gift paradigm'.[73] This somewhat essentialized and ahistorical notion of capitalist practices positing a system of exchange gendered as male, and identifying the 'selfless' act of gift-giving as female, is nonetheless partially supported by the frequent construction of female suicide as self-sacrifice in the eighteenth-century novel. To a certain extent this view is corroborated by the literary historian, Laura Brown's assessment of the effects wrought by mercantile capitalist ideology upon fiction's representation of the female figure, which subsequently becomes aligned with 'commodification and trade on the one hand, and violence and difference on the other'.[74] Since women have been 'socialized into the belief that their bodies are not theirs',[75] they may dispose of their bodies on the condition that they give of themselves for a higher purpose, thus rendering their suicides (at least in a literary form) simultaneously acts of empowerment and abjection.

In arguing that the novel assigns suicide an intermediate form of agency, I draw upon Srinivas Aravamudan's model for understanding how suicidal behaviour may serve simultaneously as an expression of agency and a strategy of containment on the part of European writers.[76] Female voluntary death in the form of suicide or self-sacrifice does not necessarily endorse victimhood or entail a capitulation to social disciplinary codes. Instead, suicide may afford a productive locus of agency complicated but not annulled by the dense nature of a discourse that can never entirely extricate itself from religious concerns surrounding the action in this period. The authors discussed in this study reveal a certain degree of ambivalence towards the potentially subversive implications of their representations of voluntary death, but their work simultaneously demonstrates the fact that suicide encapsulates a certain degree of independence, and is never entirely susceptible to authorial control in the first place. Authors may attempt to contain the disruptive effects of suicide by preventing their characters from dying, yet once invoked as a sign, suicide continues to inhere in narrative form in the form of a suicidal subjectivity. Even amid the gender constraints that appear to foreclose suicide as an option for women, female characters nonetheless engage in the 'struggle for rhetorical ownership of illness'[77] that increasingly defines discursive engagements with the idea of the English Malady.

III

Suicide was not only symptomatic of larger cultural problems that were eventually organized under the heading of the 'English Malady', but as the century progressed, debates among the *philosophes* in France and scattered remarks by prominent thinkers such as David Hume in England increasingly challenged the bases of its prohibition. A discourse of suicide thus emerges coterminously with the development of the novel as a dominant literary form and vehicle for cultural commentary. Described by Michael McKeon as 'an early modern cultural instrument designed to confront on the level of narrative form and content, both intellectual and social crisis simultaneously', the novel thematizes suicide to the extent of its representational capacity.[78] The genre's willingness to broach the subject of suicide contributed to its condemnation by critics such as Vicesimus Knox who denounced prose fiction's capacity 'to lead innocents to disease, infamy, madness, suicide and a gibbet'.[79] Many eighteenth-century English novels accommodate a kind of 'suicide narrative', a term justified by the prolific body of largely fictional writing on the subject that according to Jeffrey Timmons warrants 'its denomination as a subgenre of philosophical, historical, theological and literary discourses'.[80] Far from operating as a mere plot device or 'surface effect' the modes and means of suicide enact a performance of a death drive at work at the level of narrative, as, in undertaking what might be considered a supreme act of transgression, suicidal characters define themselves by their acts of self-extinction.

The apparent neutrality of novelistic representations of suicide in the eighteenth century has drawn the attention of critics like Timmons, who claims that the form addresses 'not so much as a word of reproach' to its suicidal characters.[81] For some time, critics and historians alike attributed this propensity to the larger forces of secularization at work within society during this period. For example, Michael MacDonald and Terence Murphy's study of the socio-cultural history of suicide in England champions the secularization theory, maintaining that 'During the early modern period attitudes and responses to suicide first hardened and then grew more tolerant and sympathetic'.[82] A central argument of this self-described 'neo-traditional' history of early modern suicide holds changes in the nature of the coroner's jury responsible for the secularization of suicide; as jury members grew increasingly literate, they were able to draw upon a wider range of cultural reference to inform their decisions in regard to suicide verdicts.[83] Mac-Donald's and Murphy's foregrounding of the role enacted by the evolution of communication technologies in altering the way people responded to suicide illuminates the relevance of a historical approach to these issues as they are mediated by the eighteenth-century novel.[84] At the same time, their claims for the secularization of suicide elide the extent to which suicide remained a discourse that could never entirely detach itself from religious considerations, as we see in the frequent conjunction of suicide and sacrifice. As the historian, Rachel Healy argues, following Susan Morrissey's cue, 'the ambivalent role of clergy, the persistence of religious sanctions against suicide, and continued efforts by the state to curb suicide all suggest that the term "hybridization" better characterizes the changes over this period than the older term "secularization".'[85] The history of suicide in the eighteenth century dramatizes a struggle, pull and counterpull, rather than the triumph of the secular over the spiritual, in keeping with the 'project of modernity' more generally, which, as the historian Jane Shaw has argued, was in many respects a deeply religious undertaking.[86]

As discussed in the preface to this book, religion continued to exert an important influence in most segments of society, and had more of an impact upon popular culture than proponents of the 'secularization thesis' often acknowledge. Although Deists and other 'freethinking radicals' sought to detach suicide from ecclesiastical authority, the notion of voluntary death as the product of demonic influence or possession persisted in popular socio-cultural attitudes. A religious strain also permeates the eighteenth-century novel's representation of suicide, which consistently explores the relations between suicide and sacrifice, thus suggesting the tenacity of Christian proscriptions in the eighteenth century. English Protestantism accommodated a nationalist vision bound up in the discourse of 'Reformation martyrology' that was already established in John Foxe's *Actes and Monuments* (1563). Although James C. W. Truman argues that the 'Protestant martyr-subject [was constituted] in discursive terms that were primarily gendered female, even as most martyrs were men,'[87] Elizabeth A. Castelli insists on the contrary that 'within the interpretative framework of sacrifice, martyrdom draws upon and generates ideals of "masculinity".'[88] Truman bases his argument upon a specific text, whereas Castelli's work evokes the tradition of gender-coding in the West according to which masculinity is positively charged in contrast with a feminine negativity that disallows sacrifice and suicide.[89] However, as Castelli notes, 'in the Christian theorizing of martyrdom as sacrifice, gender works in a number of different (and not always ideologically coherent) ways.'[90] Early novels similarly challenge these gender categories even while upholding them, and I argue that the discourse of suicide as mediated through the eighteenth-century novel consistently circles around this aporia in its alignment of (specifically) women's suicide with sacrifice.

By mid-century, suicide has been firmly established as a central feature of the plot and thematic content of the novel, which similarly absorbs a cultural interest in melancholia and mourning. A language of sacrifice that, as Benedict Anderson observes, signifies the persistence of religious paradigms in a burgeoning ethos of nationalism, in turn informs the treatment of suicide in many of the works discussed in this study. These novels represent suicide as a gift of the self, a selfless, ego-effacing social action that gives meaning to the act for both survivors and the agent. Sacrifice thus functions to obscure suicide, suggesting that it is only in constructing death as a gift that female characters in these novels obtain a degree of selfhood. In this respect, the 'system of sacrificial responsibility' articulated in the novel does not imply the 'exclusion or sacrifice of woman', which Derrida sees at work in anthropological, theological and philosophical engagements with the problem of the 'gift of death'.[91] On the contrary, women's deaths are central to a national ethos of sacrifice in the eighteenth century.

This discussion raises the question as to whether women's suicides and identities are always inherently sacrificial. In *Reflections on Marriage* (1700), Mary Astell famously described a woman's marriage to an inferior partner as a supreme 'act of martyrdom',[92] while the vast majority of recent theorists suggest that women can never escape the logic of sacrifice in any aspect of their personal lives. The process of exclusion and repression that constitutes female identity in Judith Butler's view is itself inherently sacrificial, while Julia Kristeva actively solicits a rewriting of the 'sacrificial contract' that binds women to a socio-symbolic order.[93] Accordingly, contemporary feminist engagements with the hermeneutics of female suicide question whether, in the words of Susan M. Wolf, 'women's decisions to commit suicide, and society's acceptance of those decisions as appropriate, may be skewed by a long history of cultural images revering women's sacrifice and self-sacrifice'.[94] Conversely, an alternative perspective, articulated by Diane Raymond, argues that since 'women's historical role has been to endure selflessly all forms of labor and abuse, particularly in the domestic sphere, suicide may for women be the ultimate transgressive act'.[95] This question as to whether suicide represents a disciplining of the female body or an assertion of agency is explored but never quite resolved in the novel. The texts that I focus on in this study express some ambivalence towards this concern; even as they suggest that suicide represents a source of agency, in their attempts to render death symbolically resonant, these authors assimilate self-destruction into the very continuum of sacrifice that was seen as the end of agency in some views. At the same time, many of these works circumvent a strict either/or approach altogether in positing as a third option a hybrid form of sacrificial suicide. Because this notion of sacrifice, predicated on traditional religious notions of voluntary death still persisted in popular thought and practice, suicide could be accommodated under the rubric of sacrifice. Secular and nationalist developments heralded an increasing emphasis on the political sacrifice, involving the subordination of the individual to the collective will, rather than to a conception of divine will, as seen in Charlotte Smith's *Desmond*. Within this shift, a notion of suicide emerges that is nebulous, vague and increasingly difficult to define, notwithstanding the apparent concreteness afforded by the invention of the term.[96]

In his late nineteenth-century consideration of this ambiguity Durkheim observes, 'Because altruistic suicide, though showing the familiar suicidal traits, resembles especially in its most vivid manifestations some categories of action which we are used to honouring with our respect and even admiration, people have often refused to consider it as self-destruction'.[97] However, as Durkheim goes on, this distinction breaks down when one considers its basis in the intentionality and motives of the act, which are difficult to read from the outside, and the fact that even an 'egoistic' suicide, to borrow his term, might have 'its own morality' in its sentiment of individual autonomy.[98] In eliding the distinction between suicide and self-sacrifice (or altruistic suicide), Durkheim is able to bring both forms of voluntary death into his case study. Although he predicates his research upon findings related to the social classifications of nationality and age, avoiding 'innately established' categories such as race and heredity, it becomes increasingly evident over the course of his study that Durkheim's understanding of nationality is deeply imbricated with religion, as seen particularly in his treatment of altruistic suicide.[99] Initially England represents an anomaly, given his fairly conventional argument that the relative freedom accorded to the individual in a Protestant as opposed to a Catholic society renders him or her more susceptible to suicide. Durkheim's statistical findings that by the late nineteenth century the English were less disposed to take their lives than their European Protestant peers initially confute this hypothesis. However, he eventually attributed this anomaly to the fact that the Anglican hierarchical organization of clergy and traditionalist emphasis actually curtailed the subject's liberty and integrated her into society to a degree that discourages flight from the group in the form of suicide. While Durkheim's study ostensibly puts to rest the myth of English suicide, it raises a larger problem in respect to the centrality of other forms of voluntary death more readily accommodated in this culture.

The apparent irreconcilability of Protestant individualism with sacrifice prompts further questions integral to a historicization of female suicide. The scholar of religion, Ivan Strenski, has observed the difficulties that a nationalist ethos creates for the 'traditional Protestant resistance to the ideal of self-effacing sacrifice'.[100] With the emergence of an idea of the 'nation', the individualism associated with Protestant England must somehow find a way to reconcile itself with the needs of the state, thus striking a balance between the community and the subject. Yet, suicide is typically interpreted as a supreme assertion of individuality, one that betrays the larger community in leaving behind survivors to mourn and dependents to support themselves in alternative ways. In this respect, self-accomplished death can be viewed as antithetical to the concerns of a nation that can only endorse voluntary death in the form of sacrifice for the greater good. The novel inscribes a nationalist imperative to frame suicide as self-sacrifice, not just for the purpose of circumventing religious proscriptions, but also in order to advance the idea of the nation that was so central to the form. To a considerable extent, this sacrificial motif is organized around the image of the 'allegorical mother' whose offspring, according to feminist critic Julie Mostov, 'belong to the entire country's guardians, heroes and martyrs ... Th[e] pain, suffering and sacrifices [of individual mothers] are recognized only as part of the nation's sacrifice; their individual plights are relevant only to this extent'.[101] The role of the maternal as a controlling image for the praxis of mourning generally deemed constitutive of national consciousness is present to a certain extent in the novels discussed within this study, particularly in Charlotte Smith's *Desmond*. However, many of these works opt for a more generalized version of femininity that demands a reassessment of 'gender blind' studies such as Anderson's *Imagined Communities*.[102] Although, as many recent accounts have argued, the importance of a monolithic idea of the nation has been rather exaggerated at the expense of a coexisting ethos of transnationalism, the novels considered within this study nonetheless often present their suicides as sacrifices to a national idea that takes shape within the spaces of their narratives.[103] At the same time, the cult of Wertherism that I discuss in Chapter 4, and England's and France's skirmish over their respective national rates of suicide, which is the subject of Chapter 5, reaffirm that national identity is as often fabricated in conjunction with as against a hostile 'other'.

Despite its social concerns, the novel has traditionally been viewed as an essentially 'individualistic and isolationist form'.[104] Conceding that this form represents 'humankind in society', J. Paul Hunter insists that it typically represents a 'single individual – alone – pursuing and reflecting upon his or her place in that society'.[105] However, characters' relations to the larger social contexts in which they are embedded remain crucial, as seen in the intersubjective aspect of suicide.[106] In this sense, the novel, as an aspect of culture, suggests a way of looking at the 'symbolic identity' individuals fabricate when they see themselves as members of a collective, described by the social psychologists, Clay Routledge and Jamie Ardnt, as 'something larger, more meaningful and ultimately, longer lasting than their own physical lives'.[107] Novels afford a crucial space for fantasizing this 'symbolic identity'; they go beyond Benedict Anderson's claim that they help imagine a 'community', for they allow for an imaginative encounter with and transcendence of death through this national identification. As Routledge explains,

> Secular ideologies also make us feel less finite... national and other social identities allow us to feel like we are part of something larger and more meaningful than ourselves. In this way, contributing to our nation, community, company, family and other groups makes us believe that though we will die, part of us will live on through these institutions.[108]

It is this identification that explains the sacrificial impulse, and in particular the tendency to translate self-destructiveness into self-sacrifice. The fact that social identities are so difficult to transcend accounts for this degree of slippage between suicide and sacrifice.

This category of sacrifice, however, is as elusive as an understanding of suicide. Strenski contends in his book on the rhetoric of sacrifice in French politics and political culture that sacrificial language is historically embedded in public discourse, and is inescapable.[109] Pointing to a 'lack of conceptual consensus' about the meanings of sacrifice in theories articulated by Claude Lévi-Strauss, René Girard and Susan Mizruchi,[110] Strenski poses the following set of compelling questions in a slightly later work: 'Is sacrifice a total giving up or a giving *of*? Is it gift, consecration, scapegoating, source of transcendent power, or abomination?'[111] Can it be all of these things at once? As Strenski's work suggests, situating suicide in relation to larger communal and national structures does not necessarily serve to sanction sacrificial models or victim positions; instead, it is possible to locate an alternative form of agency within an understanding of suicide as an act that always partakes of a sacrificial structure: the suicide is both a casualty of society (or biology) and an individual engaged in making a personal decision that also asserts a profound social relevance. A narrative of suicide – told either from the perspective of the suicidal individual, as in the epistolary/dialogical situation constructed in works like *Clarissa* and *The British Recluse*, or from the third-person perspective of Burney's or Shebbeare's works – typically incorporates the sacrificial element ascribed to voluntary death both by its agents and those that mourn their loss. It is for this reason, perhaps, that in its 'secular form' suicide is less an individual than a profoundly social act, especially as represented in novelistic forms.

In *Fables of Aggression*, Frederic Jameson insists that 'representations of death will always prove to be complex displacements of an indirect, symbolic meditation about something else'.[112] Given its associations with the idea of the nation, voluntary death does in fact consistently figure as a sign of 'something else' in the novel, but the meaning of female suicide is never completely left behind either. The novel to a certain extent exploits the gendering of suicide in this period to refigure it as a supreme gesture of sacrifice. Addressed within the context of a range of divergent discourses, suicide eventually takes on the status of a discourse in its own right. Changing perceptions of the nature of the body, its relation to subjectivity and its susceptibility to the operation of power all necessarily shape the discourse of suicide, which also continues to be contoured by issues of gender, as fiction of this period attempts to reconcile burgeoning notions of individual rights with duties to a collective. Ultimately, national narratives and suicide narratives converge in the novel, producing a vision of England as a veritable 'Receptacle for Suicides'.

1 SUICIDE AND SPECTRALITY IN ELIZA HAYWOOD'S AMATORY FICTION

To live an entirely private life means above all to be deprived of things essential to a truly human life: to be deprived of the reality that comes from being seen and heard by others, to be deprived of an 'objective' relationship with them that comes from being related to and separated from them through the intermediary of a common world of things, to be deprived of the possibility of achieving something more permanent than life itself.[1]

In Hannah Arendt's view, an entirely private identity is inherently phantasmatic, lacking empirically verifiable and tangible reality, without permanence and without a future. By the same token, a 'life spent entirely in public, in the presence of others, becomes, as we should say, shallow. While it retains visibility, it loses the quality of rising into sight from some darker ground which must remain hidden if it is not to lose its depth in a very real, non-subjective sense'.[2] For Arendt, both the public and the private are indispensable aspects of the human condition; while the public is artificial and constructed, it is nonetheless the arena in which one emerges fully realized as a citizen, with all the rights and responsibilities integral to this identity.[3] The eighteenth century, described by Adam Ferguson in his *History of Civil Society* (1767) as 'the age of separations',[4] saw a sharpening of the division with the formation of a public sphere,[5] although as Michael McKeon writes, this distinction clearly 'antedate[s] Ferguson's age by many centuries'.[6] Witnessing the emergence of two major cultural constructs – the nation and the novel – the eighteenth century brought the public and the private into productive tension with each other, raising new questions concerning gender identity in the process.

In being relegated to what Arendt terms the 'intimacy' of the private sphere, women lose the ability to relate to the so-called 'real', which is figured as a site of national identification. Even at the moment of Britain's inception as a nation with the 1707 Act of Union, women exist in an uneasy relation to this totality. Feminist theorists like Lauren Berlant contend that Enlightenment discourse veiled 'white male privilege' through the 'rhetoric of the bodiless citizen, the generic "person" whose political identity is a priori because it is, in theory, noncorporeal'.[7] Inevitably, heightened consciousness of national belonging in the wake of the 'birth of Britain' as an official entity in turn raised questions regarding how segments of the population identified with the private sphere might imagine their roles within this entity – the construct of the nation – which has been described by Jacques Derrida as a 'primitive conceptual phantasm of community'. For Derrida, a 'specter belongs to the structure of every hegemony', meaning that every nation is haunted by the minority populations it seeks to eject, an argument that Arendt also makes in relation to her work on totalitarianism.[8] While women in eighteenth-century Britain did in fact live public lives in contrast to their Victorian counterparts, their writing illuminates the ways in which the modelling of a national subject left them without a viable position of their own, in essence rendering them spectral. The 'secret history', a subgenre of amatory fiction that flourished at the beginning of the eighteenth century, represents a kind of ghostly 'internalization of public concerns',[9] according to McKeon, expressing an ambivalence towards national identity characterized by both a yearning for and a resistance to belonging. This writing predates the literature of 'female complaint' that Lauren Berlant traces back to the nineteenth century, but it nonetheless like other 'complaint genres of "women's culture"'... foreground[s] a view of power that blames flawed men and bad ideologies for women's intimate suffering, all the while maintaining some fidelity to the world of distinction and desire that produced such disappointment in the first place'.[10] Suicide figures largely in this writing as a metaphor for women's displacement within the social body.

Female characters in novels like Eliza Haywood's *Love in Excess* (1721) and *The British Recluse* (1722) inhabit precisely the Arendtian illusive private space; Haywood, however, renders it a site of subversion and meaning making. Part of the 'triumvirate' of early eighteenth-century women novelists in England, Haywood's affinity for offering a personal and intimate chronicle of a woman's life is reflected in the titles of many of her early works. These novellas typically construct a 'secret' history of voluntary death in which the female desiring subject emerges as a crucial agent in the course of human affairs. Aligned with the ordinary and the commonplace, suicide in Haywood's novellas marks an abridgement of the fantastic strain of the amatory plot in favour of a more expansive concern with women's experience in the public and private spheres. In this respect, Haywood's early fiction employs the modes of amatory fiction and the closely related secret history, but it also draws upon the cultural realities of its contemporary situation in foregrounding the act of suicide as not just a feature of plot – a convenient exit strategy – but rather as a critical social and national concern.

Voluntary death is a defining feature of Haywood's amatory fiction, and the explanation for its presence extends beyond the standard cliché that as victims of a patriarchal system which treats them merely as objects of desire, women are left with no option beyond self-destruction. Considering the gender-related implications of the 'love suicide' and arguing that suicide functions as more than a mere trope of amatory fiction, this chapter focuses upon Haywood's early works, since they best exemplify the suicidal strain in amatory fiction of the early eighteenth century. Haywood introduces a specific kind of 'suicide narrative' to the early novel through amatory works and secret histories such as *Love in Excess* (1719–20), *The Injur'd Husband* (1722–3), *The Double Marriage* (1726), and *The British Recluse* (1722), all of which inscribe a death drive of sorts in their female characters. Taken together, these works render self-destruction a quintessentially feminine activity, the teleology of the romance genre and the ultimate expression of desire.

Where suicide in most amatory fiction signifies either excess or extreme lack, in *The British Recluse* Haywood associates it with a different kind of excess: that represented by spectrality.[11] In this work, Haywood's female protagonists are represented as spectral beings, 'haunting' the nation and thereby illuminating the public and national aspect of woman's suicide in the early novel.[12] Choice and constraint become blurred in a disturbing manoeuvre that tries to carve out some space for agency within the inevitability of women's marginalization. Sacrifice is one of the means by which this gambit occurs; as Valashini Coopan writes, all 'national subjects' live:

> in the mode of loss for all must contend with the difficult process of identifying with something that is not entirely there, that exists in the present yet recedes into the deep past of national history, and that seems to promise future inclusion but constantly works by present exclusion.[13]

For women, this loss is voluntary, looking more like forfeiture of identity itself, which we see staged in *The British Recluse*, in particular. In Haywood's works, suicide – or, perhaps more accurately, parasuicide – is the trope by which female characters embrace and actualize their spectrality. Haywood flirts with a kind of quietism in deploying this strategy, and risks reifying her female characters' impermanence by rendering it a condition of permanence. However, her writing functions as a revelation rather than a ratification of women's spectral identities vis-à-vis the nation.

Economies of Sacrifice and Excess in Haywood's Amatory Fiction

In all of her works, and perhaps most programmatically in *Reflections on the various effects of love* (1726), Haywood distinguishes between male and female experience of physical and emotional desire, identifying women as almost exclusively susceptible to the kind of all-consuming attachments that often destroy the characters of her fiction. These texts construct male desire as ephemeral, transitory and addicted to variety, and female love as permanent and almost obsessively fixed on a single object. In her 'Explanation of Love', a central chapter of *Reflections*, Haywood's narrator muses:

> how much greater Force that Passion influences the Minds of Women, than it can boast on those of a contrary Sex, whose Natures being more rough and obdurate, are not capable of receiving those deep Impressions which for the most part are so destructive to the softer Specie [*sic*]'.[14]

In this metaphor, the mind itself takes on the physical characteristics of individual bodies and becomes hyper-essentialized in a fusion of the mental and the corporeal. Both male and female are heavily embodied in Haywood's trope, which presents desire as an external force acting upon a passive surface and thereby diminishes the extent to which individuals may truly be deemed free agents in matters of love.

Haywood's works suggest that because men and women desire differently, they inevitably react differently to the removal of the object of love. Men, according to Haywood, prove incapable of sustaining meaningful attachments.[15] As the rake of Haywood's *The City Jilt* (1726) reminds his cast-off mistress, 'The very word desire implies an impossibility of continuing after the enjoyment of that which first caused its being'.[16] According to this construction, masculine desire is short-lived indeed. Women, on the contrary, unable to retain the objects of their affection, and typically unable to avenge themselves upon the removed object, redirect these violent impulses onto their own bodies, in a literary enactment of the Freudian thesis that suicide represents a redirection inwards of anger harboured toward an exterior object.[17] Thus, the British Recluse's observation in Haywood's novella of that title that 'Not all the Ills ... which Fortune watches to oppress [women] with are half so ruinous, so destructive as this one Passion!' is validated by her interlocutor's confirmation that 'Nothing indeed is to [the female] Sex so fatal'.[18] Haywood's premise is logical: women feel more deeply than men with the result that the consequences of their passion are often 'fatal' (one of Haywood's preferred catchwords). Indeed, love itself is described as a 'gilded poison, which kills by slow degrees, and makes each moment of [a woman's] life a death!',[19] suggesting that the poison which Haywood's heroines so frequently ingest is merely a metonym for the infatuation that is killing them already. As the narrator of *Reflections* remarks,

> Wanting ... those amusements which a variety of company affords the other sex, [women] have more leisure ... to indulge their thoughts, and soothe deluded fancy. Thus do they, self-deceiv'd, supply feul [*sic*] to the unceasing Fire which consumes their peace, and rarely is it extinguish'd but by death.[20]

This statement emphasizes the role of women's experience of everyday private life in configuring a highly gendered conception of desire. In this context, suicide becomes the inevitable result of leisure, or of the divide between the public and the private. According to this construction, male mobility cultivates a taste for variety that in turn breeds detachment, whereas female immobility fosters monomania and excessive attachment unto death. The basic facts of women's ordinary experience in Haywood's account posit their radically different relation to time, which ultimately becomes responsible for the dire effects of unrequited desire. Living in the bustle of the public sphere, men's exposure to the distractions of variety keeps them anchored to a kind of reality principle; on the other hand, the leisurely pace of the private sphere breeds in women a melancholic attachment to the object of desire which, when lost, leads to an almost insurmountable sense of despair. In this manner Haywood bases her distinction between female and male experience upon both biological and cultural determinants, thereby developing a fatalistic pathology of love that sees suicide as its necessary corollary. At the same time, however, she presents desire as a cultural product, rather than a biological imperative intrinsic to a sense of 'femaleness'. Love is women's 'work', according to this narrative, a form of 'repetitive attachment', to borrow Lauren Berlant's term, constituted more by a 'binding relation to time' than 'a steady state of object desire'.[21] In her rationale for aligning love-suicide with women, Haywood pathologizes the private sphere (rather like Hannah Arendt), and seems on the surface of things to vindicate male infidelity. However, a closer look suggests that this gendered division of experience is itself to blame for the death drive that appears to be built into her understanding of desire.

Although Haywood's frequent representation of the tragic repercussions of female desire might appear somewhat fatalistically to promote a sense of female victimhood, one can also build a case (as many critics have) for a reading of her narratives that identifies them instead as scripts for women's survival in patriarchal society.[22] To this end, many of her texts concentrate upon teaching the proper mode of revenge, one that consists of mortifying the fickle lover rather than mortifying the body. Thus Haywood's persona in *The Female Spectator* (1744–6) intones, 'I heartily wish ... that all women who have been abandoned and betrayed by men ... would rather contrive some means to render the ungrateful lover the object of contempt, than themselves, by giving way to a baseless grief'.[23] Revenge becomes the study of several of Haywood's novellas, which propose numerous stratagems by which abandoned women may regain the upper hand. Accordingly, in a tale from the *Female Spectator*, a woman takes her revenge by pretending to poison both her ex-lover and herself. Her lover's response suggests that this is in fact an expected gesture, consistent with the narrative conventions of amatory fiction. Meanwhile, the protagonist of *The City Jilt* punishes the man who spurns her in favour of a more lucrative alliance by acquiring the mortgage of his straitened estate and holding it in trust. In a gesture of economic supremacy, Haywood presents the incursion of the woman into the sphere of credit as a condition for her empowerment and escape from the sacrificial logic of suicide to which her full immersion in a continuum of desire necessarily subjects her. Revenge, rather than suicide, then, appears to be a consistent recommendation of Haywood's plots.

Yet despite these exhortations that women survive the decay of their love, the majority of Haywood's female protagonists either commit suicide or seriously contemplate the act. Voluntary death figures so prominently in these narratives that they draw upon a singular vocabulary to refer to the act.[24] While the ethical philosopher Gavin Fairbairn critiques the 'impoverished language and conceptual apparatus available for discussing suicide and related acts' in today's society,[25] Haywood demonstrates that the eighteenth century afforded a much broader range of terms prior to the common acceptance of the word 'suicide'. In Haywood's narratives, the circumlocution 'lay violent hands on one's own life' becomes a favoured mode of expressing a suicide threat or death wish.[26] Thus, finding herself abandoned by her lover, the protagonist of *The City Jilt* attempts 'to lay violent hands on her own life, but [is] prevented by a serving-maid',[27] while the chief character of *Idalia* (1723) similarly contemplates 'laying violent hands on her life' when disappointed in love.[28] So pervasive is this formula that it becomes a virtual refrain in Haywood's narratives. Yet, apart from the adjective 'violent', which is arguably somewhat morally neutral, this formula is descriptive rather than judgemental. It lacks both the criminal connotation of the harshly clinical term 'suicide', and the dramatic emotive power of 'self-murder', the term favoured by moralizing sermons and conduct books, especially in the early decades of the eighteenth century. Haywood's formula intensifies the sense of self-objectification, as the body becomes figuratively dismembered, with its individual parts working to destroy the whole. The phrase also suggests the mind's ability to conceive of the self as an object – a relation facilitated by the impingement of the marketplace on the consciousness of the individual – that facilitates the act of suicide in these narratives, and in a sense explains a popular eighteenth-century characterization of suicide as 'a duel with oneself'. Meanwhile, 'life' itself comes to represent an abstract condition, a state of being, when it becomes the mere object of an action as a result of Haywood's formula.

Perhaps owing to this affinity for repeating stock phrases, John Richetti insists that 'Haywood's voice is entirely and deliberately formulaic, a breathless rush of erotic/pathetic clichés that is in a real sense unreadable'.[29] However, I am more inclined to agree with Kirsten T. Saxton's assessment that 'Haywood's hyperbolic prose ... reveal[s] her astute manipulation of text and context, of genre and gesture'.[30] Haywood's use of formulae is deliberate and complex; more often than not an expression of astonishment that the suicide was not completed accompanies the euphemism, as characters confide 'nothing is more strange than that I did not lay violent hands on my own life'[31] and 'nothing was ever more deserving wonder than that [she] did not lay violent hands on her own life'.[32] In expressing surprise that a suicide attempt does not follow abandonment, these texts inscribe a death drive even as they naturalize the notion of a 'death wish'.[33] Formulaic utterance makes of suicide a logical and ordinary occurrence of which disappointed love becomes a necessary antecedent, suggesting the extent to which speech participates in Haywood's representation of desire as a kind of drive over which individuals (or literary characters) have limited control.

In her astute analysis of Haywood's complex demonstration of the politics of desire, Margaret Case Croskery locates an alternative model of agency at work in Haywood's fiction. Comparing Haywood's representation of female desire with David Hume's adumbration of moral sense philosophy, Croskery attempts to restore the degree of agency that seems to get lost in considerations of Haywood's focus on the involuntary component of this configuration of desire. Croskery argues that 'It is because passion is a "controller of the will" that the heroine's constancy remains steadfast. In true Humean fashion, Haywood's definition of both female virtue and agency are motivated and defined by the passions'. According to this reasoning, constancy becomes analogous to obsession and functions as a drive, affirming the single-mindedness of purpose on the part of the Haywoodian desiring subject. Yet Croskery's account does not wholly explain the source of this empowerment, leaving the issue, as Ros Ballaster argues in respect to Haywood's fiction as a whole, 'at best an ambiguous form of mastery'.[34] The complex relationship between desire and agency is articulated with particular effectiveness in Haywood's first novel, *Love in Excess* (1719–20).

Unlike the bulk of Haywood's fiction, *Love in Excess* focuses upon the trials of an apparently irresistible male figure, Count D'elmont. At first eagerly and later involuntarily inspiring a host of women to love him to excess, his sympathy for their sufferings at his expense eventually instils in him not only a conscience but also a knowledge of what it is to love *and* desire. Excessive love for him elicits suicidal tendencies from several women, including D'elmont's wife, Alovisa, whose jealousy of a perceived rival motivates her to be 'reveng'd on her, then dye [her]self, and free [her] from pollution'.[35] Before she can execute her plan, however, she runs 'by accident' on her husband's sword,[36] thus achieving the voluntary death she craves, albeit by unpremeditated means.[37] In her aggressive pursuit of D'elmont and open declaration of her passion, Alovisa bears considerable resemblance to Ciamara, the casualty of 'the too fatal influence of [D'elmont's] dangerous attractions',[38] who ultimately does accomplish her suicide by swallowing poison.[39] At first glance Ciamara's death appears to be sanctioned by the text as a just penalty for her indiscretions, which include her open declaration of her love in defiance of social codes that prohibit female expression of desire.[40] The notion that suicide resulted from precisely this stifling of expression was endorsed by both Lydia Grainger, who in *Modern Amours; or, A Secret History of the Adventures of Some Persons of the First Rank* (1733), insists upon the urgent necessity of 'a sincere and faithful Friend, to whom one may relate the secret Recesses of the Mind',[41] and John Shebbeare, who in his *Letters on the English Nation* (1755) dwells at length on the utility of the rite of confession as a deterrent to suicide in predominantly Catholic countries.[42] In much of the fiction of this period, a woman's articulation of her desire often incurs a sense of shame that cannot be survived; Violetta, the final victim of D'elmont's charms whose death concludes the narrative, internalizes this proscription as she declares that 'life, after [her] shameful declaration [of love], would be the worst of punishments'.[43] Violetta's willed death at the end of the narrative not only exposes the thin conceptual divide between voluntary death and (passively) willed death, but also demonstrates the extreme fragility of life itself in Haywood's fictional universe, given the absolute nature of social protocols.[44] In this and other Haywood texts, death is the penalty for such transgressions, indicating the correlation between speech acts and death drives in Haywood's fiction. Yet, according to the literary critic Toni Bowers, Haywood does not problematize sexual desire so much as sexual agency. Bowers argues that 'the aggressively desiring women in *Love in Excess* earn not only rejection but misery and death ... Not just d'Elmont, but also Haywood, it seems, delivers a strong disciplinary message to sexually "forward" women'.[45] The fact that in another early work, *The Injur'd Husband* (1722), which once again centres closely on a male figure, an aggressively desiring woman also takes her life would seem at least partially to support Bowers's claim.[46] This text features an *homme fatal* whose rejection of the 'Baroness', a woman cast in the fierce mould of Ciamara, drives her similarly to swallow poison. At least in Haywood's early novels, it would seem that suicide serves as the narratively endorsed fate of the passionate woman.[47] However, the fact that the narrator intervenes to supply the information that the 'wicked Baroness, impatient of her fate, desperate, and as some say struck with remorse, and terrified in conscience, hopeless of mercy here or hereafter ... ended her shameful life by as ignominious a death'[48] appears to at least mitigate somewhat the harshness of this position: suicide appears in this context as the expression of contrition as opposed to the just deserts of an amorous and intriguing woman. Moreover, the theory that Haywood metes out death to actively desiring characters such as the Baroness and Ciamara fails to acknowledge the scope of Haywood's preoccupation with the place of suicide in women's experience. For suicide is a fate common to both her female villains and passive heroines, owing perhaps to the fact that Haywood utterly refuses to endorse perfection as an ideal in these narratives. Even Melliora, the ostensible exemplar of female virtue in *Love in Excess* – her name signifies her superiority to her rivals for D'elmont's affections – is not above considering 'laying violent hands on her own life'[49] when her desire conflicts with her sense of duty.[50] The closest that Haywood comes to presenting an 'ideal' figure, Melliora, like Richardson's carefully constructed paragon Clarissa, is not exempt from the experience of suicidal fantasy. Haywood's amatory fiction refuses to espouse the idealizing tendencies that J. Paul Hunter identifies in early novel characterizations such as those offered by Richardson.[51] Accordingly, her characters' suicides are left unjudged and uncensored. Furthermore, female characters author their own deaths in these narratives, suggesting that a death drive of sorts is one drive over which they assert a degree of control.

In establishing excess as virtually the signature of femininity, these works elevate the love-suicide to a genre-defining status. Although Haywood's female characters appear to support the claim of the eighteenth-century physician and pamphleteer Bernard Mandeville that 'shame is the only reason people kill themselves',[52] their suicides of passion typically involve a sacrifice of the self to an unworthy lover. Haywood's *The Double Marriage; or The Fatal Release* (1726) subscribes to precisely this 'economy of sacrifice'. The narrator begins the tale with the exclamation, 'How little answerable to the *Beginning* is the End of some People!',[53] demonstrating that from the outset, the narrative's teleology is oriented towards death, following what Nancy Miller dubs a 'dysphoric plot'.[54] After her secret marriage to the weak Bellcour has been superseded by his public union with Mirtamine, Alathia, the tale's beleaguered heroine, confronts her perjured husband in the guise of a man. Haywood's rendering of the scene borrows from the stuff of tragedy: 'You shall no more be persecuted with *Alathia, cry'd she*, (drawing her Sword, and plunging it hastily into her Breast;) thus I deliver you from the upbraidings of an injur'd, but too tenderly loving Wife'.[55] The dramatic gesture awakens Bellcour's conscience, who, finding 'he could not live and bear it, ... snatching suddenly his Sword, which happened to lie on a Table in that Room, put a period to his Life by the same way his injur'd Wife had done'.[56] Evidently enough, this scene contains multiple reversals of gender roles. Alathia dresses up as a man, and it is precisely this disguise that enables her to commit a stereotypically masculine, violent suicide.[57] Alathia constructs her suicide as a sacrifice to her husband, albeit executing it in a strikingly masculine manner, while Bellcour is left to imitate his wife and follow her to death, as even his suicide is described in euphemistic and aestheticized terms.[58] Yet the question remains as to why Alathia *must* sacrifice herself to the cause of her husband's bigamist impulses, or, perhaps even more pertinently, why she must become a man to do so? The two questions are intimately linked: in a legal sense, Bellcour's bigamy cannot permit Alathia to remain a 'woman', and Alathia's sacrifice of her gender identity anticipates her sacrifice of her 'being' itself. In Haywood's fiction, sacrifice invariably exists as part of a continuum: one sacrifice always belongs to a series of sacrifices ultimately leading to death. Accordingly, the 'release' referenced in the work's title connotes the means whereby the central male character is delivered from the charge of bigamy; modified by the adjective 'fatal', the term becomes a euphemism for suicide.

When male characters kill themselves in Haywood's fiction, it is usually a mimetic act in response to a female suicide. Like *The Double Marriage*, Haywood's *The Fatal Secret; or, Constancy in Distress* also constitutes a tale of a double suicide. In this narrative, a woman, having been betrayed by her husband and violated by her father-in-law, stabs herself with a sword.[59] As the narrator observes, Anadea 'snatch'd the Sword [her husband] wore by his Side, and plung'd it in her Bosom with such an incredible strength and swiftness, that had any of the company been apprised of her intent, it would have been scarce possible to have prevented her'.[60] The suicide of the marquis (the offending father) swiftly follows, and the husband himself is 'with Difficulty restrained' from 'laying violent Hands on his own life'.[61] To some extent, the text suggests that the woman's suicide authorizes that of the man, and it passes no real censure upon either 'act of horror'.[62] Moreover, as she lies dying, Anadea declares 'now ... the shameful story may be told'.[63] Death in this instance obviates the necessity of preserving the 'fatal secret' of the violation that has led to suicide in the first place.

According to theorist Elizabeth Grosz, 'The fantasy that binds sex to death so intimately is the fantasy of a hydraulic sexuality, a biologically regulated need or instinct, a compulsion, urge, or mode of release'.[64] To a considerable extent, this notion of sexual drive as inextricably connected to suicide (both are conceived as essentially end-directed acts) plays itself out in Haywood's construction of female desire in her amatory fiction. Her female protagonists' involuntary experience of desire in turn elicits an almost irresistible impetus towards death that, even when thwarted, as in the case of *The British Recluse*, nonetheless results in a persistent suicidal subjectivity. Juliette Merritt finds in this experience of 'compulsive desire' a 'source of Haywood's feminism', arguing that 'In the surrender to an unconquerable passion, female desire can be viewed as a form of resistance to the ideological constraints of women's lives'.[65] While I agree with Merritt's assessment of Haywood's refusal to endorse her heroines' victim status, I argue that the 'transgressive' potential of her scheme is persistently undercut by her endorsement of a notion of 'drive'. Although Haywood's refusal to produce a disciplined body (such as that which Mary Wollstonecraft calls for at the end of the century in her insistence that women submit their passions to the control of reason) resists locating the grounds of women's empowerment in a kind of recuperated Cartesian dualism, her model of a corporeality organized or constituted by a number of related drives is not entirely fruitful either. Yet does Haywood do more than cast women as unthinking beings capable of aspiring merely to sex or death? Far from condemning suicide in her fiction, Haywood rather renders it a means of revenge, rebirth and corroboration of desire. While Haywood's model of desire is somewhat problematic, her representation of suicide recuperates the transformative potential of her heroines' narratives to a limited extent. In her work on domestic fiction, Nancy Armstrong claims that women in the period were urged to relinquish their desire in order to become part of the domestic sphere;[66] however, in Haywood's fiction, women can neither relinquish desire nor fully integrate themselves into society. Accordingly, in *The British Recluse*, Haywood represents an alternative form of desiring and existing in society that I will discuss at length in the next section of this chapter. I have lingered over these texts in an attempt to establish the centrality of suicide to Haywood's early fiction, and in the subsequent section I shall focus more broadly on the implications of Haywood's preoccupation with suicide for both her gender politics and participation in the construction of a sense of nationhood.

Suicide, Narrative and Nation in *The British Recluse*

The British Recluse; or, The Secret History of Cleomira, Supposed Dead, features Haywood's most resolutely suicidal *and* secretive character. From the outset, Cleomira's character is contoured by absence. Shrouded in mystery, her empty place at the dinner table renders her identity and the motives for her seclusion the subject of conversation among the guests at a suburban lodging house. Despite the landlady's belief that 'to discover the Mystery of her concealing herself [is] an utter Impossibility',[67] Belinda – 'a young Lady of a considerable fortune in Warwickshire'[68] – manages to gain access to Cleomira, who has 'excite[d] her Curiosity to a Desire of knowing as much as she could of [her] adventure'.[69] The ensuing narrative divides itself into first-person accounts of the suffering of two women at the hands of the same man; yet Belinda's story, as the very title of the text makes clear, is merely ancillary, serving to reinforce and validate Cleomira's own narrative of suffering and her particular method of dealing with rejection.[70] The revelation that marks one of the novella's climaxes, when the women discover that the villain featured in their stories is one and the same, merely corroborates the baseness of the male, while preserving the women from censure.[71]

The narrator of *The British Recluse* describes the text as a 'little history (which [she] can affirm for Truth, having it from the Mouths of those chiefly concerned in it)'.[72] Interestingly enough, this statement appears to counter the opening maxim that 'Of all the *Foibles* Youth and Inexperience is liable to fall into, there is none, I think, of more dangerous consequence, than too easily giving Credit to what we hear'.[73] However, Haywood's appeal to an oral account as a mark of authenticity attempts to substantiate its truth claims through recourse to a secret alternate history of gendered experience that privileges the anecdotal.[74] Both narratives follow a similar pattern: a young woman is seduced in the country (where, ironically, Cleomira's mother has brought her in an effort to protect her from sexual predators), then follows her lover to the city. The parallel histories also both have nearly tragic consequences, with each teller sharing 'one fatal source of woe'.[75] Belinda's tale, however, constitutes a 'little history'[76] even when supplemented with that of Miranda (another casualty of Bellamy's desire), whereas Cleomira's account, we are told, 'takes up much of the night'.[77] *The British Recluse* consists in large part, then, of a tale told by a survivor in a first-person account by a woman who has with deadly seriousness attempted suicide and failed.

For once, then, the self-destructive subjectivity of the desiring woman commands both a voice and the sympathy that exists as a necessary corollary of this confessional mode. In effect, Haywood constructs a confessional apparatus that incorporates an ideal listener in the form of Belinda, whose commiseration with Cleomira's plight the text clearly establishes: as the narrator affirms,

> Belinda had conceived the highest Esteem and Friendship imaginable for this *fair Unfortunate* and was willing to offer everything in her Power for her Consolation, yet she could not disapprove the Justice of her Lamentations or the Resolution she had taken of concealing herself.[78]

Belinda performs the dual function of validating Cleomira's experience and confirming her account of it at the same time. Cleomira functions as a cautionary tale to Belinda, herself a representative of the normative woman who might easily have suffered her friend's misfortune if circumstances had been different. Yet without having herself 'fallen', Belinda nonetheless shares the fate of Cleomira, representing sorrow reduplicated, an affirmation of the irresistibility of the man who occasions both characters' misery and who eventually blots them out of social existence.[79] Belinda also figures the excess we encountered in Haywood's first novel, which similarly offers a treatment of female rivalry through its representation of a single rake as the focus of multiple women's desire. In *The British Recluse*, however, women's excess does not represent an empty rhetorical gesture, but rather acquires a much deeper significance by virtue of Belinda's relationship with Cleomira.

Belinda's curiosity sets in motion the narrative machinery of *The British Recluse*.[80] Even after she has met the Recluse, the narrator suggests that 'She would have given one of her Eyes to have been let into the Secret of [her] whole Affair but durst not attempt to ask, for fear of disobliging her'.[81] Various impediments to narrative progress arguably belong to the structure of the secret narrative as a series of deferrals that generate suspense and chronically resist inquiry. The text preserves its own secrets, shrouding even its title in enigma and ambiguity. Belinda's persistence thus serves as the narrative's motor, as she conversationally gathers 'histories' that are 'illustrated with many Circumstances, which aggravated the foulness of [Bellamy's actions]'.[82] But it is Cleomira who synthesizes the material and eventually deduces that they share an antagonist.[83] The story follows the general trajectory of Haywood's suicide narratives, yet, owing to her use of the first-person account, the element of suspense that the text constantly strives to generate is overdetermined, given the reader's awareness that this text cannot conclude in typical Haywoodian fashion. Furthermore, if we accept the critic Elisabeth Bronfen's claim that '[S]uicide implies an authorship of one's life, a form of writing the self and writing death that is ambivalently poised between self-construction and self-destruction',[84] Cleomira's self-narration represents a form of self-construction; at the same time, her suicide attempt demonstrates her ability to view herself as an object.

The compartmentalizing of the narrative into two distinct sections (supplemented with a preamble by an independent narrator) in *The British Recluse* signals Haywood's experimentation with first-person narrative. Although none of Haywood's short fiction fully assumes the first-person perspective, she offers insight into characters' interiority through the inclusion of letters in semi-epistolary narratives, which render the novella a 'composite text'. The suicide note constitutes one such epistolary device ostensibly operating within 'the tradition of female complaint'[85] and simultaneously recognizing the cultural currency of the subgenre of the farewell to life that was being popularized by the periodical press. For, as Terence Murphy and Michael MacDonald observe in their social history of early modern self-destruction, 'suicide notes were very rare in the seventeenth century, but as literacy became more widespread many more people explained their deaths in writing'.[86] Although suicide notes appear elsewhere in Haywood's corpus, usually incorporating a wistful regret that the perfidious male lover had not seen fit to end the writer's life before she was driven to the extreme of suicide, this text is unique in that it contains not one, but two suicide notes. These documents, composed over an interval of some months, attest to the resoluteness of Cleomira's suicidal mentality, and reinforce the oral threats that she repeatedly issues. In Cleomira's hands, the suicide note operates as a posthumous mode of writing and an essential device affording access to the conjoined desire for sex and death so central to her narrative.

The first of the suicide notes addressed to Bellamy appeals to historical precedent as a means of sanctioning voluntary death: 'History is not without Millions of Examples of Women who have dared to die, when Life became a Burden; and sure, if any ever could justify Self-murder, the wretched Cleomira may – None ever loved – none ever despaired like me, or had so just a Cause for both'.[87] This collective of suicidal women authorizes Cleomira's attempt and even attests the sincerity of her intentions. The terms in which suicide is described constructs it as an act of daring usually associated with the male paradigm of heroic suicide of the Western classical tradition. The appeal to precedent indicates that Cleomira draws upon a history of female voluntary death, part of which is imaginatively reconstructed by the narrator of Haywood's *Reflections on the Various Effects of Love*. In a grim catalogue of women that meet precisely this end, Haywood's 'reflections' initially appear to celebrate women who commit suicide upon the deaths of their husbands, although it later becomes clear that she in fact seeks to affirm female capacity for heroic self-sacrifice. Her list resembles one that Nahum Tate compiles in his *Present to the Ladies*, itself inspired by Michel de Montaigne's 'Chapter of Three Illustrious Examples of Female Vertue',[88] all of which feature the self-sacrifice of women. Cleomira strives to enrol herself in this canon of self-sacrificing women, even while elevating herself above them by virtue of the singularity of her suffering.

Despite Bellamy's scornful reception of the two suicide notes they nonetheless bear the mark of authenticity as Cleomira's subsequent suicide attempts confirm. In an effort to convince her nurse of the sincerity of her intentions, Cleomira declares:

> If I cannot die the way I choose, still I will *some* way – if not by Poison; there are Knives or Cords – My Garters may be my Executioners – Or if denied these Instruments, you cannot hinder me from strangling myself with my own Hands or dashing out my Brains against the Wall – To those *resolved*, Death always is at call.[89]

The grim catalogue affirms Cleomira's commitment to her death wish, and her insistence on the interchangeability of method refutes the commonly held opinion 'that no one is promiscuous in his way of dying'; as the critic A. Alavarez insists, 'A man who has decided to hang himself will never jump in front of a train'.[90] Yet the choice of method is nonetheless quite significant in that the use of poison facilitates intervention in suicide, as seen in this narrative when a wary apothecary substitutes a placebo for the poison Cleomira requests of him. At this historical juncture, the technologies of resuscitation had not yet become widely known, meaning that alternative methods of suicide by drowning or hanging still belonged to a higher tier of lethal behaviour. Moreover, many of the proposed methods mentioned in this ghoulish inventory are those typically preferred by women, yet as Cleomira's list continues, the mode of death becomes increasingly violent and more stereotypically masculine in nature.[91] The screen of secrecy is also dropped as Haywood's graphic account reconceives the body as a weapon that may be used against the self and serve as the witness to its own self-destruction, once again indicating the recognition of the self as object that is the precondition for suicide in Haywood's texts. Thus, even though the art historian Ron Brown argues that suicide's meanings did not begin to be inscribed on the female body until later in the nineteenth century,[92] the literary record reveals a different story as early as Haywood's amatory fiction.

Hysteria, Theatricality and the Performance of Suicide

Despite her repeated insistence that 'To those resolved, death is always at call'[93] and that 'The Means of Death are always easy to be obtained',[94] Cleomira's suicide attempt ultimately fails. The assertion that death comes readily to she who desires it is confuted by the events of the text, in which the body itself acts as an obstacle to voluntary death. In her initial disaffection with life, Cleomira finds that her 'youth ... and the natural goodness of [her] constitution brought [her] through that dangerous state in which those who find most ease have little reason to be assured of life',[95] while she elsewhere expresses her frustration that '[she] could not die ... in spite even of [her]self'.[96] Her body proves recalcitrant and does not submit to death as readily as that of other female characters populating Haywood's fiction. Just as she cannot 'die' in a sexual sense, neither can Cleomira experience the ultimate death that she desires almost as a surrogate for sex.

Failed suicide has historically been read as a symptom of hysteria, owing to the logic that Gavin Fairbairn summarizes as follows: 'Since a person who really wants to die kills himself, all who act suicidally must be hysterical and over-dramatic attention seekers'.[97] Bellamy's dismissal of Cleomira's suicide notes as 'mere romantic stuff' reflects precisely this attitude, as does the non-committal indifference implicit in the title's allusion to Cleomira as 'supposed dead'. Operating within the paradigm of romance, however, Haywood's narrator cannot be so dismissive and accordingly constructs Cleomira as a character endowed with an inordinate degree of self-possession and strength. Consequently, we are told that Cleomira, 'tho' young as Belinda, was Mistress of a much greater presence of mind',[98] with her name itself signifying twin qualities of glory and wonder. Although earlier in the narrative she admits to being 'hurried to [a] rage of temper'[99] and exhibits behaviours that are typically identified as hysterical, by the time of her suicide attempt Cleomira appears rational and calm, suggesting that her attempt need not necessarily be construed as the product of hysteria. However, many critics have labelled this recalcitrant body 'hysterical', including Ros Ballaster, who insists that Haywood's romances 'locate a form of feminine resistance precisely in the compulsive re-inscription and display of the hysterical female body'.[100] Although Rebecca Bocchicchio differs from Ballaster in her assessment of the implications of Cleomira's hysteria, she too reads Cleomira's suicide attempt as a product of 'hysterical passivity'[101] that results from the internal conflict the subject experiences between yielding to desire and obeying the social codes insisting upon its repression. While Bocchiccio's account goes far towards historicizing eighteenth-century notions of hysteria, this reading elides the significance of Cleomira's suicide and ignores the intentional structure of the act. Frequently, critics read hysteria – a nervous state associated with exaggeration and inauthenticity – back onto the suicidal act precisely because of its failure.[102] The implications of the unsuccessful suicide are worth considering here, for they raise the question as to whether the failure of the attempt might retroactively mitigate or even belatedly negate the intentionality and agency of will behind the act. Arguing that 'If we wish to understand the etiology of suicidal behaviours, we must expand our vision beyond fatal suicidal acts', the historian Howard Kushner insists that 'we must not ignore the fact that strategies which do not necessarily result in death can be as "suicidal", in terms of intention, as those actions that result in death'.[103] In the eighteenth century, when failed suicide was technically as subject to legal penalty as was successful suicide, the difference between the two acts was, from a moral and legal standpoint, less recognizable than it is now.[104] The suicidal act caused considerable interpretative difficulty for judicial and civil authorities in their attempts to categorize it as *felo de se* (self-murder) or as an effect of *non compos mentis* (insanity). The failed suicide, or suicidal behaviour, retained the stigma of a completed suicide but was still more difficult to comprehend conceptually, which perhaps accounts for why Cleomira's suicide must remain a secret. Her attempted suicide contains more authenticity than does a modern-day understanding of attempted suicide and should be interpreted as an act rather than a mere gesture at killing herself. Although in many other accounts hysteria often functions to explain female suicide attempts, Haywood dismisses its relevance to Cleomira's particular case.

The fact that hysteria is often interpreted as a performance perhaps contributes to the interpretation of Cleomira's attempt as hysterically passive. Nineteenth-century theorists equated hysteria with simulation, drawing upon a tradition of conflating hysteria with the histrionic that had already been established in the previous century. Yet, for the most part, eighteenth-century attitudes accorded a greater degree of respect to hysteria, even though traces of scepticism towards the authenticity of the disease were already in evidence. In recounting the scene that follows her supposed ingestion of poison, Cleomira rereads from her belatedly enlightened perspective her symptoms as she experienced them. Consequently, she confides that 'either the draught itself, or the force of my imagination that it must be so, operated so strongly through my veins that I grew exceedingly sick'.[105] Although we might be tempted to construe this passage as a satiric sign of Cleomira's excessive credulity, her critical and dispassionate review of the episode insists that her experience was indeed 'like that of death'[106] and invites us to take it seriously. The passage fuses fantasy with reality; although the symptoms are merely empty signifiers, they are nonetheless motivated, with the result that the suicide attempt must lay claim to at least a limited degree of authenticity. The simulation of death that the opiate affords raises questions regarding the interpretation of symptoms as performance and prompts us to ask, with the theorist Jean Baudrillard, 'Is the simulator sick or not, given that he produces "true" symptoms?'[107] Eighteenth-century medical practitioners and theorists grappled with this very issue, with one pervasive viewpoint articulated by the Scots physician George Cheyne maintaining that 'Mental symptoms were, of course, real, but they were assumed to be responses to somatic occurrences'.[108] Jeremy Collier's treatment of spleen in his *Essays on Several Moral Subjects* (1702) confirms that 'the spleen and vapours are by those that never felt the symptoms looked upon as an imaginary and fantastic sickness of the brain, filled with odd and irregular ideas'.[109] Where Freudian theory later maintains that hysteria creates 'somatic expressions', physical symptoms, to stand for 'affectively marked idea[s]',[110] Collier's argument is consistent with the somatic etiologies that the period assigned to nervous disorders. According to this thinking, the body becomes the locus of reality, entirely removed from the realm of fantasy. This conception of the body, when translated into amatory fiction, subsequently acquires a tangibility that is absent from earlier romance writings, and in turn grants to the event of suicide a degree of realism that likewise was formerly lacking. In this sense, Haywood's narrative refuses the theatrical aspect of suicide typically associated with female characters in amatory fiction, but elsewhere representative of a positive source of agency.

Consequently, Cleomira's experience as the text constructs it amounts to more than a mere performance of hysterical symptoms. As she sees it, Cleomira experiences death both mentally and physically. She awakes to no rebirth and expresses 'consternation' rather than relief when she finds her attempt thwarted. In no manner of speaking might *The British Recluse* be considered the conversion story or spiritual autobiography that suicide narratives frequently become (as in the case of the memoirs of William Cowper[111]), nor does it construct the apothecary who intervenes in Cleomira's suicide attempt as a heroic saviour. Cleomira continues to exhibit signs of love-melancholy after her suicide, preferring to live as if dead and taking 'little care ... of herself'.[112] Since Cleomira neither repudiates nor repents her suicide, this act remains central to her character's living identity rather than retrospectively defining her character after death.

In many respects, Cleomira's story anticipates the representation of a suicidal female character in Lydia Grainger's *Modern Amours* (1733). In this text, a young woman named Clara overdoses on 'a vast quantity' of laudanum and is mistakenly assumed to suffer rather from 'the Spleen and Vapours, so incident to the Sex, than any real Intention [of suicide]'.[113] Although the sincerity of Clara's intentions is later established, her attempt is thwarted by the Apothecary from whom she purchased the laudanum, who, 'being suspicious what fatal Purpose it might be for, took care to put something in it to purge it off, which it did in a most violent manner'.[114] The expedient of the placebo enables Grainger to describe Clara's case in her prefatory remarks as 'a melancholy Adventure, turn'd into a Merry one',[115] thereby eliding the issue of suicide altogether, unlike Haywood, whose narrator dwells at length upon the aftermath of suicidal exertions.[116] Grainger's narrative concludes with its heroine's revelation of her failed suicide, and she 'forbear[s] further Particulars, in regard to Clara's character, she being yet a single lady'.[117] Although Haywood's text purports to be a secret history as well, her narrative extends beyond the event of her protagonist's suicide, owing perhaps to her refusal to interpret the act, as does Grainger's narrator, as 'an execrable Deed; the very Reflection on't mak[ing her] Soul to shudder'.[118] Paradoxically enough, suicide looms large in Haywood's texts, but without the attendant scandal that identifies suicide with criminality and sin in other discourses. As an essential plot device, the placebo enables the text to interrogate the meanings of suicide and secure for its central character a spectral afterlife constantly defined by this suicide attempt.

The fact that in this text and several other Haywood narratives the 'failed' suicide attempts are undertaken by women seems to support a typical gender stereotype of suicidal behaviour, articulated in the early nineteenth century by the French doctor J. E. D. Esquirol, who asserted that 'Women kill themselves more rarely than men, and when they do, more often it is [amorous] passion which impels them to this aberration'.[119] As suicidologist Silvia Sara Canetto observes, since 'suicide is viewed as a masculine behaviour ... killing oneself may be viewed as a relatively powerful act for a male in response to a debilitating failure; conversely, "attempting suicide" is regarded as feminine'.[120] In this respect amatory fiction appears to inscribe a historically constant 'gender paradox' of the act whereby women 'gesture' at suicide and men complete it. To a considerable extent, this same gender dichotomy applies to literary redactions of suicide, as, despite the fact that male characters do frequently fail in their suicide attempts in these narratives, their failures are represented and conceptualized quite differently from those of their female counterparts. For example, Mary Davys's *The Reform'd Coquet* (1724) alludes to a suicide attempt on the part of a man wracked with incestuous desire for his sister, but the text does not pursue this scene and buries the event in silence. Haywood, on the other hand, invariably thematizes suicide to the full extent of the narrative's capacity for representing it, in contrast with later English fiction. Thus, although many theorists construe the failed suicide, or 'sublethal self-destruction' as it is sometimes referred to,[121] as a commentary upon female ineffectuality, it seems more appropriate to read it as an unfolding of possibility, an opportunity for character development beyond the usually terminal point of death. *The British Recluse* derives much of its narrative energy and impact from its nature as a tale told by a survivor of an unsuccessful suicide attempt, for the very fact that her actions have corroborated her words in one crucial instance lends credibility to the rest of her account. In this respect, suicide may be said to function as the supreme guarantor of the authenticity of desire, and an index of the female figure's sincerity. A 'failed suicide' in this sense might be viewed as the most truthful candidate conceivable for a narrator.

This general tendency to equate failure with epistemological assurance of truth speaks to Haywood's tendency to redeem female suicide in her fiction, and, even more significantly perhaps, heightens the truth claims of the narrative.

The Gift that Keeps on Giving

Therefore, although suicide has been recognized historically as largely a male activity,[122] in Haywood's texts it constitutes for the most part a female mode of dying, in defiance of the popular belief that since women cannot lay claim to an ownership of the body, women are less likely to dispose of this body than are men. This logic does not operate in Haywood's texts, in which the relatively high suicide rate among female characters arguably suggests that women do in fact own their bodies. However, the predominance of the sacrificial suicide in these texts perhaps points to a countervailing notion that ownership is provisional and that the female body is an object that must be given away. From this perspective, the body is merely in the temporary possession of a woman, whose function it is to bestow herself upon another.[123] Although the critic Joseph Suglia claims that 'self-sacrifice is *constitutively* impossible inasmuch as the self cannot secure mastery over its "own" mortality',[124] texts such as *The Double Marriage* and *The British Recluse* consistently affirm a view of the body and life itself as a gift to be dispensed to another. In this sense, they remain committed to what Berlant describes as a fundamental aspect of 'female complaint rhetoric': 'the fantasy dictum that love *ought to be* the gift that keeps on *giving*'.[125]

In *The British Recluse*, women support each other in mutual resistance to the charms of the rakish Bellamy who remains an object of adoration, while in other texts Haywood suggests that the only means whereby a woman may secure the affection or attention of a man is by sacrificing any sense of a stable identity. The fantasy of self-sacrifice that these female characters indulge is intimately connected to their experience of desire, which typically amounts to no more than a desire to be desired. In *The Plague of Fantasies*, theorist Slavoj Zizek claims that 'the desire "realized" (staged) in fantasy is not the subject's own, but the *other*'s desire'.[126] In this respect, hysteria and fantasy, as theorized by Zizek, are exceedingly similar in their forfeiture of subjective in favour of objective desire. Consistent with this construction of desire, the female characters' suicide notes often express a desire that after their deaths they might at least be remembered fondly by the very individuals that initially betrayed their trust.[127] Thus Cleomira of *The British Recluse* assures the 'dear Ruiner of [her] Soul and Body' that he is 'too dear to [her] for [her] to desire to give [him] Pain' and asks only that he remember her 'with some little Softness'.[128] Like actual suicide notes from the period that MacDonald and Murphy have studied, Cleomira's parting words attempt 'to control the ways in which others reacted to their deaths'.[129] However, despite these closing vagaries, suicide appears to mark the end of one kind of fantasy and an emergence of another. In this sense, the text does not fully pre-empt Cleomira's sense of agency, in that it concedes the essence of her wish: to appear dead in the eyes of Bellamy. Once she has made herself unavailable to him as an object of desire, her own desire subsequently becomes impractical and unfeasible, according to the model that Haywood's texts typically construct. Haywood's characters eroticize suicide, the avidity with which they seek out death seeming to indicate a 'passion for dying'. Characters inform their lovers that they long 'to dye before [their] eyes'[130] and appear to derive satisfaction from the contemplation of suicide, in accordance with the generally masochistic nature of pleasure as represented in these texts.[131] To all appearances, Haywood's female characters derive a sense of enjoyment from their meditated violation of the prohibition against suicide. Not merely a conventional gesture of romance, as represented in parodies of the genre such as Charlotte Lennox's *The Female Quixote* (1752), the repetition of suicide essentially fetishizes the act by rendering it the object of everyday fantasy.

Moreover, Haywood's female protagonists repeatedly express a desire to be killed by their lovers, as seen in Cleomira's suicide notes, and in Haywood's *Reflections*, when Sophiana begs that Aranthus 'put an end to the wretchedness thou hast occasion'd, and send me from the world'.[132] To a certain extent, Haywood's texts enact the penitential drama of the female martyr through their use of sacrificial language and fervent prayers for execution. Thus Cleomira's inquiry upon her nurse's return from reporting her suicide to Bellamy, 'was he not shocked to hear I died for him?'[133] sounds suspiciously sacrificial. The female character's demand that her lover kill her also suggests a return to a pre-Christian conception of sacrifice, even as it suggests the masochistic strain embedded in the erotics of both versions of female sacrifice.[134] Female desire, as Haywood constructs it, fails to understand indifference. Since these characters vacillate between extreme passions, they cannot fathom complete detachment, a state that Haywood by no means valorizes. In her later novel, *The History of Miss Betsy Thoughtless* (1751), Haywood indeed will authorize attachment as the only valid way of reconciling affective relations with consumer culture, and the roots of this thinking are very much in evidence in her early work. In her reading of Jacques Lacan's statement that 'love is giving something one doesn't have to someone who doesn't want it',[135] Berlant explains that love and melancholy 'anxiously tangl[e] the ongoing pleasures of desire, projection, and disappointment' and are 'hauntingly aligned with the paradoxical certitudes of ecstasy (loss of self-control, or *jouissance*) ... and misery (absolute loss of the other and therefore of access to one's own idealized ego)'.[136] Haywood's suicide narratives represent a love that cannot be other than melancholic in the sense of the inability to relinquish an object, which, as Lacan would argue, can never truly be in one's possession anyway.

Even after her foiled suicide attempt, Cleomira repeatedly interrupts her narration of her ruin to express her death wish, thus forestalling the possibility that any moralizing message might be appended to her text. Indeed, at the very outset of her history, Cleomira exclaims 'O would it had been so that Love and Life might then have had an End and escaped the Woes which both have since endured'.[137] Later in her account, she confides to her audience, Belinda, 'A thousand Times in a Day I was about to put an End to Life and all its weight of Anguish: Nor was it Reason, or Religion but merely the Consideration that Death would take from me all Power of hearing what became of Lysander that preserved me'.[138] As this text demonstrates, religious considerations lack the power to dissuade an individual bent on self-destruction from acting on this impulse; in fact, the text in no way criticizes her attempt, since the textual reference to the 'act of horror' actually represents the indirect discourse of Cleomira's appalled nurse. Even once she realizes that her temporary loss of consciousness has resulted from a drug-induced stupour rather than from the effects of poison, Cleomira exclaims, 'Oh! If one were sure to enjoy that Tranquility in a real death that I did in my imaginary one, none would survive their happiness'.[139] This statement obliquely conveys a sense that the instinct of self-preservation is nourished only by a fear of the discomfort that might attend the afterlife. The masochistic nature of female desire as represented in this and other works of amatory fiction logically fosters a secular suicidal mentality that effectively prevails over all extant social and religious considerations.

'Imagined Communities of Women': Spectral Relations in the New Britain

Cleomira's extreme anxiety lest her death be interpreted as suicide informs her request that 'to spare the Infamy of Self-murder' her nurse 'keep the Deed concealed and give out that [she] died of an apoplexy'.[140] To this end, she confesses to Belinda:

> Death was my determined care, but in what manner I should apply it was now my only study; and, after a long debate in my mind, *poison* was the means I fixed on as being not only the most decent but also the most private way I could perform this deed of desperation; for I was unwilling the world should be sensible of what I had done and when I was no more, preserve my shame still flagrant with those scurrilous ditties, which actions of the kind I was about to do are always themes for.[141]

Cleomira's concern to stage her death in an aesthetically pleasing and decorous fashion produces the apparent paradox of the 'proper' suicide. She expresses a hyperconsciousness of public opinion in her insistence on her right to privacy even after her death. Moreover, her fantasy of the intrusion of print media in this affair demonstrates the extent to which suicide had become part of what

Michael Gardiner terms 'the clandestine history of the everyday'.[142] The 'scurril-ous ditties' dreaded by Cleomira allude to the street ballads or broadsheets that circulated during the period, offering satirical reports of contemporary events. Evidently enough, the unforgiving sensibility of these broadsides runs counter to the sympathetic attitude that the novella largely expresses towards the recluse's attempt.[143] Cleomira's determination that her suicide remain an entirely private event is consistent with an emergent attitude of the period that saw voluntary death as a private matter that was the business of the individual rather than a public affair, in spite of the persistent efforts of the periodical press to render each suicide a public event. Cleomira chooses poison because it preserves the body's secrets and provides her (in theory) with a measure of posthumous autonomy.

Paradoxically, Cleomira's contemplation of suicide enables her to express a sense of individualism that might otherwise remain unrealized. Haywood's nar-rative exposes precisely the extent to which meditated destruction of the self heightens awareness of one's individuality, and seems to run counter to popular eighteenth-century attitudes affirming the impossibility of suicide from a legal standpoint. Despite his insistence upon the inalienable rights of the individual, John Locke maintains that the person cannot choose death, since this would constitute an infringement upon the right to live. The fictional world materially refutes these claims, with Haywood suggesting that voluntary death may in fact be a matter of choice, gender notwithstanding.

However, the apothecary's intervention in the affair merits further scrutiny since the text never interrogates whether the figure has any right to pre-empt Cleomira's suicide. Cleomira expresses relative indifference to the matter, admit-ting: 'I was so impatient to know what Lysander had said, since I found [my nurse] had been with him, that I could not give myself much Time to reflect on what she told me concerning the Apothecary'.[144] As the nurse relates, suspect-ing that Cleomira 'designed [the poison] for some other Use than what [she] pretended', the apothecary caused '[her] to be watched home to the End that he might relate the Truth to those about [her] if anything of what he imag-ined should happen'.[145] The ease with which the apothecary deduces Cleomira's intention calls into question the degree to which any suicide can remain entirely private. Alan Wolfe has elaborated on this paradox whereby

> Suicide appears to be clear-cut as a phenomenon and to constitute one of the most private of all acts, and yet the very ambiguity surrounding its determination and interpretation speaks rather to its nature as narrative, which suggests the incipient public tenor of even the most private suicides.[146]

Even prior to its execution, suicide is a phenomenon that can be read through a concatenation of signs that prove transparent to the trained eye of a skilled practitioner in this sense, the character of the apothecary, whom tragedies such as *Romeo and Juliet* rendered commonplace in the century prior, prefigures the institutionalized supervision of human life that evolves in the latter part of the eighteenth century into organized suicide intervention by such groups such as the (Royal) Humane Society.[147] Although proscriptions against suicide undeniably dwindle in this period, the intervention of philanthropic enterprises in these matters renders suicide a public act over which the individual still possesses negligible control. In a similar fashion Haywood's narratives work to publicize the private and expose female suicide, in spite of the privacy that was 'mandated' upon women in this period.

Yet, although a public institution in the person of the apothecary does intervene in Cleomira's suicide attempt, the secrecy of the act is somehow preserved intact. The story remains a 'secret history' precisely because the truth of Cleomira's continued existence is withheld from the unsuspecting and indifferent Bellamy. Even though it is made demonstrably clear to Cleomira that Bellamy 'was inhuman to the last' in his indifference to her apparent suicide, his perspective remains all-important.[148] Consequently, Cleomira concedes that, 'as Lysander believed me dead, I was willing every body else should do so too',[149] in this manner indirectly authorizing Bellamy to represent and control public perception.[150] Accordingly, the critic Ros Ballaster's assessment that 'Haywood's novels ... present their female readers with a thoroughly melancholy view of the world of heterosexual romance'[151] appears accurate indeed. While Bellamy continues a libertine at large in elite society, Cleomira and Belinda resolve to 'abandon the world'[152] and retreat to a miniature version of the 'Protestant Nunnery' outlined in Mary Astell's *A Serious Proposal to the Ladies* (1699).[153] As the final comment of the novella indicates, 'where a solitary Life is the effect of *Choice*, it certainly yields more solid comfort than all the public Diversions which those who are the greatest Pursuers of them can find'.[154] The text's cure for suicidal melancholy is isolation, a prescription that contradicts recommendations by seventeenth- and eighteenth-century writers on suicide such as John Sym, who advocated public activity as 'life's preservative against self-killing'.[155] The text enshrines a secret existence as the source of salvation for a 'fallen' woman, as does another Haywood novella, *Fantomina*, which ultimately buries the ignominy of its protagonist in a French convent. Finally, one might argue that although both Cleomira and Belinda fortify each other's resistance to Bellamy, he remains literally haunted by their discourse owing in no small part to his 'impious' refusal to honour the dead. In this sense, Cleomira partially fulfils her earlier warning to Bellamy: 'when I am dead, my Ghost will be before you ever, haunt all your Dreams – poison your Pleasures, and distract reflection'.[156] Although her presumed death does little to abate her seducer's libertinism, the increasingly reckless and violent ways in which it manifests itself in Belinda's narrative of duels and attempted abductions betokens that his lease on life is to be short indeed.

By virtue of the significance that the text's title assigns to her 'presumed death', Cleomira in fact lays claim to a kind of spectral identity. *The British Recluse* implicitly ascribes to Cleomira partial invisibility, as the landlady admits that she 'failed to take much notice' of her mysterious tenant's appearance and consequently supplies only the vaguest of descriptions.[157] Not fully alive, Cleomira has removed herself from social circulation and has rendered herself at least symbolically dead to the world.[158] Cleomira's circumstances evoke the liminal space that the suicide typically occupied in the set of superstitious beliefs that persisted into the eighteenth century. The successful suicide was viewed as a 'transitional' being, wandering between the worlds of the dead and the living, having exited life prematurely without first obtaining a 'passport' to the afterlife.[159] Condemned to a ghostly existence, the suicide was seen as especially polluting, and for this reason the practice of burying suicides at crossroads with stakes through their hearts and stones upon their faces persisted in England up until 1824. Having undergone a symbolic death through her simulated suicide, Cleomira is a spectral being, haunting a bourgeois boarding house, languishing ethereally in a 'nightgown'[160] and appearing only to the one individual who can relate to her experience. Her narrative exposes the spectrality of suicide itself as an act that vexes the boundaries of the public and the private, of being and non-being.

Cleomira's spectral identity extends to the foundation of her isolationist community at the end of the novella, as both she and Belinda disappear from the world's eyes and retire from life. Yet Haywood represents this retreat as a pragmatic alternative to living in the world rather than an abject gesture. As she constructs it, desire remains unconquerable, since both characters require each other to strengthen their resolve to refrain from pursuing Bellamy, and their spectral existence becomes both the effect of suicide (in Cleomira's case) and the means of avoiding it.

Yet, it must be asked, does the 'British' aspect of the Recluse's identity represent merely an arbitrary denomination, or does it belong to a larger ideological agenda? The novella ultimately is about community, about a character's movement beyond a reclusive position through the companionship of another woman and their subsequent formation of an alternative, homosocial society. The Britishness assigned to the Recluse in the title denotes the story's setting, which, unlike so many of Haywood's other 'secret histories', has a local flavour, but it also suggests the *continued* national identity of the Recluse, isolated though she is from the rest of society. Although literary critic Nicholas Hudson rightly claims that the concepts of the 'public' and the 'nation' can 'hardly be separated in eighteenth-century discourse: to devote oneself to the public is to be a "patriot", a lover of one's nation',[161] Haywood's construction of the nation in *The British Recluse* suggests its alignment with the private sphere. Her work invariably presents women as public beings, to a certain extent endowed with the mobility that J. G. A. Pocock claims a 'commercially conceived society' allows women;[162] however, Haywood suggests that a greater degree of agency may be derived from the formation of 'imagined communities of women' that, notwithstanding their private nature, define a concept of 'Britishness'.[163] Located seventy miles from London, Cleomira's and Belinda's colony is physically removed from English society or at least the centre of English civilization, but it remains nonetheless tied to *greater* Britain. Female society offers an alternative to the nation, an early prototype of the sort of institutionalized exclusive society realized in Sarah Scott's *Millennium Hall* (1762). However, this community that Cleomira and Belinda form remains doggedly British, as indicated by the narrative's title. Haywood's use of the adjectival 'British' as opposed to 'English' evokes the 'vexed question of nomenclature' that historians such as Krishan Kumar have identified as one of the 'the enduring perplexities of English national identity'.[164] Katie Trumpener points out that in the wake of the 1707 Act of Union that officially created Great Britain, the terminology 'Britain' and 'British' was 'put into circulation by Lowland Scots who proposed as a marker of collective identity the term 'British', which neither mandated the assimilation of Scottishness to Englishness nor awakened accusations of undue national influence'.[165] By the time Haywood composed *The British Recluse* in 1721, fourteen years after the ratification of the Act of Union, the label 'British' was, as Kumar indicates, already being used as a shorthand.[166] Although the historian Linda Colley attaches a degree of significance to this event that has been deemed hyperbolic by some historians,[167] it is noteworthy that Haywood favours the label 'British' in both her early and later fiction.[168] In *The Husband, in Answer to the Wife* (1756), Haywood's discussion of the 'characteristics of the British nation' suggests that her more totalizing view identifies the nation as British. Typically, Haywood prefers this designation to the more specified 'English', even though her usage reflects to a certain extent the interchangeability of the terms in the vernacular of the day.

Of more interest, perhaps, is the monastic resonance of the word 'recluse', which almost exclusively denoted religious retirement in the period.[169] In his *Lexicon Technicum: or, An Universal English Dictionary of Arts and Sciences* (1708), John Harris defines the 'recluse' as 'one that by reason of his or her Order in Religion is shut up, and cannot stir out of a Cloyster'.[170] Although the monastic life was not especially palatable to Protestantism, Alban Butler's *The Lives of the Fathers, Martyrs, and Other Principal Saints: Compiled from Original Monuments and Other Authentic Records* (1756–9) does refer to a 'holy *English* recluse, named Vulgan'.[171] However, the predominantly Roman Catholic and continental associations conjured up by the figure of the recluse perhaps account for Haywood's explicit identification of the nationality of her peculiar isolationist.

Haywood's Recluse is a votary not to religion per se, but rather to a religion of love, and Belinda becomes her acolyte early on. In a sense, nationality not so much replaces as expresses itself through forms of religious affiliation favoured in the romance tradition.

From the moment she leaves her mother's house, Cleomira is rendered an excentric figure; she is first ensconced in a private residence by Bellamy, then cast out into the world pregnant and penniless, with her suicide attempt completing the process of social alienation. Her reclusiveness becomes in effect a form of social suicide. Indeed, eighteenth-century social critics equated suicide with reclusiveness, viewing both acts as failures of civic duty. Even the sometime apologist for suicide Charles Gildon argued that

> For a Recluse, lazy Contemplation may be Innocent, that is free from Injury, but can hardly be Beneficial to our Neighbour; and that is but a Lame Virtue, that reaches no farther, than our Selves, and justly is Excluded Success in the Publick, that contributes nothing to the Publick.[172]

This argument places suicide and reclusiveness on the same level, being equally destructive to the public good. Even here we encounter the stirrings of a kind of civic national consciousness, the prelude to a fully developed sense of nationalism. A sense that suicide might violate a larger duty not so much to one's divinity as to one's community or even country is central to Gildon's deist outlook and anticipates many of the arguments that moralists will mobilize against voluntary death later in the century, as the publicizing of the act enables and galvanizes the associations of suicide with national consciousness.

As Cleomira is banished from elite society, *The British Recluse* becomes a tale of confinement, expressing acute consciousness of space and geography. Initially, the novella's lack of physical description and scenic detail in part heightens the sense of expanse conveyed by the action's concern with the outdoors. This setting teems with overturned carriages, public attempts at abduction, and theatregoings, staging the concern with spectatorship so central to Haywood's spatial aesthetic, and vividly evoking the physical arrangement of Haywood's social scene. The text's emphasis on the openness of space stands in sharp relief to the narrowing of that space at its end, as the focus shifts to the confines of Cleomira's bedroom – the site of narrative exchange – which eventually becomes Belinda's space as well when she gives up her own to be with Cleomira. The narrative experiences a spatial collapse that strongly anticipates the movement of Samuel Richardson's *Clarissa*, in which self-inflicted penance resembling the Recluse's dedication to 'her whole life's contrition' eventually ends in the space of Clarissa's coffin. Despite Cleomira's utmost efforts, events do not quite realize the Richardsonian telos in that a state of internal exile substitutes for death at the novel's end. Still, this lifestyle lacks the quality of 'forced confinement' semantically associated with the Recluse, since it is described instead as a state of liberty, 'free from all the Hurries and Disquiets which attend the Gaieties of the town'.[173] Haywood's description of this retreat echoes Astell's invitation to women to 'exchange the vain pomps and pageantry of the world, empty trifles and forms of state, for the true and solid greatness of being able to despise them';[174] in many ways *The British Recluse* constitutes a rewriting of Astell's *Serious Proposal* in which women are rendered subversively spectral rather than demurely invisible.

Haywood extends the preoccupation with suicide that we find displayed in her earlier works to her configuration of a distinctive proto-feminist community at her novella's end. Suicide represents the assertion of will on the part of a character otherwise wholly controlled by her desire, a prelude to another choice that Cleomira makes to remain dead, to allow her suicide to remain a social fact (as far as Bellamy is concerned) and her death to remain a legal fact.[175] Living on the proceeds of her own will, as remitted to her by her faithful beneficiary and nurse, Cleomira's death exists as more than a gesture, conferring upon her a kind of spectral agency that in turn enables her to imagine another way of being in the world. Haywood represents Cleomira's suicide attempt as a necessary precondition for this state, suggesting that the only way that she can subdue or rein in her desire is by seeking out a surrogate death. One drive substitutes for another in this context: where earlier, suicide had been cast as an authentication of desire, now it becomes a replacement for desire.

Cleomira thus experiences a kind of exile within England, perhaps Haywood's extreme way of demonstrating the extent to which English society alienates women, estranging them even from their mothers, sisters and families, as in the cases of Cleomira and Belinda. Yet, at the same time, Haywood's advocacy of female companionship at the narrative's end appears to afford a less destructive, yet not altogether emancipatory alternative to the typically tragic effects of female desire. Noting that Cleomira and Belinda were 'happy in the real friendship of each other',[176] the narrator opposes the chimerical illusion of heterosexual attachment to the concrete reality of female friendship.[177] Ultimately, we are told, 'There grew so entire a Friendship between these Ladies that they were scarce a Moment asunder. *Belinda* quitted her Chamber, being desired by the Recluse to take part of her Bed'.[178] In *The British Recluse*, it appears that Cleomira and Belinda find their means of survival through exile and the abnegation of their desire; however, their female friendship serves as an alternative to suicide, as does the displacement of heterosexual desire. The literary critic Susan Lanser suggests that in works such as *The British Recluse*, 'female friendship emerges through women's agency as a powerful resource in the struggle for autonomy and authority'.[179] Although they describe themselves as 'two wretches fit only for the Society of each other'[180] Belinda and Cleomira retrieve a certain degree of dignity through their declaration of independence from London society.

At the same time, however, through their sacrifice of their social identities, these characters also illustrate the manner in which a nation is constituted by the loss of women's identities.

Haywood's representation of Cleomira's ghostliness suggests that the position that women occupy in relation to the nation is inherently spectral, evoking the 'dislocatedness, unhomeliness, disinheritance' associated with the condition.[181] Suicide, accordingly, accentuates the condition characterized by Zillah Eisenstein as 'fantasmatic femaleness' in her argument that

> The fantasized bodies of a homogenized 'womanhood' ... are used to mark 'the' western nation. Nation-building is already, then, encoded with a series of racialized/ sexualized/engendered silences. The symbolized woman, as mother of us all, psychically attaches the nation to family and nature with their racialized meanings.[182]

Although some contemporary theorists maintain that 'women, and all signs of the feminine, are by definition always anti-national',[183] Haywood's implicit use of spectrality as a trope posits at least a tenuous connection to a national imaginary, thereby enacting one of the many ironies of nationalist thought. As Eisenstein writes, women are 'invisibly visible as a symbolic fantasy'[184] in their capacities as mothers raising their sons to participate as good citizens in the public sphere but removed from it themselves. Present, yet simultaneously absent, neither entity nor nonentity, women assume the excentric positions similarly allocated to suicide. Cleomira's spectral maternity further vexes even this identity, given that her 'grief-killed Infant' is still-born, causing her to know 'nothing what it was to be a Mother but the pains'.[185] Contoured by exclusion and alienation expressed in their most extreme form as suicide, women's relations to the nation are thus rather precarious in this work. The British Recluse's story exemplifies the problems afflicting the English, which in the next decade are eventually classified under the rubric of the 'English Malady'.[186]

Haywood aligns an incipient notion of nationhood with death, which is consistent with Derrida's hauntology of nationalism that claims 'Between life and death, nationalism has as its own proper space the experience of haunting. There is no nationalism without some ghost.'[187] Derrida's metaphor is consistent with the 'ghostly national imaginings' that underpin national identity in Benedict Anderson's study. Both theorists expose the ways in which the construction of identity is predicated upon the displacement of an 'other', an abject being, not quite a subject. As feminist interrogations of the 'gendered nation' have demonstrated, gender itself is a phantom presence even in incipient nationalist discourse. At the beginnings of national consciousness, women hover on the margins, and in Haywood's texts, their 'suicides' enable their participation in national affairs, as voluntary death functions as a trope heightening women's invisibility in the national imaginary. Yet Haywood persists in assigning the Recluse an identity;

she is no less British than the treacherous Bellamy who remains overexposed and visible in public places notwithstanding his violation of social etiquette and the law itself. In the final analysis, Cleomira's and Belinda's Astellian retirement does not constitute an experience of abjection because, rather than being cast out of society, they leave of their own volition.

The British Recluse thus spans the geography of both the town and the country, with the narrative for the most part taking place in a boarding house precisely situated so as to afford 'at once the Charms of both the Town and Country'.[188] This detail is in keeping with the geographical specificity of the narrator's concluding remarks indicating that 'the Recluse and [Belinda] took a House about seventy Miles distant from London'.[189] Haywood's geographical range proves expansive in her narratives; her novellas are set variously in Spain, Italy, France and England, and in many instances these continental venues enable her to draw upon the claustrophobic structures afforded by the Roman Catholic religion. The monastery/cloister affords a proto-gothic setting for the assertion of patriarchal authority; in England, meanwhile, a madhouse performs an analogous function. Haywood's scope has a universalizing effect, enabling her to claim for gender struggle a global dimension; yet, at the same time, the explicitly English locales in such texts as *The British Recluse* emphasize her heroine's nationality and resituate suicide as a specifically national problem, a part of the culture of Britain, in anticipation of attitudes that coalesce in the middle part of the century, which Haywood will again comment on in her role as a social critic in *The Female Spectator*.

Kathryn King has observed that 'Preoccupation with themes of gender has, arguably, so saturated our perception of Haywood as to swamp awareness of other aspects of the texts'.[190] Yet as Eliza Haywood's early fiction effectively demonstrates, historical understandings of suicide have largely been shaped by corresponding notions of gender, rendering the two inextricably linked. Contrary to the standard tendency to view completed suicide as a uniquely male behaviour, Haywood's narratives gender the act as distinctively feminine, allowing us to situate the feminization of suicide as occurring in the eighteenth century and earlier rather than the nineteenth century. In this sense Haywood's narratives contest the notion that women lack the capacity to kill themselves, as many of her heroines either commit suicide, or experience it through contemplation or the attempt. In foregrounding the presence of voluntary death in Eliza Haywood's narratives, this chapter does not see suicide as a kind of punishment meted out by a narrator sitting in judgement upon a desiring female subject. Nor do I argue that suicide merely marks the logical fulfilment of the victim status that amatory fiction automatically accords women. Rather, suicide operates as a complex ideological and social marker that draws upon a discourse of bodily reappropriation and corroborates Richard Berman's argument that 'history is finally an activity of the flesh'.[191] Mary Fissell has gone one step further in claiming that 'women's bodies are the stuff of history',[192] and in their recovery of an everyday experience of suicide, Haywood's texts affirm precisely this truth. Thus, rather than the typical intellectual history focusing upon the writings of David Hume and Immanuel Kant, which usually informs discussion of the suicide debate in the eighteenth century, this chapter has concentrated rather upon women's lived and *unlived* experience as represented in Haywood's particular cultural idiom. Haywood's narratives afford us some insight into eighteenth-century attitudes towards self-destruction in the extreme self-consciousness that many of her suicidal characters express in the contemplation of the act. These novellas establish suicide in the prose fiction tradition of the early eighteenth century, a trend continued by Samuel Richardson in *Clarissa*, as will be discussed in the following chapter.[193] Immersed in everyday life, one might expect them to deliver a corresponding critique of everyday *death* in the form of suicide (as it increasingly comes to be viewed over the course of the century), yet this moral corrective is simply not forthcoming in Haywood's texts which privilege representation over explicit didacticism.

2 *MORS VOLUNTARIA*: CLARISSA AND THE AGENCY OF MARTYRDOM

In her remarks on Samuel Richardson's celebrated second novel, *Clarissa* (1748), the novelist Sarah Fielding finds that 'the gentle Clarissa's death is the natural consequence of her innocent life; her calm and prepared spirit, like a soft smooth stream, flows gently on, till it slides from her misfortunes, and she leaves the world free from fear, and animated only by a lively hope'.[1] Although this panegyric typifies the immediate critical reception of Richardson's massive, seven-volume work, by the last decade of the eighteenth century the cult status of Richardson's second novel had diminished just enough to expose its protagonist to the censure of critics. Thus, in her *Letters on Education* (1789), Catherine Macaulay summarily jettisons *Clarissa* from her canon of acceptable young adult reading material on the grounds that its heroine, 'though represented as a paragon of piety and moral excellence, is positive and conceited; and all her distresses are brought upon her by the adhering to some very whimsical notions which she has entertained of duty and propriety of conduct'.[2] In addition to this already scathing criticism, Macaulay identifies as Clarissa Harlowe's chief offense 'her rigid adherence to the discipline of fasting, whilst under the alarming symptoms of a deep decline'.[3] Needless to say, Macaulay's intimation that *Clarissa* stages a voluntary death marks an extreme departure from the reception that Richardson's most celebrated novel received at its mid-century publication. Given the pervasiveness of the belief in the existence of an 'English Malady', one might expect that *Clarissa*'s early readers would have been disposed to read the novel as a suicide narrative rather than otherwise. Yet Richardson's first readers register their dissatisfaction with his published ending by offering up their revised scenes of reconciliation and consummated marriage plots in its stead, objecting not so much to Clarissa's manner of dying as to the irrefutable facticity of her death itself.

Despite Richardson's frequent allusions in the text to famous suicides such as that of Lucretia, contemporary readers persisted in claiming that 'The death of Clarissa is ... the only death of its kind in any story [and] the very word death seems too harsh to describe her leaving life'.[4] Clarissa's death subsequent to her abduction and rape by the libertine, Robert Lovelace, was widely received as a

[handwritten marginal note: J's dictionary queries Clarissa under 'SUICIDE' and against 2, as if defying the charge]

sui generis occurrence, an end that eluded definition and even understanding. *Clarissa* does not simply follow a script inherited from amatory fiction, wherein death was often the fate of women exposed to sexual experience either voluntarily or against their own will. For, even though Clarissa's will to die is actualized within the narrative, Richardson constructs her demise as a form of voluntary death that does not fall strictly under the rubric of suicide. In none of its particulars does Clarissa's death fulfil Richardson's stated criteria for suicide according to the definition presented in his last novel, *Sir Charles Grandison* (1753), in which suicide is 'an act dreadful and irreversible ... a crime that admits not of repentance' the product of 'distraction', while his favourite euphemism for the act appears to be 'to rush into eternity'. Far from inspiring dread, Clarissa's death is aesthetically pleasing and even admirable, the result of calm deliberation rather than distraction.

In any consideration of the voluntary component of Clarissa's death, the question inevitably arises as to whether Clarissa is driven to suicide by the forces of society or whether the text constructs her voluntary death as an expression of individual agency and an act of resistance to dominant social codes. This chapter advances a reading of Clarissa's death as suicidal without endorsing the 'victim status' that many traditional critical treatments of Richardson's work attribute to this character.[5] In this respect, my reading does not dismiss Clarissa as a casualty of libertine vice, but rather agrees at least partially with critics like Margaret Anne Doody, who argues that Richardson's protagonist kills herself because she 'refuses to be a mere victim'.[6] Richardson certainly does not emphasize Clarissa's victimhood, and his correspondents support this assessment by hailing his protagonist as 'the triumphant Clarissa', the 'object of envy as well as pity', who presumably reaps her reward in the afterlife.[7] In its treatment of voluntary death, *Clarissa* affords a glimpse of an alternative conception of agency that, although far from empowering, still allows for a limited degree of self-determination on the part of a character circumscribed by social and familial constraints. Unlike the protagonist of Richardson's first novel, *Pamela*, who attributes her suicidal meditations at a crucial juncture to a demon tempter, Clarissa appears to justify her death wish through an appeal to natural law and necessity. Clarissa upholds her prerogative to act according to her principles, yet reserves the right to derive a license for these principles from higher authorities.[8]

In his construction of Clarissa as a 'new Lucretia', Richardson grants her a degree of agency that renders her suicide foundational to a larger sense of community and nationhood. In the process, Richardson redeems that legendary figure from the disgrace into which she had fallen at the hands of early Christian theologians like Augustine. Whereas Augustine overlooks the national resonance of Lucretia's final act, owing largely to his preoccupation with her 'chastity suicide', Richardson foregrounds this aspect of the story by representing suicide as a locus of power rather than simply a capitulation to extant social codes. Clarissa's death is an intersubjective act, predicated on a notion of a 'social self' and an epistolary form defined more by communal than individual self-definition. Paradoxically, Richardson locates the source of Clarissa's agency in the larger community, thereby imparting to her death the status of martyrdom, and in the process blurring the boundary between suicide and self-sacrifice.

Self-Fashioning, Agency and a Pure Culture of the Death Wish

Histories chronicling the 'project of the Enlightenment' have traditionally claimed that one of its primary objectives was the increased measure of personal autonomy to be secured for the individual under the aegis of Lockean liberalism. However, this account has more recently been complicated by considerations of the extent to which protestant-inspired determinism limited and circumscribed individual autonomy. To this end, the literary scholar Scott Paul Gordon persuasively argues that 'English Protestant thought … makes desirable the loss rather than the assertion of agency, subordination rather than self-sufficiency'.[9] In Gordon's view, this 'passivity trope' radically curtails the degree of agency accorded to the individual and results in a representation of the 'self' as 'more formed than forming' in the literature of the period.[10] Although his argument at first glance appears to valorize subjection, Gordon offers the following qualification: 'By guaranteeing individuals that they do not act self-interestedly, the passivity trope paradoxically enables actions that would otherwise be difficult to conceive, from revolutionary action against a monarch to public speaking by women'.[11] In this sense, Gordon's model allows for the viable conception of agency that resides at the heart of Clarissa's actualization of voluntary death, which offers at least a limited affirmation of the power of the individual to assume autonomy over her own life. The character of Clarissa could, ironically, be an assertion of the Gordonian thesis, as a positive, individualistic resistance to a life of passivity, an existence in which the denial of self-interestedness is tantamount to a kind of agency.

From the outset of the novel, Clarissa appears to cultivate a mentality that views death as the only remedy available to an individual endowed with insurmountable principles but negligible autonomy. Clarissa's inviolable will and her rigid code of virtue demand her adherence to exemplary standards of conduct at the cost of her life. Even relatively sympathetic relatives consider her capable of taking her own life if forced into the disagreeable marriage arranged for her by her father, which eventually drives her (however unwillingly) into the arms of Lovelace. In response to some dark hints offered by Clarissa regarding the drastic measures she might take if forced into marriage with her middle-aged suitor, the 'odious Mr. Solmes', her Aunt Hervey desires that Clarissa 'assure her that [she] would offer no violence to [her]self'.[12] Clarissa's response invokes the

standard Christian disavowal of the right to suicide in its assertion that 'God
... had given [her] more grace [she] hoped than to be guilty of so horrid a rash-
ness'.[13] However, the series of events – her abduction, rape, and imprisonment in
a brothel by Lovelace – that induces Clarissa to act 'out of character' and against
her nature effect a radical revision of this attitude toward voluntary death.[14] The
first instance of this readiness to challenge society's edict against 'self-murder'
appears in the suicide threat of the notorious 'pen knife' scene, in which Clarissa vows to end her life rather than be violated by Lovelace a second time. By
the novel's end, she confesses that she desires little more than to 'slide quietly
into [her] grave', which she does with a grace that somehow heightens her virtue
and quasi-saintliness.[15] Voluntary death, formulated in this manner, becomes the
mark of privilege for the being whose exemplarity places her above the reproach
of suicide.

Early on, Clarissa articulates a belief that her death will facilitate her reintegration into the society from which she had become estranged when she fled her
father's house and accepted Lovelace's protection. In her first letter, she confesses
that she has 'sometimes wished that it had pleased God to have taken [her] in
[her] last fever, when [she] had everybody's love and good opinion'.[16] As part
of her ongoing attempt to render her suicide a communal rather than a strictly
individual event, Clarissa projects her death wish onto her relations. Invoking
a common rationale of the aspirant suicide, she asserts 'I believe I am become
the object of everyone's aversion; and that they would all be glad I were dead –
Indeed, I believe it!'[17] Her subsequent death thus becomes nothing more than an
imagined fulfilment of her family's desire. In addition, she transforms her relations' imagined wish for her death into active killing, and establishes infanticide
as a patriarchal privilege, by repeatedly insisting that she would rather seek death
at the hands of her father than submit to a marriage with her suitor. Although
this declaration might seem extreme, it attests the strength of her death wish
and the extent to which she perceives herself to be at the mercy of 'the law of
the father'. The rather sweeping power over her life and death initially attributed
to her father she later transfers to Lovelace, whom she begs to end her life. This
rhetorical transfer of authority over her life is consistent with Richardson's strategy of incorporating Clarissa's death into a network of intersubjective relations.

Although she might appear to lack the autonomy necessary to act upon her
death wish, the extensive dreamwork that the narrative attributes to Clarissa's
character enables the reader to plumb the profundity of her death wish, since
her correspondence exhaustively documents and imaginatively re-enacts each
of her dreams in detail. In these dream sequences, she is alternately tumbled
into a pit, buried alive and stabbed in nightmarish scenes suggested by her consciously articulated desires. These invariably sudden and violent deaths contrast
distinctly with the passive, prolonged and emphatically non-violent death that

Clarissa ultimately experiences, even as they establish the authenticity of Clarissa's death wish. In his study of suicide, the historian Howard Kushner observes that 'All suicidal acts (fatal as well as non-fatal) involve a fantasy component', and Clarissa's dreams invariably assign to her character a kind of fantastic agency.[18] At the same time, her visions incorporate her death into a relational structure that emphasizes the participation of another individual in the act; in the process, self-murder imaginatively transmutes into murder, enabling her to experience fantastically the passive death she paradoxically pursues.

Sinfulness is typically attributed to a conflict between the body and the mind, meaning that the most expedient means by which Clarissa, constructed on the model of a good Christian, can assert her purity after her rape is to jettison the body altogether. In her case, an aversion towards somatic experience almost inevitably fosters a kind of death instinct that overcomes any innate will to live. Repeatedly claiming 'I am [God's] creature, and not my *own*',[19] Clarissa relinquishes ownership of her body and insists that her life belongs to God rather than to the society that afforded the conditions for her 'fall' in the first place. In this respect, she represents an eighteenth-century idea of the self as being governed rather than possessed, and reaffirms the stance of passivity proposed by Gordon.[20] Based on this idea, her resolution to die involves a reappropriation of her own body on behalf of the divine agent whose will she presumably follows.

The ascetic programme of bodily denial that Clarissa pursues leads some Richardson scholars to read her character as an eighteenth-century anorexic who mortifies the body which keeps her in a life that has become increasingly distasteful to her.[21] Asceticism, as Karl Menninger writes in his psychiatric work on suicide, is 'the very refinement of slow death'.[22] In Menninger's view, both asceticism and martyrdom constitute 'forms of self-destruction in which the individual commits slow suicide – suicide by inches as it were', that he labels '*chronic* suicide, or chronic self-destruction'.[23] Richardson's representation of his protagonist's decline dramatizes what Menninger terms the 'slow suicide of the ascetic',[24] as Clarissa's aversion to her body becomes a direct reflection of her weariness of life, as she frequently complains 'how this body clings! – How it encumbers!'[25] and appears impatient to shake it off. Her surrogate mother, Mrs Lovick, accuses her of abstaining from food,[26] while her doctor and apothecary warn her 'that so much watching, so little nourishment, and so much grief as [she seems] to indulge, is enough to impair the most vigorous health, and to wear out the strongest constitution'.[27] Clarissa answers these charges of self-starvation by protesting to her doctor 'What, sir ... can I do? I have no appetite. Nothing you call nourishing will stay on my stomach.'[28] Although both her doctor's and her apothecary's admonishments regarding her self-starvation persist, once Clarissa's demise appears inevitable, all such reproaches subside as medicine defers to the authority of religious testimony, which rewrites the malnourished cadaver as a miraculous body.

Clarissa's body acquires opacity as the narrative progresses, rendering attempts to diagnose the exact nature of her medical illness impracticable and ultimately futile.[29] The body becomes the site of conflict, as Clarissa's self-diagnosis vies with early statements regarding the strength and fortitude of her 'natural constitution' and with Lovelace's contention that 'her time of life and charming constitution' should support her under any circumstances.[30] Clarissa's insistence upon the frailty of her body clashes even with the view of her advocate, the reformed libertine, John Belford, who muses in a letter to Lovelace,

> Who would think such a delicately-framed person could have sustained what she has sustained? ... Such bravoes as thou and I should never have been able to support ourselves under half the persecutions ... that *she* has met with; but, like cowards, should have slid out of the world, basely, by a sword, by a pistol, by a halter, or a knife![31]

The text at this point expresses astonishment at the miracle of unlikely survival; Clarissa is a wonder of nature, able to survive her rape and demonstrate a kind of fortitude that, gender-marked as masculine, in turn renders the libertine 'bravo' rather effeminate. Clarissa's subsequent decline seems to entail a reversion to the natural order as Belford constructs it, an order in which violated female bodies decline and perish. That Clarissa does not need to resort to the technologies of suicide as listed by Belford further heightens her embodiment; although she has access to a lethal instrument as seen in her dramatic confrontation with Lovelace, she does not require her penknife, because her indomitable will eventually enables her to die. Clarissa's body evades the control of the medical establishment, of juridical authority and of narrative constraints, as it undergoes an apotheosis that sets her above the competing claims of these social institutions. Rather than the 'failed project' that theorists such as Anthony Giddens[32] argue the dead body represents in Western culture, Clarissa's emaciated corpse instead affirms her supreme achievement and triumph over life itself.

However, despite the evident indomitability of her will, up to the moment of her death Clarissa protests she is subject to the whims of a sovereign body that has apparently internalized her death wish. As early as the scene in which she is imprisoned as a result of the malice of Lovelace's accomplices in the rape,[33] Clarissa insists that she cannot swallow, that her body rejects the food that her nervous prison wardens force upon her: 'The woman brought her a glass, and some bread and butter. She tried to taste the latter; but could not swallow it'.[34] As Clarissa's 'hunger strike' continues, her insistence upon her inability to swallow the meals placed before her becomes increasingly strident.[35] Although the act of swallowing is at least partially voluntary, the text constructs Clarissa's dysphagia as entirely subject to the influence of her body; to some extent, this representation conforms to the popular views of eighteenth-century mechanism propounded by such thinkers as David Hartley, who perceived the swallowing act as a muscular motion not in fact in the control of the will, but rather governed by the power of association.[36] Accordingly, Clarissa's moral will remains irreproachable since her body, as the text represents it, consistently thwarts her attempts to take in sustenance. Somehow the death wish precedes yet does not precipitate bodily decay, since it is ultimately the body that assumes agency under these circumstances. When considered in this light, Clarissa's assertion that 'the mind will run away with the body at any time'[37] proves meaningless and contradictory, since she strives to convey a sense that a corporeal will has the upper hand in this scenario.

Concerning themselves precisely with the possible elision of choice that this sustained self-denial might entail, Clarissa's friends worry that she might carry her hunger strike too far and overindulge her grief to a degree such that she will be unable to assert her will to live when the desire asserts itself again. At one juncture, her devoted friend Anna Howe admonishes Clarissa in the strongest of terms, warning her lest she should 'ruin [her] constitution by [her] immoderate sorrow; and by seeking death when [she] might avoid it, [she] would not be able to escape it when [she] would wish to do so'.[38] This concern recurs throughout Clarissa's decline and echoes Lovelace's earlier apprehension, as expressed to Anna Howe's suitor, Mr Hickman, 'that she will ruin her constitution; and by seeking death when she might shun him, will not be able to avoid him when she would be glad to do so'.[39] The striking similarity of these remarks reflects the extent to which Clarissa's closest friends share Lovelace's perspective in this regard.[40] A notable distinction appears in Lovelace's fanciful use of the masculine pronoun in reference to death, which anticipates his satirical description of death as a suitor courting Clarissa later in the novel. However, the assertions both construe Clarissa's decline as a fully avoidable product of her own will and view her sorrow as a temporary condition. A death wish, according to this logic, can only exist as an impermanent aberration, but may assume a power of its own when indulged 'immoderately' (as Anna Howe puts it) by the body. These repeated cautions attempt to establish proleptically a sense in which Clarissa's death might be construed as involuntary, the product of an overextended death wish that confirms the validity of the maxim of George Cheyne, physician and confidante of Richardson, that ''tis easier to preserve health than to recover it'.[41] In this sense, again, Clarissa represents her body as acting autonomously once it becomes impossible for her to repeal her death wish.

Although eighteenth-century clergymen like Thomas Knaggs[42] present the death wish as highly culpable in their sermons against 'self-murder', Richardson's novel constructs the death wish and the act of suicide as incommensurate. This means that Clarissa's desire for death takes the form of a devout appeal that is ultimately answered, thus establishing prayer as a kind of intermediate form of agency. In the loosest sense of the term, Clarissa's death wish functions as a speech act, enacting its own peculiar form of agency. The theorist Judith Butler elucidates precisely this kind of agency in her claim that 'The force of repetition in language may be the paradoxical condition by which a certain agency – not linked to a fiction of the ego as a master of circumstance – is derived from the *impossibility* of choice'.[43] Demonstrating that discourse itself may operate in a formative manner, Butler's alternative mode of agency has particular relevance to the death wish. This form of locution functions as Clarissa's locus of agency, even if her expression of will in the form of wistful regret is always contoured by the negative (as in the rhetorical question 'Why did I not drop down dead on the spot?'), which constructs her death wish, an alternate variation on the theme of passivity, as a self-liberating desire for a spontaneous act of God. As the death wish comes to define Clarissa, it becomes in a broad sense of the word performative; that is, the wish takes the place of the act that we might typically expect to follow the articulation of desire. Expressed through reported dreams, meditations and other characters' testimony, Clarissa's death wish seemingly does nothing more than convey a sense of her character's misery and thus underscores the tragic and affective nature of her sufferings. Yet sheer repetition produces a sense of movement that advances the narrative along its trajectory towards death as the fulfilment of Clarissa's prayers.[44] Clarissa's reputation and honour depend upon a radical split between word and act, as she attempts to distance herself from her actions. Members of her family circle insist on basing their interpretations of her character upon the empirical evidence afforded by her actions, dismissing her allegations of rape as misrepresentations of these apparent transgressions. Yet it is inevitable, given the emphasis placed upon discourse in a text that persistently curtails the representation of action, that the text in the end privileges the mode of self-definition most favoured by Clarissa and overlooked by her family. For despite her stance of passivity, Clarissa's particular power resides in the absolute control she exerts over the interpretation of her death: the text accepts her claim that despite her frequently articulated desire for death, her decline is not voluntary. Her emphatic demand that her body not be opened after her death further thwarts the gaze of the medical establishment that would posit a cause for her bodily decay and deliver a coroner's report that her last will and testament would be unable to refute post-mortem.[45] In the absence of an autopsy, suicide thus remains firmly in the realm of the speculative. In the last analysis, the monolithic will that Clarissa leaves provides the ultimate testimonial of her 'natural' death. A voluntary death would lead to the forfeiture of her property and effects to the Crown, making it vital that her death remain involuntary and natural in appearance; her gradual death ensures that she can dispose of her material goods according to her will. The legal document of Clarissa's will is accordingly one of several discursive means by which Richardson appears to make her suicide disappear, in a manner of speaking.[46]

Although *Clarissa* refuses to recognize self-neglect as suicide, in much eighteenth-century writing this mode of dying was considered tantamount to self-destruction. In the preface to the tenth edition of his *Essay on Health and Long Life* (1745), George Cheyne asserts that 'he that wantonly transgresseth the self-evident rules of health, is guilty of a degree of self-murder, and a habitual perseverance therein is direct suicide, and consequently the greatest crime he can commit against the author of his being'.[47] Reflecting on this issue, a number of novels later in the period would also emphasize that 'To neglect the restoration of [one's] health is a species of suicide',[48] and maintain that 'it is a species of suicide to give way to a devouring sorrow'.[49] In Richardson's novel, the notion of suicide by omission is broached in the narrative itself, as in the notorious prison scene when Lovelace's cast-off mistress Sally upbraids Clarissa for her refusal to eat, asserting 'Your religion, I think, should teach you that starving yourself is Self-Murder'. This point is reiterated by Clarissa's antagonists and supporters alike, suggesting a consensus that her actions constitute slow suicide.[50] The feeling among Clarissa's relatives that her promise that she 'will not run away from life, nor avoid the means that may continue it, if God see fit',[51] conceals a radical passivity and looks forward to Emile Durkheim's rather curt late nineteenth-century statement that 'refusal to take food is as suicidal as self-destruction by a dagger or fire-arm'.[52] However, even while allowing Clarissa's antagonists to introduce the suggestion of suicide, Richardson somehow ensures that the 'authorized' version of her death remains beyond reproach and consistent with the portrayal of her unspotted virtue.

Clarissa's death is ultimately serenely feminine, thus corroborating Silvia Sara Canetto's claim in her suicidological work that successful female suicides 'adopt the self-destructive behaviours that are congruent with the gender scripts of their cultures'.[53] In the case of *Clarissa*, the eighteenth-century endorsement of a form of 'passive quietism' affords a paradigm for female abstention. George Cheyne helped popularize the notion that the slender body was synonymous with the spiritual body in his popular writing on health in the first half of the eighteenth century.[54] Cheyne urged the benefits of abstention, fasting and purging to his friend Richardson, whose representation of Clarissa's self-renunciation could not, from this perspective, appear as anything other than a triumph of the will over the body. Clarissa's gendered performance of passive suicide enables her to appear in the guise of a proto-anorexic or a latter-day 'fasting maiden'. Although this equation between an eighteenth-century fictional construct and the medieval (or seventeenth-century) female martyr might seem a totalizing and ahistorical gesture, the feminist theorist Susan Bordo has identified some 'continuous elements' in 'women's transhistorical projects to transcend hunger and desire'.[55] Appealing to enduring historical traditions that 'have dominantly coded appetite, lack of will, temptation, and, indeed, the body itself as female',[56] Bordo locates the commonality between *anorexia mirabilia* and *anorexia nervosa* in their shared quest for perfection, whether spiritual or physical (both are mutually bound up in each other, as Bordo insists), which drives the female subject to compensate for her multitude of perceived deficiencies. This is consistent with the regimen of rigorous self-discipline that Clarissa observes in ordinary life, and which Anna Howe exhaustively chronicles in her post-mortem panegyric. However, Clarissa cannot altogether claim the status of the fasting maiden since, unlike such prodigies as Martha Taylor – an adolescent who purportedly fasted for a year in 1668 – she eventually meets her death. Where the miracle of the fasting maiden resided in the ability to suspend indefinitely the moment of death, to cling to existence despite the denial of bodily needs, the wonder of Clarissa's narrative resides in her ability to precipitate death. In Clarissa's case, the model of perfection is attainable only through total self-eradication. The central paradox of Clarissa's character unfolds in the contemplation and act of suicide. On the one hand, she expresses an inveterate hatred of her self, as exemplified by her statement to Anna Howe: 'What a tale I have to unfold! – But still upon *self*, this vile, this hated *self*! – I will shake it off, if possible ... Self, then, be banished from *self* one moment'. [57] The 'moment' Clarissa refers to here is death, suggesting that death may be willed by suspending the self. On the other hand, arguably Clarissa's death occurs as a result of her unwillingness to compromise her principles and deviate from the standards of selfhood established by her epistolary practices.

In many respects, Clarissa's death wish conforms to the sketch of non-violent suicides Margaret Pabst Battin presents in her discussion of the ethics of suicide. Battin argues that these particular suicides 'contain a component of what we might, paradoxically perhaps, call self-preservation, a kind of self-respect ... They are based, as it were, on a self-idea: a conception of one's own value and worth, beneath which one is not willing to slip'.[58] Read from this perspective, Clarissa's death is predicated upon the preservation of the self; Clarissa dies not to extinguish her being, but rather to realize its full potential, in a variation on the notion of suicide as a 'corrective remaking of the self'.[59] Elaborating upon Blanchot's rather similar description of suicide as 'an exceptional affirmation',[60] Simon Critchley theorizes that 'The moment of the controlled extinction of the subject is also paradoxically the moment when the Subject swells to fill the entire cosmos, becoming ... a cosmos, and the uncreated creator of the cosmos'.[61] The notion of 'controlled extinction' approximates the affirming vision of voluntary death that Clarissa embraces, which, of course, differs considerably from the way in which suicide is often conceptualized.

However, although this conception of suicide as 'controlled extinction' might seem rather modern, it is not so very far from John Donne's provocative claim in *Biathanatos* that 'Self-preservation, which is but an appreciation of that which is good in our opinion, is not violated by self-homicide',[62] if, that is, the perfectibility rather than the extinction of the self constitutes the aim of the suicide. Clarissa's death would fulfil the admittedly narrow parameters of the acceptable suicide as Donne defines them: those modelled explicitly after the circumstances of Christ's voluntary death. From this perspective, Clarissa's death might be read as transformative and altruistic (insofar as she constructs herself as an exemplar for the community) rather than as an act of submission to an anorexic ideology, even though she performs the 'gender script' as it is written for her. In this double vision of her death, Clarissa thus demonstrates that it is possible to be a victim and an agent at the same time. Indeed, defined succinctly by theorist Ellen Messer-Davidow as 'the ability to act otherwise',[63] agency is by no means foreclosed to Clarissa, who, as the text constantly reiterates, might alternatively have chosen to continue in life, remain single, and take up residence in her inherited 'dairy'. Her death is only posited as a myriad of narrative options, and as such, must be seen as incorporating an element of voluntarism or agency. Essentially, Clarissa cloaks her agency with the very gender scripts she employs to justify and sanction her behaviour.

Although Clarissa *professes* her body's sovereignty in succumbing to this desire, she indulges in the kind of 'psychosomatic manipulation' that Caroline Walker Bynum ascribes to the medieval female martyr.[64] Clarissa does ultimately attain her wish, although she insists upon a definitive Cartesian mind/body split, given that however sincere her desire to die might be, she claims that she cannot actuate it at the level of her body. Instead, she defers to a higher authority, whose will conveniently intersects with her own. Accordingly, we find that this divide between the mind and the body is crucial to the text's evasion of the suicide question, and the text in fact exploits the distinction between the corporeal and the non-corporeal that Western philosophy adopts from Descartes, who in turn drew upon Augustine's opposition of the two categories. In this manner, Clarissa circumvents proscriptions relevant to the older category of *mors voluntaria* as opposed to the modern and semantically more violent construct of suicide, or self-murder.

Read from another perspective, Clarissa's death wish receives validation from much more modern Christian sources. One of few Richardson critics to engage directly with the problem of suicide, Cynthia Wolff reads Clarissa's longing for death as consistent with the sentiments expressed in Puritan diaries.[65] In Wolff's view, Clarissa's death wish arises from extreme Puritan introspection, which paradoxically heightens both a sense of self and a desire to escape it. Although Wolff initially aligns Clarissa's death drive with Durkheim's category of egoistic suicide, which proceeds from the exaggerated sense of selfhood that prevents the individual from integrating sufficiently into social networks, she ultimately argues that Clarissa's death does not constitute a suicide since she has wholly extinguished the exaggerated sense of self that produced her sense of isolation and accompanying suicidal tendencies in the first place. In Wolff's view, 'Clarissa's ability to overcome self in her generosity and benevolence towards others' resolves the problem of suicide;[66] however, from this perspective, suicide can exist only as a corollary of egotism. Even if Wolff is correct in assuming that Clarissa transcends the sense of self that ostensibly fuels her 'death drive', might not her death nonetheless be regarded as voluntary? Wolff's careful delineation of the secularized strains of Puritanism that inform the plot of *Clarissa* leaves the question of suicide largely unresolved by overlooking the possible interpretation of suicide as a social or altruistic act, which is to say that selflessness and suicide are not mutually exclusive categories.

It is generally agreed that suicide could not crystallize as a concept in the Western tradition until a notion of selfhood had been formed. According to standard accounts, this event could not occur until the emergence of 'the self' as a socio-linguistic concept in the sixteenth century, and as a philosophical idea with Descartes's articulation of the *cogito* in the seventeenth century. Where Augustine's discussion of suicide in *The City of God* emphasizes the role of the will, an early modern construction of this form of death foregrounds the centrality of the self. Although seemingly a minor point, it is important to an understanding of the concept as employed by Richardson. The difference between a *mors Romana* (a Roman death) and a modern Western notion of suicide resides in the fact that the first category emphasizes the social aspect of the act and the second foregrounds the element of agency.[67] Durkheim's commonly accepted sociological definition of modern suicide as a positive or negative action that fulfils a victim's death wish draws upon the newer model. The distinction between the two categories is, however, far too tidy and fails to take into account the counter-trends that complicated the picture during the early modern period. As we have seen, in *Clarissa* considerations of agency are important, especially given Richardson's investment in according some agency, however limited, to his exemplary heroine. At the same time, this emphasis upon agency should not obscure the degree to which the text constructs Clarissa's voluntary death as a social action. Richardson's representation of voluntary death enables a scene of martyrdom that is individualistic in its emphasis on the component of agency, but, as the next sections of this chapter will address, also resolutely social in its concentration on reception and performance. Suicide as self-respect and suicide as a social statement are not contradictory here; in fact, it is only by insisting on her personal integrity that Clarissa is able to fashion herself into a martyr figure.

Natural Law, Martyrdom and Heterodoxy

Richardson's own views on suicide are difficult to determine with any degree of certainty, although his correspondence at one juncture expresses a broad-mindedly sympathetic attitude. His response to Miss Collier's account of 'a poor unhappy girl in [her] village who drowned herself'[68] in the wake of the Lisbon earthquake after prophesying the imminence of similar natural disasters on English soil exemplifies this sympathetic rationality:

> Your poor frantic girl, perhaps, thought she was avoiding the evil to come, and which she had prophesied would come, when she sought her death in the water. There have been unhappy people, more in their selves than she seems to have been, who have thrown themselves into the arms of death, for fear of dying. This girl must have been earthquake-mad, as well as otherwise delirious.[69]

Although Richardson pleads insanity on behalf of the deceased, his reaction acknowledges the possibility that suicide might be committed by the relatively rational-minded; as the historian John Stachniewski affirms, the Puritan dread of death at times precipitated devout individuals to seek an end to their suspense by resorting to suicide.[70] At the same time, Richardson's suggestion that suicide stems from an estrangement from the 'self' is highly relevant to his engagement with the problem in *Clarissa*. Interestingly, in the same epistolary exchange Collier disapprovingly records the reaction of the general populace who 'believe [the woman] a saint'[71] and a throwback to the woman visionary and martyr of medieval times: the very interpretation upon which Richardson depends in his delineation of the exemplary yet suicidal Clarissa. Richardson's attitude towards this suicide expresses a sympathetic withholding of judgement, suggesting that his views on this subject were more progressive than one might expect, even though it is not the modern, secularized notion of voluntary death that Richardson endorses so much as the early-Christian permissive attitude towards self-sacrifice.[72] Moreover, the interest Richardson expresses in the reception of the woman's suicide and the process whereby it takes on the aspect of martyrdom in his correspondence with Collier directly anticipates the communal construction of Clarissa's death in his novel.

As I have shown, Clarissa attempts to justify her voluntary death by positioning it as the fulfilment of the will of others; at the same time, she licenses it through recourse to natural law. In a pivotal scene of the narrative, Clarissa defends her threatened suicide by insisting that 'The LAW shall be all my resource: the LAW ... only shall be my refuge!'[73] Having refused the assistance of positive law, Clarissa clearly refers to a higher authority. Clarissa's insistence that her initial suicidal gesture is sanctioned by natural law questions juncture the Christian proscription against the death wish. Yet, we might ask, if the threatened act of violently taking one's life might be justified by a plea of self-defence, how much more excusable is the passive 'suicide by omission' that ostensibly ends Clarissa's life? Early, pre-Augustine Christian theologians acknowledged the complexity of this question, distinguishing between acts that directly resulted in suicide and those that indirectly led to death, as in the case of Christ.[74] Yet many natural law theorists of the early modern period, following Augustine, refused to distinguish between direct and indirect voluntary deaths. As Samuel Pufendorf writes in his influential treatise on *The Duty of Man and Citizen According to Natural Law* (1673),

> Whoever terminates or throws away his life of his own accord must be regarded without fail as violating natural law, whether he is driven by the common troubles of human life, or by resentment of sufferings which would have made them objects of scorn to human society ... or in any empty display of faith or fortitude.[75]

Yet, despite Pufendorf's stern injunction, natural law in this period had become a rather malleable discourse that enables even the devout individual to evade accountability. As the work of Heather Zias and Laura Hinton demonstrates, the rhetoric of natural law in the eighteenth century endows the individual with the freedom to choose death in a manner that is sanctioned by the moral foundations of society and positive law.[76] Zias writes that 'natural law is inherently individualistic, granting to each person (in theory) the capacity to tap into one's internal guidance system and arrive at moral conclusions independently'.[77] Richardson's Clarissa demonstrates this capacity for 'autonomous reflection' throughout the text, and her observation that 'when catastrophes are consummating, what changes ... may *one* short month produce'[78] suggests that death is in fact a consequence of rape which is sanctioned by natural law.

Clarissa thus finds in natural law a legitimation of her *mors negativa* or passive suicide in a manner highly reminiscent of Donne's arguments in *Biathanatos*, which set out to expose the contradictions and inconsistencies of that very concept. Her understanding of 'the natural' inevitably differs from that of the Hobbesian Lovelace, who maintains that 'the natural course of things' involves a transformation of languishment into active resentment.[79] The epistemological systems of each character, founded as they are on differing conceptions of what constitutes the law of nature, repeatedly collide in Richardson's fictional universe that appears to ground itself on the Augustinian/ Thomistic belief that 'natural law provides the means of determining whether or not a civil law passes the ethical test and should be followed'.[80] Far from affording the sort of 'right reason' that moral philosophers ascribed to natural law, these systems rather introduce a degree of moral relativism that proves quite useful to the rising middle class of which Richardson was himself a member. In this respect, they reflect the tendency of the emergent middle class to idealize itself in natural law, but to protect itself with an 'antinatural law' once it has established power, as observed by Ernst Bloch.[81] It is at moments like this that we can see how the novel as a genre was not only produced by the middle class, but also created and sustained middle-class values in the society.

Moreover, this construct of natural law, even while it appeals to a notion of the collective good, inevitably and almost accidentally creates an autonomous, self-governing subject. While Richardson's treatment of suicide by no means incorporates the permissibility sponsored by some of his contemporaries, it nonetheless reflects the same readiness to employ the discourse of natural law to sanction individual actions that appear to contravene the tenets of positive law. The 'natural law subjectivity'[82] that contours Richardson's idealized characterizations thus comes into collision with the 'juridical consciousness' that John Zomchick identifies as the basis for eighteenth-century moral conduct, thereby creating a conceptual anomaly in the form of a legal entity that is not bound by the law.[83] According to Thomas Keymer, *Clarissa* is haunted by 'a fear of libertinism's capacity not simply to breach particular laws but to break down their ideological foundation'.[84] But like the libertine, Richardson's heroic ideal also exists outside the parameters of the law. At the same time that Clarissa, as Deirdre Lynch demonstrates, 'lacks the ability of male protagonists of epistolary fiction to augment their powers by allying their writings with the apparatus of the law courts',[85] she can justify her actions by recourse to the accommodating rhetoric of natural law as an alternative mode of discursive agency.

The libertine belief in self-determination and absolute autonomy typically embraces suicide as an act sanctioned by reason and free will. In accordance with this creed, Lovelace expresses his own death wish in a grim parody of Clarissa's unwavering resolve to divest herself of her 'corrupted' body. Yet the primary aim of Lovelace's death fantasy involves wresting power away from Clarissa's dying body and refiguring her as his 'charming widow'.[86] The fact that his own body tenaciously clings to life despite his avowed intention of avenging himself on his critics by dying suggests the triumph of the libertine body over the spirit. In a reversal of Cartesian dualist gender structures, Lovelace's sheer materiality keeps him alive, whereas Clarissa's ethereal nature secures her death. Thus, when Lovelace finds himself unable to simply will himself to death in the spirit of Clarissa, he resorts to the preferred method of self-destruction, which enables the libertine to circumvent the stigma of suicide by seeking death in the context of a duel.[87] However, Richardson condemns this practice of duelling as a crime second only to suicide in *Clarissa*, while in *Sir Charles Grandison* lengthy discourses on the subject situate both acts on the same continuum of contemporary self-destructive behaviours, as did countless moralists of the period. Richardson rejects the model of masculinist self-destructive behaviour demonstrated in duelling, even as he endorses the more 'feminine' model of self-neglect, although, as the next section will detail, he merely transfers the gender values from one mode to the other.

In his sociology of suicide, Durkheim concedes that 'though suicide is commonly conceived as a positive, violent action involving some *muscular energy*, it may happen that a purely negative attitude or mere abstention will have the same consequence'.[88] Both 'positive' and 'negative' forms of suicide have evident gender markers, and the fact that the second category is often not identified as suicide may be attributed to the pervasive assumption that women do not take their own lives. In a Christian context, the fact that Christ experienced the latter, passive death was as troublesome as the fact that it might be construed as suicide. This mode of 'feminine' self-sacrifice was, as the literary critic Wendy Jones has noted, a source of anxiety in the eighteenth and nineteenth centuries to such an extent that male authors such as Richard Steele took 'pains to establish that the virtuous male, modeled after Christ, is entirely masculine'.[89] Yet, at the same time as this enterprise evacuates the femininity of self-sacrifice, it heightens the degree of voluntarism that would encourage Christ's death to be received as suicide. Richardson to a certain extent appreciates this fact and draws upon Clarissa's gender to complicate the voluntary component of her death. In her historiography of martyrdom, Elizabeth Castelli observes that 'the martyr's death is a masculine death, even when (or especially when) it is suffered by a woman'.[90] Richardson's martyr narrative similarly illustrates gender's contingency, for Clarissa's death involves no 'muscular energy' as such, but Richardson endows her with agency precisely by masculinizing her character in a representation that simultaneously accentuates and suspends the operation of the will. In a discussion of Clarissa's 'Christlike' attributes, Peggy Thompson claims that the theological texts that Richardson draws upon to cement this identification 'reinscribe and reaffirm women's identity as ideally passive, suffering, and salvific'.[91] Thompson acknowledges the eighteenth-century view that 'Christ's own suffering is problematic' yet insists that Richardson's narrative subscribes to 'the myth of passive womanhood' by privileging the 'agonizing sacrifice ... assigned the Christlike woman'.[92] While I agree with Thompson's assessment of Clarissa's status as an eighteenth-century martyr figure, I take a different view of the nature of martyrdom as represented in the text. Rather than presenting the passive model of female submission to self-sacrificial social imperatives, Richardson draws upon various strands of heterodox discourse to present an alternative and relatively more enabling view of martyrdom.

In his negotiation of the problem of suicide in *Clarissa*, Richardson's chronic use of Lucretia as an intertext leads him to embrace an ideal of martyrdom that was ultimately rejected by the church. Just as Jean-Jacques Rousseau will style the heroine of his novel, *Julie* a '*nouvelle Lucrèce*', we might consider Clarissa, a foundational character for Rousseau as well, a 'new Lucretia'. One of the central accounts of the foundation of Rome, the Lucretia story enjoyed tremendous popularity on the eighteenth-century stage and entered the English novel primarily through Richardson. The Lucretia story was first officially recorded by Titus Livy, whose prose chronicle begins, as so many anecdotal historiographies do, with a man's idle boast during male conversation.[93] In Livy's redaction, Tarquinius Collatinus claims that his wife, Lucretia, surpasses in terms of her 'womanly virtue' all other wives. When his friends seek first-hand corroboration of this claim, one of their number, Sextus Tarquinius (son to a Roman king), becomes enamoured of Lucretia, and returns later to rape her at knifepoint in her quarters. Summoning her husband, Lucretia informs him and his friend, Lucius Junius Brutus, of the crime, and after exhorting them to avenge her, she stabs herself, thus becoming both a martyr to a despotic system and a legendary example of the virtuous *mors voluntaria*.

In the semi-legendary narrative, Lucretia's death serves to redeem her chastity and to prove unequivocally that she was violated against her will. Stephanie Jed's observation that in Livy's account Lucretia's suicide is called on as a witness to her innocence is equally applicable to Clarissa's case.[94] Since, from her perspective, marriage to Lovelace would in effect annul the rape in popular opinion, and her preservation of her single state would suggest her complacency in respect to her 'transgressions' and sufferings, death presents itself as literally the only option available to her that will certify her innocence. As Barbara Baines notes, Lucretia's death makes of suicide a 'shorthand or code to define absolute virtue'[95] in literature of the seventeenth and eighteenth centuries. According to this logic, Clarissa's identification with Lucretia – so chronic that it compromises her individuality – invites the reader to interpret her death as wholly voluntary. At the same time, Clarissa's invocation of Lucretia as a model is an attempt to salvage her reputation for virtue, notwithstanding her own awareness of blamelessness.

The Lucretia intertext dominates the post-rape mentalities of both Lovelace and Clarissa. In his letter written just prior to that of Clarissa, Lovelace infers from Clarissa's 'majestic composure' that there can be 'No Lucretia-like vengeance upon herself in her thought'.[96] The degree to which Lovelace once again misreads Clarissa's mind becomes evident in the subsequent scenes, wherein Clarissa's thinly veiled threats of suicide alternating with requests that Lovelace kill her himself culminate inevitably in her incarnation as Lucretia in what Lovelace describes sardonically as the 'history of the Lady and the Penknife'.[97] Immediately following the rape, Lovelace confesses to Belford his apprehension that 'with her own hand, in resentment of the perpetrated outrage, [Clarissa] (like another Lucretia) will assert the purity of her heart'.[98] Lovelace's repeated return to the Lucretia analogy, and his systematic rejection of its relevance to his and Clarissa's own situation, mirrors her own preoccupation with the legend. After the rape, she appropriates the narrative for her own, and cryptic statements such as 'A less complicated villainy cost a Tarquin – but I forget what I would say again'[99] suggest that she meditates self-harm in the style of Lucretia.

The ellipses and claim of forgetfulness stem from the fact that at this juncture – prior to the appearance of her cousin Morden – Clarissa lacks the familial support that would allow for the punishment of the Tarquinian Lovelace. At this point, Clarissa evidently considers her case more egregious and her suicide more justifiable than Lucretia's parallel acts. In Clarissa's view, Lucretia suffered 'a less complicated villainy' because her rape in the traditional Roman account was accomplished by violence but without the aid of narcotics. Clarissa's innocence is still more beyond reproach than Lucretia's, according to this logic, and the vengeance that she implicitly demands is dire to a proportionate degree. However, Clarissa's contrast between her case and Lucretia's overlooks the fact that in later versions of the Roman legend, including Chaucer's retelling, Lucretia's rape takes place while she is unconscious. Making note of this interpolated detail, Barbara Baines affirms that 'By rendering Lucrece virtually dead at the time of the rape, Chaucer not only negates the possibility of her carnal pleasure but suggests that the rape is a form of necrophilia'.[100] Richardson follows a similar logic in presenting Clarissa as unconscious at the time of the assault, which is carried out only with the assistance of Lovelace's gang of prostitutes. Hence, as Clarissa both claims to identify with and transcend Lucretia, her character blends with the semi-legendary figure, which is made to carry the burden of referentiality in the novel's preoccupation with voluntary death.

The repeated evocation of the Lucretia story inevitably invites direct comparisons between Clarissa's response to her violation and Lucretia's more immediate action. The persistence of this intertext, however, only complicates an already challenging hermeneutic task, since it creates a false homology between a semi-legendary suicide of ancient Rome and an eighteenth-century fictionalized representation of an *apparent* voluntary death. In his study of suicide in Roman literature, Timothy Hill points to the 'difficulties of aligning two discourses so often entirely dissimilar to each other', since the Roman phenomenon of the *mors voluntaria* appears to correspond only superficially to the act of suicide as understood in the West.[101] However, as Elizabeth Castelli's historiography of Christian martyrdom argues, the interface between ancient sacrificial practices and Christian martyrdom is more substantial than is typically acknowledged. In Castelli's view, 'The mobilization of sacrifice as a metaphor for early Christian theorists of martyrdom is enabled by the historical construction of sacrifice as a recognized practice and as a part of the Roman religious system'.[102] Buried within Christian views of sacrifice reside the traces of Roman ritual which upheld the difference between the sacrificer and the sacrificed victim eventually elided by Christianity. Richardson's persistent invocation of the Lucretia intertext suggests that behind Clarissa's self-sacrifice lurks the ghost of Roman ritualized sacrificial practices.

Presenting herself as a victim for the slaughter, Clarissa could be considered as much a scapegoat as Lucretia who, as Melissa Matthes affirms, serves as a 'female *pharmakon*' representing both 'the source of disruption and of the return of order'.[103] At the same time, however, Clarissa claims a particular degree of power by earnestly welcoming her sacrifice, at one point even desiring that Lovelace kill her 'outright ... or help [her] to the means',[104] and absorbing it into a Christian paradigm. Clarissa represents an alternative vision of Christ similar to that formulated in the theoretical work of Julia Kristeva, who posits that Christ 'offers himself to a death-and-resurrection that causes sin to be visited on all members of the community and on each individually, instead of absolving them'.[105] Likewise, Clarissa does not absorb the sins of the community but rather redistributes them; a supreme sense of guilt for the collective failure to keep her alive is the process by which the community is restored at the novel's end. Rather than absorbing social guilt, Clarissa diffuses it outward indefinitely, realizing in abjection a peculiar locus of agency.

Towards the novel's end, the Lucretia analogy once again acquires relevance as Clarissa approaches closer to death. In his defence, Lovelace sets himself the task of impugning Clarissa's actions. Lovelace demands of his relations at one point,

> [I]f ... a lady will destroy herself, whether by a lingering death as of grief; or by the
> dagger, as Lucretia did; is there more than one fault the *man*'s? – Is not the other
> hers? – Were it not so ... we either have had no men so wicked as young Tarquin was,
> or no women so virtuous as Lucretia, in the space of – how many thousand years ...
> And so Lucretia is recorded as a single wonder![106]

Lovelace attempts to complicate the issue of blame by eliding the distinction between slow decay and quick dispatch of the self. In attacking Lucretia's exemplarity, Lovelace attempts to undermine Clarissa's status as a paragon, at the same time extenuating his own guilt by presenting his crime as a fairly common occurrence. In the process, both the tone and the language of the slur upon Clarissa align Lovelace with St Augustine, who denounced Lucretia as 'the murderess of an innocent and chaste woman'.[107]

Even though a pre-Christian 'martyr figure', Lucretia's appeal to early Christian zealots eager to sacrifice their lives in emulation of their saviour forced Augustine to include her in his round condemnation of the category of chastity suicide. In *The City of God against the Pagans* (AD 413–426), a text occasioned by the sacking of Rome in AD 410, a lengthy disquisition on Lucretia and other pre-Christian 'martyrs' sought to discourage women who had been raped during the 'barbarian' invasion from taking their lives. Paradoxically, in an attempt to assure women that their souls remained pure even when their bodies had been violated, Augustine resorted to attacking Lucretia's virtue with the suggestion that she consented to her rape, thus enabling him to dismiss her suicide as an immoral rather than an heroic and chastity-validating act, as seen in the following question: 'What if she was betrayed by the pleasure of the act, and gave some consent to Sextus, though so violently abusing her, and then was so affected with remorse, that she thought death alone could expiate her sin?'[108] However, Augustine's sustained treatment of Lucretia in the context of a discussion of martyrdom resulted in an inadvertent 'Christianization' of Lucretia; where earlier she had existed merely as a fantastic figure in the mythological pre-history of the Roman republic, in Augustine's account she comes to be ranked among the early Christian martyrs – particularly the self-destructive Donatist sect – whose mania for suicide Augustine was so eager to curb. By virtue of Augustine's sustained attack Lucretia earns increased celebrity, which Richardson draws upon in identifying in this Roman legend the source of Clarissa's agency and an affirmation of her 'right to die'.[109]

Despite the fact that eighteenth-century redactions of the myth challenged the utility and even the morality of Lucretia's voluntary death, they did not necessarily question its sacrificial component. In its Lucretia-like aspect, Clarissa's death harks back to the self-sacrificial chastity-suicides that were roundly condemned by Augustine, but, as Henry Fedden observes, 'never altogether established as a "sin"'.[110] Her death might be construed as 'altruistic suicide' insofar as Clarissa hopes that it might deter Lovelace from similarly assaulting other women. Richardson reinforces the sacrificial nature of her death in his separate edition of Clarissa's 'Meditations', in which he claims by way of a prefatorial clarification that Clarissa 'Wishes [Lovelace's] repentance, and that she may be the last victim to his barbarous perfidy: and is solicitous for nothing so much in this life, as to prevent vindictive mischief *to* and *from* the man who has used her so basely'.[111] Clarissa's death does not directly preserve other women from Lovelace's corrupting influence, but it does nonetheless result in his virtual emasculation and eventual execution at the hands of her relative. In this sense, her voluntary death represents a sacrifice worthy of martyrdom; for Richardson, the fact that 'mischief' ultimately does befall Lovelace in no way nullifies or detracts from the significance of Clarissa's self-sacrifice.

The Augustinian decree against *mors voluntaria* was designed as a stop-gap measure not only to contain the early Christian zeal for suicide after the manner of their founder, but also to counter the 'spirituality of annihilation' central to the religion.[112] One might argue that Christianity naturalizes a death wish, since, as Georges Minois observes in his history of suicide,

> The ideal Christian life rests on an extremely precarious equilibrium: the spiritual individual detests the world and life, aspires to death and to the next world, but is prohibited from crossing that threshold by himself. Living in the world but refusing all its pleasures, the spiritually inclined are like the living dead and must approach death as closely as possible without inducing it.[113]

In order to sanction Clarissa's voluntary death, then, Richardson's narrative undertakes a detour around Augustinian prohibitions of suicide and recuperates earlier models of Christian martyrdom upheld by patristic writers such as Ambrose and Jerome who sanctioned chastity-suicide.[114] Clarissa represents an anachronism as a martyr who refuses to compromise on issues that engage her principles. In her cultivation of the *mors negativa*, she also allows for the conceptualization of a new kind of character subjectivity in the novel that asserts the pre-eminence of 'will'. In this sense, Richardson constructs a notion of agency contoured by rejection of life, offering a conception of 'will' that incorporates the ability to 'nill' that Augustine dismisses in his discussion of suicide. Yet, Clarissa's suicide is less direct than that of Lucretia, and accordingly less culpable. She is a modernized version of the Roman exemplar who, denied a weapon by which to secure her immediate death, instead has recourse to the lapse of time.[115] Her extended suffering in effect removes the stigma of 'sudden death' (to borrow the period's popular euphemism for suicide). Her end is not the *mors spontanea*[116] that Augustine decried but rather a slow decline into death.

In his monumental *Book of Martyrs* (1563), John Foxe limits the relevance of *The City of God*, which had occupied a central place in Roman Catholic orthodoxy, and privileges instead Protestant discourses of suffering. The historian Linda Colley observes that an enterprising printer's decision in 1732 to publish a new edition of *The Book of Martyrs* in instalments sold by subscription suddenly rendered the voluminous work accessible to a general readership.[117] Indeed, the wide readership enjoyed by Foxe's work for centuries after its publication is suggested in an ironic moment in Richardson's first novel when Pamela compares a bishop's preparation for martyrdom to her attempt to scour a pan, ostensibly alluding to a scene from *The Book of Martyrs*.[118] In Richardson's second novel, Foxe's work assumes a much more serious import, and is crucial to his representation of the national implications of self-sacrifice. With its premise that rebellion constituted 'obedience to a higher authority than that of any earthly rule',[119] the work informs the logic governing Richardson's vision of Clarissa's martyrdom. Foxe's construction of a community of martyrs supplies the basis for the national resonance of self-sacrifice found in *Clarissa*, which will be discussed more fully in the next section.

Foxe's work affords a miscellany of historical figures dying on behalf of their beliefs, and the sheer expanse of the work attests to his vision of England as an Elect nation. As he constructs a Protestant martyrology, Foxe vindicates James Hales, a Protestant judge who, incarcerated under the Papist Marian regime, stabbed himself with a penknife 'in divers parts of his body', and having survived his suicide attempt later 'cast himself into a shallow river and drowned'.[120] Although his account makes no attempt to obviate the intentional aspect of Hales's death, Foxe palliates the suicide on the possible grounds that it was undertaken so 'that he would avoid the necessity of hearing mass'.[121] Departing from the Augustinian position that one should 'not commit suicide to avoid suffering',[122] Foxe attributes Hales's suicide to a desire to remain spiritually and physically pure in a manner analogous to the virgins of Antioch, whose case Foxe subsequently invokes in the course of his defence of Hales. In this manner, Foxe recuperates what the historian James C. W. Truman describes as a 'propaganda disaster for the Protestants'[123] by validating suicide on precisely the grounds that Augustine had earlier proscribed. In spite of his aversion to 'stories of silly women and infants'[124] Foxe also incorporates anecdotes of Protestant women martyred in childbirth, attesting to the fact that the 'Herodian cruelty of ... Catholic tormentors'[125] recognized no gender boundaries, and also establishing the category of female Protestant martyr. Foxe's text conceivably provides a precedent for a martyrological reading of suicide, even as it vindicates the female chastity suicides denounced by Augustine. Although Foxe does not discuss Lucretia's case, he does invoke that of her Roman compatriot, Sophronia, who preferred to die by her own hand than be 'defiled'. In this way, Foxe inaugurates a counter-tradition that assimilates suicide into the pattern of holiness from which Augustine had banished it, and imagines a national English identity founded upon Protestant sacrifice.

Historians eager to locate the incipient stirrings of an English national consciousness in the sixteenth century evoke this aspect of Foxe's work in support of their arguments. For example, the historians Liah Greenfeld[126] and William Haller identify the text's publication date as a pivotal moment in English nationalism, although their account has been challenged by Krishan Kumar, who finds in Foxe's work rather an expression of 'an apocalyptic tradition that is international or global in the fullest sense of the word'.[127] Although Kumar is correct to point out that religion rather than nation constitutes Foxe's primary concern, the sixteenth-century writer's preoccupation with the stories of predominantly English martyrs weakens Kumar's claim for the work's internationalist bias. As Foxe declares in his concluding remarks, his focus centres on the 'acts and proceedings of the whole church of Christ, namely of the Church of England'.[128]

Although a genealogy of English nationhood is outside the scope of this work, we can see how Foxe's vision of England as an elect nation in fact affords a model for political or national martyrdom. Foxe renders suicide central to the Protestant martyrology and to his construction of a nationalist ethos contoured around suffering, which bears a strong resemblance to the model of suicide found in *Clarissa* and is articulated most forcefully (and counter-intuitively) through Richardson's intertextual references to Lucretia.

Like Foxe, John Donne affords a template for the erasure of the difference between suicide and self-sacrifice, in his posthumously published *Biathanatos* (1647). The influence of Donne's writing on Richardson's composition of *Clar-*

issa has been traced by G. Gabrielle Starr who dwells at length upon Richardson's use of Donne's lyrics in his representation of the scene of 'holy dying' at the narrative's end.[129] However, it is plausible that Donne's prose treatise *Biathanatos* also lurks in the background of Richardson's work. As the subtitle of this controversial work declares, Donne sets out to prove that 'self-homicide is not so naturally Sin that it may never be otherwise'. In his construction of a 'martyro-loge [*sic*] of all which have perished by their own means for religion, country, fame, love, ease, fear, shame',[130] Donne places self-sacrifice on behalf of one's country and one's religion on the same continuum, pointing to a secularization of martyrology that renders a slippage between suicide and sacrifice more readily attainable. Donne also declares permissible the 'enormous witherings of our bodies' involved in death by fasting,[131] thereby assimilating the *mors negativa* into his definition of *biathanatos*, which literally signifies 'violent death' in Greek. As Donne suggests, death by fasting performs no less violence upon the body of the subject than does hanging or other more direct means to death. Regardless of the degree of influence Donne's text may have had on Richardson's, the fact that its heterodoxy complicates the picture of suicide in the eighteenth century renders it relevant to the cultural background of Clarissa's own death.

Not surprisingly, *Biathanatos* gained a notoriety that persisted into the eighteenth century when it was blamed for inciting melancholics to suicide. Moral treatises against suicide launched polemical attacks on Donne's arguments when *Biathanatos* was published for a second time in 1700. That year John Adams responded with his magisterial *An Essay Concerning Self-Murther*, which presented the permissive attitude towards suicide championed by Donne as fundamentally absurd in all its permutations. Adams's denunciation became a touchstone for subsequent sermon literature that similarly ignored the fact that, when closely attended to, Donne's work in fact offers a qualified advocacy of suicide under certain circumstances and for particular ends. Donne construed 'self-homicide' for the 'wrong reasons' as a sin, yet sanctioned voluntary death in emulation of the crucifixion with a view to achieving spiritual perfection on another plane. In Donne's view, suicide does not contravene the tenet of 'self-preservation' but rather fulfils it insofar as a spiritual death advances the 'best part' of the individual elected. As Susannah Monta observes in her work on the impact of religious changes upon early modern literary culture, by 'taking martyrdom as a primary instance of suicide, Donne naturalizes and demystifies martyrdom'.[132] Moreover, he affords another precedent for authorizing voluntary death on religious grounds that early Christian theologians had sought to preclude. Both Foxe's and Donne's texts offer an unorthodox and antinomian view of martyrdom that at times appears rather similar to suicide. In his letter *Against Gaudientius*, Augustine had argued that the cause rather than the penalty was constitutive of martyrdom,[133] and both Foxe and Donne to a certain extent preserve this argument in their focus on intentionality, even while they broaden the field of acceptable causes for voluntary death in a manner that would prove highly useful to Richardson in his reintegration of mortality and the voluntary in *Clarissa*, through the useful metaphor of Lucretia.

A New Lucretia and 'a National Point'

An essay that Richardson putatively wrote in collaboration with Ralph Courtville, a journalist for the *Gazetteer*, begins with the acknowledgement that '[T]here is nothing which hath brought greater reproach on our Nation, or that is still more frequent among us, than Suicide', which is subsequently identified as England's 'new Religion' among those 'who are addicted to melancholy'.[134] Despite its concluding exhortation that the suicidal individual entrust his or her destiny to God, the tone of the essay is secular rather than doctrinally prescriptive, as it lays out techniques for avoiding melancholy and suicide. Even though the authorship of this essay is only speculatively attributed to Richardson, it demonstrates the identification of suicide with national identity that obtained in this period, and which arguably finds its way into *Clarissa* as well.

This publication makes no reference to women's suicide, yet despite the general tendency to omit mention of women almost altogether in discourses on 'self-murder', some periodical writings indicated that women were by no means immune to the general 'trend'. Consequently, a 'concerned citizen' urges the editor of *The World* to 'keep a strict eye on [his] countrywomen', claiming that he knows 'one or two, who already wear pocket-pistols; which, considering the tendencies of their natures, can only be intended against their own persons'.[135] This contributor then proceeds to cite violation of virtue as the only excusable grounds upon which a woman might take her own life, and (albeit sardonically) holds up Lucretia as a 'pattern of her sex'[136] in an attempt once again to rewrite female suicide as sacrifice. Lucretia clearly permeates the public consciousness of eighteenth-century England, affording one means by which female suicide was linked to national concerns. Lucretia's association with Clarissa in public memory brings to mind important arguments about general perceptions and treatment of women in public discourses during the so-called Enlightenment. The feminist scholar Anne McClintock, for example, makes the salient observation that 'women are not seen as inhabiting history proper; but existing, like colonial peoples, in a permanently anterior time within the modern nation'.[137] Richardson taps into such a 'conservative repository of the national archaic'[138] in constructing Clarissa, and partially for this reason, his construction of suicide is itself atavistic and counter-Enlightenment, looking back for a model of virtuous self-sacrifice to the Roman Lucretia.

In many accounts, the most significant part of the Lucretia story takes place after her death. In these narratives, her husband Collatinus and his friend Brutus declare war upon the Tarquin royal family and, having overthrown the kings and established the republic of Rome, become its first consuls. Lucretia's corpse fades into the background as the heroic narrative proceeds, and at its end, her death becomes no more than a pretext for the foundation of a new political order, one of several Roman legends that unfold in this way. In her treatment of the 'transhistorical' relevance of the Lucretia story, political theorist Melissa Matthes interrogates 'the logic that seems to demand the rape of a woman in order to found a republic'.[139] Although Matthes pays some attention to the significance of Lucretia's suicide, interpreting the act as an assertion of 'female power',[140] her discussion submerges suicide in the rape itself, thus neglecting its socio-political significance and instrumentality as a vehicle for nationalism.[141]. According to most accounts, the 'erotics of ravishment' that shape national consciousness cannot typically accommodate the death of the female subject. If the symbol dies, she acquires her own signifying power external to that of the men fighting on behalf of her honour. Perhaps this is why treatments of the story take as their starting point the male boast and as their end point the avenging of Lucretia by her male kin, burying her suicide in an indeterminate middle ground. Richardson's variation on the old tale extends this hazy middle area to such an extent that one cannot but acknowledge the event of Clarissa's decline. When Richardson draws upon the Lucretia myth, he dwells particularly upon the significance of her suicide. Although the rape affords the primary basis of comparison, Clarissa's thinly veiled threat and other characters' apprehension of her suicide resonate more strongly in Richardson's invocation of the myth. Like Lucretia, Clarissa dies neither for shame (as Augustine would have it) nor for virtue but rather to make a 'national point' and to achieve maximum social, communal and national visibility. I will address this making of a 'national point' in more detail shortly, especially in connection to Lovelace's commentary on the Lucretia story and his non-Augustinian *anagnorisis* at the end of the novel.

Despite both Lovelace's and Clarissa's recurrence to the Lucretia narrative, the text's ostensible 'ideal reader' dismisses its applicability. Lovelace protests:

> Her innate piety ... will not permit her to shorten her own life, either by violence or neglect. She has a mind too noble for that; and would have done it before now, had she designed any such thing: for to do it like the Roman matron, when the mischief is over, and it can serve no end, and when the man, however a Tarquin, as some may think him in this action, is not a Tarquin in power, so that no national point can be made of it, is what she has too much good sense to think of.[142]

By sardonically invoking the 'national point' to be made of Lucretia's suicide, Lovelace voices a conventional eighteenth-century attitude toward Lucretia, which views her suicide as a futile, irrational act that runs counter to modern values of refinement and sensibility. Yet, as we have seen, the reception of her self-inflicted death was by no means uniform, and during this period disputes regarding Lucretia's motives and justifications continued to polarize prominent thinkers. Lovelace's protest succeeds only in interrogating the principles of the Roman legend, and fails to address its relevance to Clarissa's situation. For Clarissa is cast explicitly in the Lucretia mold, but rather than affording the basis for the foundation of a republic, she consolidates affective bonds on the national level.

Clarissa's martyrdom lays claim to a certain degree of political power that the Lucretia figure realizes only symbolically; this is the post-mortem, uncircumscribed power that in the nineteenth century Søren Kierkegaard will attribute to the martyr, whom he constructs as the natural successor to the tyrant. Although Kierkegaard does not invoke Lucretia as an exemplar of this narrative, the ancient story's progression from tyrant rule to a republic predicated on martyrdom closely corresponds to his account. As Kierkegaard writes, 'The martyr, in himself unconditionally obedient to God, compels through his own sufferings. So the tyrant dies and his rule is over; the martyr dies and his rule begins.'[143] In much the same way, Clarissa secures for herself an afterlife of power that accords her a degree of posthumous agency predicated upon passivity. In this respect, she realizes the capacity for women to exist as 'both active subjects and subjects of domination' in what amounts to a relatively realistic reading of women's agency.[144] Similarly, Castelli's observation that 'martyrdom has to do foundationally with composing ideas about the character and legitimacy of different systems of power'[145] suggests the viable form of resistance that Clarissa locates in the very experience of her death.

Evidently uncomfortable with the implications of the Lucretia legend that magnifies his crime even as it accords to Clarissa a degree of power and metaphorical significance that in turn renders him fairly inconsequential, Lovelace attempts to rewrite the history of his relations with Clarissa along the lines of the Dido and Aeneas epic romance. In the process, he substitutes one foundational legend for another. In his attempt to prove that he is '*comparatively* an innocent man',[146] the self-styled '*pius* Lovelace' demands,

> Should Miss Harlowe even break her heart for the usage she has received (to say nothing of her disappointed pride, to which her death would be attributable more than to her reason), what comparison will *her* fate hold to Queen Dido's? And have I half the obligation to her that Aeneas had to the Queen of Carthage?[147]

Lovelace's 'preferred' Roman narrative involves the suicide of the woman figure, but the offense of the 'hero' to whom Lovelace likens himself is comparatively less egregious. Since the abandonment of Dido, the Queen of Carthage, is a necessary precondition for the foundation of Rome, Lovelace's identification with Aeneas attempts to restore the masculine agency that is not immediately apparent in the Lucretia analogy. To his libertine sensibility, the narrative that Lucretia embraces in order to understand the rape is problematic insofar as it presents the scenario of a woman giving birth to a nation rather than a man; as Pettman observes, 'Nationalism, war, sacrifice and death are associated with the birth of the nation ... men are the agents and what they birth – the nation – is feminised'.[148] The Aeneas analogy enables Lovelace both to recast his relationship as an amorous one and suggest that Clarissa's potential suicide ensues from thwarted passion. Appropriately enough, Lovelace's substitution privileges a foundational story about the establishment of Rome by a Trojan aristocrat; the Lucretia narrative, on the other hand, chronicles the transformation of Roman government from a monarchical to a republican model. As a libertine deriving much of his claim to sexual power from his class superiority, Lovelace would of course favour the aristocratic over the more egalitarian narrative. Moreover, Lovelace's proclivity for rehearsing these narratives suggests the libertine affinity for the suicidal impulse fostered by Graeco-Roman heroism, which corresponds roughly to the 'suicidal strain' at the heart of Christianity that Clarissa favours instead.[149] These competing strains of thought work together to reinforce the suicidal 'ideation' that characterizes the subjectivities of Clarissa and Lovelace in the novel.

As seen, repetition of the Lucretia metaphor foregrounds the allegedly self-sacrificial nature of Clarissa's death, but more importantly, assigns it national significance. Lovelace equates Clarissa's 'lingering death' with the violent Roman suicide, while Clarissa in turn insists upon the similitude of her and Lucretia's sufferings. Ian Donaldson, however, argues for the ultimate disparity between the two narratives in his assertion that

> Clarissa's dying request for amnesty stands in significant contrast to Lucretia's dying request for vengeance, marking yet another change of sensibility, a new hesitation over the value and propriety of revenge, a sense that true power may express itself in other ways than in blood feuds.[150]

But Clarissa's divulgence of certain particulars of the Lovelace plot in her last will and testament seems calculated to incite the duel that eventually accomplishes what Lovelace himself construes as a 'Christian revenge' upon him.[151] Although Lovelace's death at the hands of Clarissa's cousin Morden might appear to reaffirm masculinity, Clarissa achieves a measure of success in making of her suicide 'a national point': exactly the effect that Lovelace himself, in his dismissal of the Lucretia analogy, denied was possible. In this respect I agree with Ewha Chung's argument that the sacred community consolidated by the expulsion of Lovelacean libertinism at the end of *Clarissa* symbolizes the nation as a whole.[152] Clarissa's death resonates across the imaginative nation figured in the readership of the novel, united in its repudiation of Lovelacean libertinism and parental despotism. In this sense, Clarissa's suicide is foundational to the 'republic of letters' represented by the epistolary novel.

Clarissa's death grants her the symbolic signifying power denied to her in life; as the centre of an extended and seemingly interminable scene of mourning, Clarissa moves beyond the typical 'feminine position' that constructs woman as the quintessential mourner in nationalist contexts.[153] In these accounts, the woman mourns the loss of a father, brother or son and participates in national events in a purely indirect and domestic manner. While the novel might to a certain extent be read as a nationalist allegory, Clarissa does not embrace as a miniature version of this structure the idea of the family, which, as the feminist geographers Mona Domosh and Joni Seager put it, 'helps to secure the "naturalness" of social hierarchies within nations'.[154] On the contrary, as seen in this early statement, Clarissa repudiates the insularity of her family and foregrounds the centrality of forgetfulness to the constitution of (inter)national loyalties: '[T]he world is but one great family. Originally it was so. What then is this narrow selfishness that reigns in us, but relationship remembered against relationship forgot?'[155] In this passage, Richardson suggests that identifications are founded upon the loss of memory in a way that prefigures Ernst Renan's insistence that forgetfulness (in this context of sacrifice) forges national and international bonds.[156] Clarissa proposes a feminized model of memory that advocates almost a melancholic attachment to the past, rather than the 'narrrow' or selective mode more familiar to masculine paradigms. Although Clarissa is seemingly beyond national identifications, the scene of mourning that she inaugurates through her constructed self-sacrifice enables the consolidation of national identity and ensures her memorialization.

Defined throughout the novel by superlatives that take the nation as the limit of identification, Clarissa certainly represents a paragon not only of her family but of the nation as well. The rhetoric that constructs her exemplarity deals in unqualified superlatives, with even Lovelace insisting that there is 'Not such another woman in England!'[157] As Ewha Chung points out, 'Clarissa personifies the "Sincere Ideal", which emerged and became part of the national character in England around the 1740s'.[158] Clarissa defines the national ideal, whereas as 'one of the greatest profligates in England' Lovelace represents the opposite limit.[159] Clarissa's suicide both re-establishes and transfigures the community of mourners at the novel's end while the contrast of Lovelace's unmourned foreign slaying only heightens the Englishness of Clarissa's own death.

Ars Moriendi: Aesthetics and the Psychological Autopsy

Several years after the first edition of *Clarissa*, Richardson published separately the text of Clarissa's *Meditations* that asserted a meta-textual yet non-material presence in his novel. Masquerading as a 'found work', this booklet was intended to grant the reader access to a kind of interiority which even Clarissa's personal letters so often deny. Arguably, however, the fact that these meditations represent largely a tissue of quotations from scripture mitigates the degree of personal intimacy with Clarissa's subjectivity ostensibly offered by the text. Richardson certainly uses them to make it unequivocally clear that 'CLARISSA WAS A CHRISTIAN'[160] as his bold capitals early on in the appended notes to the meditation unambiguously insist. Drawing upon the books of Job, the Wisdom of Solomon and Ecclesiastes, the excerpted passages also underscore the profundity of Clarissa's death wish, as they plaintively question 'Why died I not from the womb?'[161] and 'Wherefore is light given to one that is in misery; and life unto the bitter in soul?'[162] While their very biblical origins absolve their transcriber of any culpability, they simultaneously naturalize self-starvation as an acceptable response to extreme suffering. Throughout the narrative, Clarissa self-consciously identifies with the Hebrew Scriptures' exemplar of resigned suffering, but this text enables Clarissa to articulate her misery indirectly with Job as a mouthpiece.[163] Although Jonathan Lamb argues that Clarissa 'is beyond the need of a supplement because she is beyond any positive concept of identity, having been broken into pieces with words, precipitated as a negative being, and reconstituted as fragments of text',[164] Richardson clearly renders Clarissa's identity contingent on that of Job in an effort to authorize female self-expression and complaint. As Donne affirms in *Biathanatos*, Job openly indulges his suicidal despair in his meditations and 'strayed thus far towards killing himself as to wish his death and curse his birth, for his whole third chapter is a bitter and malignant invective against it, and a violent wishing of his own death'.[165] The theorist Slavoj Žižek similarly insists that 'Job is NOT a patient sufferer, enduring his ordeal with the firm faith in God – on the contrary, he complains all the time, rejecting his fate'.[166] In this manner, the meditations bury Clarissa's death wish (and her will itself) within that of Job.[167] Richardson's supplementary text serves as an extension of Clarissa's salvific death by reproducing her meditations as an aid to any individual seeking spiritual solace.

Although granted minimal interiority by the text towards the end of her life, Clarissa's character is formulated by the praise of other characters who describe her as a saint and a 'divine being', as her immaculate opacity thwarts attempts to locate intentional meaning in her death. The 'hermeneutical anarchy' that proliferates within the novel's epistolary networks facilitates this sense of indeterminacy; meanwhile, this epistemological quagmire is populated by what

Terry Castle describes as 'a cacophony of voices, a multiplicity of exegetes strug-
gling to articulate different "constructions" of the world',[168] which combine to
confuse the issue of agency in respect to Clarissa's death.

Richardson's layering of narrative perspective enables Clarissa's suicide to
exist as a lacuna or visible absence that no one wishes to discuss or acknowledge.
In this work, suicide becomes a virtual non-signifier, an act that is unnatural in
its execution but natural in its contemplation, bearing the double culpability of
felony and moral sin in the perception of institutional authority, yet ultimately
lacking an absolute value.[169] So heavy a burden of false blame has Clarissa been
made to shoulder throughout the novel that the act for which she may be culpable above all others (according to the very ethical code to which she subscribes)
is left uncensured in what may clearly be identified as a triumph of narrative
control on Richardson's part. Clarissa's suicide falls neatly into the cracks left
open by a continuum of letters that are still being organized at the novel's end.
Indeed, Richardson so effectively forecloses debate regarding the sincerity of
Clarissa's motives that scrutiny of his saint's psychology appears almost akin to
sacrilege; Richardson's strategy effectively precludes a literary equivalent of the
'pyschological autopsy' that routinely follows suspected suicides in an attempt
to determine motive and sometimes mode of death. Hence, a 'writerly reader', à
la Roland Barthes, might become as reluctant to deliver the *felo de se* verdict as
was the mid-eighteenth-century coroner's jury. A reader's complicity with this
virtual erasure of the act of suicide might therefore stem from a reluctance to
interrogate too closely a social reality that challenges the sanctity of life and the
illusion of an integrated and contented society.

Richardson provides an additional incentive to read the text 'properly' by
implicitly cautioning the reader who adopts the 'cynical' viewpoint (by raising
questions regarding the circumstances surrounding Clarissa's death) that she
risks aligning herself with the libertine perspective. Richardson's friend and fellow writer Edward Young makes this point explicitly in reassuring Richardson
(of the correctness of his plan to render Clarissa extinct) that 'Christians of taste
will applaud your plan, and they who themselves would act Lovelace's part, will
find the greatest fault with it'.[170] According to this logic, readers must either
accept that Clarissa merely succumbs to a divine will or reject this notion with
a libertine cynicism worthy of Lovelace. This position is carefully constructed
by Richardson, whose anxiety that his heroine and her intentions might be
misread lead him to emphasize her blamelessness in subsequent editions and to
publish the extracted *sententiae* as moral correctives to any possible misread-
ings.

In most recent critical assessments, Lovelace appears as the only character
endowed with any degree of 'rational' insight into the implications of Clarissa's determination to die, even amid his temporary insanity. Lovelace's mania

inevitably discredits his interpretative position, and his assessment of Clarissa's suicide is never commented upon, yet never, as we find, wholly contested either. Although Lovelace's reading of Clarissa often proves specious, we might nonetheless detect some elements of sincerity in his insistence that Clarissa models herself after the suicidal Roman *matrona*, Lucretia in seeking out her death so resolutely. Lovelace has been a witness to Clarissa's previous suicide gesture, and this experience does qualify him to assess her capacity for self-destructiveness more accurately than we might wish. Lovelace's insistence that 'a death desired merely from worldly disappointment shows not a right mind'[171] makes of suicide a pathology, in anticipation of the modern attitudes that coalesce in the latter part of the eighteenth century. Even though the libertine perspective celebrates suicide as an act of reason and an affirmation of personal autonomy, Clarissa's prolonged embrace of death cannot be fathomed by Lovelace's demystifying sensibility, and therefore meets more readily with acceptance.

Lovelace's scepticism in respect to the voluntary aspect of Clarissa's death maintains the suggestion of illicit behaviour in the text. He also endorses an alternative hermeneutic of martyrdom, indicating the extent to which practices of reading *mors voluntaria* were contingent upon one's religious affiliation in the period. As Susanne Monta affirms, the Catholic tradition asked its followers to accept martyrs' claims that they died in good faith or for a higher purpose, where Protestants adhered to a practice of reading martyrs' consciences.[172] The hermeneutic tradition espoused by Protestant martyrology is more dynamic and resembles more closely the rigours of Lovelace's unremitting scrutiny; in contrast, other characters in the text follow a typical Catholic practice of accepting on faith Clarissa's 'martyrological' professions. Paradoxically, Clarissa's epistolary confessional deflects scrutiny and blocks psychological autopsy, while she presumably derives her particular discursive agency from counter-traditions of martyrology that are unexpectedly represented by Lovelace.

Clarissa's sedulous cultivation of the *ars moriendi* prompted Richardson's most sympathetic reader and correspondent, Lady Bradshaigh, to exclaim: '[never] did I behold the duties of a Christian in so clear, so striking, and so amiable a light: they make even life a trifle, and death look lovely'.[173] Richardson expends a considerable amount of creative energy in rendering the death scene iconographically and aesthetically perfect in order to rule out the suggestion of suicide. This is an aesthetic choice that the nineteenth- century European novel at the acme of its realism would resolutely abandon for the sake of a nauseating, unadorned reality of things. A good example of this unabashed realism can be seen in Gustave Flaubert's *Madame Bovary*. Trapped in a tedious marriage and feeling superior to her fate, Emma Bovary eventually commits suicide by ingesting arsenic: '"Look at her", said the innkeeper, sighing; "how pretty she still is!" ... Then they bent over her to put on her wreath. They had to raise the head a little, and a rush of black liquid poured from her mouth, as if she were vomiting.'[174] Evidently, Emma is not Clarissa; she is not an innocent protagonist endowed with a sensible vision of a world whose rightness condemns the experience life offers. But they both meet at the fateful intersection of what Georg Luckacs describes as the *Grunddissonanz* of the novelistic form, that is, the alienation of the heroine who finds that the meaning she supposes immanent in the world refuses to penetrate empirical life. However, unlike Emma's Nietzschean nihilistic finish, Clarissa's serene attitude towards death accounts for the reception of her death as a holy event, which in no manner of speaking conforms to conventional understandings of suicide. In this sense, Clarissa fully realizes the aspect of martyrdom that, as described by Castelli, 'is not simply an action, but requires an audience (whether real or fictive)'.[175]

While Flaubert vulgarizes and deliberately frustrates any attempt at beautifying death, Richardson aestheticizes it in having his characters make of it a virtual fetish. According to the literary critic Jolene Zigarovich, both Richardson's Clarissa and Lovelace 'actually fetishize, are aroused by and obsess upon, the exquisite corpse. Both, in their own manner, are necrophiliacs.'[176] Indeed, Richardson's representation of Clarissa's 'ecstasy of pain' suggests the erotic component of martyrdom that, according to Karl Menninger, is corroborated by clinical experience and historical accounts, both of which 'give us the impression that in some instances there is a physical pleasure even in this kind of suffering associated with gratification of the sexual instinct'.[177] In Richardson's rendering, fetishism becomes yet one more means by which the narrative occludes the act of suicide, as the eroticizing of death places suicide behind a sexualized screen and enables both literary characters and readers to accept a death that might otherwise appear rather unpleasant and unattractive in the level of its stark determination.

Far from 'rushing into eternity' – the conventional circumlocution for the suicidal act – Clarissa creeps towards her grave. Clarissa's assurance that she 'will do everything in [her] power to prolong [her] life, till God in mercy to [her] shall be pleased to call for it'[178] foregrounds the violation of temporal norms that is often tied up with suicide: a suicide rushes to death precipitately, rather than embracing 'Christian' values of patience and resignation. The abridgement of time that the voluntary death typically entails does not assert itself in this context; instead, the narrative evokes what the philosopher Simon Critchley refers to as the 'interminable temporality of dying' in alluding to death more generally.[179] Clarissa's pursuit of death appears to be decidedly non-dramatic; marked by inaction, her final life-ending act is the culmination of an exhaustive series of non-acts. Unlike the dramatic tragedy, which exalts the dramatic potential of the suicide but cannot effectively portray suffering extended over time, the voluminous epistolary novel can attenuate a suicide into an almost natural death.

Clarissa's appreciation of the category of time as a form of deferred power is reflected in the assurances she provides to her confidantes: '[A]lthough I wish not for life, yet would I not like a poor coward desert my post, when I *can* maintain it, and when it is my *duty* to maintain it'.[180] This statement offers a qualified moral imperative in the repetition of the adverb 'when', which suggests that circumstances might obviate the performance of duty. Moreover, this passage invokes conventional military rhetoric that designates the individual as sentry, posted as a guard over one's own life. Clarissa embraces the rhetoric of duty, which Immanuel Kant later in the century transforms into a categorical imperative. In embracing death, Clarissa finds a method of discharging her duties toward her family and society at large, for her painstaking decline affords her sufficient time to draft her exhaustive will, to attempt reconciliation with her family, and, failing that, at the very least to acquaint them with her impending death. Her last duty – to herself – involves paying her devotions to religion, and that she has ample time to do. [181]

Richardson's manipulation of narrative temporality possibly facilitates the cloaking of suicide, as time becomes an index of the natural, in a manner of speaking. The individual letter carries the burden of generating narrative interest, and an ever-expanding chorus of voices absorbs any tension that Clarissa's voluntary demise might generate. The narrative hence constructs a deontology of voluntary death that is intimately bound up with the fictional representation of time. The practice of 'writing to the moment' presumably facilitates the production of a seemingly stable subject, or at the very least a psychology that is directly accessible to the reader, yet it also affords the means by which certain pertinent questions are repeatedly deferred or ignored. This method generates a vacuum of meaning in which suicide has neither status nor presence as an object of knowledge or representation; but it is the duration of the decline that guarantees the rational component of the act, for the choice of death under such conditions must be reiterated every day, an activity that Clarissa does not fail to undertake for the duration of the novel.

Many critical investigations read epistolarity as a highly subjective mode, one that allows for the realization of a conception of the individual.[182] According to these interpretations, epistolarity offers access to both an interior space and a subjectivity that remain impenetrable in alternative, third-person narratives. Essentializing epistolarity as a feminine form, critics often align the letter with the private, the personal and the intimate. While this approach to the novel-in-letters is tenable to a certain extent, it concomitantly elides the highly intersubjective aspect of the subgenre. Works like *Clarissa* in fact strive to shore up the communal through the device of the letter and enable the discovery of the 'other'.[183] This strategy not only secures Richardson a sizeable network of literary patrons but within the novel itself also creates a community of reader-correspondents unified in their resistance to the libertine tradition. In this sense, the discourse of suicide in the novel is highly contingent upon epistolarity to generate personal agency and social ties simultaneously.

However, Clarissa's death would seem to threaten the community in its suggestion that at any moment, a citizen may 'opt out' of the social contract either through emigration, self-imposed exile or simple withdrawal from the community or by the extreme method of suicide. According to the French philosopher Ernst Renan, 'A nation's existence is ... a daily plebiscite, just as an individual's existence is a perpetual affirmation of life'.[184] Renan renders the existence of the nation contingent upon an ongoing affirmation on the part of its citizens to its right to life, drawing a parallel between that action and the individual will to live. Renan foregrounds the issue of will and voluntarism, rendering the nation a contingent and almost impermanent entity, subject to erasure at any point if the nation's citizens cease to consent to its existence, or, as we encounter in *Clarissa*, discontinue their own existences. Yet this dreaded scenario does not transpire in Clarissa; instead, those characters that opt to stand by Clarissa's deathbed do find themselves participants in her death. The complex relation between will and temporality enables suicide to become a communal event as Clarissa's will to die produces a national subject of an entirely different order: her will is subsumed into the 'grand narrative of will' that, according to post-colonial critics like Homi Bhabha, governs a national collective[185] and ultimately demands her death. If Clarissa's will to die is reinforced by sheer repetition of the death wish, the notion of citizenship that Richardson would develop more fully in *Sir Charles Grandison* similarly is constructed by the repetition of acts. The prolongation of Clarissa's suicide forces all other characters to participate in and legitimate the act, rendering it a communal event, and even one that can be extended outwards to the nation at large.

In *Clarissa*, Richardson's gender politics arrive at an inevitable impasse, as his desire to retrieve a measure of autonomy for his heroine by enabling her to slip passively into death leads him to valorize the traditional roles of both female passivity *and* self-sacrifice. Clarissa's interminable dying aestheticizes female suffering and patient submission to one's fate, even while it foregrounds the logic of female sacrifice so intrinsic to gender ideology. Yet Richardson questions neither his heroine's right to die nor the possibility that death might be an object of will. Clarissa's staging of her death scene, her scrupulous attention to the iconography of mortality, and her mastering of the *ars moriendi*, all affirm her unwavering resolution to 'wean' herself from a temporal existence.[186] Her exemplary death similarly affirms the ease with which an individual may die, in a humbling deathbed spectacle of Christian piety.

Needless to say, Richardson's exhaustive manipulation of the imagery of death is calculated to underscore Clarissa's unwavering determination to actualize her death wish. In this respect, Richardson clearly operates under an ideological system that contradicts contemporary tendencies to preclude the notion of free will in their insistence that voluntary death is an irrational act, the product of a constellation of mental and nervous disorders that suppress the will to live. In fact, Richardson's recuperation of a cult of female voluntary death masquerading as martyrdom would seem rather to support modern society's drift towards what theorist Jean Baudrillard refers to as 'resacralization'.[187] In this respect, *Clarissa* involves a return to earlier codes rather than a movement forward. Richardson reverts to an understanding of voluntary death that is more nuanced than Augustinian proscriptions, at once more modern in its acknowledgement of a 'right to die' and more obsolete in upholding an ideal of a female martyr invested with agency. Ultimately, Clarissa's death constitutes a suicide, but one that legitimates itself through detours around Christian proscriptions, as Richardson's narrative reveals the religious foundations for both the conception and the destruction of the self that were entertained during the period of the Enlightenment.

3 ENGLISH MALADIES AND MATERIAL CULTURE AT MID-CENTURY

Although suicide was never deemed a wholly personal affair, as attested by the post-mortem desecration of the suicide's corpse, which persisted in Britain as a practice up until 1834, the act became increasingly the 'nation's business' in direct proportion to England's increasing derivation of its character from suicide. By mid-century, the English Malady – the notion that the English suffered inordinately from melancholy and that as a result the per capita rates of suicide were much higher in this country than elsewhere – emerged as a complex, troubling and often contradictory index of national character.[1] Each instance of suicide confirmed popular opinion regarding the pathological character of the nation, while England's attempt to define a national identity necessarily foregrounded certain critical issues of the period. By 1791, the persistently suicidal poet William Cowper could lament that he 'should be born in a country where melancholy is the national characteristic' and subsequently confide, 'To say the truth, I have often wished myself a Frenchman'.[2] Cowper is just one of many writers in the eighteenth century to attach a degree of determinism to national character: one is melancholy because one is English, according to this view. However, other writers downplayed this sense of fatalism by representing melancholy as an affectation. Arguing from precisely this position, a contributor to the 17 November 1738 issue of the *Daily Gazetteer* announced, 'I cannot do a more charitable, or publick spirited Thing, than to examine the *Validity* of this *Plea*, which I shall do very candidly, and with no other View, than to convince those, who are addicted to *Melancholy*, that they have no Right to *Indulge* themselves therein'. The writer identifies a perverse strain in the psychology of the English, whom he represents as willfully indulging a state of mind ultimately detrimental to the welfare of the public. Both positions, however, locate in English identity a strongly passive element that serves as an obstacle to the recovery of 'national health'.[3]

English acceptance of the stigma and resignation to the label might be construed as a symptom of the English Malady insofar as a melancholic temperament fosters precisely the passivity that would have enabled the English to constitute their sense of national character on the basis of other nations' perceptions of

[handwritten margin note: cf. American English tendency to ascribe to suicide – the colonists took it with them?]

them. National identity, according to this construction, is a collective project, a complex amalgam of self-imaging from within and absorption of views from without. This view of national character leaves little room for agency, as it presents identity as a set of defining characteristics imposed from above. Indeed, a further sign of this passivity is the fact that, rather than attempting to prevent and curb melancholy, physicians of the time like George Cheyne focused on rehabilitating melancholy into a dynamic and civic principle of social behaviour.[4] As recent revisionist accounts of the history of pathology have illuminated, 'Whig' interests adopted a 'functionalist' approach to social illness and disease that contained and recuperated 'deviance' by constructing it as a mark of civility or progress and an indication of the affluence of English commercial enterprise.[5] This position embroiled the Whigs, and their ideological and political opponents the Tories, in a debate regarding the relative merits and demerits of luxury and commodity culture in mid-eighteenth-century England.

A representative of the Tory position opposing Whig functionalism at the middle of the eighteenth century, John Shebbeare, a physician by training, gained a reputation for his political pamphlets and scattered 'minor' novels including the polemical *Marriage Act* (1754) and *Lydia; or, Filial Piety* (1755).[6] Active in his resistance to the government of Robert Walpole and outspoken on the social issues of his day,[7] Shebbeare engages with the problem of the English Malady and its relevance to a developing sense of national identity in *Lydia* and his other work of the mid-century, exploring the socio-cultural implications of the pervasiveness of the perception that the English were more afflicted by melancholy and hence more inclined to take their lives than citizens of other nations. In his writings, Shebbeare responds specifically to Cheyne, one of the chief proponents of this view, who, in managing the health of a number of London's elite, inevitably became an apologist for some of their excesses. Shebbeare's response to Cheyne presents the English as characterized by a kind of passivity that is inherently self-destructive. For Shebbeare, melancholy and suicide exist together on a continuum of behaviour that, far from having its roots exclusively in the nervous system of the individual, as Cheyne would have it, is instead a sign of a more critical social problem indicating an inescapable connection between the condition of the individual, whether male or female, and the health of the nation. Until the health of the nation receives proper treatment, the individual cannot hope to thrive.

Shebbeare's argument is of a piece with that of the opinion printed at the beginning of this chapter: as a social act, suicide represents an indictment of society's inequities, and hence demands a fundamental reformation of its very structures and systems. Far from being what historian Richard Cobb has termed 'the most private and impenetrable of human acts',[8] suicide for Shebbeare is wholly transparent and public, with its origins in the individual's relations with society rather than in any physical, medical or nervous condition.[9] His novel

Lydia expresses a sympathy for the plight of women driven to the point of suicide by the excesses of society – a constellation of vices that for him constitute a peculiar figuring of the English Malady – which are themselves represented as effeminate in nature. In this respect, Shebbeare holds out suicide as an option for both sexes (even though he recasts it to a certain extent as sacrificial), even while gendering the English Malady as resolutely feminine. Shebbeare's reconfiguration of English national identity resembles John Hutchinson's concept of the 'cultural nationalist' – typically an artist or scholar rather than politician – who seeks to affect a form of moral regeneration through his or her writing.[10] In Shebbeare's case, this moral regeneration is sought through a complex relationship to materiality, which represents the body as a political resource and re-visions English landscape as a symbolic space integral to imagining identity.

John Shebbeare's 'Civic Humanism'

In his *Practice of Physick, Founded on Principles of Pathology Hitherto Unapplied in Physical Enquiries* (1755), Shebbeare advises sufferers of the 'spleen' or melancholy to read Fielding's *Joseph Andrews* as an antidote to the affliction.[11] Far from promoting melancholy through sedentary behaviour, novel-reading, according to Shebbeare, has therapeutic effects that counter any ill effects associated with the practice. In this view, he is joined, at least ironically, by Laurence Sterne, whose hero, Tristram Shandy, insists that if his 'memoir' is 'wrote against anything, 'tis wrote, an' please your worships, against the spleen' in the hope of driving 'the *gall* and other *bitter juices* from the gall bladder, liver, and sweet-bread of his majesty's subjects ... down into their duodenums'.[12] Citing Sterne's passage but overlooking its satirical thrust, the literary critic Oswald Doughty observed in 1923 that 'We might indeed, but with little exaggeration, seek to show that the necessity for distraction from spleen was one of the influences leading to the creation of the modern novel'.[13] Like other writers of his time, Dr Shebbeare supposed that a novel's briskness of plot and narrative convolutions could quicken the imagination and counteract the inertia typically associated with the act of reading. His own mid-century novel, *Lydia* (1755), published the same year as his medical treatise, presumably performs precisely this function, as it mingles high-seas adventure and urban intrigue in a sprawling plot that affords fictional corroboration of the problems, economic, social and moral, besetting the English people. Interestingly enough, however, Shebbeare's novel bears more resemblance to Fielding's *Amelia* (1751) than to *Joseph Andrews* or his other earlier, considerably less sentimental work. In the final section of the novel, Amelia describes her attack of the 'vapours' as 'a sort of complication of all diseases together, with almost madness added to them', and in this sense she anticipates the afflictions of Shebbeare's own exemplar of feminine sensibility, Lydia Fairchild.

Transatlantic in its scope, the novel begins 'on the banks of the great river, Cataraqui ... deep embosomed in the eternal woods of America' where a fictional version of Canasatego, the famous Onondagan leader, diplomat, and Iroquois Confederacy spokesman, is cast as a romantic hero in the mould of Aphra Behn's 'noble slave' Oroonoko.[14] After pledging to take up the plight of his people with the King of England and 'lay the story of [his people's] woe before him', he falls in love with a Cayugan, Yarico, and becomes embroiled in a conflict between love and honour.[15] After a brief romantic interlude, honour prevails and Cannassetego (Shebbeare's spelling) embarks for London, where his own unspotted virtue stands in sharp contrast to the fallen state of the English people, whose collective debauchery draws a decidedly unflattering portrait of national identity.

The exception to the general state of English corruption is Lydia Fairchild, who emerges as the novel's protagonist when she embarks on the same ship as Cannassetego for London. A woman of modest origins and means, Lydia returns to England after a tenure with a guardian in the colonies to find her mother in financial distress and her lover, Mr Probit, elevated above her expectations to the status of an earl. She enters into service as a 'lady's maid' to the sympathetic Arabella Thrifty, whose husband, the debauched and decrepit Viscount Lord Flimsy, immediately begins to pursue Lydia. After she is framed for theft and cast in prison owing to her rejection of the lord's advances, Lydia withstands a series of assaults on her 'virtue', which only serve to tarnish her character and intensify the poverty into which she and her mother have fallen. Powerless to relieve her mother's distress and believing her to be in her death throes, Lydia sets out at the narrative's climax to end her own life. Her suicide attempt in St James's Park is thwarted by her accidental meeting with her newly titled former lover (Probit, now the Earl of Liberal) who marries her despite the difference in their stations, and the remainder of the narrative relates their marital contentment and good works, which include sending Lydia's deeply disillusioned Amerindian friend, Cannassetego, back to his people in the Americas.

In his characteristically scathing indictment of English society, Shebbeare employs the device of an outsider in the character of Cannassatego to assess all the more vividly the differences between the two civilizations. Through an Amerindian 'other' defined by physical cleanliness and moral purity, Shebbeare offers a critique of the various conditions that had by this period become synonymous with Englishness and the sensible body of the nation. Initially setting up two parallel 'histories' of virtuous couples, one aboriginal and the other English, Shebbeare then transfers his focus almost exclusively to his English characters as his contrast between the ideal and the corrupt eventually gives way to a single-minded and dogged critique of English depravity informed by an overarching concern with the meanings of Englishness and their connection to disease. Although he is quickly eclipsed by Lydia Fairchild as the novel's central figure, this Amerindian character is the chief means by which Shebbeare's novel illumi-nates the connections between nervous disorders, venereal disease, femininity and class forged in the process of national identity formation.

Shebbeare seems to elide the distinctiveness of each of the First Nations in his contrast of the uniformly virtuous aboriginal peoples with the almost wholly corrupt British populace. However, Cannassetego's Onondagan 'race' is none-theless singled out for its particular share of acclaim:

> In all the oral history of this ancient race, delivered down from sire to son, no instance is to be found of broken faith with other nations; no anecdote of friends betrayed, or allies deserted in the hour of danger and distress; their words are sacredly preserved; their lives offered up in battle are the proof of it.[16]

Idealized even beyond his representation in history, Cannassetego stands out as 'eminently superior' to his 'fellow countrymen'.[17] As the historian Barbara Mann observes, Shebbeare's fictionalized Cannassatego serves as 'judge and jury of all that is corrupt in mid-eighteenth-century England'.[18] However, Shebbeare, departing from the convention of the outsider topos, scarcely grants Cannas-setego a voice, allowing his critique of the English to operate instead by way of contrast. An inhabitant of 'uncontaminated lands',[19] Cannassetego represents an exemplar and standard of virtue unfamiliar with the diseases of culture afflicting the English, and his decision to return to his home in the Americas constitutes the most critical action of his narrative. Thus, although the novel begins with a frame narrative establishing Cannassatego as its ideal reader of the English national character, it abandons this viewpoint midway, ultimately allowing con-taminated Englishness to represent itself without mediation.

To a large extent, Shebbeare's work reflects the contemporary trend of defin-ing Englishness through pathological discourse. At first glance, Shebbeare's novel seems to act as an antidote to the apparent idealization of the melancholic, suicidal disposition in works such as Cheyne's *The English Malady* (1733), but *Lydia* also absorbs suicide into the paradigm of sacrifice so intimately tied to con-temporary constructions of nationhood. However, where Cheyne addresses the problem on an individual basis, assuming that a simple prescription for health-ier living will limit the dire effects of luxury and curb the inclination towards suicide, Shebbeare maintains his focus on the national problem by insisting on radical measures and the immediate treatment of society itself.

Cornering the market on 'fashionable disease', Cheyne's work presents an iatromechanical view of the body as a machine that may be regulated by strict diet, frequent exercise and the measured use of salts. Although Cheyne acknowl-edges the dire effects of nervous disorders, analyses of his work on melancholy and the English Malady typically overlook his preoccupation with suicide, in large part as a result of largely aestheticized treatment of the disorder. Although as seen in previous chapters, the notion of an English Malady predates the work of Cheyne, it was his popular medical treatise, *The English Malady; or, A Treatise of Nervous Diseases of all Kinds. With the Author's Own Case*, that consolidated this aspect of English identity. In 1733, Cheyne claimed that 'nervous disorders [are] computed to make up almost one-third of the complaints of the people in England',[20] and proceeded in the next sentence to encourage the belief that suicide had reached epidemic proportions just a few decades into the eighteenth century. Yet in *The English Malady* Cheyne constructs an elaborate explanatory machinery in order to exonerate the English, never questioning the basic premise that they killed themselves more than did most nationalities.[21]

In *The Female Spectator* (1744–6), Eliza Haywood complained that melancholy and suicide had 'not only undone the nation, but rendered us extremely ridiculous to Foreigners who are Witnesses of it'.[22] Cheyne addresses this reputation specifically in *The English Malady*, and openly acknowledged that he derived the title of his treatise from the derisive generalizing label that Europeans assigned to nervous disorders in the period. The international audience that *The English Malady* commanded no doubt also contributed to the spread of this reputation beyond England's borders. A contributor to *The London Magazine* (1762) observed that 'the frequency of suicide in this island is so notorious, as to have become among Foreigners almost proverbial; scarce a week passes without some melancholy intelligence of this kind [being] circulated'.[23] So pervasive was this reputation that a reviewer of the satirical comedy *The Suicide* (1778) could claim that when suicide occurs 'on the continent of Europe, it is usual to say – such a one has killed himself à l'Angloise – according to the English fashion'. In this spirit, Pierre Grosley in his *Tour to London* (1772) identified the numerous corpses found on the bottom of the Thames as 'monuments of the eternal disposition of the English to suicide'.[24] The art historian Ron Brown has written persuasively about this trend in *The Art of Suicide* (2001), in which he asserts:

> That suicidal death should be exteriorized, displaced, or relocated on to a regime, or on to one national body, is explicable as a symptom of cultural pressure, where suicide, England and the English were posited by other nations as 'what-we-are-not'. By operating to cement together other national identities where suicide was not so readily put to press, England became a mirror that offered stability and control for others.[25]

Yet this assessment inevitably prompts the question as to why the English themselves so readily embraced the stereotype, self-diagnosing their nation as inherently suicidal. How in fact, and in what terms, did the English assess the state of their national 'health'?

Although the English did for the most part accept the notion of an 'English Malady', it received some opposition from contemporary writers such as George Colman, who protested that 'From reading the public prints a foreigner might be naturally led to imagine, that we are the most lunatic people in the whole world'.[26] Similarly, William Chaigneau's novel *The History of Jack Connor* (1752) features a lengthy debate on this very subject between a Frenchman and an Englishman. Jack Connor contradicts his interlocutor's assertion that 'suicide and madness are much more common in England than in France' by attributing the misconception to different styles of reporting and the greater liberty that the English press enjoyed. Connor appeals to the universality of humankind, rejecting the theory of climate influence popularized by Montesquieu and attributing England's reputation for 'frantick disorders' to the fact that 'if a poor wretch hangs or drowns himself, the Newswriters immediately give the circumstances and his Name to the whole Kingdom. Such an affair in Paris is seldom known beyond the District he liv'd in'.[27] Chaigneau and several other writers blame the stigma on the sheer overexposure of suicide reporting in the country, but rather than rejecting the idea that the English as a people are given to suicide, they suggest that it is in fact a pan-European phenomenon which is simply underreported elsewhere. Media, in these works, are credited with the power to shape national character and public opinion in historically unprecedented ways.

The papers' penchant for 'canvas[sing] the misfortunes of mankind without endeavoring to discover some expedient to relieve them' is consistent with the general attitude of passive resignation so lamented by this anonymous contributor to the *London Magazine* (1762).[28] Rather than simply sensationalizing events with mere reportage, the contributor urges that the 'hypochondriackal' subject receive medical treatment and hospitalization, and after providing a brief history of the 'absurd' theories of the condition popularly assumed to foster suicide, he wonders whether 'melancholy is indeed irremediable'.[29] In this respect, he follows the example set by Cheyne, who claims to have published *The English Malady*:

> upon the late frequency and daily Encrease of wanton and uncommon Self-Murderers, produced mostly by this distemper ... to try what a little more just and solid Philosophy, join'd to a Method of Care, and proper Medicine, could do, to put a Stop to so Universal a Lunacy and Madness.[30]

Although Cheyne characterizes the condition as universal at this early stage, over the course of his study it becomes increasingly apparent that the English Malady afflicts only the elite of society. In his attempt to rationalize the reputation that England had already acquired for suicidal mania, Cheyne acknowledges that the English are particularly inclined to suicide, but ties the problem to a specifically economic cause, downplaying the effects of climate and 'freethinking' that were so often held responsible for the apparently nationwide affliction. Identifying nervous disorders as 'the diseases of the wealthy, the voluptuous and the lazy', Cheyne proceeds to attribute them to 'the wealth and abundance of the inhabitants ... the inactivity and sedentary occupations of the better sort'.[31] The construction of England as a prosperous, economically flourishing nation thus emerges as an important subtext of *The English Malady*, even as it obscures the paradox that precisely this wealth leads to disease. Although Cheyne prescribes radical adjustments to dietary regimens and lifestyle as a cure for the malady and preventative to suicide, he offers no such remedy for the plight of the poor and disenfranchised. Clearly, as Roy Porter observes, 'unlike many "civic humanists", Cheyne never sought to use the critique of over-sophistication implicit in his formulation of the "English Malady" as a stalking-horse for political reform'.[32] Attributed to 'the Inactivity and sedentary Occupations of the better Sort (among whom this Evil mostly rages)', Cheyne's definition instead constructs the classic melancholic as a blue-blooded patrician whose wealth accorded him or her ample leisure to refine the sensibilities and wind up the nerves to a pitch of delicacy too exquisite to allow for continued existence in the world.[33] The association of melancholic suicide with a particular class was somewhat ironically invoked by a 'well born' contributor to *The World*, who confessed 'pedigree is my distemper and, having observed how much the mode of self-murder prevails among people of rank, I grew to think that there was no living without killing oneself'.[34] By implication, the labouring classes were viewed as too insensible to feel the effects of melancholia, and as largely impervious to the suicidal impulses that afflicted the elite; as Cheyne observes, 'Fools, weak or stupid Persons, they of dull Souls, are seldom much troubled with vapours or spirits'.[35] The notion that suicide was virtually unheard of among the lower classes was promulgated in specialist and popular writings alike in the period. In an article published in the *Gentleman's Magazine*, Sir John MacKintosh claimed that 'suicide is rarely the crime of the poorer classes occupied with their daily labour. It is the effect of wounded shame, the result of false pride, and the fear of some imaginary degradation.'[36] Clearly, as Minois affirms, 'Freedom to kill oneself seems to have been confined to a privilege of the nobility' since members of the labouring class were viewed as lacking the necessary developed sensibility.[37] Almost inevitably, then, the construction of the English Malady as a fashionable disease of the affluent suggests that the poor who killed themselves were viewed as being somehow less English than the self-destructing aristocrats and members of the rising middle class. National identity, in this and most other cases, is determined by the wealthy and elite.

In his study of the national nervous disorder, Cheyne's patients become proto-neurotics that help reshape a stigma into an aesthetically appealing and more socially acceptable category. In particular, Cheyne transforms the melancholic from an antisocial recluse into a communicative being, anticipating Freud's study *Mourning and Melancholia*, which also, contrary to expectation, claims that the melancholic exhibits a 'trait of insistent communicativeness which finds satisfaction in self-exposure'.[38] In Cheyne's view, over the course of becoming a social being, the melancholic becomes integrated into national identity. Furthermore, the exhaustive and highly personal excursus on the 'Case of the Author' at the end of *The English Malady* not only lends Cheyne's medical system credibility but assimilates him into the elite society to which he caters.

Unlike Cheyne, Shebbeare might be included among the ranks of the aforementioned 'civic humanists' in that he concentrates upon the *effects* of a so-called English Malady. After apparently meeting with little success in his initial profession as a physician, Shebbeare resolved 'to write himself into a pension or the pillory' by taking the health of England as his primary concern.[39] Like Cheyne, Shebbeare in his writings diagnoses his patient (England) as a victim of systemic disease, both in a physical and emotional sense. However, his assessment of the causes of the disease differs dramatically from that of his colleague. Where Cheyne characterizes melancholia as an internal, somatically based complaint, Shebbeare adopts a sociological perspective and attributes the disease to England's policymakers, even while adhering to familiar medical terminology and metaphor. In his *Second Letter to the People of England* (1755), Shebbeare labels the passivity of England's domestic and foreign policies as suicidal, and towards the outset of the treatise he demands,

> Ought not that Nation ... which, unremonstrating, permits her servants to assassinate her, or runs on that sword which she has given into the hands of others for her protection, though she does not stab herself, to be deemed equally guilty of suicide, with men who commit that unnatural Act? And like those self-destroyers, will it not be ignominiously buried in Rubbish on the highway?[40]

Representing the chosen mode of death as that favoured by the noble Englishman wishing to emulate the heroic Roman, this dire image constructs a suicidal nation as quintessentially aristocratic in nature. It is only in its allusion to burial practice that Shebbeare's metaphor deviates from its aristocratic tenor, for the ignoble burial was generally reserved for the obscure and lower-class suicide. The image is also consistent with the apocalyptic tone of the entire work, which diagnoses England's fatal 'symptoms of impending ruin' by appealing to its 'similitude of manners' with those of ancient fallen civilizations.[41] Over the course of Shebbeare's argument, England transforms metaphorically into a giant body, debilitated by the 'stream of poison which rises destructive in the Head [and which] still run[s] on the same, thro' the conduct of all that Body which lies beneath him'.[42] Rather than the objects of his care, the aristocrats and statesmen represent to Shebbeare the chief carriers of the disease afflicting England on the level of its national consciousness. According to Shebbeare's metaphor, a nation may not only derive its identity from suicide, but may also commit suicide, as if some sort of death drive manifests itself at the level of national consciousness.

This image of a nation being consumed by infection is a popular metaphor in the writings of the period's social critics and conveys their apprehension that England's emergent sense of nationhood was increasingly defined by the negative and, more disturbingly, the self-destructive.

Elsewhere, in his 'translation' of *Letters on the English Nation by Batista Angeloni, a Jesuit, Who Resided Many Years in London* (1755), Shebbeare continues his diatribe against the ministry, employing the persona of an outsider as a platform from which to launch his critique.[43] In a letter devoted exclusively to a discourse assigning 'The causes of suicide in the old Romans and modern Britains', Shebbeare's persona, 'Angeloni', vehemently rejects the theory of climate influence espoused by numerous writers attempting to account for England's suicidal tendencies.[44] Although he accepts that this 'phaenomenon' is 'characteristic of the manners of [the] nation', Angeloni dismisses the excuse that 'external nature' might 'explain the appearance and effects of internal' by dictating the system of government chosen by each nation and in turn affecting the general disposition of the populace.[45] As in Shebbeare's other works, *Letters on the English Nation* establishes the problem of suicide as a political and social issue in contrast to Cheyne's *The English Malady*, which scrupulously avoids any suggestion that the government might be responsible for the 'moral character' of the nation it administers. To bolster his argument that no correlation exists between a nation's climate and its adopted system of government, Angeloni adduces the homology of aboriginal systems of government across 'the Americas' notwithstanding drastic differences in 'winds, soils and climates' throughout the continent.[46] In this way Shebbeare counters one generalization with another, and displays a homogenizing tendency also seen in the early chapters of *Lydia*.

While persisting in holding the government accountable for the 'uneasy countenance' of the nation, Angeloni attributes English suicide rates primarily to 'poverty, from which [self-murderers] saw no way of retrieving themselves'.[47] The line between Shebbeare's persona and his own pamphleteering voice grows rather indistinct at this point, as we are reminded elsewhere of his indictment of an England in which 'everything is venal, where the laws become partial and tyrannic, where virtue is held in disgrace, and poverty, honest poverty, is the only thing which remains considered as a sin, amongst the people of Great Britain'.[48] According to popular opinion, in cases of aristocratic suicide the presence of material wealth posed an obstacle to the psychological autopsy[49] while in the instance of an indigent labourer, poverty sufficed as a cause, and no examination into the victim's emotional or mental state was deemed necessary. The *non compos mentis* plea of insanity, then, becomes a viable defence only in the presence of wealth in a society that (at least in much of the period's discourse) cannot comprehend unhappiness joined with affluence. Yet Shebbeare's *Lydia* presents a counter-history of the realities of the poor that conforms to the account afforded by outside sources condemnatory of the English malaise, even as it foregrounds the experience of women that often gets overlooked in considerations of national stereotypes and trends.

In his *Second Letter to the People of England*, Shebbeare compares the 'Greeks sunk into effeminacy, luxury and disease' with the present-day suicidal English, an observation that he conveys more implicitly in other works of the period such as *Lydia*.[50] Shebbeare follows others in viewing the English Malady as one of 'the corrupting forces of England's nation character' that undermined the cult of 'manliness' central to the construction of British nationalism in this period. Even apologists for the English Malady like Cheyne called attention to the 'feminine' qualities of the afflicted. As the historian of science Anita Guerrini observes, Cheyne's 'detailed physiognomic description of the weak-nerved patient emphasized feminine qualities: the nervous tended to be small-boned and white-skinned, with "soft and yielding" flesh, fat rather than muscular, low and soft in voice'.[51] However, interestingly enough, Cheyne obscures the suspected emasculating nature of melancholia by including at the end of his tract just as many case histories of men as of women. The continued cachet of an upper-class ailment rests upon a precarious foundation, for Cheyne must establish the delicacy of temperament essential to the melancholic, even while taking care not to 'over-feminize' this disposition. Inevitably, however, such a balance could not be maintained, and the English Malady was increasingly viewed as one of 'the corrupting forces of England's nation character' that undermined the cult of 'manliness' central to the construction of British nationalism in this period.[52] If, as these sources suggest, the normative suicidal individual suffered egregiously from a strain of melancholia, then suicide would have been typed as feminine by association. Thus, by the middle part of the eighteenth century, the 'feminization' of suicide was already intimately bound up with a sense of national identity.

The narrative of *Lydia* revolves around a female character whose perfection is unimpeached by her contemplation of suicide. At the structural centre of this novel, bridging the conclusion of volume two and the beginning of volume three, we find Lydia's prolonged suicidal *psychomachia*. The novel's second volume concludes with a cliffhanger of sorts as, having resolved to drown herself, Lydia sets out for St James's Park. Reduced to indigence by Lord Flimsy's predatory ruthlessness, Lydia can imagine no alternative to death by her own hand. Suicide, in this case, results from social pressures as opposed to individual malaise, for Shebbeare holds society at large accountable for Lydia's resolution to die. Almost as an afterthought, the narrator appends to the first volume's last page Lydia's suicide note in which she implores divine mercy and social sympathy. The assumption immediately upon the discovery of this letter that she has 'wandered to the Canal in St. James's Park' contributes to the realism of the scene.[53] Ironically, while en route to ending her life, Lydia is accosted in the park as a prostitute, a circumstance that only reinforces both her conviction that 'the world is no longer a place for virtue' and her subsequent determination 'to walk directly to the canal and end her miserable life'.[54] The heightened sense of social realism that distinguishes this scene humanizes suicide in a manner that is rather unusual even in novelistic representations of the period.

Lydia's contemplation of suicide does not, however, compromise the novel's chief moral concern of 'filial piety', since Shebbeare clearly demonstrates the mutual accord between mother and daughter on this subject. After yet another test of Lydia's virtue, her mother insists that it is 'better to perish by Famine, even to be guilty of Suicide, than live indebted to the Loss of Virtue for Existence'. Lydia's reply, that "'Tis true ... tho' Self-Murder is a detested Crime; yet surely Life, preserved at the Price of all that is delectable in the Eyes of Heaven, is yet more criminal', suggests that her suicidal deliberation has already commenced at this juncture, under the perceived sanction of her mother.[55] In an earlier moment both mother and daughter mutely contemplate suicide, as the narrator suggests that 'each would have found but little Difficulty in finishing their miserable Days'.[56] Mrs Fairchild implicitly licenses Lydia's suicidal impulse both in this tacit exchange and through her own near attempt instigated by her discovery of her daughter's suicide note. The narrator clearly establishes the sincerity of Mrs Fairchild's death wish, as 'with her trembling Hand seizing a Knife which lay before her, she was sinking to her knees to address the supreme Being and finish her Distress and Life together' before being interrupted by an unexpected visitor.[57] In fact, Lydia's contemplation of suicide is taken as evidence of both her unassailable virtue and her filial devotion. Her suicide note, in conjunction with the 'wretchedness about [her], this Resolution of Death, this paternal Fondness, and filial Piety' convinces her lover, Probit, that 'Lydia Fairchild is still the virtuous Maid [his] Soul first knew her'.[58] The text constructs Lydia's suicidal contemplation as a testament to her character and withholds the condemnation that prevailed at this time in clerical and periodical discourses on voluntary death. In this manner Shebbeare naturalizes self-destruction, severing suicide from the affectation of melancholy with which it was implicated. In calling attention to her poverty, moreover, Shebbeare reveals its status as a major motivation of suicide in the period.[59] Lydia's predicament dramatizes the 'massive cracks' in the eighteenth-century welfare network 'that too many people fell through', according to the historian Kevin Siena. Explaining the tendency in the period to read suicide as an effect of mental rather than bodily illness, Siena observes that it was 'safer to dismiss the sick who killed themselves as deranged than to confront the implications if they were not'.[60] Shebbeare's fictional representation reveals his own practical experience as a physician with the plight of the poor when confronted with debilitating disease. Suicide crosses class boundaries in Shebbeare's rendering, which foregrounds both the impoverished body that had been rendered obscure by contemporaries' focus on elite corporeality, and the material conditions of eighteenth-century existence.

In addition to her poverty, Shebbeare constructs Lydia's suicidal impulse as a response to a particular 'female difficulty'.[61] Drawn in some respects as a second Clarissa, Lydia's poverty results from her unwillingness to sacrifice her virtue; like her Richardsonian antecedent, albeit for a much shorter interval, Lydia finds herself detained in a brothel (specifically here a bagnio), lured there under false pretences by an older woman. Although she succeeds in extricating herself from the situation, her reputation is nonetheless tarnished by her visit to the premises, with the result that acquaintances previously disposed to relieve her financial distress opt to direct their charity elsewhere, seeing her 'in the ready road to become an abandoned Prostitute'.[62] At this point in the text, the issue of poverty is eclipsed by compromised virtue, as Shebbeare succeeds in conflating the two suicide motives to the extent that it becomes unclear whether the suicide 'attempt' results from Lydia's extreme indigence or from her solicitude for her blemished reputation.

In a further attempt to demonstrate the complexity and ultimate futility of any effort to determine a clear motive for suicide, the text introduces yet another contributing factor to Lydia's suicide resolution. This takes the form of her grief at her mother's supposed death and her inability 'to give her the last duties of interment'.[63] In her suicide note she begs that she not be condemned for deserting her mother 'without paying the last filial office to her ashes',[64] and explains that 'Deprived of wherewithal to execute this last Duty, [her] soul ... possessed not Firmness sufficient to attend that awful Moment'[65] when her inability to finance her mother's funeral would be exposed. Lydia's suicide in this sense is not conceived of as a wholly individualistic act, but is instead tied up in her mother's own suffering, which she feels all too acutely. In order to avoid the humiliation of seeing her mother sent to a pauper's grave, Lydia herself risks an ignominious burial of the sort described at the beginning of this chapter. The distress in this passage highlights the issue of proper and improper burial so central to the narrative's concern with the relation between luxury and national decadence, which Shebbeare links directly to his re-visioning of the English Malady in the context of eighteenth-century material culture.

Monuments, Collecting and the Luxury Debate

Shebbeare's treatment of monument culture, beginning with the elaborate tomb commissioned for Lord Flimsy upon his demise, marks the novel's entry point into eighteenth-century luxury debates. In part, Shebbeare parodies the lavish monument culture that had sprung up in the cloisters of Westminster Abbey, driving the Dean of St Paul, Thomas Newton, to protest that 'the gothic structure is encumbered and overloaded with ornaments'.[66] Meanwhile, Horace Walpole's complaint of the 'crowds and clusters of tombs in the Abbey'[67] signals the monument's elevation to a form of conspicuous consumption by mid-century. As historians David Bindman and Malcolm Baker observe, 'monuments were ... fully enmeshed in the luxury debate' and 'were a target for those who believed that pursuit of unnecessary goods led inevitably to national decline...[and] prepared the minds of the people for corruption'.[68] As mentioned earlier, however, the Janus face of luxury in this period meant that it could be viewed, on the one hand, as a corrupting influence or sign of pre-existing decadence, and on the other hand, as a sign of economic prosperity and affluence. The burgeoning of monument culture in mid-eighteenth-century England, accompanied by the vogue for 'graveyard poetry', complemented and catered to the melancholic disposition of the English. At the same time, owing in part to its strong ties to consumption and materiality, this culture of melancholy was easily dismissed as affected, insincere and indulgent by social critics like Shebbeare, who offers an alternative form of commemoration grounded in an aesthetics of authenticity, restraint and humility.

Inevitably, a critique of class accompanies this critique of culture, as we see in poems by 'graveyard poets' like Thomas Gray, whose critique of the lavish ornamentation on display in places like Westminster Abbey[69] takes aim at the fact that social inequality extends to the realm of death. The wealthy received commemoration regardless of the circumstances of their death, where the poor, as we see represented in *Lydia*, are condemned to ignominious oblivion.

In this vein, in 1755 George Colman complained that

> a penniless poor dog who has not left enough to defray the funeral charges, may perhaps be excluded the church-yard, but self-murder by a pistol genteelly mounted or the Paris-hilted sword qualifies the polite owner for a sudden death, and entitles him to a pompous burial, and a monument setting forth his virtues in Westminster Abbey.[70]

Self-destruction exposed the extent to which the disposal of the suicidal body was increasingly the subject of concern and death not in fact a leveller of class difference. By the time the Parliamentarian Lord Castlereagh took his life in 1821 and his burial in the Abbey sparked a national furore, decades of dispute in public life and in the realm of fiction had already thrust the issue into the forefront of national consciousness.

In *Lydia*, funereal monuments serve as an unmistakably material emblem of the English Malady as perceived by Shebbeare. An embodiment of all that is wrong with England, Flimsy is honoured with an elaborate monument, the propriety of which *Lydia* openly interrogates. Recounting the details of a lavish funeral bestowed upon the memory of Flimsy, the narrator dryly remarks:

[A] dead Lord, blasted with a Life of Infamy, is always to receive honourable Interment, and a panegyrical Epitaph; he was therefore ... enclosed in a Velvet Coffin,
and then in a Hearse with nodding Horse-hair formidably graced, and follow'd by
six Coaches in Mourning; which Machines grieved for him as much as anything.[71]

All that is wanting to complete the tableau of mourning, is a 'very superb Monument'[72] that subsequently being 'bespoke at Mr. —'s, the Cardinal-virtues were
placed weeping round his Lordship's Urn, and Fame writing his History'.[73] The
maudlin display of represented grief compensates for the absence of authentic
mourning, while the absurd figure of the panegyrical scribe represents a parody
of monumental iconography popular in the period. Upon reviewing the effu-
sively complimentary epitaph, his much injured widow recommends that there
be 'something added at the End of it, to tell the Readers that it was written
in complaisance to the Custom of attributing every Virtue to those Noble-
men when dead, who never possess'd one of them when alive'.[74] The widow's
disclaimer [ensures] that society at large bears the responsibility for the incom-
mensurability between merit and material recognition.

Although monuments are also erected by the novel's more upstanding characters, these represent private and personal testimonials of affection, correctives to
the empty testaments to personal vanity that proliferate in Shebbeare's novel. To
this end, the last will and testament of Probit (the Earl of Liberal) stipulates that
'his Monument should be plain, consisting of a marble Urn, and an Inscription
below'.[75] Probit's urn lacks the iconography surrounding that of his unworthy
peer, while his epitaph complements his monument in its simplicity, running
less than a third of the length of that inscribed on Lord Flimsy's tomb. Erected
in the Parish church, the monument meets with uniform disappointment from
the 'commoners' who, familiar with national sites such as Westminster Abbey,
expect a similar display of extravagance. In a concession to popular opinion, Probit's heir 'orders a statue of his father to be made by Mr. Collins in London',[76] as
a companion to the statue that Probit earlier commissioned Michael Rysbrack
to sculpt 'after that woman who truly deserves the Honour, Lydia, Countess of
Liberal',[77] using Reynolds's portrait of her as a model. Rysbrack was celebrated
for his Westminster Abbey works, among which, according to Philip Connell,
his monument to Nicholas Rowe best typified 'the sentimental sculptural representation of private, familial grief' that had become highly regarded in the
mid-eighteenth century.[78] Shebbeare involves prominent designers of Westminster Abbey monuments in the production of his text's commemorative statuary,
but the narrative focuses both on the aesthetic merits of the pieces and the kinds
of death they memorialize.

After placing these statues in a 'Temple of Fortitude', the Liberals' heir com-
missions 'in the upper Range of Pieces, which surrounded the Temple ... Basso
Relievos of the most remarkable Passages of [Lydia's and Probit's] Lives to be

carved on Marble'.[79] The passage offers a covert critique of Westminster Abbey in its assertion that the Temple 'exhibited to view' nothing but 'the mild Lessons of Religion, Virtue and Humanity' as opposed to 'ransacked Cities, slaughtered Thousands, Temples prophaned, weeping Widows and Orphans, the wretched Victims of Ambition'.[80] In case the point was lost on an unheeding reader, however, the narrator exhorts '[M]ay the Doers of good Work receive the Reward which is due to them alone'.[81] Clearly, then, the Temple of Fortitude exists as an antithesis to Westminster Abbey. Rural and private, it navigates a middle ground in the debate, advocating a modest monument accompanied by heartfelt grief of the sort expressed by the Liberals' steward, whose melancholy response to Lydia's death eventually results in his own demise, while the Earl of Liberal as swiftly follows his wife to the grave. These expressions of sincere grief render the monument more than an empty signifier, just as suicide itself is surcharged with meaning in this text. The statuary that adorns the Temple of Fortitude commemorates Lydia's suffering in a material show of sympathy marked by a refusal to cast judgement upon an act of desperation, featuring carvings of 'the most distinguished Events of the Countess's Life' that depict 'the severe Trials which this deserving Lady sustained in her youth'.[82] A highly secularized *via dolorosa*, these frescoes elicit universal sympathy from their observers and praise for the 'superior Goodness' of Lydia in her distress, in a manner that memorializes Lydia's contemplation of suicide without at any point casting aspersions on her conduct. On the contrary, the trials of Lydia represent a *Stations of the Cross*, suggesting that, had she completed her suicide, she might have achieved the martyr status the text appears partially to grant her.

The chronicling of the Liberals' biographies in statuary at the novel's end is consistent with the general preference expressed by the narrator for representing emotion with the assistance of sculpture. Hence, indicating that Lydia 'felt an Agony of Grief beyond all power of painting', the narrator proceeds to describe her face as a 'Magdalen from the Hands of Guido'.[83] Even the descriptions of Cannassetego and Yarico are assimilated into the aesthetics of Western sculpture. Yarico is 'form'd like the Statue of a Grecian Sculptor',[84] while Cannassetego is likened to the 'beauteous Statue of Apollo, which adorns the Belvedera Palace at Rome', endowed with a perfection of form and 'visage' that 'the *Grecian* Sculptors of the famed Statue of *Laocoon*, or the fighting Gladiator, might have studied him with Instruction and Delight; such was the Figure of Cannassatego'.[85] Shebbeare's preferred descriptive strategy reflects the affinity with the neoclassical that he cultivated during his travels in Europe, establishing a 'standard of taste' and aesthetic purity that distinguishes between authentic and inauthentic art, a standard that he perceives to be threatened by the mania in the period for collecting and curio-cabinets.

Not surprisingly, Flimsy's avidity for collecting aligns him with the pro-luxury side of the debate and results in his acquiring a 'Reputation for Taste in *Vertú*'.[86] Having become a 'deep Virtuoso' over the course of his Tour, he acquires 'no less than Seven undoubted *Raphael*'s, Six *Dominchino*'s, Five *Corregio's*, Ten *Titian's*, Seven *Annabel Carrache*'s, all sworn to be true Originals by the People who sold them'.[87] Flimsy's exhaustively catalogued collection attests to the spirit of excess and uninformed taste that eighteenth-century critics saw as distinguishing features of luxury. His ostentatious presentation of a 'Silver Kettle and Lamp' to the obsequious spouse of his future wife's guardian is extensively satirized as a mark of empty luxury. Collecting in this novel thus serves as a kind of shorthand for debased character. To this end, Flimsy compliments Muckworm's own sizeable collection as 'the most elegant Piece of Virtu' he has ever seen, thereby introducing a semantic confusion between virtu and virtue that cuts to the heart of the novel's social critique in its suggestion that commodities stand in for actual moral qualities, just as the monument ostensibly compensates for the lack of worth of the individual it commemorates. Ranged on the side of vertu, both the bourgeois Muckworm and aristocratic Flimsy represent the debasement that critics feared was coming to define the national character, largely as a result of commodity culture.[88]

National Pathologies and Corruptible Bodies

Apart from the suicidal disposition of its primary character, *Lydia* represents an England that is unequivocally suicidal in temperament, openly sowing the seeds of its destruction in much the same way that, as we shall see, the character Flimsy actively seeks out death in the form of venereal disease. Shebbeare concludes the fourth and final volume of the novel with a sardonic apology that his work has failed to conform to accepted generic constraints (as he perceives them) which 'display the whole Art of Woman, the soothing, frowning, fondling, scolding, sickening, deceiving, dying, recovering Female, in a series of Histories, as practiced in the Revolutions of that illustrious Lady'.[89] To compensate his supposedly disappointed reader, he offers a parodic advertisement for a new work 'proving beyond Contradiction, that every Gamester who shoots himself through the Head, drinks Poison, hangs himself, or runs his Sword through his Body, is really a Lover of his Country, and absolutely doing it great Service by that Action'.[90] In one stroke, Shebbeare denigrates both the putative conventions of the novel and the values of English society, while establishing suicide as a central component of both the textual and the social realm. Most interestingly, however, this final paragraph satirizes the notion that the suicidal act is available to women solely as a gesture, while serving as an index of patriotic zeal for their male counterparts. Shebbeare alludes to the common tendency to reconstitute the male suicide as the kind of sacrifice typically seen as central to an understanding of nationalism, which also enables the suicides of national figures such as Sir Charles Romilly and Lord Castlereagh to be construed in this century and the next as almost patriotic acts.

In her study of Romilly's self-accomplished death in 1818, Donna Andrew reveals that responses ranged from viewing it as a sin or the result of a long career of public service that ultimately took a toll on his mental and physical health. The latter camp, as Andrew observes, 'evoked the image of a warrior fallen in battle – a victim of the sacrifices he had to make'.[91] According to this perspective, Romilly's public identity allows for his final action to be assimilated into the series of sacrifices made during his life, as the ultimate sacrifice. A career of public service negates the element of self-interest required for his death to be labelled suicide; sacrifice, in this sense is a malleable discourse, easily conscripted on behalf of men in the public sphere. In connecting the rhetoric of sacrifice to the material realm, Shebbeare exposes the inauthenticity not only of this discourse, but also that of national character itself.

According to Shebbeare, the assimilation of sacrifice into material culture undermines its authenticity. At the same time, recognizing that there is no venturing outside of this materiality, Shebbeare appears to recuperate monument culture through the construction of the iconic Temple of Virtue, at an important juncture of the narrative, as a corrective to the debauched public taste. Private virtue is put on display in this country landscape garden, which comes to stand in symbolically as a sanctuary or refuge for English values. Mapped large on to this landscape, Lydia refigures national character in a manner consistent with the symbolic spaces of nationhood that Rachel Crawford, John Barrell, and others associate with the English landscape park of the period. In the process, national character remains firmly embedded in materiality, suggesting that there is no outside of material culture, especially in imagining national identity. In this respect, Tim Edensor's work connecting popular culture and national consciousness seems salient: 'national identity', he argues, 'is not only a matter of will and strategy but is also enmeshed in the embodied, material ways in which we live'.[92] But Shebbeare rehabilitates the material realm, in his imagining of the English countryside as a kind of 'purified space'.[93] Constructed as what Edensor would term 'an ideological rural national landscape' charged with 'affective and symbolic meaning',[94] the Liberal estate offers a moral geography of England that stands as a corrective to the fallen culture associated with Lord Flimsy in both his life and his death.

The monument that will be conferred upon the predatory Flimsy after his death at the midpoint of the narrative aligns him directly with the character of the nation, standing for both him and the country notwithstanding the fact that 'his mind was thoroughly convinced that Love of our Country is a Folly'.[95]

Shebbeare's affirmation in his first *Letter to the People of England* (1755) that 'the purest soul is foremost in offering up life a sacrifice to its country, whereas the contaminated skulks to save itself in cowardice'[96] attests to the central role accorded to sacrifice in the ethos of nationalism. However, the funerary monuments of a literary character like Flimsy and a historical figure like Castlereagh inscribe sacrifice in terms of self-destructive. A kind of ironic martyr, Flimsy, whose very name underscores his feeble and effeminate nature, wields the power accorded to the elite over self-presentation in the public sphere.

If interpretation of the suicide of the male public figure was a complicated task, the hermeneutics of women's suicide was also a difficult business. In their capacity as private beings, women could not as readily construct their deaths as sacrificial in the grand sense of a Romilly or even a Castlereagh. However, as previous chapters have argued, eighteenth-century constructions of femininity did not accommodate the capacity for independent agency required for suicide. Citing Durkheim's late nineteenth-century sociological work on suicide as an example, Howard Kushner highlights the fact that women have historically been viewed as having a 'natural immunity' to suicide.[97] The reasons for this immunity are manifold, but the case of the double suicide of the married couple discussed by Sarah Chapone presents one common explanation. According to Chapone's account, the jury's verdict found the husband guilty but exonerated the wife on the grounds that she was merely obeying the commands of her husband. In this sense, the wife's death underscores her lack of the capacity for self-determination required for auto-destruction. However, her 'obedience' need not preclude her agency, especially if we consider her death as sacrificial in the sense elucidated by M. D. Faber, who argues that, in the previous century, 'the ideal Renaissance wife was willing to embrace self-destruction for her husband's sake ... she was willing to carry her loyalty to the furthest possible extreme ... she was willing in short, to become a martyr'.[98] If we accept that this willingly gave her life as a gift to her husband, we must read her death as both sacrifice and suicide, notwithstanding the judgement of the court.

This notion of self-sacrifice as an integral component of the love suicide is validated in Shebbeare's novel. In an early scene, the Cayugan princess, Yarico, attempts to kill herself in her apprehension that Cannassatego, her lover, has been poisoned. Like Lydia, however, her attempt is aborted just as she is 'extending her Arm to plunge the Shaft within her Bosom' and realizes that Cannassetego has survived his snakebite.[99] Yarico's contemplation of the deed is represented not so much as an act of desperation as a proof of her devotion: 'the life you gave I sacrifice to follow thee', she exclaims as she prepares to take her life beside what she perceives to be her lover's corpse.[100] Drawn as she is from Shebbeare's romanticizing primitivist perspective, her suicidal ideation would seem to contradict eighteenth-century popular beliefs that 'self-murder is an act highly unnatural, and men who do not live in a state of civil society will never be guilty of it'.[101] The notion that suicide is foreign to a 'state of nature' was consistently reiterated over the course of the century, but it was often refuted in novels such as *Lydia*, when contact with aboriginal cultures disproved the idea that suicide was exclusively a phenomenon of consumer culture. Yet in constructing Yarico's suicide attempt as a kind of idealized self-sacrifice, Shebbeare succeeds in both maintaining her innocence and distinguishing her from the fallen English.

Similarly, despite his constant railing against the English predilection for suicide, Shebbeare does not critique Lydia's suicidal contemplation. Rather, the novel censures the complex of social forces that drive the individual to acts of desperation. Just as Yarico's 'New World' home insulates her from the effects of the English Malady, Lydia is similarly held distinct from English society throughout the novel. Her name literally signifies a geographical region in Asia, while her characterization as being 'more impregnable than Gibraltar, an Island of Virtue not touching the Continent of Vice by the least Particle', further suggests the extent to which she is consistently distinguished from corrupt English society.[102] As discussed in the previous section, Shebbeare positions Lydia as a quasi-martyr figure whose contemplation of suicide does nothing to mitigate her virtue. Shebbeare's construction of female suicide as sacrifice bears some resemblance to Richardson's strategy of salvaging his heroine's reputation in *Clarissa* and enables him to represent her as a victim of rather than an active participant in the English Malady, which, as the final section of this chapter discusses, Shebbeare recasts as a sexual ailment, synonymous with the many 'English maladies' that medical discourse generated in its attempt to rationalize the act of suicide in eighteenth-century Britain.

Cultures of Disease and the Secret Malady

In contrast to common eighteenth-century practices of assigning non-European geneses to all manners of disease, Shebbeare constructs England as a virtual breeding ground for disease, whether biological, psychological, or social. In Shebbeare's novel, Flimsy's passion for collecting vertu, or fine objects of art, is by no means confined merely to art objects, with the result that '[a]t Naples he had been honoured with a Crown from the Hands of Venus herself'.[103] As the narrator indicates, the syphilitic Viscount 'had but one way of considering Objects; which was whether the Possession of them would be agreeable to himself',[104] and the satisfaction of his desire typically leaves him with a material memento of the transaction. Shebbeare coyly conflates physical markers of venereal disease with luxury items throughout his treatment of the mouldering Lord who, after an affair with a prostitute, 'discovered some Symptoms of a Present which was likely to remain some time, in that very Place where [his] Gold Watch was accustomed to be placed'.[105] Lord Flimsy constitutes a walking embodiment of what was on the continent popularly referred to as the 'English Malady', as he succumbs to a mysterious venereal disease that accelerates his physical decay and eventually deprives him of his olfactory sense and his nose itself. Yet even this loss is somehow converted into profit, as the narrator remarks that 'he might have said of his Nose, what is cut on some Tombstones, *Mors mibi lucrum* [death is a gain/profit for me], with more Truth than that Sentence is always added to an epitaph'. The narrator repeatedly couples his abuse of the lord with a critique of commodity culture, specifically that which generates the example of the insincere epitaph. The noble nose (or the absence thereof) becomes the object of a sustained attack and the basis of Arabella Thrifty's initial refusal to marry the lord, notwithstanding one generous title-struck character's reassurance that the disfigurement 'may be a Mark of the nobility to distinguish them from Common People'.[106] According to this logic, physical decay becomes a sign of rank, a move that contradicts Cheyne's attempt to substitute a more aesthetically desirable malady for the ravager of the body that was commonly stigmatized as English. Roy Porter affirms that Cheyne's endorsement of an invisible nervous condition as characteristically English enables him to 'sidestep' the 'physically disgusting features and the shameful implications of scorbutic, glandular, or venereal disease'.[107] Possibly Shebbeare's reputation for scurrilous writing was owing to his preoccupation with venereal disease and willingness to portray its debilitating effects upon the body of an aristocrat. Despite attempts to assimilate it into a visual aesthetics of aristocratic physiognomy, the abject body of Lord Flimsy figures social degeneration on a grand scale. From Shebbeare's perspective, the effort to aestheticize the diseased body by virtue of its social status suggests that order itself is decayed, as a disease of culture in turn becomes translated into a culture of disease.[108]

The narrative traces the beginnings of Flimsy's self-destructive sexual practices back to his Grand Tour, over the course of which his 'Body had been three Times purified from all Dross, like Gold, by Quicksilver, [and] his voice had contracted a foreign Tone, by a small Accident which happened to the Organs of Speech'.[109] English detractors of the Grand Tour betrayed their national prejudices in attributing a continental origin to the pox that accompanied the travellers home.[110] However, as withering as Shebbeare's commentary on the benefits of the Tour undoubtedly is, he reserves most of his censure for English tourists' aptitude for spreading contagion. Similarly, he discounts other popular theories regarding the 'New World' origins of syphilis, which many British medical writers considered the necessary trade-off for imported luxuries.[111] The opening chapters of *Lydia* definitively establish the purity of the indigenous Onondagans and the Cayugans, whose corruption as a result of exposure to 'European manufactures' and moral depravity Cannassetego seeks to combat by tracing the evil to its source: London and the court of George II. However, this mission only leads him into the hands of an amorous Lady who demonstrates conclusively for Cannassetego and the reader the appropriateness of an English provenance for the pox, given the fact that venereal disease had been almost commodified in England, according to Shebbeare. Shebbeare's depiction of this debauched aristocrat nationalizes the 'pox' as an English Malady notwithstanding the aesthetically objectionable associations that accompany the disorder. *Lydia* in this sense reveals the slippage between the idea that the English Malady represented a nervous disorder and the opposing interpretation of the pathology as a venereal disease.

Increasingly in this period, nations' identities derived from the diseases they were seen to propagate. Although in France syphilis was popularly known as the 'English Malady', writers such as Cheyne attempted to remove the stigma by appropriating the term for another, more socially acceptable 'nervous complaint'.[112] Cheyne's *English Malady* embraces England's reputation as a high-strung, melancholic nation and displaces the less desirable reputation for sexual licentiousness among the upper classes. Yet the similarities between melancholia and syphilis constantly lead to an identification of the two afflictions.[113] Both diseases were commonly treated with mercury during the period – Cheyne specifically recommended mercury as a 'potent purgative'[114] – with the result that the designation of Lord Flimsy as one of the *virorum mercuralium*[115] might as readily identify him as suffering from melancholia. Either way, the condition was frequently labelled as distinctively English. In a 1718 'Letter Concerning the Antiquity of the Venereal Disease', William Beckett credits the English with inventing the common mercury treatment for venereal infection; in her work on early modern syphilis, McAllister construes this statement as a bizarre nationalist gesture on the English doctor's part, given the dominant eighteenth-century belief that the origin of a disease was synonymous with the cure.[116] If mercury was viewed as a common English remedy, that is, then the malady that it treated must necessarily also partake of this national identification.[117]

In his work on the relation between religious despair and Puritanism in the eighteenth century, the historian John Sena points out the irony in the fact that 'although Englishmen demonstrated an almost obsessive concern over the malady, they were not able to define precisely the nature of the disorder'.[118] Writers on the subject achieved little or no consensus as to whether the malady might be considered a syndrome, a disorder or an actual disease, and as a result of its nebulous nature, melancholy was often described as 'protean [and] able to transform itself into the shape and representation of almost any Distemper'.[119] An affliction of this nature has the capacity to absorb the symptoms of myriad other diseases, perhaps accounting for its identification with venereal disease.[120] Moreover, the fact that both melancholy and syphilis (although somatically based) constitute 'diseases of civilization' productive of mental disorders also might account for their easy conflation. In a scene laden with symbolic significance, the Viscount Flimsy is driven from the bed of a prostitute by a man posing as her husband and subsequently 'straggle[s] into St. Michael's churchyard',[121] where, clad in nothing more than his nightshirt, he is mistaken for a ghost by a nightwatchman. This inadvertent churchyard escapade places sexual experience in a setting that during this decade in particular was associated with a peculiarly English brand of melancholy. While in other novels of the period, such as Eliza Haywood's *The History of Miss Betsy Thoughtless* (1751), Westminster Abbey becomes first a scene of flirtation and then of near rape, in *Lydia* St Michael's churchyard becomes hyper-sexualized by the presence of Flimsy's scantily clad body.[122] The transformation of these *loci mori* into sexualized spaces demonstrates the conceptual layering at work in this novel and also affords a proleptic glimpse of the lord's imminent demise.

Shebbeare's construction of Lord Flimsy as a ruthless transmitter of disease and contagion confirms his diagnosis of venereal disease as the true English Malady. The novel charts Flimsy's course from the 'stews' of France, through Europe, and back to England where, despite his physical disintegration, he continues to infect with impunity those who cross his path. The sinister intentions that the narrator ascribes to Flimsy unequivocally attest to the pervasive belief that held women responsible for the spread of the 'secret malady'.[123] Accordingly, we are told,

> Such was [Flimsy's] disposition, he would have slept with his Lady on purpose to have given her the Distemper, that the Proof from which Side the Infection began might be dubious in some minds, and that the Fame of Beauty of that lovely Creature might be blasted, whom he beheld the Darling of all the World that gazed upon her.[124]

Venereal disease becomes a means of revenge in the hands of Flimsy, who similarly attempts to 'contaminat[e] the lovely Body of *Lydia Fairchild* with the most loathsome Disease, and blast her Character with universal Infamy'.[125] Not only does this novel consistently refuse to label venereal disease as a female pathology, but it also reverses the typical oppositional understanding of sexuality, according to which, as Mary Springborg notes, 'The male body came to represent the standard for health, [while] the female body came to be seen as an aberration from the norm'.[126] From this perspective, Lady Flimsy's resistance to infection attests to her spiritual and physical purity, just as the debauched, 'corruptible bodies'[127] of the nobility are re-visioned as carriers of disease rather than exemplary figures.

After Shebbeare has re-established venereal disease as the English Malady par excellence, the related matter of the English predilection for suicide suddenly appears less the result of a complex nervous disorder and more a social phenomenon demanding specific attention. This is in contrast to the work of Cheyne, which implicitly annexes suicidal impulses to a nervous disorder, thereby lending credibility to the notion of a death drive, or less anachronistically perhaps, to a mental condition that overrides and suppresses the life instinct that moral philosophers and clergymen alike invoked in the eighteenth century in their campaign against suicide. Cheyne's promulgation of a nervous stimulus for suicide arguably bolsters *non compos mentis* verdicts that coroners' juries regularly delivered in the cases of suspected aristocratic suicides. The susceptibility on the part of the nobility to a suicidal melancholia necessarily exonerates them from any degree of culpability in their self-accomplished deaths. In Cheyne's treatment, both melancholy and suicide are distinctly upper-class phenomena, while the suicides of the lower classes are essentially invisible. But Shebbeare thrusts suicide into the foreground as an option for the poor as he contrasts his indigent yet physically pure heroine with the wealthy yet physically debauched aristocratic Flimsy, whose self-destructive lifestyle attracts the full share of his censure, and extends well beyond Flimsy's death in the text itself.

Although a physician, Shebbeare's focus remains fixed on the sociology rather than the biology of suicide. Hysteria, melancholia and other nervous afflictions frequently identified as part of the psychology of the suicide are nowhere present in his characterization of Lydia, whose moral and spiritual purity sets her apart from her society, in a way that aligns her strongly with her antecedent, Clarissa. However, rather than retracing the tragic narrative arc of Richardson's exemplary figure, Lydia eludes rape and death at the hands of a libertine, experiencing a rebirth of sorts as Lady Liberal, equipped with the means of working the social reform that Shebbeare could only see realized in fiction. The second half of *Lydia* chronicles the charitable works and benevolent deeds performed by Lydia and Probit after their marriage, and stages in its final chapters the 'good deaths' of the couple and their faithful steward. Indeed, the entire second half of the novel imagines a nation in which benevolence, justice and (virtual) equality prevail. The Liberals' estate is rendered in essence an island of mercy set apart from the rest of the country.

Unfortunately, Shebbeare's vision of a utopia is rather limited in scope and reflective of the chauvinism that informs his resistance to the naturalization of England's Jewish population and his contempt for Scots and other groups constitutive of Great Britain.[128] Although his praise of aboriginal nations is sincere, it is somewhat mitigated by his valorization of the notion of the 'noble savage', in anticipation of romantic primitivism. Consequently, his narrative sedulously returns its Welsh characters to Wales, sends its First Nations figure to his 'New World' home and dispatches colonists back to England, evincing a nationalism that is narrowly English rather than comprehensively British. In this respect, Shebbeare supports the historian Rosemary Sweet's argument that English subjects in the period did not necessarily privilege their British nationality over more local identities and patriotisms.[129] Indeed, despite the superficial cosmopolitanism of novels like *Lydia*, Shebbeare remains committed to articulating an idea of English identity that is restrictive rather than comprehensive. At the same time, Shebbeare's account of identity formation attempts to counter the passivity he viewed as endemic to the national character. Some theorists of the nation suggest that this process is fundamental to the construction of national identity; Eric Hobsbawm's notion of 'invented tradition', for instance, represents individuals consenting to 'a set of practices, normally governed by tacit or overtly accepted rules, and of a ritual or symbolic nature, which seek to inculcate certain values and norms by repetition'.[130] Tim Edensor critiques both Hobsbawm and the social theorist Ernest Gellner for endorsing a notion of national subjects as passively accepting the 'knowledge and identities' imposed upon them by 'all-powerful national cultural organisations'.[131] Shebbeare similarly resists cultural imperatives, offering the special insight that although nations are artificial constructs, they need not be inauthentic.

As we have seen, notwithstanding Shebbeare's satirical treatment of his medium's affinity for representations of voluntary death, suicide permeates his work, marking the beginning, middle and the end of *Lydia*. Shebbeare's novel features three women on the verge of committing the act. They are prevented by male intervention; nonetheless, the will to die remains a matter of textual import, and its centrality suggests the paradox whereby suicide comes to be seen as productive of a national identity at the same time as it works to jeopardize the stability of society itself.[132] The view that suicide posed a threat to the very fabric of civil society finds support from thinkers such as John Adams who, in his *Essay on Self-Murther* (1700), insisted that 'suicide would destroy the force of society's laws',[133] and a good many others, who warned that a man capable of murdering himself would have nothing to lose and consequently nothing to prevent him from wreaking havoc in the streets prior to his self-execution. Discourse of this nature easily reassimilates suicide into the realm of criminality on the grounds of relaxed inhibition as opposed to heightened intentionality.[134] Yet just as other eighteenth-century writers imagine a productive albeit melancholic mode of being in the world, so too do the hosts of writers committed to rendering the English Malady socially acceptable find in it the means of consolidating a sense of nationhood. I do not of course suggest that the work of nation-building amounted to a conscious project on the part of this particular writer, but merely point to the effect produced by this body of writings on the subject. Ultimately, Shebbeare rejects Cheyne's model of sensibility and instead views suicide, melancholy and venereal disease as existing on a continuum of social behaviours that define the national character. Behind the 'corruptible' decaying bodies of Shebbeare's English characters looms the image of an afflicted nation that opposes the construction of the English Malady as an aesthetic category, a sign of culture and of status.

4 THE PATHOLOGY OF SENTIMENT: POLITICS, SACRIFICE AND WERTHERISM IN THE ENGLISH NOVEL OF SENSIBILITY

Suicide is a phenomenon of human nature that demands everyone's attention and needs reassessment in every epoch, however much it may already have been discussed and treated.

Johann von Goethe.[1]

In his compendious *A Full Inquiry into the Subject of Suicide* (1790), Charles Moore sets out to 'free this island from the imputation under which it has so long laboured, of producing more self-murder than any other nation'.[2] Citing the high suicide rate of Geneva as evidence that other countries are at least as suicidal as England, Moore nonetheless acknowledges that his compatriots are exceedingly prone to suicide and have 'a dreadful propensity to its commission'.[3] For Moore and other social critics concerned by the stigma of the English Malady, the publication of Johann Wolfgang von Goethe's *Die Leiden des jungen Werther* (*The Sufferings [or Sorrows] of Young Werther*) in 1774 must have seemed fortuitous indeed. Not only was the German novel inordinately preoccupied with suicide but its narrative also concluded with its hero's self-destruction. A bourgeois youth of an artistic temperament condemned to the lot of a bureaucrat, Werther flees a romantic attachment only to discover in the obscure village of his refuge a woman whom he finds irresistible. However, much to his despair, Werther discovers that Charlotte (or Lotte, as he refers to her), the unfortunate object of his attraction, is unavailable, owing to her engagement and, ultimately, her marriage to another man. His sorrows come to an end when Werther acts upon the death wish he has articulated throughout the narrative. However, Werther goes on to experience an afterlife in the eighteenth-century popular imagination, becoming a kind of 'cult hero' to the youth of Europe.

Although the enormous popularity of *Werther* might have been viewed by Moore and others as a potential means of neutralizing the stigma of the English Malady, the phenomenon of the 'copycat' suicide quelled any such optimism. Goethe's work was perceived to have triggered a 'Werther-effect' (*Werther-Fieber*) that spread like a contagion throughout Europe and, in particular, Britain.[4] Newspapers ran accounts of young people casting themselves from windows and overdosing on laudanum, all the while clutching the book that had been so fatal to them, which was subsequently seen as an accessory to their deaths.[5] The fact that these cases were fairly few in number and spread out over Europe either did not register or did not signify to those who believed that suicide could be spread through social contagion. Moreover, *The Sorrows of Werther* gave rise to a notion of *textual* contagion, as works carried across the channel were Anglicized by virtue of their translation into the English tongue, despite the fact that translators of the work were vigilant to append the qualifier, 'A German Story', to the titles of their editions. The English novel readily accommodated Werther by reproducing his character in an ever-expanding panoply of suicidal heroes in works ranging from Herbert Croft's *Love and Madness; or, A Story Too True* (1780), to Jacobin novels such as Charlotte Smith's *Desmond* (1792). Werther rapidly became a symbol for all that the anti-Jacobins execrated in English and European societies, conveniently allowing them, as literary critic Peter Mortensen observes, to 'pathologiz[e] foreign cultural influences [and] bran[d] continental romance's inchoate phantasms a "drug", "disease", or "infection", which, with its seemingly unlimited ability to diffuse itself, already threatened to influence Britain's entire body politic'.[6] The perception of suicide as a contagion thus positioned it as an imported vice fostered through exposure to pernicious foreign influences like Goethe's first novel. Not only does this view limit the agency of English authors, but it also invites us to question why Werther should constitute a watershed of such magnitude if suicide (as previous chapters have demonstrated) was already palpably present in novels prior to this period?[7] If works such as Eliza Haywood's *The British Recluse* and John Shebbeare's *Lydia* had already supplied ample material for the discussion of suicide, why was *Werther* considered so inflammatory?[8] Finally, how was the concept of contagion – moral, social, textual, and biological – understood in this particular instance?

As with the case of the English Malady, even if no empirical evidence in the form of statistical data was immediately forthcoming to validate the existence of the 'Werther effect', the very fact that this phenomenon was corroborated by media reports lent it at the very least a kind of textual reality.[9] If the 'Werther effect' barely registered in the realm of everyday existence, it nonetheless infiltrated the public imaginary through newspaper accounts of Werther-inspired suicides, treatises that in their very denunciation of Werther magnified its effect and novels, which displayed symptoms of the contagion in their representation of explicitly Wertherian figures. In their treatment of *Werther*, critics increasingly espoused the position that contagion might be transmitted through the act of reading or even through mere exposure to textual phenomena. In this manner, the power of print both to forge social bonds and to undo the ties of the individual to the community achieved full realization in early epidemiological considerations of suicide.[10] Held responsible for promoting first the English Malady and then the Werther effect, the press and the novel were thus constructed by their critics as almost anti-nationalist media. In response to this trend, Herbert Croft redeems the singularity of his own form by framing his anti-Wertherian story of love and madness as that of a Christian hero and nationalist narrative dedicated to dismantling the myth of the English Malady. Croft anticipates the identification between the 'Werther effect' attributed to the novel and Jacobinism that will be sustained by his chief supporter, Charles Moore, in his dissertation upon suicide. Parodying this attempt to align Jacobinism with Wertherism in her 1792 novel, *Desmond*, Charlotte Smith holds newspapers responsible for the national fear of suicidal contagion and clears the novel of any blame. This ideological struggle to define the aesthetics, moral principles and national aims of the novel establishes Werther as a pivotal figure; in this debate, the concept of suicide remains in flux, but it is ultimately subject to a consistent narrowing of its array of socio-cultural significations. For even English Jacobin novels limit the possibilities of suicide, on the one hand affirming individual agency and on the other hand always keeping suicide firmly within the domain of the 'other', constituting it as a decisively *non*-English malady. While Croft struggles to dislodge the label of the English Malady and reassign suicide's nationality, Smith literally renders Werther a woman in one characterization and nationless in another. In the works of both authors, suicide becomes absorbed into the gendered discursive matrices of sacrifice and sensibility, and into a larger deterministic structure worked out at the level of plot in the form of positive and poetic justice.

Social Contagion, Blame and Gender Contamination

Although Goethe's detractors were eager to hold him accountable for the apparent predilection for suicide that was already an established facet of English society from the beginning of the eighteenth century, it seems more reasonable to assume that the 'Werther-mania' inspired by the controversial work was as much a product of this pre-existing national culture of suicide.[11] With his passion for English authors and his adoption of the signature yellow vest and blue coat, a style of dress modelled upon English fashion, Werther was as indebted to the English novel as he was to the early strains of German romanticism.[12] As the literary critic Max Novak observes, 'If Werther's tale of woe was advertised as a "German Story", it was quickly seen as the kind of tale of emotional excess that was extraordinarily English'.[13] His prototype was already present in the work of Frances Sheridan,[14] and even Henry Mackenzie's *The Man of Feeling* (1774) presents a model of tragic sensibility that anticipates the self-destructive affectivity of Werther. Although anti-Jacobin writers conveniently blamed Goethe for the popularity of the suicidal hero in novels of the century's final decade, clearly this figure could trace his genealogy back to earlier English novels, suggesting that the vector of textual contagion, contrary to the claims of Moore, Croft and others, in fact originated in England rather than Germany.

Goethe's rendering positions Werther as a continental 'man of feeling', characterized by an extraordinary degree of sensitivity to emotional experience and responsiveness to external stimuli, a capacity that was alternately celebrated and pathologized in the period under the general term 'sensibility'. Charles Moore viewed sensibility as a dangerously malleable concept, 'deceitful in the extreme; being as often applied to dangerous as to honourable purposes',[15] whereas others viewed it as a natural outgrowth of the 'moral sense' expounded by the Earl of Shaftesbury. However, as Werther demonstrates, sensibility is also constructed as a profoundly physical experience, with the body's nerves and 'fibres' allowing one to experience sensation in a direct and at times excruciating way. The literature of sensibility is to an extent a literature of the body, which both registers and communicates affect. For detractors of sensibility – those who characterized it as a kind of 'cult' – this sensitive body is particularly susceptible to and capable of spreading moral and spiritual contagion.

The body is also in many accounts responsible for the kind of 'madness' leading to suicide. In his *Treatise on Female, Nervous, Hypochrondriacal Diseases, with Thoughts on Madness and Suicide* (1788), William Rowley draws this connection explicitly while dealing in the standard English truisms regarding suicide and national character. From Rowley's perspective, the vaunted English freedom has an unfortunate side-effect, given that 'The agitations of passions, this liberty of thinking and acting with less restraint than in other nations, force a great quantity of blood to the head, and produce greater varieties of madness in this country, than is observed in others'.[16] Civil and religious constraint, according to this logic, are productive of both a healthy citizen and national body, whereas freedom is somehow pathological in this bizarre intermingling of the medical and the political. Yet Rowley also assigns a positive value to Britain's pathology of liberty; in contrast to other nations whose subjects 'are educated from infants in implicit submission and non-resistance; in Britain every one thinks and acts as he pleases; this produces all that variety and originality in the English character, and causes arts, sciences, and inventions to flourish'.[17] According to this thinking, both suicide and the novel emerge from this unique brand of British liberty. However, while accepting (and medically sealing) England's reputation as a nation of suicides, Rowley takes to task largely foreign advocates of suicide, reaching back into Roman history to rebuke Cato, and geographically across the channel to censure Rousseau. Moreover, Rowley attributes the fact that '*The Sorrows of Werther* were a general topic of conversation' to readers' propensity for suicide.[18] Rowley's account mingles acknowledgement that the British are 'constitutionally' (both in a political and physical sense) afflicted by madness and suicide, with a statement that they are also susceptible to the contamination of foreign influence. Hence, in Rowley's construction of national character, blame and praise alternate in a slight modification of the usual rhetorical position, presenting the British as both free agents and victims, at once strong-minded and independent and melancholically vulnerable. Indeed, the internal contradictions of Rowley's account reflect the incoherent nature of imaginings of national identity more generally. The historian Geoffrey Cubitt argues that 'however institutionalized nations become, and however well established the symbolism that denotes them, nations remain elusive and indeterminate, perpetually open to context, to elaboration and to imaginative reconstruction'.[19] In relation to eighteenth-century national identities, this flexibility leads to disorder, ambiguity and even, as seen in Rowley's account, a good deal of contradiction when trying to define a country's character.

Interestingly, Rowley bases his discouragement of female suicide upon an inclusive and ostensibly ungendered construct of the political sphere, even while he pathologizes suicide as one of the many female diseases he addresses in his treatise: 'Suicide is a crime ... where the duties of *every* individual are politically considered' given that in 'a political view, it robs mankind of those services, whether corporeal or mental, that society at large has a right to expect of each member forming a part of a whole'.[20]

For Rowley, every suicide, whether the action of a man or woman, is a political and highly public act. It may seem surprising that, as a medical professional, Rowley would persist in viewing suicide as a crime even while acknowledging it as the product of madness, but for him, the two positions are not mutually exclusive. His representation of his patients as to some extent accountable for their conditions is not entirely singular, although it is somewhat at odds with the 'popular "medical" (or rather, emotional, philosophical, and pragmatic) interpretations' in circulation during this period, according to the historian Rab Huston.[21] Although Huston characterizes Rowley's argument as a 'fashionable philosophical, rather than a medical, one, even if he dressed it up in technical terms', he does acknowledge that it reflects contemporary tendencies to 'mix different levels of explanation' with a 'pure' medical interpretation of suicide not emerging until 1835.[22] As a result of this 'mixing', suicide is caught within the nexus of intermingled political, medical, literary and social interpretations, all of which inform and often contradict the other, which in turn has a bearing on attempts to read suicide through the pseudo-medical lens of contagion.

Despite anxiety expressed by writers like Rowley regarding the transmissibility of suicide via bodies of sensibility and print culture, prominent figures of the period like Germaine de Staël nonetheless dismissed the notion that *Werther* was a dangerous book, insisting that 'The example of suicide can never be contagious'.[23] From Staël's perspective, *Werther* 'is an undiluted presentation of the harm a bad social system can do to an energetic mind'.[24] Staël's assessment transfers the blame for a 'Werther effect' of sorts from sensibility, and the susceptibility to contagion that this condition was thought to foster, to society at large. In this sense, she anticipates the late nineteenth-century sociological work of Emile Durkheim who claimed that 'suicide ... is precisely one of the forms through which the collective affection from which we suffer is transmitted'.[25] Although in his landmark study Durkheim drove a wedge between contagion and imitation, regarding the former as a sociological phenomenon (and therefore worthy of study) and the latter as a psychological aberration, no such clear-cut distinction exists in the eighteenth century. Imitation was thought to transpire as a sort of contagion, potentially occurring both through the faculty of sympathy, as expounded in the writings of David Hume, and through the permeability of the body, as outlined in the medical writings of Tissot and his eighteenth-century colleagues.

In his *Treatise of Human Nature* (1740), Hume elaborates an idea of sympathy which was seen an integral feature of sensibility. Emphasizing the involuntary in his account of the communication of sympathy, Hume attempts to explain how individuals can affect each other in a disinterested way. For Hume, the idea of an emotion is sufficient to produce the equivalent of that emotion in the individual considering it:

> When any affection is infus'd by sympathy, it is at first known only by its effects, and by those external signs ... which convey an idea of it. This idea is presently converted into an impression, and acquires such a degree of force and vivacity, as to become the very passion itself, and produce an equal emotion, as any original affection.[26]

Drawing on Spinoza's theory of the 'imitation of affects',[27] Hume's representation of sympathy operates as a complex affective response involving a series of substitutions and translations that eventually enable one to experience an analogue of the other's emotion. Hume's fellow Scot Adam Smith frames a concept of contagious sympathy in more somatic terms in his *Theory of Moral Sentiments* (1759):

> [Another person's] agonies ... when we have thus adopted and made them our own, begin at last to affect us ... Persons of delicate fibres and a weak constitution of body complain, that in looking on the sores and ulcers which are exposed by beggars in the streets they are apt to feel an itching or uneasy sensation in the corresponding parts of their own bodies.[28]

Posited as a physiological experience, sympathy appears as a kind of contagion over which the individual has little control. This model connects sense perception to an idea of intersubjectivity that provides some insight into eighteenth-century approaches to understanding the 'other'. In its emphasis on achieving a kind of understanding from within, Smith's and Hume's model of sympathy bears resemblance to what we would understand as empathy; as the literary critic Brigid Lowe observes, the coining of the latter term in the earlier twentieth century 'took over much of the earlier meaning of sympathy'.[29] Affective identification is carried to an extreme in this construction, and Smith even goes so far as to suggest that if one wants to mourn the dead, one must imaginatively inhabit the grave they occupy. Hence, the phenomenon we refer to as the 'Werther effect' might more accurately be termed a 'Werther affect', given the fact that it is largely a product of eighteenth-century models of sympathy and sensibility. However, these same critics struggled when attempting to demonstrate how affect could transfer from a character to a person.

Despite the fact that, as the critic Marthe Robert observes, 'The relation between [*Werther*] and reality only exists on paper',[30] Werther was embraced as a model for imitation largely owing to the realistic aspects of his character. A reason for this ready slippage between reality and illusion is provided in part by a significant footnote in which Charles Moore clarifies his intention 'to fall in with the common opinion, that Werther is not a fictitious, but a real character; which opinion, whether it be true or false, is of no consequence to the point at hand; only that its being read as a true story more engages the attention and increases the mischief'.[31] That Werther was a composite of a youthful, lovesick Goethe and his friend, Karl Wilhelm Jerusalem[32], who ultimately did take his life in 1772 in despair over his love of a married woman, was of little relevance to those who realized that no Werther as such had ever existed in the world. *Werther* blurs the distinction between the original and its imitation, between a literary character and an actual person. In this sense, it can be taken as yet another example of a work supporting Michael McKeon's thesis that the eighteenth-century novel 'challenges the priority of the real'.[33] Werther is, in a sense, hyperreal; a product of a group fantasy, he is contagious not because he is fictive[34] or real, but because he is neither.

Jakob Michael Reinhold Lenz's defence of the work in a series of letters simultaneously praises his compatriot Goethe for the seemingly authentic humanity with which he injects his character, at the same time as it censures readers for receiving Werther as anything more than 'an image [that] it is physically and metaphysically impossible to imitate fully'.[35] Lenz transfers moral responsibility from the author to the reader while acknowledging the power of the image, which according to this construction is invested with a kind of virtual reality. Explaining in similar terms the process by which Werther engenders sympathy, Caroline Welbery argues, 'Both the exclusive substitution of the imagined for the real and the characterization of the subject as the victim of desire play a crucial role in designing a reader who collaborates in image-making'.[36] The vividness of Werther's rendering engenders sympathy, although critics such as Brigid Lowe would argue that sympathy is an animating principle of novel reading in a more general sense.[37] Regardless, Werther overcomes the distance of fiction in order to impress eighteenth-century readers with an acute sense of his own constructed melancholia.

But were some readers more susceptible to the 'Werther affect' than others? A gendered idea of contagious sympathy is seen in the influential medical writings of the eighteenth-century French thinker Samuel Auguste David Tissot. Tissot's insistence that 'all living things transpire' suggested a bodily permeability or porosity that rendered a being susceptible to contagion. Since women from the time of Hippocrates and Galen were seen as more porous than men, it follows that a female body would be more readily infected than a dense male body. In her interrogation of the historical construction of the body, the feminist critic Carole Pateman confirms the way in which women's bodies in particular have been pathologized. For Pateman, the male body is 'tightly enclosed within boundaries, but women's bodies are permeable, their contours change shape and they are subject to cyclical processes'.[38] According to this construction, the woman's body is an ideal viral carrier, the site of infection and symbolic of the very self-destructive forces that are simultaneously withheld from women by the same discourse. In this context, women are both physically and emotionally more permeable than men and hence more susceptible to the so-called 'Werther-effect'.

In his essay on suicide, Charles Moore bases his condemnation of *Werther* on charges that

> it has been known to have been made the express groundwork for suicide also. Many a wretched self-victim to his passions has been found, grasping with equal avidity in the awful moment his sword and these *Sorrows;* and many a deluded female has been discovered in her hour of self-destruction to have reclined her aching head on this poisonous tale.[39]

Notably, Moore indicates that both sexes were susceptible to Werther's influence and ready to emulate his example, thus rendering his gender-transcending appeal doubly injurious. Yet, although many of Werther's emulators were in fact male, Moore directs his dire warning exclusively to the female reader, advising her to

> be assured, that whatever tale of tender woe arrests the feelings without the approbation of the judgment, or even contrary to its dictates ... tends when encouraged only towards delusion, disquietude and torment; robbing the soul of its innocence and ease, if not conducting it at length into the paths of gross error, vice, and wickedness.[40]

According to Moore, a woman's sensibility and underdeveloped sense of will render her more vulnerable both to the novel's corrupting influence and to contagion than a masculine sensibility. A 'contaminated femininity' more readily absorbs the influence of Werther, and perhaps for this reason, critics of the novel were especially wary of the influence it might assert upon its increasingly female readership.

Moreover, the affectation of sensibility on the part of men of fashion inevitably generated gender trouble. William Preston's xenophobic *Reflections on the Peculiarities and Style of Manner in the Late German Writers, Whose Works Have Appeared in English* (1802) charged that Goethe's and his compatriot's writings 'feed and diffuse a prevailing malady of the times, which has taken too full possession of the female world, and, indeed, of many men, under the name of sentiment; a malady, which … exalts a morbid and absurd sensibility'.[41] The 'feminization' of sensibility, as Claudia Johnson writes, 'fundamentally unsettled' gender, 'leaving women without a distinct gender site' and in effect rendering them 'equivocal beings'.[42] As men of feeling adopted or were ascribed traits typically associated with women, female behaviour was pathologized to a still greater degree, as both femininity and effeminacy become gender markers of suicide and sensibility in the latter part of the eighteenth century.

Predictably, Preston and other detractors insisted that an assertion of masculinity might serve as an antidote to the effete suicidal sensibility that Werther indulges, while medical writers like William Rowley similarly claimed that suicide and madness might be curbed by a 'masculine habit of body and mind'.[43] Interestingly, Lotte enjoins Werther to 'be a man!', while Goethe, after he himself began to believe in the 'Werther effect', appended an epigraphic disclaimer to a later edition that echoes this call for masculine forbearance.[44] The art historian Ron Brown confirms that '[L]iterary scholars such as Charles Moore began attempts to establish the masculinity of staying alive and the femininity of death and suicide'.[45] However, this tendency actually stretches further back into the eighteenth century, to John Adams's *Essay Concerning Self-Murther* (1700), which represents suicide as a female weakness unworthy of men of true spirit and strong character. Wertherism is thus simply a development of the notion that a feminine temperament generates suicidal despair, whereas a masculine assertion of the will presumably quells any form of spiritual malaise.

Werther's critical reception in England thus often rendered him effeminate, an exaggerated or excessive form of himself. Yet this very effeminacy creates precisely the conditions that preclude the consummation of his death in English reworkings of Goethe's story; as seen in earlier chapters, women in literary representations may attempt but seldom ever accomplish self-destruction. Croft and Moore represent Werther's so-called deficiencies (for example, his inability to conquer his passion) as excesses, marks of a being whose gender has become unmoored. In contrast, Smith's more sympathetic portrayal of Werther dwells upon his femininity, and in fact heightens it by transmuting him into the heroine Geraldine Verney, in *Desmond* after first rendering him both an English and feminine 'Werter'. The vagaries of political affiliation inform and are inextricably tied up with Smith's and Croft's construction of gender in national contexts, as will become clear in the remainder of this chapter.

Sensation, Spectacle and Discipline in Croft's *Love and Madness*

On 7 April 1779, a woman was fatally shot as she stepped into a waiting carriage outside the Covent Garden Theatre in London; the young man responsible then turned a second pistol on himself in an unsuccessful attempt at suicide. This event sparked considerable interest in the media, owing both to its public nature and to the fact that the victim, Martha Ray, was the long-term mistress of the Earl of Sandwich. Long after the trial and execution of James Hackman, Ray's suspected lover, the scandal persisted in numerous literary and paraliterary representations, including Herbert Croft's *Love and Madness; or, A Story Too True*, which, while not the most sensational of contemporary representations, is by far the most self-conscious in positioning itself in relation to *Werther*'s impact on late eighteenth-century print culture.

An unabashedly sensational 'potboiler', Croft's narrative masquerades as the authentic correspondence between Ray and Hackman over the three-year interval of their alleged clandestine relationship. Playing on the public sympathy for Hackman as a 'man of excessive feeling', Croft establishes Hackman's exemplarity in the text's final pages in a way that provides a testimony of the latter's forbearance during his trial and in the days leading up to his execution.[46] As such, the work intervenes in the archival accounts and public memory of the event in order to vindicate and 'rehabilitate' Hackman by casting him as a martyr and reconstructing an identity contoured around a contagious form of 'madness'.[47]

Croft sets out to present his protagonist as mentally ill, and therefore not fully accountable for his so-called 'crime of passion'. Even before the epistolary correspondence (which runs to sixty-five letters in total) gets underway, the novel's prefatory material chronicles a series of 'true crime' events, some of which are inspired by the Hackman/Ray story. Croft uses these newspaper accounts of 'love and madness' to place Hackman in a tradition or continuum of passionate murderers, but he also seeks thereby to palliate the severity of Hackman's crime by establishing numerous precedents. During his actual trial, Hackman had agreed to allow the plea of insanity to be entered in his defence, but the notion that he killed Ray in a moment of frenzy was rejected on the grounds that his possession of two pistols implied premeditation.[48] In Croft's novel, however, the proliferation of 'newspaper clippings' points to the author's favoured methodology of constructing an identity for Hackman based on a dense layering of crime upon crime and multiple instances of madness. Croft's elaborate textual apparatus constructs a post facto defence for Hackman in order to exonerate him by pursuing the insanity plea posthumously. These prefatory 'true crime' narratives are supplemented by fictional equivalents in Croft's novel, as we witness in the text Hackman's subjectivity actively feeding on such stories, whether they take the form of ballads, songs, drama or tales of passionate crimes. Using his authority as 'editor' of Ray's and Hackman's correspondence, Croft manipulates print culture as a strategy for characterization and identity formation while he attempts to clear Hackman's name through various forms of 'constructed evidence'.

In the novel, Hackman's letters chart the progress of his madness; a reasonable tone at the opening gives way to jealousy by the third letter and passionate violence by the tenth. Croft anticipates the tragedy by attributing such early admissions to Hackman as, 'My passions are all gunpowder! Though, thank God, no Othello, yet am I'.[49] The urgency of the letters' tone steadily escalates until Hackman declares that he 'would massacre all mankind sooner than lose [Ray]'.[50] Read chronologically as a narrative about the onset of mental illness, these letters contradict the supposed purpose of the text: to redeem Hackman by proving his crime was committed while in the throes of a merely momentary 'frenzy'. In fact, Croft works against the temporary insanity plea to establish a history of mental disorder, suggesting that Hackman's murderous 'frenzy' is the natural culmination of his passion for Martha Ray.[51] In Croft's text, mental illness is integral to a theory of identity as a fluid entity subject to the caprices of external events and circumstances. Early in the correspondence, Hackman tells Ray: 'I am not the same identical man I was three months ago. You have created me ... created me anew'.[52] Croft's model of identity is perfectly consistent with his construction of Hackman as a 'man of feeling' or exemplar of sensibility, which is a radically unstable and unbalanced way of being in the world, according to other detractors such as Charles Moore.

As early as the fourteenth letter, we see clearly the proceedings of a disordered brain, as Hackman's attention swings rapidly from a Scottish ballad, to the black hole of Calcutta, to questions of literary 'realism', back to Holwell's account of the black hole, to the origins of Robinson Crusoe, to the double suicide of two Italian lovers. Mental illness figures in these free-associating letters as a kind of manic hypergraphia, which is why it's important to note that most of the letters of the correspondence are composed by Hackman.[53] But 'madness' also becomes increasingly associated with suicide as Hackman's desperation mounts. For, even though Croft foregrounds Hackman's murder of Martha Ray as his primary scene of investigation, the legal and moral aspects of 'self-murder' eventually overwhelm the text and even take priority over the author's attempt to highlight the actual Hackman's passionate sensibility as a factor in his crime.

Although in this period individual cases of suicide had already become enshrined in casual discourse and helped perpetuate the notion of an English Malady, Hackman's murder-suicide created a sensation that truly propelled the phenomenon onto the centre stage of contemporary debate. Hackman's actual suicide attempt was publicly witnessed by a multitude of passersby in addition to the crowd of theatregoers exiting Covent Garden Theatre. Unlike the self-inflicted death that occurred quietly in the privacy of the home or in a sheltered corner of a park, Hackman's suicide attempt afforded a visual spectacle to the crowd. By employing the sidewalk as a lethal implement when he hurled his temple against it after his pistol jammed, Hackman fully integrated the public space into his suicide attempt. Moreover, the bloody spectacle heightened the criminality of suicide through its close association with murder.[54] In fact, however, Croft's reconstruction both acknowledges the centrality of suicide to the public reception of the scandal and attempts to contain its implications for his reformed hero.

Croft's attempts to redeem his fictional Hackman accompany a larger project of rehabilitating an English national character rendered notorious by its own print culture for melancholic and suicidal tendencies. Croft's effort to highlight the transnational dimension of suicide was recognized by the *London Magazine*'s review, which praises the work for demonstrating that suicide 'is not to be confined to any one country'.[55] Hackman, as represented in Croft's novel, bolsters this transnational stance in his insistence that the reputation of 'the English propensity for suicide is not true, though a very popular idea'.[56] In his challenge to the notion of an English Malady, Croft returns repeatedly to the problem of suicide, qualifying every anecdote of English suicide with one of European origin. Late in Croft's story, Hackman dwells at length on the infamous double-suicide of Richard and Bridget Smith (mentioned already in this study owing to its strong effect on the popular imagination of the day), the 'freethinking' couple who in 1732 took their lives and that of their child in the belief that the world was not a fit place for human residence. Hackman's interest lies with their suicide note, which he finds surprising for the 'calm resolution, the good humour, and the propriety with which it was written'.[57] Introducing this event to his reader, Martha Ray, as an instance of 'English suicide much more cool and deliberate than any you have ever heard',[58] he subsequently glosses his account with the claim that he had recounted 'This tragedy ... because I think France, lively France, in which language suicide is an Anglicism, can supply me with an anecdote, as authentic, of something still more cool, and more deliberate, since the motives for the crime were so much weaker'.[59] After combatively satirizing the stereotypical French demeanor, Croft's Hackman narrates the story of the suicide of two French soldiers who, after dining sumptuously at an inn, coolly and efficiently dispatched themselves on Christmas day. In this digression on duelling anecdotes, Croft contrasts the English case of domestic suicide with the military 'heroics' of the French, a political manoeuvre that, without actually denying the prevalence of British suicide, defuses the stigma of the English Malady by assigning to the French a predilection for a more disreputable form of voluntary death. Recognizing that the reputation of the English predilection for suicide may not be altogether refutable, Croft's version of 'damage control' thus subtly seeks to vitiate the French style of suicide and highlight not only the share of other nations in the phenomenon but also their influence on the suicide rate in Britain.

Of course, the notable influence emerging from the European literary scene for Croft was Goethe's controversial work, *The Sufferings of Young Werther*. Betraying an inordinate preoccupation with suicide, and concluding with its protagonist's self-destruction, Goethe's novel afforded Croft a convenient means of de-Anglicizing suicide. After its German publication in 1774, *Werther* was translated into French a year later, but the English would have to wait until 1779 for a direct translation from the German text.[60] Moore's account of the complicated history of *Werther*'s transmission from Germany to England runs as follows:

> This pernicious publication was first broached in German by one Goethe; then trans-
> lated into French; and a few years since into the English from the French copy; when
> it met with astonishing encouragement under the title of the 'Sorrows of Werther'.
> The last English translation of 1788 is said to be from the original German. It
> assumes the less interesting title of 'Werther and Charlotte', a German Story. It is also
> somewhat preferable to the original translation, as it contains occasional notes and
> strictures on Werther's conduct, and condemns his suicide; but its preface contains
> much objectionable material.[61]

In a manner typical of late eighteenth-century Europhobic discourse, Moore places an emphasis on the alleged partnership between Germany and France in introducing Goethe's work to England. France's mediation of the transmission of *Werther* to England acts as a conduit of contagion that serves to heighten the particular animosity between the two countries (Moore published his work in 1790, roughly a year after the storming of the Bastille). Despite the absence of a 'pure translation' and the fact that the transmission of the text in Britain was invariably mediated, whether by virtue of double translation or by the intervention of an English moralizing voice, Moore insists on the detrimental impact of *Werther*'s textual presence in England. One of the subscribers to the first edition of *Love and Madness*, Moore thus works in tandem with Croft to delegitimize *Werther*.[62]

Not surprisingly, the 1779 account of Hackman's execution in the *London Magazine* was followed on the very next page by a review of the first English translation of Goethe's novel, *The Sorrows of Werther; a German Story, Founded on Fact*. The reviewer observes that 'the familiarity of this story to that of the late Mr. Hackman and Miss Ray renders this performance more interesting at this time'.[63] Even though Goethe's work predates the fatal events of 1779, the London journal assumes its virtual unfamiliarity to an English audience owing to the lack of a translation.[64] And ignoring the fact that this translation came some five years after the 1774 publication of the original German edition, the reviewer invites British readers to draw parallels between the London crime and the German narrative. Evidently, the publishers of the English translation of *Werther* based the appeal of the work on its contemporaneity with Hackman's case, and in turn rendered Goethe's novel newly relevant for England. From the time of their English geneses, the destinies of *Love and Madness* and *Werther* are hence inextricably linked, as Croft and numerous other eighteenth-century commentators attribute Hackman's suicide attempt to a so-called 'Werther effect'.

Disregarding the fact that in the narrative, Hackman's suicidal and manic propensities predate his reading of the text, both Croft and Moore hold Goethe's novel responsible for somehow infecting Hackman with a temporary madness culminating in his murder of Martha Ray and his suicide attempt. In this sense, reading functions as a kind of pathology on which translation has no bearing. Prolonged exposure to the textual is itself a problem for Croft, and for this reason, the novel's lengthy digression on Thomas Chatterton, the gifted and penniless Bristol poet who took his life in 1770, is highly relevant. On the pretext of an assignment to uncover all available information pertaining to the case, Hackman in Croft's novel writes a dissertation in miniature on the work of Chatterton, which exonerates his 'forgery' of the Rowley poems, even while presenting him as being 'holden up to shame' for his suicide.[65] Over the course of this long letter to Ray, Hackman ascribes Chatterton's disorder to the 'wear and tear of the imagination' caused by excessive study. Here he quotes the French medical theorist Tissot, who, in his 'Essay on the Diseases Incident to Literary Persons', insists:

> When the mind, long time occupied, has forcibly impressed an action upon the brain, she is unable to repress that forcible action. The shock continues after its cause; and, reacting upon the mind, makes it experience ideas which are truly delirious, for they no longer answer to the external impressions of the object, but to the internal dispositions of the brain.[66]

Croft cites this very passage in specific reference to the case of Chatterton (and, by association, Hackman), whom he incorporates into Tissot's catalogue of melancholic geniuses. In this sense, both Croft and Tissot present melancholia as a product of habit, or lifestyle choice, produced in this instance by overexposure to texts like Goethe's *The Sufferings of Young Werther*. In Croft's assessment, the physiological effects of the prolonged immobility occasioned by reading are as harmful to the psychology of the individual as the pernicious examples afforded by the texts themselves.

In his emphasis on Chatterton's story, Croft appears anxious to demonstrate a wider range of literary influences upon his hero, while maintaining Werther's primary influence. Chatterton and Werther occupy the same discursive space and were consistently linked in the public imagination, despite their significant differences and the fact that, as Michael MacDonald observes, 'Werther killed himself from love; Chatterton died for want of recognition'.[67] Both figures fashioned themselves as poets, and their deaths were viewed as particularly tragic owing to their youth.[68] However, an eighteenth-century British audience would have viewed Chatterton's case as rather singular, whereas Werther's case of unrequited love was at once more familiar and susceptible to imitation. According to Croft's version of events, both Chatterton and Werther coalesce in Hackman's mind to produce his 'mental imbalance'. But despite his preoccupation with the story of Chatterton, Hackman appears to be moved more by the fictional example of Werther than by the real-life suicide of the young poet. As Max Novak asserts, 'Hackman is presented as a person who sees his world through examples, both literary and real' and he adopts Werther as the 'dominant text for the way in which he conceives of the world'.[69] Indeed, the extent of Hackman's identification with Goethe's protagonist is indicated by his ability to enter Werther's interiority and compose a set of 'Lines found, after Werther's death, upon the ground by the pistol'. Hackman's imaginative assumption of Werther's identity through this form of prosopopoeia reflects his real-life attempt to emulate the character, albeit with some embellishments of his own. Croft's text consistently blurs the distinction between fact and fiction, presenting itself from its very subtitle (a 'Story too True') as a work that lays claim to a privileged relation to the 'truth' and even somehow exceeds it.

In many ways, Croft frames his work not so much as a novel as an enlightened corrective to contemporary interpretation of events. Objecting to the stigmatization of suicide as an English Malady, Croft blames the fiction industry (both foreign and domestic) for producing novels glorifying suicide and the avidity of the press for perpetuating these accounts.[70] Accordingly, the fictionalized Hackman hypothesizes that

> Perhaps, if these instances of desperate cowardice did not go out of this country, through the channels of our papers, by which means they are stored up as authorities against the disappointment of a gloomy day, suicide would with less propriety, be considered an Anglicism.[71]

In a statement fraught with contradiction, even as Croft's Hackman denies any basis for the stigma, he blames the media that promotes it for instigating suicide within England.[72] In this respect, he affirms the status of suicide as a public phenomenon that effectively pathologizes the social body through the transmission of texts.

Precisely because of the significance that Croft attributes to print culture, he downplays the sensation caused by Chatterton's death in Britain during this period in comparison to the effects of the fictional example of Werther. Dismissing Werther as a 'very bad man',[73] Croft blames Goethe chiefly for his failure to remove 'the edge of the dangerous example' supplied by his novel through some

sort of disclaimer or a moralizing qualification to 'take the edge off the representation'.[74] In this respect, Croft renders the admissibility of suicide narratives
contingent on their inclusion of a sufficient number of precepts condemning
the immorality of the act. Despite his protagonist's vehement protestations to
Ray that he is not 'fool enough to pistol himself because a thick-blooded German has been fool enough to set the example, or because a German author has
feigned such a story',[75] his suicide attempt supplies incontrovertible proof that,
from Croft's perspective, Goethe's Werther is a principal accessory to his 'crime'.

Similarly, in the view of the eighteenth-century suicidologist Charles Moore,
the step from 'approbation' to imitation is a small one, and the reader must take
care 'lest compassion unrestrained should blend a mixture of excuse, of countenance, and at length, of imitation'.[76] The process of contagion presented by
Moore moves systematically from textual exposure, to an example of suicide,
to active imitation. Eventually, in both Croft and Moore, the case of Hackman
recedes in order that their texts can address Werther against the backdrop of
a more general engagement with literary criticism. Much of that discussion
turns on the uncoupling of precept from example, which, as the literary critic
Michael McKeon has demonstrated, constitutes a central issue in eighteenth-
century debates pertaining to the moral and epistemological foundations of the
novel.[77] *Love and Madness* proposes itself as an antidote to moral contagion by
privileging anti-Wertherian precepts over the mimetic appeal of example. Moore
corroborates this agenda in his insistence that Croft 'seems anxious through the
whole to show a pointed abhorrence of suicide in every shape'.[78] Moore presents
Love and Madness as an antidote to the 'pernicious example of *Werther*',[79] and his
citations of Croft are so extensive that they present almost an expurgated version
of his novel. Despite the fact that James Hackman is a murderer and a failed suicide, his reincarnation in *Love and Madness* as a mouthpiece for its author's own
moral preachings (that Hackman, like Croft, was an Anglican minister in part
accounts for the ease of appropriation here) enacts Croft's strategy of using the
novel as a didactic device to promote a more felicitous kind of social contagion.

By holding Werther primarily responsible for Hackman's suicidal intentions,
Croft locates the source of suicidal contamination outside of England, suggesting that his protagonist has merely been corrupted by a foreign body. Although
Moore also cites 'Hackman's own opinion of the great danger of publishing
sorrows such as Werther's',[80] it has been generally agreed that the 'real' James
Hackman probably did not read *Werther*, and that it is highly unlikely that the
text would have incited him to murder. However, Croft's claim that Hackman
imitated Werther contributes to a perception of ideas as something akin to 'viral'
and supports the idea that social contagion may be promoted intertextually. As
a character based on a non-fictive model, Hackman dramatizes the evils of read-

ing too closely and too sympathetically, especially material originating outside of England.

Much of the suicide narrative's impetus in *Love and Madness* derives from the eagerness of Croft's protagonist to read the French version and from Ray's anxious determination to keep it from him. After imploring Hackman never to read *Werther*,[81] Ray construes his month-long silence as a sign that he has ignored her appeal and subsequently ended his life. Croft's Hackman later admits that he has read Goethe's novel and he does ultimately attempt suicide, albeit unsuccessfully. Croft's text explicitly supports the notion of suicide as a form of contagion in its insistence through Hackman on the 'indisputable magnetism' of the influence of the phenomenon.[82] This metaphor underscores the involuntary nature of a 'Werther effect' and its suppression of the functioning of the will. Also implicit in the notion of an English Malady, this view emphasizes human impressionability and the notion that suicide is a suggestible and hence exceedingly dangerous phenomenon. This model of suicide as social contagion constructs the act as a communal rather than an individual event, one conceived within the confines of clubs and the literary space of print culture. As the anecdote of the French soldiers' suicide mentioned above illustrates, suicide may take place in solidarity and companionship, as an interpersonal relation that undermines the sovereignty of the state to a greater extent than the solitary, private suicide. According to this logic, the act of suicide forges social relations even as it resists containment on the part of the state, and it is in this way that it can be viewed as exerting an impact on national character.[83] Even as Croft works to counteract the notion of the English Malady, his text nonetheless demonstrates exactly how group behaviour may be taught and national identity defined through a form of social contagion.

Sacrifice and Martyrdom

Another means of imagining national identity was staged at the execution of James Hackman on 20 June 1779. On this day, the *London Magazine* published an account of the execution that was subdued, matter-of-fact, but affecting, emphasizing the piety and dignity of the condemned in his final moments. Although the execution was public, the reporter presents it almost as a private affair, emphasizing Hackman's last devotions and sidelining the spectators almost altogether. The respect accorded to Hackman transforms the execution from a public to a private event, yet one that paradoxically generates public commendation and sympathy. As John Brewer observes, 'Hackman's repeated enactment of his exquisite sensibility, the legibility of his feelings as they manifested themselves in his conduct, fashioned bonds of sympathy, despite the crime he had perpetrated'.[84] In Croft's text, meanwhile, even the juridico-political function of justice is personified as a person of sensibility, as indicated by the apostrophe to Hackman that appears in Croft's final letter: 'That justice which condemned thee to death cannot refuse a sign, a tear to thy virtues'.[85] As Croft's postscript avows, 'That he was a lover, his martyrdom denounces, and proves that his heart was sincere'.[86]

Hackman's execution thus elevates him to the status of a martyr and is constructed as a national sacrifice in many accounts, including William Dawes's *The Case and Memoirs of Mr. James Hackman* (1779).[87] Dawes's version of events goes to great lengths to exonerate Hackman, refusing to use the word 'murder' in reference to the killing of Ray, and even acquitting Hackman of the crime 'which the law rigidly condemned him for'.[88] The same author casts aspersions on Ray's 'character and condition', suggesting that the considerably older and more experienced Ray exploited Hackman's naïveté.[89] This elaborate smear campaign cements Hackman's position as victim and rewrites his act as a sacrifice.

The language that both Dawes's apologia and Croft's own one-sided work (to a lesser extent) employ readily lends itself to the interpretation of Hackman's downfall as the result of his ill-treatment by a kind of femme fatale.[90] Dawes construes Hackman's 'unbounded love for Miss Reay [*sic*] [as] a kind of virtue',[91] pleading that he has merely 'fallen a sacrifice to love at an unguarded moment'.[92] Where Werther's suicide is reduced to mere posturing, Ray's death is wholly nullified in Croft's version. Amid the panegyrics that Hackman's conduct attracts, the dead woman remains unaddressed, rendered essentially invisible by Hackman's heroics. At the narrative's conclusion, Ray is present only through the spots of her blood and remains that stain Hackman's unchanged clothing. Although the justice served at the narrative's end presumably avenges Ray's murder, in effect she disappears in the valorization of male death.

Even as the lady gradually vanishes in Hackman's case, so too does the act of suicide itself, as Croft effectively annuls Hackman's suicide attempt through his focus on the latter's recantation. Although he incorporates the act into the broader cultural history of suicide that unfolds as a thematic backdrop to the novel, Croft nonetheless tries to present it as an isolated event, singular in the circumstances surrounding it, and inimitable. The elaborate intertextual tapestry that Croft weaves in his reclamation of Hackman serves to distinguish him all the more vividly from his peers, enabling him, as Brewer notes, to make 'the case into an exploration of an individual pathology rather than a complex social drama'.[93] Hackman's recantation sanctifies Croft's publication, while the plea of insanity renders society irreproachable. Croft's rendering of Hackman's case places his protagonist above and beyond society as he undergoes a veritable apotheosis. Ultimately, Hackman distances himself from his literary model and indeed exceeds it by declaring that he has more cause to commit suicide than his antecedent, as expressed in his apostrophe, 'Unhappy Werther! Still less pretense hadst thou for suicide than I after quietly seeing thy Charlotte marry another man'.[94] Hackman's redemption comes at the expense of Werther, of whom it is said, 'though a Werther pretends to sacrifice himself ... it is only an excuse (by which we deceive ourselves) to justify our own impetuosity, our own despair, under the specious pretext of preferring another's life to our own'.[95] Not only does Hackman claim for himself a greater degree of suffering than Werther, but he also sets himself up as a martyr for *not* committing suicide: he achieves his redemption by denying the public the example of suicide, notwithstanding the fact that his attempt was apparently sincere.[96] Precisely because he withholds the example of his suicide, Hackman absolves himself from all culpability and distinguishes himself from Werther.

Despite Hackman's rejection of the German character's claims to sacrifice himself as disingenuous, Werther's appeal for the eighteenth-century reader stemmed in part from the sacrificial construction of his death; his victimhood elicited the sympathy of an audience already primed for the reception of such a hero and eager to assimilate him into its canon of popular martyrs that already boasted the likes of Lucretia and Cato.

In fact, Werther's advocates easily salvaged his reputation by comparing him to Cato, whose suicide was deemed honourable by some because of its ostensibly patriotic motives.[97] However, as Tobin Siebers notes, although 'The logic of sacrifice is indeed critical for Werther's act; it is not the pagan variety, in which a victim is killed by a priest, but the Christian variety, in which the victim sacrifices himself or herself'.[98] An update of the classical ideal, Werther distinctively and scandalously Christianizes suicide by espousing the attitude of messianic altruism, particularly towards the end of his letters. Werther informs the unfortunate Lotte, 'I am sacrificing myself for you', and constructs himself as a Christ figure in one of his last letters, echoing his words on the cross and likening his suffering to that of the Christian figurehead.[99] Goethe reminds us of early and more recent interpretations of Christ's death as quasi-suicidal on the basis of interpretations of the Gospel of John.[100] Werther, however, is not a Christ figure, and encapsulates the paradox of the self-sacrificial individual, the being who, as Roland Barthes observes, is simultaneously 'the suicide but also, perhaps, the lover, the utopian, the class heretic, the man who is "ligatured" to no one but himself'.[101] Embracing the half-derogatory label of a 'man of sensibility'[102] assigned to him by his rival, Lotte's husband, Werther reveals himself as a being extraordinarily attuned to the needs of others, yet simultaneously mired in the egotism that sets him above his peers. This is perhaps the paradox of suicide itself: the agent of suicide might see sacrifice as a critical motive, but those judging the suicide after the fact might not so readily accept this interpretation.

Croft's task is to refute the interpretation of Werther's death as self-sacrificial, while insisting upon the martyrdom of his own fictionalized Hackman. Thus, even though Hackman writes to his friend Charles from Newgate to request that he send him poison, he disowns Werther, telling Charles that 'I never persuaded myself, unlike many of my fellow creatures, that I had any right over my own life'.[103] In his final words he claims to be desirous that 'his countrymen know how [he] abhor[s] this part of [his] crime, how thoroughly [he] was ever convinced (except during my phrenzy), and how perfectly [he is] now persuaded, that our lives are no more at our disposal than the lives of our fellow creatures'.[104] Moore similarly comments that 'in the midst of his ungoverned passions, he never intended to defend the principle or lawlessness of suicide (like the more guilty Werther), or to make it appear to be the result of judgment and deliberation'. Deliberation, of course, is the word that Hackman dwells upon earlier, in his comparison of the suicides of Richard and Bridget Smith with the French soldiers, and its recurrence here reaffirms Croft's own call for the *non compos mentis* verdict in regards to both Hackman's murder and attempted suicide.[105] Moreover, Croft strives to obscure the fact that despite the failure of Hackman's suicide attempt, he nonetheless realizes his death wish via his execution, an instance of the detour around suicide proscriptions that individuals undertook in this period.[106] *Love and Madness* contains the problem of social pathology by reasserting the supreme individualism of his English hero, who is produced within the cultural nexus of Dawes's *Account* and Croft's reconstruction of his correspondence. However, despite Croft's attempt to rehabilitate his character at the expense of Werther by subsuming suicide into the paradigm of sacrifice, and despite Werther's transnational status in eighteenth-century print culture, Croft's efforts do little to combat the problem that suicide continues to present for perceptions of the British national character at the end of the eighteenth century.

The spectre of justice that overshadows the work's end in effect counters the notion that suicide may be construed as a natural and therefore legal act. For one of the more unpardonable aspects of the Wertherian defence of suicide was its attempt to locate the act in the realm of nature. In one of his many extended meditations on the act, Werther alludes to 'a noble race of horses, which, when they are terribly overheated and excited, instinctively bite into a vein to breathe more freely. So it is often with me, I'd like to open a vein to gain eternal freedom.'[107] This view was, in part, shared by Jacobin writers such as Robert Bage, who, in *Hermsprong* (1796), rejects the idea that suicide is a proof of insanity and hence unnatural given that 'the fear of death itself is a lunacy, for to a reflecting mind, at least, death is not an evil'.[108] The medical position that no rational being seeks his or her own extinction contradicts the philosophical viewpoint that suicide can in fact be an object of the will and the choice of a reasonable individual. Jacobin discourse circumvents both positions not by necessarily endorsing suicide, but by giving expression to a suicidal subjectivity through the English Werthers that abound in these writings, and especially the novels of Charlotte Smith.

Jacobinism, Revolution and the 'English Werter'

In the midst of his censure of Goethe, Charles Moore pauses to denounce:

> the plaintive Charlotte Smith, who seems to have bestowed too much honour on Werther, by presenting no less than five of her tender elegiac sonnets in [his] person ... The last of these is supposed to have been written by Werther just before his death; which, though well aligned to the feelings of its supposed writer, yet tends to increase and give (sanction to the act).[109]

The sonnet that Moore cites alludes to Charlotte's visit to her lover's tomb, the imagined scene that was commemorated so frequently in eighteenth-century visual culture. Perhaps more objectionable was the affirmation that Smith offered of the sacrificial aspect of Werther's death in ventriloquizing his last address to Charlotte, which opens with the apostrophe: 'O thou, to save whose peace I now depart' (Sonnet XXV). Smith's controversial interest in Werther continues into her novels, which incorporate the figure into their later political narratives and demonstrate the extent to which the German text intervened in the British processing of French events in the last part of the century.

France emerges as a significant force in the transmission of Werther as the century wears on. Given that Werther had become the polarizing site for the nationalization of suicide, the stakes here are clearly ideological. This political dimension of Werther became increasingly tangible in later Jacobin, or at least sympathetic, reworkings of his character in novels like Charlotte Smith's *Desmond*. The participation of a German literary figure in British discussion of French politics is ironic, given the fact that, as E. J. Clery affirms, 'The French Revolution was itself being written, and consumed by a paranoid British public, like a gripping romance translated from the German'.[110] To the British, Werther became almost an emblem of the French situation, epitomizing the spirit of class rebellion and transgression. While Werther appeared to bolster the cause of the detractors of suicide by shifting attention away from Britain, British writers' assimilation of the Germanic figure into their own narratives undermined this enterprise, hence eliciting an outcry from anti-Jacobin periodicals. 'Jacobinism added a new urgency to the incrimination of the novel',[111] as M. O. Grenby asserts, and the heroes of German novels in particular were decried by leading anti-Jacobin activists like William Preston as 'robbers, cut-throats, suicides, poisoners and parricides'.[112] By all accounts, the phenomenon of suicide is integral to late eighteenth-century British politics, which are framed around a philosophical debate over the meaning of death and of life. The Jacobin position that life is unacceptable under certain circumstances, drawn from Jean-Jacques Rousseau's statement that 'when life is an evil to us and a good to no other person, we may then get rid of it',[113] was easily interpreted by its detractors as an endorsement of suicide.[114] Ranging the Jacobins on the side of voluntary death, atheism and amorality, the *Anti-Jacobin Examiner* (1799) identified as one of the stakes of the conservative cause the resolution of the question 'Whether human existence, which has always been seen as a subject of thanksgiving, will be seen as a blessing or a curse?'[115] Meanwhile, the rival publication the *London Corresponding Society* countered that 'He who draws his sword for the destruction of liberty, commits an act of suicide, – or worse than suicide, for in rendering himself the instrument of slavery, he becomes in reality the worst of slaves.'[116] According to this logic, the anti-Jacobins were guilty of consigning themselves and society at large to voluntary death. An ideological struggle to define life emerges, at the centre of which resides Werther and his insistence that he can take his life at any moment. In a letter featuring a sustained analogy between existence and imprisonment, Werther confides that 'However circumscribed [an individual] may be, he always preserves in his heart the sweet feeling of freedom and the knowledge that he can leave this prison whenever he wants to.'[117] Evidently, Werther conceives of existence as a form of voluntary incarceration and posits suicide as the logical and inevitable product of such a condition. Although the Jacobin position in France paradoxically cultivated 'sublime individualism' and 'communitarian sacrifice' in the form of suicide,[118] this position is not authorized by English Jacobins such as Smith, Helen Maria Williams, Thomas Holcroft or even Robert Bage in their novels, who rather attempt to discover the means of rendering life more palatable to the alienated and disenfranchised.[119] At the same time, however, the priority these texts place upon sacrifice, upon giving one's life over to a worthy cause, necessarily endorses voluntary death.

Smith's first novel, *Emmeline* (1788), presents the stock situation of an orphan cast on the fortune of the world and the charity of her relations.[120] When first introduced to her aristocratic cousin, Delamere, she finds herself the unwilling recipient of his 'unguarded sallies of unconquerable passion' and his 'phrenzy of almost hopeless love!'[121] Her unexpected rejection of his advances overwhelms him with 'transports of agonizing passion which he could neither conceal nor contend with. He wept, he raved like a madman.'[122] During one of her critical encounters with this unreasonable suitor, Emmeline carelessly takes up a copy of the second volume of *The Sorrows of Werther*, and is admonished by Delamere that if she had read it, she 'might have learned the danger of trifling with violent and incurable passions.'[123] His subsequent demand whether Emmeline could 'ever be reconciled to [her]self if [she] should be the cause of a catastrophe equally fatal?'[124] confirms *Werther*'s status as a cautionary tale that the lover can manipulate in pleading his case. Although Emmeline rejects Delamere's self-identification with Werther, he nonetheless maintains that 'without [her], [his] life is no longer valuable, – if indeed it be supportable.'[125] Furthermore, he warns, '[S]hould I ever be in the situation this melancholy tale describes, how do I know that my reason would be strong enough to preserve me from equal resolves? Beware, Miss Mowbray, of finding an Albert at Woodfield'.[126] Although Delamere's emotional blackmail procures Emmeline's grudging promise to remain unmarried, he ultimately realizes the fate that he had always threatened, albeit in a slightly indirect way. The duel in which he engages with a former admirer of Emmeline and current paramour of his sister may constitute the gentlemanly alternative to suicide, but the practice was generally considered a species of voluntary death in this period, and as such invites the reader to view it accordingly.[127] Delamere's duel enables him to construct his death as a sacrifice on behalf of his sister, notwithstanding the trajectory towards self-destruction that he manifests throughout the narrative. Like Werther, whose passion for Lotte merely serves as a catalyst for his suicide, Delamere is suicidal from the outset.[128] Although Diane Long Hoeveler characterizes Delamere as 'an antediluvian form of the hero, emotional, self-involved, passionate',[129] he is clearly modelled on the Wertherian protagonist.[130]

With the exception of *Emmeline*, Smith's narratives repeatedly teeter on the brink of suicide, only ultimately to disavow the act. Her courtship novel *Celestina* (1791) features no fewer than three desperate lovers apparently cast in the same mould as Werther. The most obvious of these would-be Werthers is Montague Thorold, a young man of a poetic sensibility whose lengthy mysterious disappearance in the middle of the narrative wrongly arouses suspicion that he has acted upon his oblique suicidal hints.[131] The second Werther receives his introduction to the narrative via a copy of the actual book: the ownership of a 'torn book' that is rescued from the fire to which it had been committed on the charge of 'trumpery'[132] is traced to an unhappy character named Cathcart who identifies himself explicitly with Werther. Self-referentially summarizing the novel as the 'story of a poor young man, who was as unfortunate as I am; but [who] had the resolution to end his calamities; he indeed was not enchained to life as I must be',[133] Cathcart initially interprets the book as a licence to kill himself, although a fortuitous alteration in his circumstances effects a corresponding change of heart. As in anecdotes attesting to the 'Werther effect', the sheer physicality of the book in this passage is represented almost as a vector for contagion. Although Smith does not altogether suggest that Cathcart has actually been contaminated by the book, the narrative does represent its confiscation as a somewhat providential act, even while refusing to condemn Cathcart for his suicidal deliberations.[134] *Werther* circulates as a commodity, burned and abused but ultimately rescued and redeemed in Smith's Anglicization of the text. Finally, the text's more central Werther figure, Mr Willoughby, reacts to the perceived alienation of Celestina's affections in so frantic a manner that he elicits the apprehension of suicide on the part of his servant. Although this crisis is eventually averted, along with the other examples it hints at suicide, as Smith presents the development of the Werther figure without the actual consummation of the plot. In this respect, *Celestina*, like many of Smith's other novels, repeatedly threatens suicide only to retreat from its narrative possibilities.

Smith's personal letters account at least partially for this tendency to abandon the suicide narrative just when it would appear that events cannot resolve themselves in any other way. Smith appears to adhere to a principle of poetic justice in her plots, if only for marketing purposes:

> Another year is coming when I must by the same motives be compelled to a renewal of the same sort of task. A Tragedy would most undoubtedly be more honourable and profitable. But it still appears to me an effort in which I should fail. And it is a very discouraging circumstance that the taste of the modern world is not for Tragedy.[135]

Although Smith alludes to a meditated stage production, her statement is just as relevant to the form of the novel, which in her view cannot readily accommodate suicide, at least not by English characters.[136] Interestingly, when suicide does occur in her novels, it is the act of a foreigner: in the *Wanderings of Warwick* (1794), the Italian exile, Villanova, shoots himself, while in *The Banished Man* (1794), the French expatriate, the Marquis de Touranges, indulges his despair, thus becoming another one of the 'victims of the Revolution'. But Smith's central characters invariably survive, despite the strong undercurrent of suicide that runs through her writings, which in effect sacrifice suicide to the demands of her market.

In *Desmond*, the political valency of the Werther figure finds its most revolutionary apotheosis. In the words of the preface, *Desmond* 'represent[s] a young man, nourishing an ardent but concealed passion for a married woman'.[137] Lionel Desmond's attachment to Geraldine Verney, the wife of a degenerate spendthrift, drives him to France, where he finds an outlet for his revolutionary sympathies but no permanent cure for his passion. Desmond's concerned confidante, Erasmus Bethel, labels him an 'English Werter'[138] when his erratic behaviour and solicitude for Geraldine threaten the integrity of his reputation.[139] Providing an ever-wary voice of reason, Mr Bethel demands of Desmond 'why is it that the strongest minds ... those who have examined whatever is offered to them with acute reason ... shall yet sink under the influence of images impressed on the brain by a disturbed digestion, or a quickened circulation?'[140] Bethel's assessment of the obsessive disorder that afflicts Desmond echoes Rowley's treatise on female nervous diseases, which asserts that anyone who commits suicide is delusional, subject to 'false images of the mind' produced possibly by the 'acrimony of the blood'.[141] According to Rowley, the body is accountable for madness, and ultimately, for suicide as well. Both Smith and Rowley draw upon the iatromechanist understanding of the body's influence on the mind popularized by George Cheyne, according to which the various bodily functions dictate to the mind the objects of its reflection. This theory reduces imagination to a corporeal function, and promotes a notion that ideas may be contagious. The representation of Desmond as a kind of 'body at risk' from an early point ominously but misleadingly launches a suicide narrative, which is never in fact fulfilled.

Furthermore, Desmond's admission that 'I wander about like a wretched restless being'[142] echoes Werther's complaint that 'I am indeed but a wanderer, a pilgrim on earth'.[143] But, although Desmond's unconquerable passion aligns him with Werther, rather than yielding to the inertia that afflicts his Germanic literary counterpart, he sublimates his passion into a cause that he apparently pursues on behalf of Geraldine.[144] In Bethel's estimation, an 'active spirit and feeling heart preserve [Desmond] from th[e] palsy of the mind'[145] afflicting his fellow Wertherians. While Desmond's stance as a 'man of feeling' inevitably results in the feminization of his character, his hectic activity (so different from Geraldine's passivity) re-masculinizes him sufficiently to prevent him from engaging in the quintessentially feminine act of suicide. From this point of view, Werther dies because he is too feminine to resist suicide, lacking the strength of comparatively masculine English characters.

Each of Desmond's actions is ostensibly motivated by concern for Geraldine's welfare, thereby allowing him to translate his romantic interest into a political cause and absorb it into the French Revolution. Accordingly, his 'disinterested' concern for Geraldine's welfare is characterized as a form of 'Platonism'[146] by his friends, while he himself entertains 'a most flattering and soothing idea, that [he] was deputed to watch over this angelic woman, with the fond affection of a guardian spirit'[147] and declares that he feels himself 'ennobled by the charge, and would not have exchanged the sublime place it accorded [him], for any less elevated indulgence an epicurean could offer'.[148] By integrating his desire into the sublime, Desmond, like Hackman, also transcends his Wertherian model. Inspired with this lofty sense of purpose, Desmond returns to France 'to protect [Geraldine] if possible, from the wretch who would thus basely avail himself of his legal right to render her wretched'.[149] In his discussion of the 'nexus of the political and the sacrificial' realized during revolutionary events, the historian Jesse Goldhammer identifies martyrdom as one of the 'important form[s] of political sacrifice to appear during the French Revolution'.[150] Desmond's 'sacrifice[e of] his life to save [Geraldine]'[151] is wholly assimilated into this ethos, as he is consecrated as 'the victim of that generous and exalted spirit which led him to hazard his life'.[152] In this respect he reflects the trend identified by the historian Vera Lind, who claims that 'the considerable number of individuals in the later eighteenth century who viewed their self-afflicted deaths as a form of sacrifice were all males'.[153] Desmond's principles will not permit his suicide, but they will allow him to sacrifice his life to the same cause for which his French friend, Montfleuri, declares himself ready 'to draw the sword once more. [For] he must be a desperate wretch, who, in such a cause, would refuse to sacrifice his life itself'.[154] The spirit of sacrifice that the narrative promotes is not, as in the case of the English Malady, aligned explicitly with national identity, but rather with the cosmopolitan principle that the English Jacobins espoused. As their chief periodical, the *London Corresponding Society* affirmed, their cause was 'but the echo of the wisdom and the experience of all ages, and of all nations'.[155] As a 'citizen of the world', Desmond's disaffection with English society, self-imposed exile to France and ready embracing of revolutionary politics complicate his national identity, rendering him less an 'English' than a transnational Werther. This is in contrast to Geraldine, whose double in the person of Josephine Bois-belle, a French woman trapped in a bad marriage and also in love with Desmond, allows her to remain staunchly English.

The novels discussed in this chapter engage with the pervasive notion that sui-cide is a transmissible disease afflicting primarily those rendered susceptible to its influence by virtue of their exaggerated sensibility. If passion is 'unconquerable', as Werther, Hackman and Delamere all plead, then suicide might be deemed defen-sible. Yet Smith for the most part represents the feasibility of 'regulating passion' by channelling it into a political cause. This gradual transmutation of 'Werther' (through Desmond) into a political being marks the beginning of his distancing from suicide and the dwindling of his intertextual signifying power. Although literary critic Eleanor Wikborg insists that 'the political and the romantic are fundamentally incompatible' in *Desmond*,[156] the Jacobin novel's incorporation of Werther into its narrative structure demonstrates the interconnectedness of the domestic and the revolutionary.[157] Significantly, Desmond's optimistic belief in the viability of a 'controlled' revolution is somewhat tempered by his friend Bethel's apprehension that violence is inevitable under such politically volatile conditions. However, the violence stems from the mercenary mobs that shift allegiance according to whichever party is in the ascendancy, rather than from the more moderate Girondin-Jacobins, with whom Smith and her fellow English sympathizer more readily identified.[158] In many respects, the novel's attempt to substitute a 'well-regulated affection' for the unrestrained sensibility characteris-tic of Werther is analogous to its advocacy of a disciplined revolution. Desmond's self-imposed ascesis prevents him from embarking on the route of Delamere (or, for that matter, Werther), and the reward for his self-discipline is marriage to his Lotte equivalent with, astonishingly, the blessing of her dying husband. The consummation of the love plot thus renders suicide unnecessary in Smith's novel. Desmond's sacrifices are not mandated to the point of death, and a principle of poetic justice intervenes to save him from the fate of Werther.

Although it has been argued that 'the figure who occupies the place of the sexually transgressive heroine of sensibility is actually Desmond',[159] the male Wertherian hero serves as a foil to the narrative's truly suicidal character, the married woman who loves from within the confines of her immediate domestic situation. At the outset of the narrative, Geraldine Verney represents a Lotte figure,[160] appealing to the English Werther audience that took an intense interest in the fate and subjectivity of Werther's beloved, which Goethe withholds in the story.[161] However, as the narrative proceeds, and hints of Geraldine's partiality to Desmond begin to surface, Geraldine increasingly appears as a refraction of Werther. Upheld as a paragon of virtue, Geraldine nonetheless acquires a taint of scandal through her frequently articulated desire to die.[162] At the height of her misery during her sojourn in France while awaiting the instructions of her husband (who has embraced the cause of the aristocrats), she articulates her death wish directly in such statements as: 'I know not how I find resolution to proceed from day to day in this career of misery. – My children, for whom I ought to live, alone support me; nor have I in the world another motive to wish my existence prolonged'.[163] Maternity serves as a deterrent to suicide, although Geraldine also confides that 'there are moments when I most sincerely wish that I and my babies were all dead together'.[164] In Smith's text, children both foster Geraldine's melancholia and anchor her to life; this compulsory existence comes about through a kind of biopower that naturalizes women's maternal identities[165] and affords immunity to contagion. Women are anchored to life both by their bodies that are too weak to destroy themselves and by the products of their bodies.

Geraldine's catalogue of the ills she would sooner avoid than death concludes with her assertion that 'there is hardly one situation in which I can *now* be placed, to which death would not be preferable'.[166] In her affecting portrayal of Geraldine's death wish, Smith reappropriates the rhetoric of martyrdom that had been taken up by writers as disparate as Goethe and Croft. Even Geraldine's mission to the most unstable region of France in search of her wounded husband suggests the resignation of the martyr. External descriptions of her facial expressions, particularly in reaction to the insults of her husband, reflect the self-correcting and abasing tendencies of a martyr: 'It was contempt, stifled by concern – it was indignation subdued by shame and sorrow'.[167] Her later behaviour is consistent with that view, for she occupies the narrow iconographic space allotted to female heroics within the context of French Revolutionary politics in maintaining her pose of static virtue.[168] Geraldine performs martyrdom, scripting her behaviour upon that of earlier long-suffering novel heroines like Clarissa, with the French Revolution serving as a dramatic backdrop to her suffering.

However, the text implicitly critiques Geraldine for her passivity and quiet resignation, even as it establishes her as a female Werther, dramatizing the plight of a woman trapped in an oppressive marriage and half-conscious of an attraction to someone other than her spouse.[169] In spite of her distaste for her husband, Geraldine maintains her blamelessness, insisting 'I was obedient – very obedient; and in the four years that have passed, I have thought only of being a quiet wife, and a good nurse, and of fulfilling, as well as I can, the part that was chosen for me'.[170] Geraldine's allusion in this statement to Desdemona's defence of her conduct to Othello draws upon an intertext that, as we have seen, was highly integral to Croft's portrait of Hackman in *Love and Madness*. Geraldine depicts herself as the good wife, sacrificed to a violent husband, and intimates that she desires to die Desdemona's death. In this sense, she is passively masochistic like Werther, and also highly reminiscent of Sidney Bidulph, Frances Sheridan's martyr figure in her 1761 novel. Geraldine explicitly accepts her identification with this Sheridan character in her correspondence with her sister in which she asks if she 'recollect[s] in the novel of Sidney Biddulph [*sic*] (one of the best that we have in our language) how poor Sidney is treated in her adversity by the haughty wife of her brother, Sir George?', reflecting 'Perhaps there is a little similarity in our destinies – But *I* have *no Faulkland!*'[171] This highly allusive moment involving one literary character modelling herself on another literary character suggests the extent to which the discourse of sensibility is permeated with the intertextual. The superimposing of a literary character's subjectivity upon her own also indicates that the cult of sensibility has deprived Geraldine of a valid response to her immediate situation. Although elsewhere Geraldine claims that 'she set out in life with too great a share of sensibility'[172] and altogether denies that she possesses any amount of stoicism, Geraldine identifies most strongly with the adamantly stoic and comparatively emotionless figure of Sidney Bidulph. While the dominance of Werther in the popular imagination of the eighteenth century denies Geraldine the capacity to articulate her emotion, her intertextual identification with another literary character in Sidney Bidulph also limits the possibilities of her character. Furthermore, her hypersensitivity identifies her to a greater degree with Faulkland, Sidney's hapless lover who eventually takes his life, although her gender denies her his expedient.[173] As Katharine Rogers observes, the culture of sensibility fostered an ethic of self-sacrifice in women,[174] an attitude that disenfranchises Geraldine both emotionally and literally, as, buffeted about by patriarchal and matriarchal authorities, she is unable, like Desmond, to employ political affairs as an escape, and even the option of suicide is foreclosed by her maternity, as she herself suggests.[175] The fatalism at work within her character finds expression in her identification with both Sidney Bidulph and Desdemona.

Geraldine's attitude towards suicide to a certain extent resembles the materialist approach to suicide articulated in *Werther*. As William Donoghue points out in his treatment of Werther and the sceptical strain of Enlightenment thought, the text assigns a subjective limit to an individual's threshold of suffering, which attained, dictates the surrender of that individual to voluntary death.[176] To some degree, this theory absolves the individual of responsibility for his or her own suicide by imposing a sort of automatic control or trigger on the psyche of the individual. Not quite a death drive in the deterministic sense posited by Freudian thought, this theory nonetheless suggests that suicide under certain conditions, and depending on the biological and emotional makeup of the individual, is inevitable.

Claudia Johnson provides an explanation for the emotional plight typically endured by the heroine of the novel of sensibility in her observation that 'If the man Werther is already the culture's paragon of feeling, then any feeling differentially attributed to women must be excessively delicate, morbidly *over*-sensitive'.[177] Johnson's analysis meticulously details the implications of male co-optation of woman's normative stance of sensibility; the construct of the man of feeling necessarily entails the 'abjectifying' of woman through her relegation to the borders of sensibility, as in the novels of Frances Burney, or the emotional and corporeal paralysis of the sort we find in *Desmond*. A strain of morbidity is a by-product of the gendering of sensibility, as, deprived of a legitimate subjective standpoint, women instead occupy the space of death: suicide is paradoxically a feminine act, yet an act that is at the same time denied to women, since it requires both an assertion of will and a display of courage, both of which are typically seen as residing outside the purview of a female mentality.[178] In a sense then, Geraldine's narrative, and indeed that of the normative female character, enacts a kind of gendered morbidity drive, which articulates a death wish without an accompanying act of suicide.[179] Accordingly, Geraldine can resign herself to being 'doomed to be the unresisting victim of a man, whose conduct is a continual disgrace to himself, his family and his country'.[180] Moreover, at the outset of the novel, Geraldine, as one already 'sacrificed' to marriage, presents herself in all her abjection as already dead.[181] Since Geraldine's suffering has already exceeded anything that she may have encountered in death, suicide appears as the sole rebellion she can offer at this juncture, although morbidity is the only attitude that the text allocates to her, which subsequently seeps into and comes to define her correspondence.

The access to Geraldine's interiority secured by the epistolary form to a certain extent belies the passivity that her actions attribute to her character. Although I agree both with Watson's argument that epistolarity functions 'as an oppositional discourse – a potential disruptor of the existing social or symbolic order'[182] and with Bowstead's observation that Smith favours 'letters' over 'narrative' owing largely to 'the political and didactic import of the novel',[183] I would also attribute Smith's choice of the epistolary mode to her debt to the sentimental tradition of the *Werther* narrative, which (in conjunction with Rousseau's *Julie*) renovates the 'novel-in-letters' and proves particularly accommodating to the character subjectivity formed over the course of the suicide narrative. The epistolary form marks the convergence and compatibility of the sentimental and the political, and in the case of *Desmond*, offers a forum for women to define themselves as political beings and participants in the interpretation of national and transnational events. To this end, a sympathetic appraisal in the *Monthly Review* commended Smith for her recognition that the great events which are passing in the world are no less interesting to women than to men, and that in her solicitude to discharge the domestic duties, a woman ought not to forget that, in common with her father and husband, her brothers and sons, she is a citizen.[184]

This relatively progressive review accredits a dual responsibility to women, demanding that they discharge both private and public duties, co-opting some of the particular agency typically aligned with the masculine public realm, while continuing to hold sway in their own.

Once Geraldine leaves England, her interiority becomes increasingly accessible to the reader, owing to her heightened vulnerability and identification with the 'miserable slaves' of France. Accordingly, the events that she witnesses in her travels through the French countryside are all filtered through her suicidal subjectivity. At one point, Geraldine pauses to observe a 'process of priests ... carrying the host to some sick person'.[185] The spectacle inspires her envy of the invalid about to receive with reluctance 'a passport to the bosom of ... God!'[186] Geraldine's language evokes the terminology of standard proscriptions against suicide, which urge the need for a divinely issued permit in order to gain entry to a higher sphere. As potentially controversial as is the fact that a glimpse of the ministering of a 'holy rite' elicits Geraldine's suicidal fantasy, still more scandalous is her subsequent imagined apostrophe to the invalid, lamenting that she,

> a wretched wanderer, in a wretched world, would most willingly exchange situations with you; and with your faith and your prospects, lay down, even with pleasure, a life which, according to the course of nature, may be very long, according to all present probability, must be very miserable.[187]

The transition from a hypothetical 'may' in the penultimate clause to the emphatic imperative of 'must' in the statement's final clause heightens the sense of Geraldine's desolate relationship to time. Geraldine expresses a readiness to turn apostate (in the eyes of her church) and risk damnation (should this be the fate of her counterpart) sooner than live out the course of her life. This crack in Geraldine's piety suggests that she does not altogether dismiss suicide as an option, a means of conquering time, for, as she admits, 'I see no end of calamities but in the grave ... long lingering years, varied only by different shades of wretchedness, is all my prospect'.[188] Geraldine's lamentations regarding the length of her sufferings appear to discount the principle of justice, whether poetic or providential, according to which (at least in the providential scheme followed by fiction in the tradition of Henry Fielding) the suffering of central figures is limited and finite. However, Geraldine's defence of the novel would seem to refute the relevance of any such claim on the literary plane as she demands whether 'in every well-written novel, vice, and even weaknesses that deserve not quite so harsh a name, are not exhibited, as subjecting those who are examples of them, to remorse, regret, and punishment?'.[189] This statement identifies a principle of retribution at work in the novel, which necessarily constructs suicide as a form of narrative punishment. According to this logic, a harsh notion of poetic justice serves an inherently cautionary purpose by discouraging imitation, simultaneously mitigating the effects of contagion and negating the possibility for emulation. By Geraldine's standard, her husband's death would represent no more than his just reward for past behaviour. Smith's affirmation of poetic justice serves as a justification for her recasting of Werther in her narratives. Ultimately, however, this same principle precludes this figure's defining act of suicide and calls instead for the sacrifice of the novel's villain, who dies the death that the narrative requires in order to unite the parted lovers, as the text evacuates the Albert figure rather than eliminating Werther.

Predictably, given Geraldine's attitude of resigned pessimism, her view of poetic justice is considerably one-sided, omitting altogether the idea of 'virtue rewarded' typically associated with less austere versions of poetic justice. Whereas poetic justice logically precludes acts of martyrdom, Smith's vision accommodates a notion of sacrifice, but only up to the point of death. Smith reconciles the narrative ideology of poetic justice with a corresponding advocacy of self-sacrifice, which, through the mediation of her Werther figures, she shows to be exceedingly proximate to suicide both behaviourally and discursively. Hamstrung by the facticity of his materials, Croft in *Love and Madness* does his utmost to elevate Hackman from a debased position of murderer/failed suicide by reconstituting him as a martyr figure, thus transforming a potentially tragic story into a Christian hero narrative. Werther is thus assimilated into the punitive/remunerative model of poetic justice principle shared by Croft and Smith.

Although in many respects, Geraldine appears as a promising candidate for the Clarissa club for martyred women, she disavows the influence of *Clarissa* in her reflection on Richardson's novel, scenes of which she considers 'infinitely more improper for the perusal of young women ... than any that can be found in the novels of the present day'.[190] Geraldine bases her critique of the dispensation for earlier fiction upon the fact that it is based upon 'a kind of hereditary prescriptive deference'.[191] Geraldine's phrasing evokes the rhetoric of Jacobin resistance to inherited authority, as it fuses literary criticism with the political in a manner similar to that of *Love and Madness*. Yet Geraldine's own rebellion remains unrealized in the text, as only this protest of novel-censoring leads her to her 'slide' into 'egotism'.[192] In the context of this same debate –strategically placed at the structural centre of the novel – *Desmond* reflects the tendency of novels to 'host a self-reflexive meditation on their own practice' to an exaggerated degree, as the literary critic William Donoghue has observed.[193] Accordingly, Smith presents an acutely self-conscious treatment of the censoring of young women's reading materials on the part of tyrannical mothers and 'severe female censors' who decide that novels 'convey the poison of bad example in the soft semblance of refined sentiment'.[194] The difference between the metaphor of the novel as a poison in this context or as a malady in others is relevant, for, as Mortensen writes in his study of anti-Jacobin polemic, poison suggests an active malice at work, an element of deliberation not necessarily associated with the idea of a malady, which is almost self-generating.[195] Although Mortensen possibly over-states his case somewhat, the notion of a literary malady does complicate the question of accountability. The anti-novel's and anti-Jacobin's (for Geraldine's mother and her censor board clearly affiliate themselves with the reactionary stance) retention of the poison metaphor enables them to trace the origins of the poison to a definable, in this sense, foreign source. Moreover, since poisoning was historically seen as a woman's occupation, the very process of transmission is itself irrevocably feminized.[196] The basis for the censor board's condemnation of the novel is subsequently provided in the following terms: 'One contains an oblique apology for suicide; a second, a lurking palliation of conjugal authority; and a fourth, against religion'.[197] The use of the descriptor 'oblique' suggests the 'deceptive indirection' that, as McKeon argues, characterizes the strategy of the novel and further aligns the genre with femininity from the perspective of an eighteenth-century public.[198]

In her spirited defence of the novel, Geraldine insists that she 'cannot imagine that novel reading can, as has been alleged, corrupt the imagination or enervate the heart – at least such a description of novels as those which represent human life nearly as it is'.[199] The prohibited material described could plausibly refer to the content of Werther, but it also speaks to the pervasive tendency to associate the novel with suicide. Tragically, Geraldine invokes her own case as evidence that novel reading has little impact, in a positive or negative sense.[200] Meanwhile, pointing out that the newspapers and the annals of history present 'a mortify-ing detail of crime and follies' offering an 'argument ... that heaven created the human race only to destroy itself',[201] Geraldine's sister Fanny posits the existence of a kind of cultural death drive. Her confession that 'the pretty soothing tales of imagination are prohibited while the hideous realities of human life affright [her]'[202] suggests that the 'real' itself exceeds representation and is infinitely more horrifying than anything that fantasy can produce, thus nullifying the argument that literature like *Werther* produces examples that lead to their imitation in life. Smith's intra-textual defence of the novel dismantles the argument regarding the form's dissociation of example from precept by pointing to the realm of 'real' experience as chronicled by the periodical press, which abounds in examples of suicide and self-destructive behaviour that far exceeds the representational capacities of the novel. Reality itself is posited as a contaminating influence, thus reversing the blame for suicidal contagion.[203]

Yet given the tacit approval of Werther in these contexts, why was this figure such a bane to English Jacobins like Mary Hays who frequently represent suicide in their novels? In her *Letters and Moral Essays*, Hays expresses her regret that her friend's daughter is reading Goethe, and objects to the fact that Werther 'dignifies his excesses by the names of sentiment, delicacy, and tenderness'.[204] Although she acknowledges that the 'enthusiastic' style of the work readily excites sympathy, she maintains that 'calm reflection' prompts the critique that the work deserves.[205] Hays illustrates the extent to which the concept of sensibility had become highly problematic by the late 1790s for writers of every political stripe (including Smith, who later recanted her endorsement of the Revolution), as, according to the eminent historian, E. P. Thompson, the violent turn of revolutionary progress inspired the 'pathos of thwarted heroism'.[206] Accordingly, a trait that decades earlier had been viewed as a mark of refinement had now become dangerous by virtue of its association with the excesses of the revolutionaries.

Yet, earlier in the decade, Werther was still allowed to be a sympathetic figure. In Helen Maria Williams's only novel, *Julia*, its central character's contemplation of one of the engravings of Lotte at Werther's tomb that enjoyed so much popularity during this period elicits an extended debate concerning the merits of the novel.[207] Julia, an analogue of Rousseau's Julie, expresses disapproval of the work, claiming 'few will justify its principles'.[208] Yet her opinion is not defended in the text, which privileges the view of its Werther figure, Frederick Seymour, as he appeals to the blending of virtue and vice in 'the great book of nature'.[209] His demand whether 'any person, when pleased with a book, immediately determine[s] to imitate the hero of it in every particular?'[210] ominously fails to receive an answer, as Julia is suddenly obliged to leave the room. This assertion disputes the cause-and-effect argument that representation demands imitation. Williams's and Smith's defence of the novel advances an understanding of a non-mimetic aesthetic *and* ethics, which reject the idea of the imitability of suicide and dismisses the notion that suicide can operate according to a paradigm of contagion.

While curtailing the agency of the individual, the model of contagion espoused by these discourses does not altogether absolve her from responsibility. As Christopher Forth observes in his historical treatment of moral contagion,

> [M]oral contagion represents a double capitulation to the outer world of contagious ideas and to the inner world of affects and drives: the external 'other' seemed to form an alliance with the sensual 'other' within ... indicates that on an unconscious level the individual welcomed the collapse of the will that contagion entailed.[211]

Forth's work focuses specifically on contagion in a nineteenth-century context, after the medical establishment had departed from the model of a porous and permeable body that the work of Tissot and others had popularized in the century prior. However, in its insistence that some individuals are more susceptible to contagion than others, the discourse of sensibility invoked both internal and external affects, suggesting that part of the individual assents to contagion. This model represents a way of preserving guilt, even while partially denying the autonomy of the will, and in effect tries to have it both ways by preserving individual accountability and limiting personal autonomy.[212]

Yet, if the autonomy of the will is so far eroded in these novels, the question arises as to how they manage to preserve a paradigm of sacrifice? The particular logic of self-sacrifice depends upon the cooperation of the will; as previous chapters have discussed, the very denial of free will to women limits their ability to take their own lives. In contrast, the masculine paradigm endorses political suicide and martyrdom. To some extent, men's sacrifices are more in keeping with an older, pre-Christian model, as rather than giving themselves in sacrifice, they are the sacrificed: Werther is driven to his death by his sensibility, Hackman must submit to divine will, and Desmond must sublimate his desire. Geraldine's options, meanwhile, are foreclosed by both her maternity and sex. Self-sacrificial suicide, which had been repressed by Thomistic proscriptions based on natural law, returns as a political gesture as revolutionary politics celebrates the individual yet at the same time assimilates him (for it is always a male this model demands) into a collective, demanding a sacrifice for the whole.

Eighteenth-century England enshrined sacrifice as an act intrinsic to nation-building, and Charles Moore distinguished it (in a military context) from suicide on the grounds that its immediate result was involuntary and unpremeditated. Across the Channel, the French Revolution recuperated a more ancient notion of sacrifice, one that demands both sacrifice of representatives of the old order and the self-sacrifice of proponents of the cause.[213] With its emphasis on the principles of fraternity and equality, the revolution negates death in the form of suicide, even while it heightens the prestige of sacrifice. This event further serves to politicize suicide, a process that was already well underway with the increasing authority the medical establishment claimed over determination of death on both sides of the English Channel.[214] Werther resides at the centre of this shift; slowly and imperceptibly, he becomes bound up with English national identity as he is Anglicized by the English Jacobins and ultimately assimilated into their political narratives. Werther's suicide is written as a gesture of sacrifice in these works, which do not actually demand the performance of the deed. Literary critic Jay Fliegelman argues that 'Before 1774, the deaths of sentimental heroes and heroines were, on the model of Clarissa, cautiously semi-voluntaristic; after 1774, the suicide becomes a common figure in the sentimental novel; passive resistance gives way to active resistance'.[215] However, suicide narratives after *Werther* remain resistant to representation and frequently repress suicide altogether. These texts typically present violence as an off-stage and concealed event. Hence Martha Ray's bleeding body, Hackman's executed body and Delamere's slain corpse, all remain unrepresented. Werther's death alone is described with all the accuracy of a coroner's report in a graphic extended scene at the end of Goethe's novel.[216] The English novel consistently denies this form of suicidal violence, which lurks beneath the surface of the narrative and, in effect, aestheticizes voluntary death out of the genre almost altogether.

Yet, aesthetics is never entirely separated from the novel's engagement with politics. As Werther's textual body organizes the discourse of suicide in the novel, his suicidal subjectivity brings to the foreground of national debate the reality of suicide, which subsequently produces the idea of a transnational community that was inimical to British conservatism. Although Werther's is presumably a genderless body, imitated by men and women alike, suicide remains the affliction of a foreign or effeminate body, as English novelists attempt to circumscribe the Werther effect on the novel by assimilating the figure into multiple gendered discourses of sensibility and sacrifice. To this end, Smith affirms the expression of individualism as an antidote to contagion in her self-reflexive remarks on the novel. Positing that the will of the individual renders him or her resistant to the contaminating effects of suicide, Smith unfolds an anti-mimetic aesthetic that emphatically rejects the model of contagion. In a curiously similar manner, Croft endorses a kind of individualism through his support of exemplarity yet does not venture so far as to afford an explicit endorsement of individual will. Both authors afford an abridgement of the Werther plot: constrained by his materials, Croft nonetheless undertakes to rehabilitate his character at the expense of Werther, a manoeuvre that inevitably involves the subsuming of suicide into the paradigm of sacrifice. Although all of these works privilege the suicidal male over the suicidal female, the gendering of the act remains constant, as the version of suicide they represent performs a kind of femininity that is eventually subsumed into effeminacy. Even as Werther 'goes' transnational, demonstrating the universality of self-destructive tendencies, suicide continues to define national identity in England at the end of the century.

5 'THE DEATH OF REASON': VITALISM, TRANSNATIONAL IDENTITY AND FRANCES BURNEY

> The definition of life is usually sought for in abstract considerations; it will be found, if I mistake not, in the following general expression: Life consists in the sum of the functions, by which death is resisted
>
> Xavier Bichat[1]

The diligent attempts of researchers to isolate an organic cause for suicide reflect the consternation with which society and the medical establishment more specifically reacted to voluntary death at the beginning of the nineteenth century. This project also led medical researchers such as Xavier Bichat to speculate on the existence of a principle that sustained life and enabled the body to resist death. Similarly, the pathologist F. J. V. Broussais remarked, 'it is necessary to recognize in mankind the existence of a propensity for staying alive. I do not know the seat of this propensity, nor what its organ. I believe only that it exists. I believe that because I feel it in myself and see its effects in others'.[2] According to Broussais, in the absence of a 'suicide organ', one could not effectively overcome an instinct of self-preservation, thus explaining why some individuals were unsuccessful in their suicide attempts.[3] This theory constructs the body as far from self-destructive and instead anchored to life, the antithesis of the Freudian notion of the death instinct and a reflection of the vitalist philosophy that was in the ascendancy at the turn of the nineteenth century owing to the work of doctors like Bichat.[4] One might expect that the linking of suicide to the body would preclude voluntary death from being identified as a national phenomenon, but debates as to whether suicide belonged to the French or the English nevertheless occupied the medical establishment on each side of the channel, and became inextricably linked to vitalist philosophical and physiological ideas of the time.

Fostered by the French in medical centres like Montpellier and popularized by *philosophes* such as Denis Diderot, vitalism gradually gained a foothold in Scotland and England, in spite of the pervasiveness of the iatromechanical model so popular among British physicians like George Cheyne and philosophers like

Joseph Priestley and David Hartley.[5] Vitalism rejected the mechanistic under-standing of human functions and ascribed to organic matter a force that kept it alive even under duress.[6] Although necessarily retaining a materialist compo-nent by virtue of its emphasis on organic matter, vitalism nonetheless placed an emphasis upon the soul, thereby rendering it a welcome alternative to the atheistic doctrines many associated with mechanism.[7] In representing nature as 'a powerful, vital force',[8] vitalism further presented a contrast to the morbidity of mechanism, in a sense substituting a culture of life for a culture of death in the early nineteenth century.[9]

In 1814 a widely publicized 'vitalist controversy' erupted in Britain between John Abernethy and William Lawrence, two physicians who, although both espousing vitalist views, disagreed fundamentally over the spiritual implications of their respective theories. Whereas Abernethy maintained that a vital principle motivated physiological functions, Lawrence contended that physiology itself was reducible to this vital force; his omission of an external 'prime mover' of sorts led to the public outcry that eventually forced a recantation of this theory by its originator.[10] Taking the form of an exchange of lectures delivered to the Royal College of Surgeons and sensationalized to a certain degree by the period-ical press, the debate indicates the extent to which vitalist views had permeated the English medical establishment and public consciousness by the early decades of the nineteenth century.

In the same year as the 'vitalist controversy', the prominent novelist Frances Burney published her fourth and final novel, *The Wanderer, or Female Difficul-ties,* a text that features a lengthy meditation on the nationality of suicide and its connection to gender. Set during the French Revolution, the novel involves perilous channel crossings and considerable interchange between characters of French and British extraction. Although catering to the popular taste for the his-torical novel that was characteristic of early Romanticism, *The Wanderer* resists the temptation to recount these events from a mainstream perspective. Married to a French exile, Burney inevitably sympathizes with the plight of the French aristocrats, but she also disparages simplistic pro-British, anti-Jacobin attitudes towards the Revolutionaries generally, and towards the subject of suicide more specifically. In this sense, the *Wanderer* is considerably more transnational in its focus than any of Burney's earlier writings.

Burney's resistance to nationalistic typing appears in her treatment of sui-cide as a phenomenon that transcends national boundaries. Although suicide figures prominently in her novels, its representation does not perpetuate the idea of an English Malady. In presenting English women as consistently thwarted in their attempts to take their own lives, both *The Wanderer* and Burney's earlier novel *Camilla* (1796) – which is important to an understanding of the last work – express an overarching concern with life, and specifically with the body that cannot die. Their depiction of the body as infused with a life essence residing in the nerves, fibres, tissues or organs of the body counters contemporary conceptions of the human as a mere machine. In this sense, both *Camilla* and *The Wanderer* move beyond the borders of Britain both geographically and conceptually, thus allowing for a broader European dialogue about the viability of a mechanistic outlook in an age desperately seeking to regain its faith in the wake of the French Revolution.

Burney's refutation of the mechanistic justification for suicide in *The Wanderer* is influenced (whether directly or indirectly) by the vitalist principles that inform the attitudes of her contemporaries, such as Germaine de Staël, towards the nation and suicide. The persistence of the body in *Camilla* and *The Wanderer*, despite clearly pronounced desires by both protagonists to die, suggests the operation of an insuperable life principle enforced at the biological level. Vitalism in this sense emerges as a form of 'biopower' dedicated to keeping the individual alive; as Ian Marsh explains in his Foucauldian historicization of suicide, 'within a bio-political economy of power suicide represents something of a challenge to those techniques and strategies that aim to foster health and vitality (in short, life itself) in the face of disease and decay (and ultimately death)'.[11] The vitalist notion of the individual as bound organically to life by the forces of society constructs self-preservation as an almost irresistible instinct, overcome only by a perversely colossal assertion of the will. In this sense, vitalism supersedes consciousness to exert an impact directly upon the body itself. Vitalism in Burney's novels thus constitutes a form of corporeal agency, co-opting both voluntary and involuntary processes, and ultimately incorporating a degree of agency in life's resistance to death.

Burney's last two novels present alternative models of agency intricately tied to suicide and the survival of the death wish. The fact that suicide is relevant to the fate of Burney's female characters yet suspended as an exit strategy raises the question as to whether suicidal ideation accords a temporary agency to characters, or exposes with grim seriousness the literal dead ends that women encounter as they circulate through society. The 'radical ambivalence' that characterizes Burney's gender politics frustrates attempts to resolve these questions conclusively.[12] However, a curtailed degree of agency is nonetheless discernible in Burney's work, which exposes the flaws of male authoritarian structures. This chapter suggests that Burney advances a survivalist platform predicated on vitalist principles; although her text imposes constraints upon the female body, it does not carry a form of narrative discipline as far as death. Instead, the devices of fantasy and dreamwork assume much of the burden of the didactic agenda. At the same time, Burney's work suggests the interrelations between suicide and national consciousness, although she rejects the notion of an English Malady and indeed denies her characters the power to die. In the midst of a struggle to align suicide with national character, an awareness of identity beyond the national increasingly informs the conversation surrounding voluntary death, as suicide is increasingly absorbed into a matrix of affective relations that helped define an idea of the 'transnational' in the period.

Camilla and 'The Picture of Death'

Although suicide pervades *The Wanderer* as the subject of exhaustive (and arguably inconclusive) debate, it emerges as a prominent concern only towards the conclusion of *Camilla*, at the height of its heroine's crisis. In a protracted episode centring on Camilla's suspense and despair, she finally resolves to die, having become an alien 'to [her] family, a burden to [her]self ... an excommunicated wretch'.[13] A catastrophic series of events brings Camilla to this precipice: she forfeits the affections of her suitor, Edgar Mandlebert; her father is imprisoned for non-payment of the debts that Camilla assumes from her brother; her uncle is turned out of his estate and her mother returns from abroad to find her family in turmoil. Camilla's alienation from her family results from this chain of disastrous events. From this point on, Camilla's desperate attempts to restore herself to the trust or at least to a form of correspondence with her mother tax her sanity and ultimately precipitate her confrontation with 'death in a visible figure' at the novel's climax.

Camilla, like each of Burney's other novels, features young female characters whose public exposure fills them with 'mortification', an evocative term that underscores the extent to which their social embarrassments affect their 'psychologies'. The term became synonymous with personal humiliation in the seventeenth century, but its alternate signification of 'subjection of the flesh' claims a longer etymological history that continues to resonate in Burney's usage. Protocols of behaviour become incorporated into Burney's female characters to the extent that minor deviations from the social code produce a sense of shame so acute that they lose control of their bodily functions, having been rendered 'more dead than alive', as we find in *The Wanderer*.[14] Burney suggests in each of her novels that manners themselves have been rendered mechanical in this period, and *Camilla* (1796) in particular presents the automaton as the consummate socialite in a strange blending of mechanization and mortification.[15] *Camilla* explicitly constructs its naïve young protagonist as an automaton when she is deprived of her reason and the adverb 'mechanically' becomes a veritable refrain. Once the trials that define Camilla's 'coming of age' begin, the narrator indicates that she 'mechanically follows' counsel,[16] she 'mechanically complies' with her advisers,[17] and 'mechanically rather than designedly' roams the countryside.[18] Burney exposes the repercussions of social strictures placed upon the mind but is not necessarily complicit with them; she employs the man-machine trope to critique the particular effects that culture, in its most sterile and vacuous form, asserts on the body. Fashion, affectation and the sensibility of what the novel refers to disparagingly as the *ton* all detach the mind from the functioning of the body, rendering it no more than an automaton controlled by the external forces of social etiquette and prescribed behaviour.

An intensified desire for death accompanies the multiplication of Camilla's difficulties. In a fit of agony, Camilla intones 'O that I could die! That I could die!' before 'madly advancing to the window, and throwing up the sash, yet with quick instinctive repentance pulling it down, shuddering and exclaiming, "Is there no death for me but murder – no murder but suicide?"'[19] Only the timely assertion of a life principle of sorts prevents Camilla from flinging herself from the window. This death wish becomes a refrain, accompanied by frequent musings on the part of the narrator such as 'A wish for death, immediate death, in common with every youthful mourner, in the first paroxysm of violent sorrow, was the sole sensation which accompanied the reading, or remained after the finishing of this letter'.[20] The narrator here and elsewhere imputes suicidal desire to immaturity, analogous to madness or irrationality, but ultimately overcome by the body's refusal to die. In effect, Burney naturalizes the death wish, rendering it an inevitable consequence of women's financial crises. At the same time, she affirms the ability of characters to survive conditions that appear to preclude continued existence. Hence, in an end-of-the-novel apology, Burney's narrator attributes both Camilla's meditation and triumph over suicide to the 'elastic period of youth'.[21] This elasticity was viewed by the French anatomist Xavier Bichat as one of the properties of 'living tissues' that maintain the vital existence of the organic being, and was an integral component of vitalist physiology generally.[22] According to this construction, elasticity prevents suicide; as a kind of biological failsafe, it resists the outside pressures that would destroy life. Although Burney's expression is metaphorical, it speaks to her 'survivalist' position that advocates female perseverance without necessarily soliciting social change. In this line of thought, female characters, and hence female character, are robust enough to prevail over the most challenging of circumstances.[23]

In her insistence on the relative commonness of what she refers to elsewhere as the 'fatal wish',[24] Burney makes of the Shakespearean caveat a virtual cliché in her textual meditations upon suicide, as reflected in her narrator's assertion:

> The wish of death is commonly but disgust of life, and looks forward to nothing further than release from worldly care – but the something yet beyond … the *bourne whence no traveler returns* to prepare succeeding passengers for what they may expect, not abruptly presented itself to her consideration …but came to scare not to soothe.[25]

But the narrator's reflection transcends the commonplace in its refusal to entertain the notion of an ideological or mental 'life principle', which clerics and anti-suicide polemicists invoked in their arguments for the 'unnaturalness' of the act. Burney implicitly rejects this stance by acknowledging the common develop-ment of an apathy toward life, and she concerns herself more in both novels with a Pascalian[26] notion of suicide as a 'gamble' that may or may not pay dividends. Similarly, in her *Réflexions sur le suicide* (1813), Staël insists that 'There are only two ways to think about existence. Either it is a game of chance in which winning or losing stakes are the goods of this world, or it is a novitiate for immortality'.[27] In her novel of the following year, *The Wanderer* (1814), Burney will revisit this notion of suicide as aleatory and ultimately employ it as the basis for her narra-tive's conversion of Elinor Joddrell. At the same time, however, Burney locates a deterrent to suicide at the corporeal level. After denying herself both food and sleep over a period of four days, Camilla dejectedly finds 'life still in its vigour, though bereft of its joy, and death no nearer to her frame, for being called upon by her wishes'.[28] The obstinacy of her body elicits her lament 'I have lived too long, and yet I cannot die!'[29] Camilla's corporeality rather than her mental or spiritual fortitude hence precludes the possibility of her suicide. Accordingly, Camilla's most severe self-accusation is that she has rejected her 'life, her vital powers'[30] and thereby knowingly rendered herself a machine. Like Clarissa, Camilla finds her body an obstacle to her death wish. However, according to most interpretations, in *Clarissa*, the body eventually breaks down and is made to carry the burden of blame for the heroine's demise, rendering her death involuntary. Camilla, on the other hand, lacks the requisite allotment of time to turn her death wish into actuality. To a degree, then, the physical fortitude of Burney's heroines suggests a resilience that contrasts with the passivity of earlier figures like Clarissa. Whereas Richardson constructs suicide as a form of agency, albeit in a sacrificial sense, Burney rejects the long-suffering martyr stance of the exemplary figure, or 'fault-less monster', as she refers to the paragon in the preface to *Evelina*, and in effect integrates the vitalist position into her survivalist agenda.

The catalyst for Camilla's vision comes in a gothic scene that finds her trans-fixed by the image of a bleeding corpse on a bier. The corpse is not exposed as a mere waxen replica (as in Anne Radcliffe's 1794 blockbuster, *The Mysteries of Udolpho*), but is rather revealed to be the victim of an accidental self-murder and, coincidentally, Camilla's brother-in-law. The bloodied corpse mirrors back to Camilla an image of her own fate, and her confrontation with her suicidal inten-tion realized in material form affords a *memento mori* that underscores the gulf between the idea and the image of death that exists in her mind. The narrator at this point intones that 'the mortal being requires use to be reconciled to its own visible mortality; dismal is its view, grim, repulsive, terrific its aspect'.[31] A recanta-tion of her death wish swiftly follows, but ironically, the phantasm of death that haunts Camilla's nightmare appears only after she has repented, and she finds that 'the corpse she had just quitted seemed still bleeding in full view'.[32] The vision scene that follows arguably represents 'a breakdown of the limit between life and death' that, according to literary critic Terry Castle, is typical of a Gothic (specifically Radcliffean) vision.[33] After willing herself to die over the course of successive chapters, Camilla confronts death as a form of wish fulfilment. What follows is essentially a bifurcation of the self, as Camilla becomes divided between her death drive and her will to survive, a scenario that does not take place in *Clarissa*, despite her relatives' conviction that her life instincts will eventually override her death wish. In some respects, Burney's representation of suicide takes on the structure of the 'female gothic', which, conventionally, results in the triumph of reason over irrationality. Just as a Radcliffe plot cannot conclude until rationality has been re-established, so too Burney's plots cannot conclude until the instinct of life-preservation has resumed its hold of the suicidal character.

In the climactic nightmarish scene, 'a visible figure' of Death compels Camilla to record what she believes to be her final confession 'with a velocity uncontrollable' in the 'Volumes of Eternity'.[34] Although constructed as a dream vision, the scene dwells extensively upon the act of writing, as, 'unlicensed by her Will', Camilla is forced to 'seize [an] iron instrument', which, to her horror, 'makes no mark on the page' as 'death in a visible figure, ghastly pallid, severe, appear[s] before her, and with its hand, sharp and forked, [strikes] abruptly upon her breast'.[35] A 'force unseen, yet irresistible' subsequently thrusts into her hand a 'pen of iron' and forces her 'to write [her] own claims, [her] merits to mercy'.[36] The passage suggests the extent to which the violence of writing substitutes for the repressed violence of Camilla's willed decline into death. Camilla has surrendered her volition to death, and in a kind of uncanny manoeuvre, her will returns to assert itself directly on Camilla's body in a sadomasochistic gesture of irrepressible violence. The dream sequence may thus be read as a textual disciplining of Camilla for her contemplation of suicide and her presumption of autonomy over her body.[37] Once again we are reminded of *Clarissa*, in which the violence of dreams conveys the actual violence that Clarissa's character wishes to inflict on her body. In *Camilla*, however, fantasy assumes the entire burden of censoring the heroine that is demanded by the social codes Burney appears intent on upholding. In this sense the dream serves a productive function, becoming the means of reaffirming Camilla's existence, for unlike Clarissa, Camilla awakes to reconciliation with her estranged family and a recovery of her social identity. The dream represents a device whereby Burney can assert a mode of narrative discipline yet preserve her heroine in the space of the 'real' as represented in the narrative. Domestic ideology in this respect actualizes itself on the level of fantasy, whereas the main narrative conveys a kinder, gentler but nonetheless problematic reality.

Camilla elevates the figure of the automaton to the status of a metaphor for the fate of the female subject exposed to the rigors of social ideology and unremitting surveillance. What had been represented as an object of scrutiny in Burney's first novel now becomes the subject of her third, as she represents in vivid and appalling detail Camilla's metamorphosis into a *femme machine*.[38] Ultimately, Burney attributes Camilla's self-destructive tendencies to the follies of youth and conveniently dismisses them with the conclusion of the narrative. It is her final work that offers her most comprehensive, in-depth and deeply conflicted treatment of the subject of voluntary death. An issue that in *Camilla* lurks in the background is brought to light in *The Wanderer*, which returns frequently to the relevance of suicide to the construction of a national character, where the concern expressed in the background of *Camilla*'s world of debt and credit has more direct and vivid implications for an understanding of national consciousness.

The Wanderer and the 'Death of Reason'

The Wanderer ventures beyond the domestic and casts its narrative against a broad historical backdrop.[39] The opening line explicitly locates the narrative's action '[d]uring the dire reign of the terrific Robespierre',[40] although the physical setting, initially on 'the coast of France', abruptly shifts permanently to the south of England, towards the shores of which a 'small vessel' bearing English fugitives from the 'Great Terror' has just embarked. The novel's opening lines also feature a desperate young woman pleading with the vessel's passengers to grant her passage across the Channel. Only after the novel's hero, Albert Harleigh, intercedes do the other passengers reluctantly take in the supplicant and set sail for England.

In this dramatic opening, the narrative ostensibly establishes Great Britain's peace as a contrast to the violence of France, but it quickly dispels this illusion, as the terrors that the refugee, the titular 'Wanderer', must endure while in the society of her shipmates, quickly establish the racist, sexist and classist attitudes endemic in British society.[41] The gothic element of terror that the narrative inspires wafts across the English Channel along with the refugees from the historical Great Terror. The persecutions by the Wanderer's fellow passengers arise from the power that her financial vulnerability accords them and from their unrelenting curiosity regarding her identity. For the greater part of the novel, the Wanderer's identity remains a mystery, and she embraces the pseudonym, Ellis, conferred upon her by her shipmates. Only at the novel's end does she disclose her true identity as Juliet Granville, a British expatriate of aristocratic stock. An accidental disclosure reveals that Juliet Granville's perseverance in preserving her anonymity (even to Albert Harleigh whose affections she covertly returns) was motivated by her flight from a Robespierre henchman whom she had married to save her legal guardian from the guillotine. This undesirable spouse later resurfaces to claim the fortune pledged to Ellis/Juliet by a recently deceased English lord who had secretly married her mother.[42] Predictably, the text both disposes of the tyrant husband and thwarts attempts to discredit Juliet's claims to her paternal inheritance, thus restoring the Wanderer to social respectability through her marriage to Albert Harleigh and reunion with her natural family.

Although nominally defined by mobility the Wanderer appears just as constrained as Camilla. Both are straitened by circumstances and cast upon the charity of strangers, and each must devise extraordinary means of coping with catastrophe. As in *Camilla*, Juliet in the *Wanderer* finds herself in desperate circumstances (the paternal figure in each novel is cast into prison as a result of his connection to the heroine), but she does not once consider taking her own life, whereas Camilla becomes altogether consumed by the idea. *The Wanderer* displaces this death wish onto Elinor Joddrel, a volatile and unstable character whose unrequited passion for Albert Harleigh leads to her obsession with suicide. If the existence of Juliet's pseudo-husband does not constitute a sufficient deterrent to a relationship with Harleigh, the spectre of Elinor and her ever-present threat of self-murder certainly does, and it is not until this threat is laid to rest that the marriage plot can be consummated. Elinor, however, appears as a sort of overdetermined obstacle to the main thrust of the narrative. Her role as 'blocking character' in the romantic plot is somewhat superfluous, given that Juliet's union with Harleigh is already rendered impossible by her secret marriage. Juliet's own story constitutes a botched manual for survival, as her numerous endeavours to procure a subsistence from tutelage or manual labour ultimately fail, and the prospect of becoming a 'humble companion' to a tyrannical patrician is all that is left to her. But Juliet's situation reinforces an inexorable life principle of sorts, since only her continued existence ensures the survival of her legal guardian, an elderly French bishop. Elinor, by contrast, perceives herself as wholly unfettered, and represents suicide as the supreme expression of this power of self-determination. The glory of suicide from her perspective resides in the fact that it is wholly voluntary – literally, a 'death of reason'[43] – for she disdains natural death as passive, animalistic and altogether unworthy. The suicidal violence represented by the actions of Elinor stands in for the violence of the French Revolution, which ever lurks beyond the realm of representation as the historical backdrop of the novel.

In the midst of the text's central discourse on suicide, Elinor demands of Harleigh whether he can

> wish to doom half [his] species to so degraded a state [as marriage] to look down upon the wife, who is meant for the companion of [his] existence; and upon the mother, of whose nature [he] must so largely partake; as upon mere sleepy, slavish, uninteresting automatons?[44]

Elinor's vindication draws heavily upon the language of mechanization that Burney associates with social abjection and it echoes Mary Wollstonecraft's *Vindication of the Rights of Women.*[45] While many critics identify Elinor as a fictional analogue for Wollstonecraft, they base this assessment largely upon the early, unsuccessful suicide attempt precipitated by the abandonment of her lover, Gilbert Imlay. For Wollstonecraft's views on suicide were decidedly more ambivalent than those expressed by Elinor, and unlike the fictional character, she did not subscribe to atheism. In her *Letters Written during a Short Residence in Sweden, Norway and Denmark* (1796), a vision of an embalmed corpse prompts an extended meditation upon suicide and the fate of the body after its demise that concludes, 'Surely something resides in this heart that is not perishable – and life is more than a dream.'[46] Wollstonecraft's leap from Putney Bridge subsequent to the desertion of Imlay, the addressee of the *Letters*, of course attests to the ineffectuality of such meditations to reinforce a 'life principle', but her reflections nonetheless reveal a more complex attitude toward voluntary death than that expressed by Elinor, resembling more closely the anti-materialist sentiments voiced by Albert Harleigh, the chief opponent to suicide in *The Wanderer*. Moreover, Wollstonecraft's condemnation in her second *Vindication* of excessive sensibility and of love exceeding the bounds of reason, as well as her recommendation of serene friendship over passionate attachment, also strongly resemble Harleigh's remarks on the subject in the novel, which I will address later in this chapter.

An alternative model for Elinor Joddrel may have been Germaine de Staël, who befriended Burney at the time of her first exile from France. Their relationship was short-lived, however, owing to the interference of Burney's father, who disapproved deeply of Staël's lifestyle. Staël's *Influence of the Passions on the Happiness of Individuals and Nations*, published the same year as *Camilla* (1796), was read to Burney in manuscript at Juniper Hall while the two women were still friends. Despite their considerable personal and political differences, Burney and Staël shared a lifelong preoccupation with the problem of suicide; Staël claimed that suicide 'is at the heart of mankind's moral organization'[47] whereas Burney allowed her later novels to articulate her preoccupation with voluntary death.[48] Suicide recurs in Staël's novels, surfacing in *Mirza* (1795), *Delphine* (1802) and *Corinne* (1807). In embracing suicide as a 'sublime resource', Elinor appears to echo Staël's controversial remark that 'nothing is so horrifying as the possibility of existing simply because we do not know how to die'.[49] Although Staël was never the committed materialist that Elinor purports to be, she nonetheless bears a strong resemblance to Burney's character. Yet, by 1813, Staël had moved away from her favourable view of suicide, recanting her earlier opinions and offering an argument against suicide that prefigures the central debate in *The Wanderer*. Although Burney expressed an eager interest in Stael's *Refléxions sur le Suicide* (1813), she claimed not to have read this surrender to orthodoxy, and would have been familiar only with earlier statements of the sort articulated in *De la Littérature* (1800): 'excellent creatures hounded by ingratitude and slander may very well wonder if any virtuous man can stand life as it is, and if the whole organization of society does not weigh down on sincere, tender souls, making their existence unbearable'.[50] This assertion finds an echo in *The Wanderer*, in which Elinor frequently questions the value of life in similar terms. Although Burney's philosophical development roughly follows the trajectory of Staël's thinking on suicide, her characterization of Elinor Joddrel echoes the remarks on the subject that appear in the early writings of her Swiss counterpart.[51]

In addition to a shared interest in suicide, Burney and Staël both appear to have been drawn to contemporary vitalist ideas. Both Staël's salon and the 'hôpital' founded by her mother, Madame Necker, welcomed noted vitalists, including the Montpellier vitalist Dr Fouquet.[52] During her last illness in 1817, Staël was visited by R. T. H. Laennec, a celebrated physician who believed that a 'vital force' inherent in all living matter acted as a curative agent. Earlier, in *The Influence of the Passions*, despite her apparent endorsement of suicide as the end result of the indulgence of the passions, Staël suggests the existence of 'a sort of instinct of preservation, closer to physical nature than moral sentiment, even when every instant of life brings new pain with it'.[53] In this respect, she is not far from the vitalist assertion of the tenacity of life. Staël's positing of a bodily instinct that informs, rather than being guided by, morality strongly suggests a vitalist position that Burney will similarly incorporate into *The Wanderer*. Staël's work, like Burney's, reveals the complex mutual imbrications of suicide and vitalism in the discourse of the period.

The gradual displacement of the mechanical body by a vitalist, organic model was so current and widespread in the thinking of the period that Burney herself might well have been influenced by it.[54] Her ten-year residence in France and marriage to the French émigré Alexandre D'Arblay would have inured her to 'the negative associations of vitalism' that, according to the science historians Caroline Hannaway and Ann F. La Berge, 'tended to go hand in hand with royalism and Catholicism'.[55] Burney's own perception of her miraculous survival of her mastectomy in 1810 may have made her sympathetic to the vitalist belief, articulated early by the German animist Georg Ernest Stahl, that 'the soul of man governs disease' and prompts quick recovery.[56] The ability of the body to survive acute physical suffering becomes subsumed into an accommodating vitalist ethos in Burney's works, as in her preoccupation with the preservation of the suicidal woman she eschews the tragic endings favoured by earlier novelists like Richardson. Despite strongly articulated death wishes on the part of her characters, Burney's 'bodies' are resilient and tenaciously vital. This in itself does not supply sufficient evidence for a vitalist position, but it speaks to an increasingly prominent concern in the early nineteenth century with the management of life, which finds expression in the valorization of suffering in both Burney's and Stael's works.

Despite persistent attempts to take her life in Burney's *The Wanderer*, Elinor is kept alive by a vitalist principle, suggesting that only a 'natural death' is possible for the female character lacking the physical and intellectual strength necessary to complete suicide. Yet this scenario does not foreclose her agency altogether since, as the feminist theorist Linda Birke affirms, 'To see organisms/bodies as having agency and the ability to be self-organizing ... also implies that social constructions and experiences of gender can themselves be part of a process'.[57] Exposing the mechanistic principles informing physiological language, Birke recovers a view of the body as transformative and 'lived' in opposition to the 'dead, or inanimate body' that the philosopher of the body Drew Leder argues resides at the heart of medical discourse in the West.[58] Whereas corporeality is typically seen as the seat of 'unreason', Burney succeeds in countering the belief in what Elizabeth Grosz refers to as 'the fundamental passivity and transparency of the body' so intrinsic to Cartesian thought by according to it an agency derived from lived experience itself.[59] Elinor possesses a corporeality defined by survival and aligned with life as a direct result of the failed suicide.

Performing Suicide: Cross-Dressing, Spectacle and the Death Drive

By inflating her contemplated act to mythic proportions, Elinor attempts to demonstrate the possibility of female heroics in suicide, even while remaining in a masculinist paradigm of actively sought out death. Whereas in *Camilla*, the protagonist's passive desire for death resembles the feminized category of suicide, Elinor's unwillingness merely to decline into death proves consistent with the 'noble, though ... masculine spirit' attributed to her character throughout the narrative.[60] In a scene orchestrated to present Juliet's beauty as an object of spectacle when she is forced to raise money by performing publicly, Elinor appears 'in full masculine attire' that includes a scarlet 'wrapping coat ... half mask ... slouched hat, and embroidered waistcoat'.[61] Thus, while Juliet appears fully exposed as 'an object of tumultuous delight'[62] to the audience convened for her musical performance, Elinor, by contrast, is initially fully obscured. She outperforms Juliet, yet simultaneously preserves her from the shame of public self-display as she stabs herself in full view of the audience, becoming at once a spectator and a performer in a scene that evokes the production of a divided self that suicide is typically viewed as entailing.[63]. Although this performance ostensibly serves to heighten Elinor's sense of will, the body rebels and cannot execute the part that Elinor scripts for it, as it remains obstinately alive, owing in part to the ministrations of local physicians.

The 'masculinization' of Elinor Joddrel through this performance is in keeping with the figuring of suicide as a male act in Burney's works. In contrast to the 'female difficulties' that the passive 'Wanderer' endures, Elinor's monomaniacal 'death drive' is gendered as strongly masculine, as underscored by her cross-dressing practices. Elinor's failure stems precisely from the fact that she crosses gender boundaries, as she appropriates a script taken from outmoded classical and obdurately male models. In her heroic staging of suicide, she self-consciously emulates the picturesque death of Pliny, and she recites Cato's soliloquy as adapted from Addison's play. Elinor's orchestration of her suicide as mimicry is doomed to failure, a product of Burney's pessimism regarding the ability of individuals to transcend the gender roles allocated to them on the basis of their sex. Claudia Johnson identifies the problem in this scene as Elinor's attempt to 'unsex herself' rather than recover an authentic site of female empowerment,[64] and I agree that Burney may countenance limited modes of resistance that are understated and subtle but do not allow for transgression of what Vivien Jones terms the 'constraints of acceptable femininity'.[65] At the same time, however, Elinor's transvestism serves to emasculate patriarchal authority, even as it under-scores both masculine and feminine incapacity.[66] Ultimately, Elinor's attempts at performance align her with the femininity she strives to transcend, thus reveal-ing the inherent limitations of her performance strategy.

Elinor's failure to complete suicide has been construed as a mark of her inau-thenticity by numerous critics, including Katharine Rogers, who claims that the character's lack of success 'suggests unconscious insincerity in her wish to die'.[67] With its Freudian overtones, this argument elides Elinor's genuine desire to die, which is only strengthened by her friends' reactions to her suicide attempts. The argument also suggests two factors at work in Elinor's death wish: a conscious and an unconscious. However, how do we measure such a thing as 'unconscious insincerity' when her so-called 'failure' could be more or less an act of conscious-ness? Distressed that the 'abortion of [her] purpose' may have made her appear 'a mere female mountebank', Elinor insists:

> I have meant all that I have seemed to mean: though, by waiting for the moment of the most *éclat*, opportunity has been past me, and action has been frustrated. But I can die only once. That over, – all is ended. 'Tis therefore I have studied how to finish my career with most effect.[68]

In a manner reminiscent of Staëlian protagonists such as Delphine and Corinne, Elinor expresses a heightened consciousness of the public reception of her actions and indisputably manipulates circumstances and other individuals to serve her own interests. However, interpretations of her will to power as mask-ing insincerity of intention overlook the fact that Elinor's desire for death and her quest for autonomy are inextricably linked.[69] Elinor's persistent repetition of the suicidal act suggests a complete overcoming of the life principle, which even the philosopher David Hume, despite his insistence on the rationality of suicide, considered strong enough to deter an individual from a second attempt once a suicide has initially failed.[70] Similarly, in her recantation of her earlier position on suicide, Staël insists that '[M]ost people who have attempted suicide and failed do not try again, because in suicide – as in all reckless acts of the will – there is a sort of madness that quiets down when it gets too close to its own goal'.[71] Yet Elinor's horror of life exceeds her horror of death, and her repeated suicide attempts both authenticate her desire and underline her conviction that suicide is an intellectual act that may be entered into with all one's rational powers intact. The emphasis in this remarkable scene on performance amplifies rather than detracts from the sincerity of this character's desire to die.

As we've seen, Elinor constructs herself as a 'Tragedy Queen' intent upon staging her suicide to optimum effect. She makes of suicide a project that, as in *Clarissa*, only serves to amplify the very sense of 'selfhood' that she strives so sedulously to eradicate. Furthermore, she 'studie[s] how to die without torture, by inflicting a wound by which she might bleed gently to death, while indulging herself, to the last moment, in pouring forth to the idol of her heart, the fond effusions of her ardent, but exalted passion'.[72] Suicide, in this paradigm, involves a conscious construction of the self that is contoured by its confrontation with death. In this sense, voluntary death figures in the performative conception of the self that Elinor appears to espouse. This understanding of selfhood was not unusual in the period; in his *Treatise on Human Nature*, David Hume conceived of the self as a theatre 'where several perceptions successively make their appearance, pass, repass, glide away, and mingle in an infinite variety of postures and situations'.[73] Fully embracing a theatrical notion of the self, Elinor's subjectivity constructs itself in both the performance and the public reception of suicide. Ultimately, Elinor stages a suicide that, like Clarissa's martyrdom, incorporates the public into its very structure and thereby erodes the individualism of her act.

Accordingly, when Elinor upstages Juliet's starring role at the concert by plunging a dagger into her breast, the audience gathered for the performance consumes this spectacle in its stead, with 'the men, though all eagerly crowding to the spot of this tremendous event, approaching rather as spectators of some public exhibition, than as actors in a scene of humanity'.[74] Conscious of the reception of her public act of self-violence, Elinor comments upon society's appetite for sensational accounts of suicide that render it marketable. To this end, she advises Juliet, 'If I were poor myself, I would engage to acquire a large fortune, in less than a week, by advertising, at two-pence a head, a sight of the lady that stabbed herself'.[75] In facetiously recommending that Juliet exploit the scene of her suicide, Elinor constructs her death wish as performative and ironically situates it within a continuum of consumer exchange. Her ability to commodify herself renders suicide a marketable spectacle that dramatizes the extent to which a consumerist mentality might undergird even attitudes to subjects deemed as 'taboo' as suicide in the eighteenth century.

Electrified Bodies and the Argument against Mechanism

Burney infuses the performative aspect of Elinor's death wish with the rhetoric of enthusiasm, and explicitly characterizes the would-be suicide as the act of a 'self-devoted enthusiast'.[76] To this end, Harleigh cautions Juliet to take care not to irritate Elinor's 'enthusiasm, or to excite her spirit of controversy'.[77] One might expect this spirit of enthusiasm to contradict the representation of Elinor as a mechanical being, 'completely governed by impulse ... who considers her passions as her guides to glory'.[78] However, as the philosopher and historian Michael Heyd has noted, 'Whereas in the seventeenth century mechanistic natural philosophy was seen as an effective antidote to enthusiasm, in the eighteenth it could be coupled with an active interest in prophecy and "enthusiastic" movements'.[79] This 'favorable, or at least indulgent attitude towards enthusiasm'[80] on the part of mechanistic thinkers suggests the compatibility of the two 'movements', which of course, is corroborated by Elinor, a character driven at once by the 'subjective sentiment' with which enthusiasm became associated in the eighteenth century and by the mechanistic worldview. Moreover, Burney's novels conflate the discourses of enthusiasm and sensibility and establish suicide as a corollary of both outlooks. While Elinor is a victim both of her own passions and of the Enlightenment rationality that informs her worldview, it is her mechanistic philosophy that comes under specific scrutiny in the novel. In this sense, *The Wanderer* explicitly engages with issues of materialism and mechanism that remain implicit in Burney's earlier work. An extended debate between Harleigh and Elinor regarding the separability of the soul from the body consistently refers to the body as a 'fragile corporeal machine', or alternatively as a 'wretched machine of clay'.[81] As in *Camilla*, the female body literally takes on the mechanical functions ascribed to it by the 'iatromechanist' view of the body, which the physician and medical writer George Cheyne classically defined as 'a machine of an infinite number and variety of different channels and pipes, filled with various and different liquors and fluids, perpetually running, gliding, or creeping forward, or returning backward, in a constant Circle'.[82] This conception of the body seeks to render it intelligible and transparent, a mere piece of equipment that lends itself readily to the management of both its immediate owner and society at large.

Arguably, this perception of the body as mechanical mitigates the stigma of suicide, since it invests the flesh with even less sanctity than is found in the traditional Christian contempt of corporeality. The fact that the Church condemned suicide while simultaneously (albeit indirectly) inculcating a desire for death through mortification of the body was derided as a doctrinal paradox by Enlightenment *philosophes*. Despite her avowed atheism, Elinor's violence suggests a self-loathing consistent with the attitude of the Christian penitent; she attempts to sublimate her desires through a masochistic disciplining of her body, and strives to translate these actions into the rhetoric of heroic asceticism reminiscent of Clarissa's labours in Richardson's novel. However, as seen in both *Camilla* and *The Wanderer*, the body is far from the 'fragile machine' that Elinor describes, since it resists both main characters' attempts to destroy it. In this respect, the body proves more robust than either the sanity or intellects of the protagonists, and is imbued with a life principle that almost renders it impervious to voluntary death. Indeed, a doctor's diagnosis that Elinor's 'imagination is yet more diseased than the body' lends support to this view.[83] Accordingly, it becomes increasingly evident that Burney's text does not accommodate a notion of a biological death drive that writers on melancholia like George Cheyne and Bernard Mandeville appeared to advocate a century earlier. On the contrary, the body is kept alive by a vital force that resists all attempts to destroy it before its time.

Like Camilla, Juliet in *The Wanderer* is referred to as mechanized, but almost exclusively in the context of her dealings with tyrant figures who attempt to deny her right of self-determination. Moreover, while Burney's chronic characterization of Camilla's movements as mechanical might conceivably arise from her desire to underscore the susceptibility to the inertia that necessarily occurs in an individual so dependent upon an external source of impulsion, the mechanistic philosophy of Burney's 'secondary' heroine, Elinor, is targeted in *The Wanderer* as a menace to the religious and social status quo. Elinor's ideological opposite, Albert Harleigh, attributes her disbelief in 'a future state ... her defiance of all revealed religion ... her high approbation of suicide' to these very mechanist ideas, complaining 'so boundless is the license which the followers of the new systems allow themselves that nothing is too dreadful to apprehend. Religion is, if possible, still less respected than law, prescriptive rights, or any of the hitherto acknowledged ties of society.'[84] Yet, these connections between mechanism, atheism and permissibility toward voluntary death were recognized as tenuous by many thinkers of the period. Automatism, as the eighteenth-century philosopher David Hartley indicates, accommodates the metaphysical world in its mechanisms, since it locates the source of movement in an external entity.[85] Moreover, even the staunchest mechanist of the period, Julien La Mettrie, stridently denounced the person who attempted or completed suicide as a 'monster'.[86] Although one might think that Humean thought informs the arguments put forth by Elinor, hers are openly atheistic while Hume adopted a staunchly deist position, perhaps in part to protect himself against ecclesiastical reprisals.[87] Clearly, in *The Wanderer* Elinor's suicide catalyses a philosophical debate, which in *Camilla* had been entirely subordinated to the religio-mystical treatment of suicide that dominates the scenes of crisis.

The concern with the relation between automatism and agency that informs Burney's narratives might suggest that she subscribes to the *non compos men-*

tis diagnosis of suicide. Just as she attributes Camilla's death wish in her earlier novel to mere youthful folly, in *The Wanderer* she assigns Elinor's suicide quest to delusive madness. Elinor's use of the phrase 'death of reason' in the context of her apostrophe to 'suicide! Triumphant antidote to woe!' is ironically undercut by the ambiguity of the grammar, which suggests the very annihilation of rationality that suicide entails from Burney's standpoint.[88] Thus, where Elinor views voluntary death as the ultimate expression of rationality, the text indicates that reason itself breaks down and perishes in the suicidal act. This identification of suicide with mental illness also indicates that the act cannot constitute an authentic object of the will, and must necessarily arise from either demonic possession (according to earlier beliefs) or insanity.

However, even while one strain of the text works to establish Elinor's mental instability and hysteria, another operates to reaffirm her rationality.[89] For instance, Harleigh insists that Elinor's abortive 'fatal deed' has 'no excuse to plead from sudden desperation; she came prepared, decided, either to disprove her suspicions, or to end her existence!'[90] The emphasis on calculated deliberation suggests a woman in control of her intellect and capable, furthermore, of countering theological arguments for the sanctity of life. In one such debate, Elinor describes life as a 'donation made without our consent or knowledge',[91] simultaneously drawing upon and refurbishing the imagery of the Christian tradition that constructs the body as a kind of divine 'gift', which it would be discourteous to reject. In this respect she assumes a standard 'freethinker' position, one that reasons, in the words of the scholar of French philosophy and literature Lester Crocker, 'that life being a gift or favor, we have the right to give it up when it becomes onerous'.[92] While the rationality of this argument is unequivocal, Burney predicates Harleigh's argument upon the essential indeterminacy of the fate of the body after death, as he shows 'nonentity itself to be as doubtful as immortality'.[93] In relying substantively upon the factor of fear, this argument constitutes an appeal to the irrational, suggesting that even presumably detached and speculative discourse concerning the subject can never be entirely rational.[94]

In a sense, Burney conceives of suicide as an inevitable product of a 'mad' materialist system of thought that views the body as a mechanical entity. Elinor's insistence that the soul is a material entity no less subject to death than the body precludes for her the dread of death that Burney views as a necessary deterrent to suicide. Albert Harleigh contests Elinor's insistence on the identity of soul and body in his claim that 'the connexion between mind and body, however intimate, is not blended'.[95] In its insistence on the capacity of 'corporal force for supporting the bitterest grief of heart with uninjured health; and mental force, on the other side, for bearing the acutest bodily disorders with unimpaired intellectual vigour',[96] Harleigh's argument resembles vitalist conceptions of the body as an entity 'powered by internal forces and vital energies which steer it unconsciously and independently to well-being, ease, and health'.[97] Endorsing the notion of a vital principle but otherwise distancing himself from materialist thinking, Harleigh conceives of the body as an obstacle to suicide in a way that counters the morbidity that Burney typically aligns with mechanist thought. In this sense, Burney's deactivation of her *femme-machines* involves the assertion of a vitalist principle that in effect discounts the possibility of suicide.

Although the resolution of the characters' debate involves merely a substitution of agnosticism for atheism, Elinor capitulates to her antagonist's argument with the exclamation 'Harleigh, you electrify me! You convulse the whole train of my principles, my systems, my long cherished conviction!'[98] Like *Frankenstein's* inert corpse, Elinor has been restored to life, revitalized by Harleigh's anti-reductionist argument, which significantly invokes the case of 'renovated beings' – those individuals, many of them suicidal, resuscitated by the techniques promulgated by the Humane Society in the late decades of the eighteenth century – as evidence for life after death. Moreover, Elinor's language recalls the means of energizing dead matter that Mary Shelley herself had borrowed from the 1790s experiments of Luigi Galvani and Alessandro Volta. Galvani's research focused on the convulsions experienced by electrified bodies, and, as the historian Bruce Clarke observes, provided 'the clue to vital phenomena'.[99] Strikingly enough, once revitalized, Elinor speaks in the language of the vitalists, no less a 'renovated being' than Frankenstein's monster himself.

Elinor's reanimation at the hands of her doctors demonstrates the collusion of science with nature, a representation likely informed by the kind of modified life instinct espoused by the vitalist members of the Humane Society.[100] Founded in 1774 to promote the resuscitation of 'persons apparently drowned', the Humane Society promulgated the belief that life instincts might, even if overcome temporarily, assert themselves belatedly, and presented empirical evidence confirming the operation of these self-preservative instincts. In his *Sermon on Suicide Presented on the Anniversary of the Royal Humane Society* (1797), George Gregory insisted that 'no person intending to commit suicide, who was indebted for recovery to [the Society's] exertions has ever attempted it a second time'.[101] This claim was bolstered by an appendix to the published version of the paper that attested to the remarkable success of the society in 'restoring despairing culprits to themselves' at a rate of 350 out of 500 attempts.[102] The anecdotes that further corroborate the society's 'ardent zeal for the preservation of human life'[103] dwell upon observers' comparison of the resuscitation attempts to 'a resurrection from the dead'.[104] The members themselves deemed their interventions at the scenes of suicide 'providential', as they merely activated a temporarily dormant life instinct, or a 'small spark', as their official motto proclaimed. At the same time, in its efforts to intervene in suicide attempts by British subjects, the Humane Society saw itself as doing the 'work of the nation', rehabilitating its reputation and preventing depopulation, which was a nagging concern of the period. The Society's work was officially recognized in 1793 when it received royal patronage, and the techniques of resuscitation (and associated vitalist theories) were widely disseminated to such an extent that they were represented in works of fiction such as Thomas Holcroft's *Anna St. Ives* and Burney's *The Wanderer*. The sermons and medical writings of clerics and doctors involved in the Society's work promulgate strongly vitalist theories that view resuscitation efforts as assisting a body more inclined to live than to die. Yet the Society's intervention in suicide attempts represents one more assertion of 'biopower', as an arm of the state managing and preserving the lives of its subjects even against their will. As the next section of this chapter will make clear, Burney's novel highlights the extent to which 'medical nationalism' of the sort promoted by the Royal Humane Society became integral to an understanding of suicide in the early nineteenth century.

The Suicidal Sublime: National Character and Gothic Nomads

Whereas *Camilla* makes use of gothic interpolations in its attempt to underscore the terrors of death, *The Wanderer* casts as its primary character the supremely gothic and archetypal figure of the Wanderer, an enigmatic figure estranged from her adoptive country and society at large. The Wanderer's existence is typically rendered insupportable by particular circumstances, and early eighteenth-century versions of this figure, such as that which appears in Richard Savage's poem *The Wanderer* (1721), either commit suicide or contemplate the deed. Although not the nominal nomad of the narrative, Elinor Joddrel embraces the role and heightens its gothic possibilities; with each appearance Elinor grows increasingly 'pale, meagre, and wretched', but a sense of immortality clings about her haggard form that obstinately refuses to submit to her death wish.[105] Gradually, she comes to resemble and anticipate other gothic Wanderers of the period like Charles Maturin's *Melmoth the Wanderer* (1820), as her search for self-actualization through death is steeped in all the psychological horror of the genre. Whereas in *Camilla* the terrors of death are personified in an allegorical figure of mortality, in *The Wanderer* Burney allows death to speak directly through Elinor.

An inevitably conflicted, paradoxical and deeply complicated character, Elinor represents a vigorous mind 'distorted' by the brand of 'freethinking' materialism that leads her to proclaim the sublimity of suicide:

> In the dauntless hour of willing death, I proclaim my sovereign contempt of the whole race of mankind! of its cowardly subterfuges, its mean assimilations, its heartless subtleties! Here, in the sublime act of voluntary self-extinction, I exult to declare my adoration of thee, – of thee alone, Albert Harleigh![106]

Invoking a kind of 'suicidal sublime', Elinor thus constructs voluntary death as a revolutionary act that defies both religious codes of conduct and perceived notions of a social contract, thereby aligning her with the Wertherian suicidal stance detailed in Chapter 4. Elinor's attitude is consistent with Edmund Burke's formulation of the sublime as evoked by the threat of death and dissolution of the self. In *A Philosophical Enquiry into the Origins of Our Ideas of the Sublime and Beautiful* (1757), Burke claimed

> But as pain is stronger in its operation than pleasure, so death is in general a much more affecting idea than pain; because there are very few pains, however exquisite, which are not preferred to death; nay, what generally makes pain itself, if I may say so, more painful is, that it is considered as an emissary of this king of terrors. When danger or pain press too nearly, they are incapable of giving any delight, and are simply terrible; but at certain distances, and with certain modifications, they may be, and they are delightful, as we every day experience. The cause of this I shall endeavour to investigate hereafter.[107]

Burke's aesthetic category predicates itself on the paradox that no actual 'idea of danger' is connected with it; as E. J. Clery avers, 'The sublime is an apprehension of danger in nature or art without the immediate risk of destruction'.[108] According to this paradigm, an element of inherent inauthenticity would necessarily inform Elinor's conception of a 'suicidal sublime'. Elinor's relentless striving to inflict pain on her body simultaneously actualizes the violence that resides in most eighteenth-century concepts of the sublime and negates the very principles of security and self-preservation so intrinsic to this category. To a large extent the exalted nature of suicide, as Elinor constructs it, is analogous to the 'Sublimity of Revolution'[109] since death in the context of both events produces 'an unacknowledged, and unoffered sacrifice',[110] rather than the openly acknowledged sacrifice that Elinor demands.

Elinor's state of perpetual decay suggests a sort of 'negative sublime' involving a fall into and confrontation with the abject nature of the body rather than an expansion of the mind. Elinor consistently conjures up the medieval 'food for worms' topos that points to the dissolution of the corpse and reminds the individual of his or her mortality. Her appropriation of the motif embraces the abject body and invests it with the sublimity she assigns elsewhere to suicide.[111] Hence, the narrator at one crucial juncture describes Elinor as having 'flung off her bandages, rent open her wounds, and tor[n] her hair, calling, screaming for death'.[112] In graphic depictions of self-inflicted violence, Elinor offers a preview of decomposition ghastlier even than Camilla's bodily deterioration. Elinor carries the marks of her first suicide attempt about her body, and repeatedly threatens to tear open these wounds to demonstrate her fixity of purpose. Intended to serve as a prolepsis of suicide, the wounded body instead signifies Elinor's lack of success, reproaching her for her failures. Elinor is separated from her corporeality precisely by these gashes; in this respect, wounds represent the alienation of self from body, staging the 'self-betrayal' so integral to the experience of physical suffering described by Elaine Scarry in her landmark study of 'the body in pain'.[113] Pain, Scarry argues convincingly, involves an experience of 'double agency', rendering the subject simultaneously the victim and the agent, for in physical suffering 'suicide and murder converge ... one feels acted upon, annihilated, by inside and outside alike'.[114] In much the same manner as Scarry's trope, Elinor's wounds also, paradoxically, figure as the site of her agency, signifying resistance to the institutions that strive to keep her whole. At the same time, Elinor's only partially healed wounds emblematize her intermediate position between life and death that heightens her sense of gothic spectrality. It is these wounds that keep suicide materially present to Elinor.

Elinor's aestheticization of the sublime aspect of suicide raises the question as to whether any action may ever actually aspire to the status of Burke's exalted category. In his reformulation of the sublime, which dethrones it from its lofty position in Burkean aesthetics, Immanuel Kant acknowledges that the paradox whereby we 'must find ourselves safe in order to feel this exciting liking' might *seem* to controvert the genuine 'sublimity of our intellectual ability'; however, Kant insists upon the mind's capacity to transcend the limitations imposed upon its authentic experience of the sublime through the very 'exercising' and 'development' of this ability.[115] Kant exposes the fallacy of attributing sublimity to an object, insisting instead that 'all we are entitled to say is that the object is suitable for exhibiting a sublimity that can be found in the mind'.[116] Thus, the sublime exists purely at the level of 'ideation', a condition altogether purged of sensibility and suffused instead with a 'higher purposiveness'.[117] Read from this perspective, Elinor's sublimation of suicide into an ideal arguably aligns itself with the Kantian rather than the Burkean category, although her exalted aestheticization of voluntary death fails to observe Kant's vital imperative of duty and lacks the cognitive rationality and the categorical imperative so integral to Kant's thinking as a whole. Her recasting of the sublime involves mere annihilation and constitutes precisely the opposite of the expansion of the 'self' typically associated with the experience.

Perhaps owing to his equation of duty with sacrifice, Kant avers that 'Even war has something sublime about it', before offering the qualification 'if it is carried on in an orderly way and with respect for the sanctity of the citizens' rights'.[118] If war might be conceived as a sublime undertaking, then might not also suicide, or at least the heroic or self-sacrificial version that Elinor contemplates? In 'Duties towards the Body in Regard to Life', Kant insists that 'a suicide opposes the purpose of his Creator, he arrives in the other world as one who has deserted his post; he must be looked upon as a rebel against God'.[119] This rather conventional military rhetoric borrowed from the Greek philosopher Pythagoras is echoed by Albert Harleigh in *The Wanderer*, as, interrupting Elinor's characterization of suicide as a

'Straightforward, unerring route to rest, to repose!', he demands 'Repose? – rest? ... how earned? By deserting our duties? By quitting our posts? By forsaking and wounding all by whom we are cherished?'[120] The cluster of military metaphors that appears in Harleigh's and in Kant's discussion of suicide might seem counter-intuitive, since suicide apologists invoked the fact that homicide was condoned in the context of war to negate the warning 'grafted' onto the sixth commandment (since no explicit prohibition against suicide is to be found in either the Hebrew or Christian scriptures). To this end, in his tract on suicide, Hume explicitly turns the analogy on its head by insisting that 'whenever pain or sorrow so far overcome my patience, as to make me tired of life, I may conclude that I am recalled from my station in the clearest and most express terms'.[121] From this perspective, Kant's construction of suicide as a sort of moral opposite of war appears to break down, and perhaps recognizing this contradiction, he resorts to invoking a version of the categorical imperative to support his argument: 'since suicide cannot obtain as a universal law, it therefore contradicts the supreme principle of all duty'.[122] However, because sacrifice and duty are synonymous for Kant, the form of altruistic suicide that we see authorized in novels throughout the eighteenth century would be deemed acceptable.

To some extent, this reasoning is in fact accepted by Germaine de Staël, for whom Kantian idealism functioned as an antidote to materialism, fulfilling a basic human need for 'a philosophy of belief, of enthusiasm' that countered the morbidity of the dominant belief systems of the Enlightenment.[123] In *Réflexions sur le Suicide*, the converted Staël reads life itself as sublime, calling the 'gift of existence a miracle in every instance' that 'partakes of the sublime'.[124] Whereas Elinor reads the sublime as a metaphor for oblivion, Staël follows Kant's restorative view in claiming 'the first effect of the sublime is to crush man, the second is to restore him'.[125] The mechanistic worldview that Burney ascribes to Elinor prevents her from looking beyond her death wish to appreciate the true nature of sublime experience.

Meanwhile Staël's exposition of Kant uncovers the latent vitalism that led him to affirm the 'autonomy of organic life'.[126] In his reading of the 'vitalism without life' implicit in Kantian cosmopolitan theory, theorist Pheng Cheah argues that 'Although he is often regarded as repudiating vitalism, Kant is actually a critical vitalist because he safeguards the autonomy of organic life and insists on its distinctiveness from both nonorganized and technical bodies'.[127] We see these strains of a peculiar version of vitalism at work in *The Critique of Judgement* where Kant claims,

> An organized being has within it formative force, and a formative force that this being imparts to the kinds of matter that lack it (thereby organizing them). This force is therefore a formative force that propagates itself – a force that a mere ability [of one thing] to move [another] (i.e. mechanism) cannot explain.[128]

This immaterial entity is not synonymous with an idea of the soul, and Kant does not try to identify its precise nature, considering it sufficient to theorize that organisms are self-actualizing and hence wholly free. This organic body becomes a metaphor for an understanding of the political body termed 'political organicism', which Kant applies to the emergent Republican state set against the mechanical nature of the constitutional monarchy.

The 'organismic vitalism' seen in Kant is similarly discernible in Staël's thinking on national character, which led her to recover a reason for living in her identification (however tenuous) with a national body. Staël rendered the theory of fixed dispositions fostered by the vitalists the basis for her 'geo-sociology'. According to both Staël and the prominent vitalist Louis de la Lacaze, the dispositions of denizens of the *midi* differed radically from those of the north, which in turn informed the development of a national character.[129] Both Staël and Lacaze concentrate on the interdependence of national and personal *moeurs* and the need to regulate passion in order to foster social and individual well-being, an approach that conflates the moral and the physical as well as the national and the individual. Lacaze claims that 'By habits of sobriety, suitable exercise for the body, and, especially by worthy occupations, one is happily distanced from the manner of life and disposition that lead almost inevitably to excessive passions'.[130] In *Réflexions sur le suicide*, Staël similarly recommends a Protestant work ethic as an antidote to suicidal tendencies, claiming that 'hard, steady work has comforted most of those who have devoted themselves to it'.[131] Staël thus represents Protestantism as a remedy for suicidal tendencies even as she removes the obstacles that in many views rendered sacrifice irreconcilable with the Protestant ethos.

In this, her final work on the subject of suicide, Staël's concern with the connection between suicide and nations inevitably leads her to dwell on the rhetorical question of sacrifice as she demands of the suicidal individual: 'And this man who would like to die, does he not have a country? Is he not capable of fighting for her? Does there not exist any noble or perilous enterprise on behalf of which he might offer himself up as an example?'[132] According to this construction, sacrifice neutralizes male suicide, suggesting that the individual may redeem his suicide by dying on behalf of the nation. In the same discussion, Staël demands 'can one give the name of virtue to the conduct of a woman who voluntarily destroys the duties of a daughter, wife, and mother?'[133] According to this line of thought, women's duties are domestic and men's are national, although both are equally relevant to the nationalist deontology Staël develops throughout the treatise in her attempt to assert an altruistic case for remaining alive or for giving up one's life. In Staël's theorization, suicide becomes subsumed under the category of sacrifice, an instinct for patriotism being placed alongside that of self-preservation, as we see in her novels, most particularly

Jane Gray. Interestingly enough, according to her biographer, Avery Goodden, Staël's experience of exile was responsible for this alteration in her attitude to suicide: according to Goodden, Staël revised her view that 'some losses rob life of all meaning ... partly in response to what exile taught her about adapting, replacing, renewing, and regenerating'.[134] Even, or perhaps especially from her marginal position, Staël was better able to appreciate the sacrifices that one might make on behalf of a nation one held dear.

Burney, however, appears to reject the rhetoric of sacrifice, suggesting that 'egotism' is inevitably implicated in suicide. In *Camilla*, the protagonist rouses herself from her prolonged suicidal deliberations to remark on the 'cruelty of [her] egotism'.[135] Meanwhile, in *The Wanderer*, Elinor constructs suicide as a profoundly feminist, although ultimately self-serving, act, as she demands, 'Why, alone, is woman to be excluded from the exertions of courage, the field of glory, the immortal death of honour ...?',[136] and she later reiterates, 'if ever that wretched thing called life has a noble moment, it must surely be that of its voluntary sacrifice!'[137] Elinor presents a condensed version of a 'Jacobin' defence of suicide (albeit expressed in stronger terms than we find in their writings), which preserves the rhetoric of self-sacrifice so intrinsic to the *fin de siècle* revolutionary political discourse, as discussed in chapter 4. Elinor's parting words reveal her resignation to the fact that since 'neither sorrow, nor despair, nor even madness [will] kill me ... nature, in her decrepitude, alone [may] bring death to Elinor'.[138] Elinor's third-person self-reference reveals a persistent strain of egotism, as does her wistful longing for 'the single thrill of one poor moment's returning doubt' regarding both her newfound conversion to agnosticism and her realization of Juliet's intrinsic worth.[139] Her third-person reference also suggests the ability to see oneself as an object that is so often seen as a necessary precondition for suicide. Burney's representation of Elinor's mindset invokes a dichotomy of sorts, an alienating split of subjectivity, which, instead of being close and intimate with itself, posits the self as absent and distant in an effort to deepen the chasm between the object of suicide (the corporeal body) and the executor of the act (the rational/irrational mind). Her speech also conveys a theatrical consciousness of the spectacle, resembling an externalization of the protagonist's interior monologue; hence the need for a third-person reference, or a soliloquy of sorts. However one reads this passage, it is clear that Harleigh has not met with unqualified success in his proselytizing endeavours, and his partial failure confirms Burney's simultaneous critique of and concession to male authority, which we also see manifested elsewhere in her writings. Furthermore, Elinor's declaration that she 'would now suffer martyrdom!' for even a temporary return to her former 'systems' expresses a desire for relapse and rebellion against Harleigh's orthodoxy.[140] Her announcement also exemplifies the attitude towards sacrifice expressed in the novel, in which 'martyrdom' is an act of violence associated with the revolutionary sentiment of France under Robespierre.

Burney resists the rewriting of suicide as sacrifice that characterizes eighteenth-century novelistic works in general, possibly in keeping with the anti-nationalist bias that she betrays throughout the novel. If nations are organized around sacrifice, then Burney wants no part of them, as she deliberately opts to substitute a transnational for a national outlook in *The Wanderer*.

The novel also reveals Burney's resistance to a totalizing concept of Englishness, expressed in her emphasis upon the claustrophobic restrictiveness of English society, this time against a transnational backdrop.[141] In her decidedly unfeminine and uninhibited rambling across Europe, Elinor fully embraces the role of the gothic 'Wanderer'. Her early disguise as a 'strange figure, with something foreign in his appearance',[142] both evokes the alterity of women and emphasizes the transnational identifications that Elinor cultivates throughout the novel. The final protracted dialogue with Harleigh and Juliet, which ultimately convinces Elinor of the error of her ways, prompts her flight to the 'far corners of the earth', thus handily removing one of the obstacles to the narrative's primary romance plot. The narrator suggests that Elinor opts to live, although one must wonder whether the neat disposal of her character is not in itself tantamount to a narration of death. A contemporary reviewer asserted that 'the authoress leaves room to suppose she returns to the good old maxims from which she had been perverted'.[143] The reviewer also maintains that a certain degree of indeterminacy nonetheless surrounds her departure, which is characteristic of the uncertain endings of suicide narratives written by women.[144] It is thus Elinor who is the real 'Wanderer' of the story. Exiled from the narrative and the coterie established at the end by the central figures, Elinor transmutes from an avenging fury to a resigned, humiliated penitent. She departs the scene with the final imperative to her coachman: 'Drive to the end of the world!',[145] a command that could be read in either a straightforwardly spatio-geographical sense or a temporal, slightly apocalyptic one that would ultimately affirm the teleological finality of her unyielding suicidal subjectivity and establish her irreducibly stateless identity. The spirit of internationalism that the text suggests Elinor absorbs during her sojourn in France inspires a disregard of borders that is integral to the gothic incarnation of the Wanderer.

Although, for much of the narrative, as the titular 'Wanderer', Juliet is the text's outsider, positioned as a kind of *pharmakon* or scapegoat made to assume the faults of society, it is Elinor whom the text ultimately sacrifices to its code of middle-class values. Ironically, although Elinor configures her suicide as a symbolic sacrifice from a political and feminist standpoint – at one point in the text she exhorts Harleigh to behold his 'willing martyr!'[146] – she finds herself literally sacrificed, deprived of her volition, and consistently prevented from dying.

As the unstable element in the text and the embodiment of unbridled desire, Elinor is sacrificed in a figurative sense, that is, driven from the perimeter of her community and permanently exiled in order to preserve the welfare of the community as a whole.

Once Elinor has left the scene, harmony can be restored to a community that had earlier been fractured by the secret marriage of Juliet's parents and the resulting expatriation of Juliet herself. As the literary theorist Andrew McKenna states, 'Sacrifice restores order by restoring difference between the sacralized victim and the community',[147] and we can see how Juliet reinstates likeness through the assimilation into her natural family that she achieves through the final recognition scene at the narrative's end. The achievement of recognition thus proves contingent upon the jettisoning of the differential element represented by Elinor. At the same time, the reconstruction of the family unit through Juliet's reunion with her half-siblings, Lord and Lady Melbury, affords the means of establishing nationalist ties in a quintessentially Burkean manner that conceives of the family as a means of naturalizing the nation.[148] Juliet's reassimilation into her family at the novel's end sets the stage for her recovery of a national identity. Earlier, without parents, patrimony or country, Juliet had been an outcast, but now Elinor's estrangement from her family renders her the archetypal gothic outsider. Whereas Clarissa's death had been the means of securing social cohesion through the act of mourning, Elinor's prolonged (albeit displaced) existence and Juliet's survival of her misfortunes afford the means for social rehabilitation and the defeat of Enlightenment mechanistic ideas.

However, despite the fact that Harleigh attributes Elinor's mania for suicide to the impact of the 'new systems' of France, the text suggests that the anomie that infects any society disrupted by violent revolution could produce her penchant for self-violence. Accordingly, Burney argues for a universal human nature that transcends geographic borders, advising those

> who expect to find here materials for political controversy; or fresh food for national animosity ... [to] turn elsewhere their disappointed eyes: for here, they will simply meet ... a composition upon general life, manners, and characters; without any species of personality, either in the form of foreign influence, or of national partiality.[149]

This disclaimer might have been motivated by Burney's anxiety regarding the reception of her manuscript in the French customhouse through which she was obliged to pass on her return to England in 1812, but less cynically, might be the result of her prolonged residence in France and connections to that country by marriage to Alexandre d'Arblay.

Whatever the case may be, despite Burney's cosmopolitan stance, she links the issue of suicide inextricably to the question of nationalism. A character whose sole function in the narrative involves stitching up Elinor's self-inflicted wounds (and who scarcely otherwise lays claim to a voice) nonetheless delivers the text's more plain-spoken expostulation against suicide. Referring to Harleigh's unwavering refusal to capitulate to Elinor's emotional blackmail, the surgeon, Mr Naird, asserts:

> No men, however, – none at least on this side of the Channel, – can wonder that he should demur at venturing upon a treaty with a lady so expert in foreign politics, as to make an experiment, in her own proper person, of the new atheistical and suicidal doctrines, that those ingenious gentlemen, on t'other side of the water, are now so busily preaching, for their fellow-countrymen's destruction. This mode of challenging one's existence for every quarrel with one's Will and running one's self through the Body for every affront to one's Mind; used to be thought peculiar to the proud and unbending humour of John Bull; but John did it rarely enough to make it a subject of gossiping, and news-paper squibs, for at least a week. Our merry neighbours, on the contrary, now once they have set about it, do the job with an air, and a grace, that shew us as drowsy in our desperation, as we are phlegmatic in our amusements. They talk of it wherever they go; write of it whenever they hold a pen; and are so piqued to think that we got the start of them, in beginning the game first, that they pop off more in a month, than we do in a year: and I don't in the least doubt, that their intention is to go on with the same briskness, till they have made the balance even.[150]

This lengthy speech recapitulates the trend toward assigning a nationality to suicide in the latter part of the century, by setting up an absurd competition to set records for suicide casualties. Mr Naird's potted history of suicide in the eighteenth century draws heavily upon the rhetoric of 'John Bull' and engages with the culture of voluntary death as it was publicized by the papers and in the coffee-house chatter of the time. The speech also invokes the myth of the suicidal English, which constructs voluntary death as a national, and accordingly, a political question.[151]

In transferring the 'crisis' across the English Channel, Naird's discourse subscribes to the pervasive early nineteenth-century British attitude towards France. According to Naird, in the fall-out of the French Revolution, the British basked in a smug sense of their own virtues, occupying a position of superiority that naturally enabled them to displace their own problems onto the French.[152] Composing *The Wanderer* chiefly while in France during the tenure of Napoleon, Burney does not espouse Naird's sentiment, and thus refuses to articulate this position (in a manner indicative of support, at least) in her text. Her sojourn abroad would have made her aware of the fact that French institutions of power rigorously legislated against suicide at all times and with particular severity during the Reign of Terror. The National Assembly and its 'atheistical systems' had no more interest in promoting or even endorsing suicide than did the English government. Indeed, the extent to which it perceived suicide as a threat to its power is suggested by the regular guillotining of political prisoners even after their suicides. The 'Catechisme moral republicaine' called suicide a crime, and this attitude was reiterated in countless other republican treatises of the period. Despite this biopolitical commitment to the containment of suicide, the national reputation for suicide was, as Burney's text demonstrates, less subject to legislative control.

Naird's speech highlights the constructed nature of all nationalist debates, suggesting that the English Malady was a product of the papers rather than, as Staël would argue, a viable social reality. Naird's speech also exemplifies the ease with which constructed positions could be naturalized even amid recognition of their artificial nature. Both here and in her caricature of the committed anti-Jacobin, young Mr Gooch (a figure obsessed with the French despot he refers to as 'Bob Spear'), Burney ridicules the ignorance and xenophobia informing British interpretation of foreign events. The undercurrent of 'fierce democratic nationalism' that Gerald Newman detects in *Evelina*,[153] notwithstanding its mockery of English patriots such as the coarse Captain Mirvan, is nowhere apparent in *The Wanderer*, owing perhaps to the apparent non-Englishness of its central figure.[154] Juliet's ambiguous nationality drives much of the narrative; her associations with France render her a lightning rod for nationalist discourse comprised largely of the cultural slurs and disparaging stereotypes which the rural English clubs of the sort that Gooch frequents are dedicated to promoting.[155] Juliet's Englishness is consistently called into question by a text that does its utmost to destabilize all such modes of identification; the fact that Juliet is raised by a French bishop in a French convent is just one of several ways in which Burney undercuts Juliet's English identity. At the same time, just as much as Juliet's apparent foreign extraction, Elinor's passion for suicide provides an impetus to national comparisons as exemplified in Naird's speech.

In the course of the surgeon's lengthy harangue, Elinor's suicide attempt is subsumed into a totalizing national discourse of suicide. Although Elinor's character was principally construed by contemporary reviewers as a 'historical antidote to lingering remnants of poisonous doctrines',[156] Burney offers only a *partial* condemnation of Elinor's suicidal tendencies. While female suicide in this text represents neither the liberating gesture nor the submission to social commands posited by some critics, Burney implicitly critiques the fact that the doctor cannot recognize Elinor's suicide attempt as an individual act, but can only understand it in the larger context of the construction of British nationhood. In this spirit, Elinor's suicide attempts cannot be faced or acknowledged but must rather be rendered an extension of the prevailing hostilities between the French and English. Burney in this manner ironically exposes the absurdity of the attempt to incorporate suicide into a definition of national identity, especially given that nationality, as presented in this novel, is a highly unstable category.

The characterization of Mr Naird in some respects brings to mind the English physician George Man Burrows, who helped propagate the belief that by the early nineteenth century the French suicide rate had outstripped that of the English.[157] Consulting the French tables for mortality in 1813, Burrows argued in his *London Medical Repository* (1815), 'It is clearly evident that, of late years at least, suicide has been immeasurably more frequent in Paris than in London'.[158] Although the leading French epidemiologist of the time, J. E. D. Esquirol, rejected Burrows's interpretation of the tables, Esquirol's junior colleague, J. P. Falret, acknowledged that '1813 was rather a bad year for Paris suicides, but not a typical one'.[159] In 1813, Burney was completing work on *The Wanderer* in England, having carried her son across the Channel to prevent his recruitment into Napoleon's military. The ostensible suicide epidemic in France and the British commentary that it precipitated would almost certainly have been familiar to Burney, since Esquirol and Burrows had revived the 1790s dispute over the nationality of suicide chronicled in *The Wanderer*. Where in the previous century, British commentators had ascribed the *morbus anglici* to the autonomy accorded to their countrymen by their economic system and civil liberties, in the nineteenth century suicide in France was easily credited to the *lack* of autonomy enjoyed by the individual under Napoleonic rule. Dr Thomas Arnold's opinion (articulated in 1782) that France was 'a land of slaves, where the bulk and strength of a nation is depressed and impoverished ... being subject to the will of an absolute monarch' in contrast to England's 'happy land of liberty'[160] was invoked by English commentators throughout the eighteenth century in their attempts to rationalize if not celebrate their English predilection for suicide. Arnold's Cheynean findings were echoed by colleagues such as William Rowley and Benjamin Faulkner who reveal the politicized nature of the suicide debates in their rhetoric of luxury and excess. In the early decades of the nineteenth century, the same nationalist suicide debate that had been initiated nearly a century earlier and which became increasingly central to the development of an idea of the 'nation' was being waged yet again. Naird's speech, then, belongs to the historical discourse of suicide, highlighting the polemical aspect of the debate over the nationality of voluntary death. From an English perspective, suicide affirmed the advanced notion of selfhood and the autonomy that arguably accompanies this mentality, yet this celebration of pathology did not prevent the same writers from transferring this particular mark of distinction to the French when the opportunity arose in post-revolutionary France.

Interestingly, Burney declines the opportunity to diminish the stigma of the English Malady by displacing the problem of suicide onto the terrain of revolutionary France. In spite of the 'John Bullish' prejudices that she confesses to harbouring in her personal letters, Burney devotes herself in her final work to challenging the idea of an essential Englishness. Although she does not venture quite so far as David Hume in questioning the existence of an English national character, she offers a subtle critique of the very notion of a 'stationary nationality' in works like *Camilla*.[161] Burney rejects the notion of a permanent national character, and her resistance to the standard 'Whiggish' practice of defining Englishness at the expense of the French in part fuels the criticisms levelled at her last work of fiction. Burney herself attributes the work's poor reviews to 'the false expectations universally spread that the Book would be a "picture" of France', a work depicting the country at its historical nadir during Robespierre's reign of terror. Instead, Burney affords a decidedly unflattering picture of England circa 1793. She claims for her suicides or would-be suicides an unequivocal Englishness that refuses to exoticize or displace the deed, even as she resists the notion of a peculiarly English malady that was perpetuated by the popular press and other novelists of the time, including Staël.

In her concern with rehabilitating French character, Staël, in contrast, turned to England for support of her theory that Northerners were driven by pain and Southerners by pleasure.[162] As one of the intellectuals directly responsible for propelling the stereotype of the suicidal English into the nineteenth century, Staël modifies somewhat the parameters of the English Malady (by questioning the relevance of climatic influence), even as she retains its central premise that the English are inordinately suicidal.[163] Despite the fact that her attitude regarding the morality of suicide was remained ambivalent during her career, she adheres to 'a sociology of suicide by national temperament'[164] up to her final word on the subject in her 1813 treatise, *Refléxions sur le suicide*. By arguing that individuals and nations share the same characteristics and by annexing suicide to national character, Staël in effect naturalizes the act and relocates suicide to the realm of an 'other', in this case, the very England that she exalts in so much of her otherwise Anglophilic prose.[165]

Unlike Staël, whose novels turn on the problem of female nationality, Burney adopts a politically prudent cosmopolitan outlook in her final work that accords her the neutrality upon which her pension from the British Queen and her husband's good standing with Napoleon depended.[166] Thus, while Staël and her contemporaries were busy codifying national divisions, Burney was occupied with dismantling them in texts like *The Wanderer*. Yet the purpose of this argument is not to uphold an uncomplicated nationalist-cosmopolitan distinction, but rather to argue that each of these positions shares a tendency to dismiss women's suicide as something 'other'. Accordingly, even as Burney's and Staël's works implicate women's suicide in an understanding of national character, they simultaneously indicate the extent to which the gendering of suicide as a 'female difficulty' was disconnected from the naturalizing of voluntary death as an English affliction. For, even if national character was ostensibly feminized by its associations with nervous debility, this is not to say that women were actually involved in the construction of this character. As the historian Roberto Romani remarks, 'Women's attitudes were ... thought to be part of the national mind only to the extent of their influence over men' and 'Many authors of the eighteenth century, especially in Britain, regarded the mere existence of this influence as a symptom of a faulty national character'.[167] To Staël, who decried the silencing of women like Burney in English society, this influence would have been considered negligible. The fact that women's liberty was circumscribed by social constraints, let alone by the only partially sardonic yet common perception that women 'have no characters at all' as famously expressed by Alexander Pope, would work to preclude their participation in the construction of at least a notion of *English* national character. Yet in France, as the feminist scholar Anne McClintock has observed, a direct result of the *Code Napoléon* was that 'a woman's political relation to the nation was ... submerged as a social relation to a man through marriage'.[168] Married to citizens of France, both Burney and Staël would have appreciated the impact of this decree that rendered their nationality even more contingent than before. Even in Staël's work unrelated to England, we find a national subject under construction, albeit one that cannot accommodate women, suggesting that her understanding of national character is in fact constituted by the loss of women's identities.[169]

In works such as *The Influence of the Passions* (1796), Staël's argument regarding the homology between nations and persons renders the individual the basis for national identity and contributes to emergent Romantic (and in this case Kantian) views of the nation as biological rather than constructed.[170] Although Burney does not personally subscribe to the notions of national character being espoused and popularized in this period by early Romantics like Staël, her ambivalence towards the construct of a nation is figured through her representation of suicide, which draws in turn upon the very gothic mode that was itself implicated in late eighteenth-century projects of 'nation-building'.[171] The host of outsiders, enigmatic, spectral figures and wanderers that populate the gothic necessarily provokes a suspicion of national affiliation even as it works to consolidate a sense of communal identification.[172] As the literary critic Cannon Schmitt notes, 'Gothic fictions not only resisted the work of nation-building but also provided a glossary of figures and narrative conventions with which Englishness was defined and redefined'.[173] In many respects, *The Wanderer* expresses this ambivalence as Burney consistently invokes the notion of nationalism only to undermine it. By refusing to associate England with morbidity, Burney does not necessarily espouse a vitalist conception of the nation. Yet, at the same time, her representation of the suicidal body reflects the shift from a mechanistic to a vitalist outlook, for Burney grounds her rejection of suicide in its associations with mechanism. Her refusal to allow her female characters to die affirms a kind of life essence suggestive of the turn from mechanism to vitalism. Still, England continues to derive its identity from suicide in her final work, for even as Burney endeavours to dislodge the label, she ends up perpetuating it in the figure of Elinor Joddrell, who represents suicide as both a 'female difficulty' and a national problem.

With the Staël generation positing a connection between the individual (body) and the nation, the emergence of a view of the nation as organic and self-regenerating would seem inevitable. The increased naturalization of the nation is consistent with the vitalist view of nature 'as a powerful healthy force'.[174] Hence, we witness the advent of a 'vitalist ontology' of the nation that affirms the ability of post-revolutionary national bodies to recover independent of external assistance. The optimistic faith in the ability of societies to heal or at least sustain themselves, however precariously, that Burney expresses implicitly in her final novel departs from the Burkean concept of the nation as a 'fragile body'.[175] Where in the earlier part of the century (English) culture was largely pathologized and diagnosed as incurably morbid and suicidal, the perspective on culture offered in *The Wanderer* suggests a redemptive vision, albeit one that is achieved through the intervention of an individual from the outside. In this sense, Juliet, the Wanderer, might be construed as fulfilling a kind of messianic role, while her visit to the English enclave arguably belongs to the tradition of the Olympian Gods who disguised themselves as humble mortals in order to test humans' commitment to the rules of hospitality or *xenos*. By offering herself up to an undesirable marriage, Juliet saves the life of her guardian, the Bishop; through her physical and mental sacrifice of her body, she to a certain extent restores the larger community. In this sense, Juliet is Burney's most archetypal heroine and the closest she comes to creating a paragon.[176] The convergence of her French and English extended kin on the Brighton coast at the novel's end heralds the recuperation of a strong English body through the infusion of 'foreign' blood. In Burney's text, transnationalism enables a sense of nationality in a reversal of the standard position that international bonds are predicated on national identifications.[177]

In both *Camilla* and *The Wanderer*, Burney betrays a vexed attitude toward suicide. Her refusal to represent the consummation of her female characters' suicides resists both the Romanticist tendency to valorize voluntary death 'as a fashionable indicator of sensitivity and feeling', in the words of the historian Ralph Houlbrooke,[178] and suggests an insuperable life principle at work in the sensibility of her female characters. Composed during a period of unparalleled social, political and philosophical debate regarding the decriminalization and secularization of voluntary death, Burney's 'suicide narratives' establish the gothic novel as a 'vital' participant in the discussion, and moreover complicate the representation of voluntary death as a peculiarly 'female difficulty'. Burney's novels dwell specifically upon female encounters with voluntary death, perhaps because women in her texts are more readily mechanized than men, more subject to social constraints and systems of authority that drive them to attempt suicide. Impelled by external forces to end their existence, but kept alive by internal forces, women's bodies in these novels cannot simply 'self-destruct', as exemplified in Camilla's failed resolve to undergo an abbreviated version of Clarissa's death and Elinor's inability to launch herself into oblivion. Both the passive body and the active body persist, as these suicidal bodies essentially articulate both an embodiment and a repudiation of the mechanist doctrines espoused in this period. Vitalism lurks in the background, never a fully articulated idea, but presumably an influence upon Burney's anti-mechanist thinking.

As argued in Chapter 3, a notion of melancholy as both expressive and productive of a death drive invests suicide with both innate and natural properties. If some individuals were more naturally susceptible to melancholy than others, it follows that the suicidal impulse also might have an organic basis. However, Burney does not appear to subscribe to this notion of suicide as biologically determined. Like Staël in this respect and anticipating Durkheim, she sees it instead as a social phenomenon, caused either by the alienation of the individual from society as a result of early modern mercantile capitalist systems or as a result of the individual's over-integration into society and exposure to the anomie that afflicts it. In *Camilla* and *The Wanderer* women lack control over their bodies, which are both products of culture and subject to certain instinctive forces. In these novels, Burney recuperates a sense of vitality through resistance to mechanized models, even as she naturalizes a life-instinct as both a form of and mode of resistance to biopower.

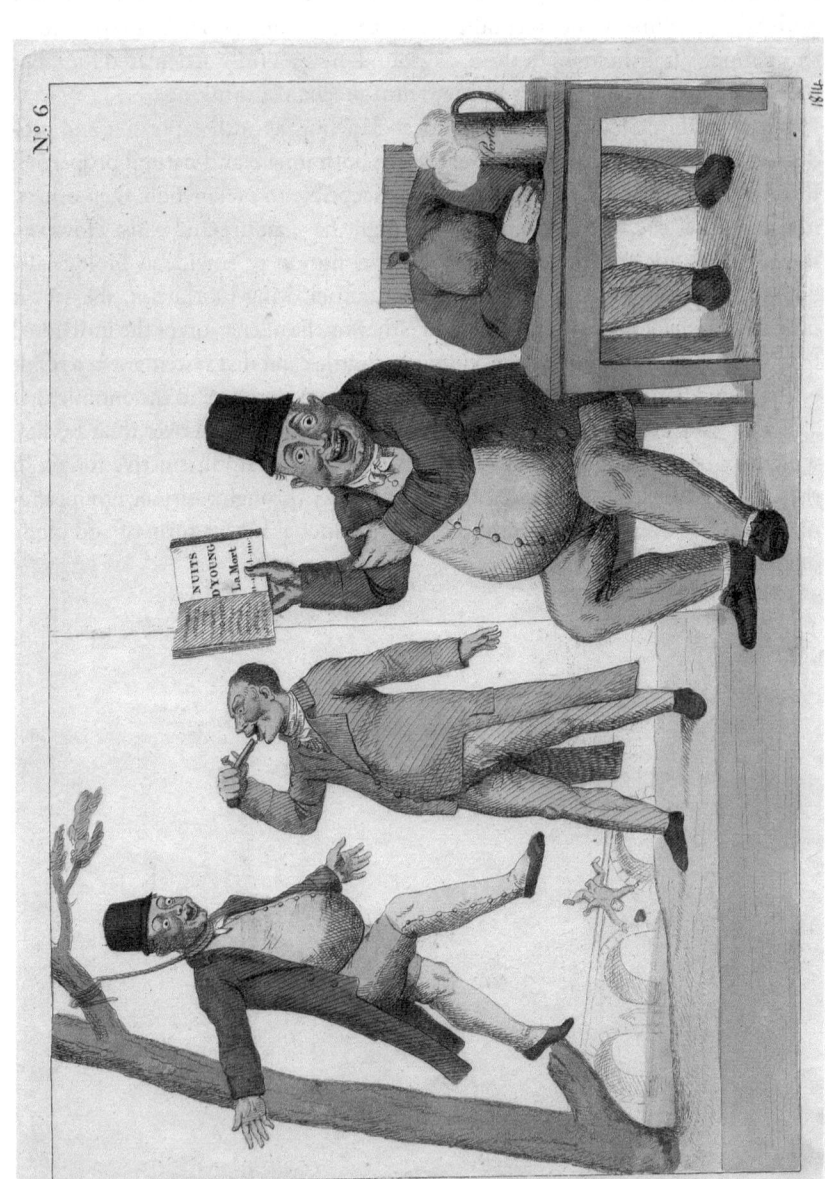

Figure C.1: Amusements des Anglais à Londres © Trustees of the British Museum

CONCLUSION

All nationalisms are gendered and all are invented and all are dangerous
Anne McClintock[1]

Although viewed today as an exploded myth and a stale relic of the Enlightenment, the eighteenth-century national cliché of English suicide has a longevity
exemplified in a 1814 French caricature with the caption *Amusements des Anglais
a Londres*.[2] The cartoon depicts Englishmen engaged in various forms of suicidal
practice. In the picture's foreground, a rather merry John Bull holds open a copy
of Edward Young's *Night Thoughts*, a mid-century poetic meditation on mortality intended to serve as a deterrent to suicide. In this context, Young's poem in
French translation appears both to afford a stimulus to voluntary death and to
confirm the English melancholic disposition. The scene behind this disconcert-
ingly jovial figure features a veritable festival of voluntary death, with one figure
engaged in hanging himself, his neighbour on the right poised to execute himself
with a pistol, another drinking himself into the grave courtesy of English ale, and
yet another plunging into the Thames, which was represented throughout the
century in French and English texts as a popular destination for people seeking
to end their lives.

Apart from the evident glee with which the various figures execute their
self-destructive designs, the lack of female participation in these 'high jinks' constitutes a conspicuous feature of the image. The cartoon presents English suicide
as an urban and exclusively male activity, the particular forte of John Bull. Given
that 'Mrs Bull' did not begin to appear alongside Mr Bull in popular visual representations until later in the nineteenth century, the fact that women figure
here as 'elided shadows' is scarcely surprising.[3] However, in the very year of the
cartoon's publication, an English celebration of victory at Waterloo featured a
woman dressed as Mrs Bull, a character that had hitherto been alien to British displays of patriotism and whose presence in this pageantry Linda Colley
reads as an indication of women's increased participation in national affairs.[4]
Nonetheless, Mrs Bull is largely a symbolic figure and, as numerous feminist
critics contend, the appropriation of women for symbolic purposes has historically resulted in a proportionate exclusion from the political arena.[5] Regardless

of the extent to which symbolic representation correlated with actual participation in national affairs, women were, as Colley points out, increasingly faced 'with the demands and meanings of Britishness', and at the turn of the century they were expected to increase the population that an 1800 census had indicated to be in decline.[6] Against this background, female suicide could be read as an unpatriotic act. Yet, as we have seen, many of these cultural demands upon the female body had already been played out through imaginative encounters with voluntary death earlier in the century. The high rate of female suicidal behaviour in the eighteenth-century English novel suggests that women's relations to the national imaginary were more than metaphorical. An increasing number of female suicides were reported in the periodical literature of the day, while medical investigations acknowledged that the 'spleen' or melancholia afflicted both sexes alike. The cultural medium of the novel affords a space for the representation of suicide, albeit in a form of self-accomplished death that does not quite conform to a modern understanding of the act. As legal nonentities, women did not breach a social contract through their voluntary deaths, yet the symbolic repercussions of the act were nonetheless manifold.

The models of civic and dynamic melancholy that scholars have found to be at work in this period warrant a reconsideration of the pathological component of the English Malady. Recent revisionist accounts of the history of pathology illuminate the functionalist approach to social illness and disease adopted by 'Whig' interests that contained and recuperated 'deviance' by constructing it as a mark of civility or progress and an indication of the affluence of English commercial enterprise. The 'rehabilitation' of the English Malady was enabled by the fact that melancholy was in itself a discursive entity. Owing partially to Robert Burton's *Anatomy*, the condition had a rhetorical dimension that rendered it a malleable discourse in the hands of those pursuing a political agenda. Melancholy could easily bear the sign of prosperity, whereas an act like suicide was less readily construed as a kind of discourse. Constructed as a symptom of English melancholy, suicide had a different status and was construed as an uneasy remainder of the rehabilitation of melancholy. If the violent act of 'self-homicide' – to borrow Donne's term – disrupted the rehabilitation project, it too eventually acquired the status of a discourse in its own right, owing partially to the so-called 'suicide debates' of the period that grappled with the question of whether suicide was a rational or irrational act, a natural or unnatural act, and even a voluntary or involuntary phenomenon.

In spite of the necessarily mediated nature of suicide, a purely discursive approach to the subject produces an effect of disembodiment that evacuates the materiality of the suicidal body, and it is this body that I have desired to retrieve and foreground. The novel is inordinately concerned with the embodied subject, and my study has attempted to reconnect discourses of suicide and melancholia with materiality. Accordingly, I have focused extensively upon medical engagements with suicide, examining the different ways in which vitalist and mechanist discourses construct the suicidal body, and how fears concerning the capacity of contagion to threaten the boundaries of the self were projected onto the suicidal body. Hypochondriacs like Samuel Richardson, a zealous disciple of Cheynean 'physick', and Dr John Shebbeare, whose concern with a national body politic was an extension of his care of the individual body, express an attitude towards suicide that foregrounds the embodied experience of voluntary death. Yet even as they naturalize the English Malady by highlighting the corporeal agency of suicide, these thinkers participate in the movement towards the diagnosis of insanity that inevitably accompanied the medicalization of the act.

Mental illness, however, has the status in this study as one of a host of contributing factors to the suicidal act. Rather than approaching suicide as an effect of social, individual or national concerns, I have tried to focus on the specific cultural meanings of the phenomenon itself. As the prominent suicidologist Antoon Leenars insists, 'suicide is not a disease ... not an immorality, not a biological anomaly, and not a neurological dysfunction'.[7] Rather, self-destruction is a constructed phenomenon, possessing a structure and internal logic contingent on historical context and profoundly demarcated by gender. Indeed, gender was a tool that eighteenth-century thinkers employed to define and understand the act, and suicide in turn arguably participated in the constitution of gender norms as well. Behaviour itself acquired a gender in this period, and since signs of weakness, excess, or folly were readily designated as feminine, suicide was accordingly aligned with femininity. That women were seen as incapable of committing suicide confirms theorists' arguments that gender floated free of sex in the incipiency of what Thomas Lacquer has termed the 'two sex model'.[8] Representing the 'part of the nation that is unchanging and "natural"'[9], on an abstract level women were viewed as being unable to undertake an act that was both unnatural and aligned with a higher tier of civility.[10]

This gender-coding necessarily reflects the devaluation of heroic models of suicide inherited from the Graeco-Roman tradition. In the wake of Augustinian proscriptions bolstered by Thomistic principles of natural law, an act that had previously brought with it shame or honour, depending upon the circumstances surrounding it, suddenly became deviant, sinful and immoral. At the same time, these proscriptions introduced a host of epistemological and hermeneutic problems in distinguishing between martyrdom and suicide, between 'wrongful' voluntary death and sanctioned *mors voluntaria*. Suicide now acquired an intentional structure: to commit suicide presupposed that one had a self that could not only be discarded but could also be interrogated after the fact. Suicide, then, as I have argued throughout this book, was productive of the self and represented a veritable technology of selfhood. The development of this sense of self, still inextricable from an idea of a soul in the period,[11] in turn introduced its own self-regulating, self-monitoring protocols that rendered external proscriptions in the form of canon and civil law superfluous. Natural law had never constituted merely an external proscription, for the principle of self-preservation that Thomas Aquinas formulated posited an internal regulator in the form of instinct. The logic of the Thomistic doctrine was fragile indeed, given that it based its proscription on an aporia: individuals should not commit suicide because they *could not.* The Foucauldian genealogical account of the shift from sovereign to disciplinary power implies that the obstacles to suicide were doubly determined on the level of the individual, owing to a notion of an instinct of self-preservation that remains with us today, and the fact that the body was now held hostage to a newly empowered soul. Natural law was not so much replaced as supplemented by biopower, which sought to render suicide a biological impossibility.

Meanwhile, even as a host of factors eroded the availability of suicide as a theoretical concept, suicide was imperceptibly translated into the rhetoric of sacrifice. Although occasionally contemporary authors challenged the notion of natural law, often through sustained attention to social phenomena such as the English Malady and the 'Werther effect' which gives way to an epidemiology of suicide and a suggestion that an analogue of a death drive might in fact afflict the human species, the rhetoric of sacrifice and a refurbished category of altruistic suicide inevitably complicate these discussions. As seen in Chapter Two, the difficulty of determining whether the discourse of martyrdom articulated in *Clarissa* reflects a residue of an older model of the Christian valorization of sacrifice or an emergent secularization of suicide results from the consistent overlapping and interpenetration of these discourses. Accordingly, Clarissa's death is simultaneously an act of martyrdom and a suicide, while suicidal gestures in the context of narratives concerned with nationalism or Jacobinism similarly at one and the same time constitute both sacrifice and suicide. The emergence of a permissive attitude towards suicide might in the final analysis reflect a cultural quandary, which renders the phenomenon both an integral aspect of the eighteenth-century novel and a defining feature of national identity. Elizabeth Castelli writes that 'martyrdom is hardwired into the collective consciousness of Western culture and is one of the central legacies of the Christian tradition'.[12] So pervasive is this concept that it informs attitudes towards suicide and pushes interpretations ever towards the sacrificial, perhaps an indication that the separation between the two acts which began with Augustine has always been somewhat forced. As formulated in the much of the literature of this period, suicide often occurs not for strictly egoistic purposes (regardless of what Durkheim might claim) but with a view to social and occasionally national benefit.

The translation of suicide into sacrifice imparts to the act a social structure, which in turn resonates with the construct of nation that, according to most accounts, had grown out of the religious and kinship systems of western culture. A Protestant nation has its own uses for sacrifice, as we have seen, which affect but do not necessarily annul individualism. But in the eighteenth century suicide vexed the very idea of social integrity; a nation in which citizens regularly withdrew their membership through voluntary death must lack a certain degree of stability. At the same time, the phenomenon was an index of progress, given that urbanization, the leisure afforded by rapid accumulation of wealth and the relaxation of ecclesiastical holds all participated in the construction of an English suicidal subject. From this perspective, suicide was formative, generating categories of identity and even, counter-intuitively, social cohesion. The structure of suicide as it was conceived at this time remained resolutely social, as the proliferation of print media prevented the most individual of acts from partaking in a private dimension. This, then, was the paradox: at the same moment that Western liberalism was giving birth to the individual, according to the standard narrative, the ultimate choice of the individual was itself precluded by the biopolitical apparatuses that infiltrated (especially) the human sciences. For this reason, suicide was a national event, and one in which women could participate in a self-sacrificial manner, even if this participation was not reflected in visual cultural representations.

Modern recuperations of the creative properties of suicide run counter to the metaphysical critique that the act obliterates an 'entire world', as articulated by Kant at the end of the Enlightenment.[13] Yet neither perspective completely captures the experience of suicide as mediated in the novel, which is at once transformative (insofar as it produces a sense of self) and intersubjective in that it is typically conceived as a social action. The extent to which suicide problematizes the relation between 'self' and 'other' becomes a central concern of novelistic engagements with the subject and is extended to a larger national and, eventually, transnational concern. Colonialist enterprise in the later decades of the eighteenth century encountered a form of female self-sacrifice in India that became the focus of intense scrutiny and received attention in a smattering of novels, which examine the impact that this 'new' form of suicide asserted upon British constructions of female suicide in their own land. Alongside the 'rehabilitation project', then, we can detect considerable anxiety surrounding suicide rates that resulted in attempts to displace the problem onto foreign soil.

In the epigraph to this conclusion, Anne McClintock voices a reservation towards Benedict Anderson's generally idealizing treatment of the idea of the nation. The emphasis that the national imaginary places on sacrifice – constituted, as I have argued in this book, as a form of voluntary death – is precisely what renders this construct so hazardous. The nation is etymologically linked to birth and, consequently, to life; yet it is also profoundly contoured by death, and in this construct women's sacrifices remain unacknowledged and are subsumed into the totality of the national community. The eighteenth-century novel reveals the problems of a community so defined and yet so threatened by the idea of voluntary death, yet simultaneously refuses to align sacrifice with the forfeiture of agency, as a gendered form of suicide closely aligned with sacrifice organizes resistance in the form of alternative communities existing alongside and within the nation. The Recluses, neo-Lucretias, Werthers and Wanderers that this book has discussed carve out alternative modes of agency and look ahead to Romantic discourse and its establishment of Antigone as a significant figure that was conspicuously absent from eighteenth-century engagements with female suicide.

The narrative of simultaneous growth and decay that this study has related views suicide as a construct forged in the same socio-cultural cauldron that produced the novel and the nation. The fact that gender attaches itself so persistently to suicide yet nonetheless remains 'unimagined' as a constituent element of national consciousness is acknowledged in an implicit manner in the eighteenth-century English novel. Viewed by its detractors as a symptom of the national malady, suicide in the novel also exposes the transnational constitution of English identity based upon its citizens' supposed suicidal proclivities. In the course of turning suicide into narrative, the eighteenth-century English novel translates the English affinity for casting themselves as martyrs to climate, nerves and newspapers into a productive rhetoric of suffering and in the process produces an early idea of a gendered nation.

NOTES

Introduction

1. 'A Receptacle for Suicides', *The World*, 9 September 1756, p. 169.
2. Ibid., p. 174.
3. Ibid.
4. Ibid., p. 172. Clearly, suicide was not so taboo that it could not be taken as a subject of satire, mock bills of mortality etc. W. Withers published a mock 'how to' manual on voluntary death early in the century entitled *Some Thoughts Concerning Suicide, or Self-Killing, with General Directions for the More Easie Dispatch of the Affair. Written for the Benefit of all Malecontents in Great Britain* (1711). Towards the end of the century, a comedy called *The Suicide* enjoyed enormous popularity on the London stage.
5. Eighteenth-century philosophers and social theorists employed a transliteration of the Latin term, *mors voluntaria*, to emphasize the centrality of the role of will in such deaths. The term occurs sporadically throughout the novel, although self-murder, initially, and later suicide, are the favoured terms. As Daube notes, 'Latin *mors voluntaria* stresses the voluntary nature of such dying, English "suicide", self-killing, the fact that oneself is the object'. D. Daube, *The Linguistics of Suicide* (Princeton, NJ: Princeton University Press, 1972), p. 14.
6. See Z. Bayatrizi, *Life Sentences: The Ordering of Mortality* (Toronto: University of Toronto Press, 2010), p. 98, and Daube for an account of the linguistic history of suicide.
7. For the etymology of the term, see B. Barraclough and D. Shepard, 'A Necessary Neologism: The Origin and Uses of Suicide', *Suicide and Life-Threatening Behaviour*, 24:2 (1994), pp. 113–24.
8. Nineteenth-century medical researchers in France sought out both a suicide organ and a 'stay-alive' organ (as will be discussed in Chapter 5), while ongoing current research attempts to isolate a 'suicide gene'.
9. While Foucault's approach might afford an understanding of suicide's simultaneous subjection and resistance to the operations of power, his suggestion that the politicization of suicide does not properly begin until a notion of biopower has been firmly established treats the act as a metaphysical rather than an anthropological phenomenon. (For a critique of Foucault's failure to explain how it is that power impinges on bodies, see G. Agamben, *Homo Sacer: Sovereign Power and Bare Life*, trans. D. Heller-Roazen (Palo Alto, CA: Stanford University Press, 1998), p. 5.)
10. B. Jennings, 'Biopower and the Liberationist Romance', *The Hastings Report*, 40:4 (2010), pp. 16–20.

11. M. Foucault, *The History of Sexuality. Volume One*, trans., R. Hurley (New York: Vintage, 1990), p. 139.

12. I. Marsh, *Suicide: Foucault, History, and Truth* (Cambridge: Cambridge University Press, 2010), p. 99.

13. Ibid., p. 142.

14. In his reading of 'bare life' in *Homo Sacer*, Agamben argues that biopower predates modernity. In his critique of Foucault's understanding of the biopoitical, Agamben points out that Foucault fails to adequately explain how it is that power impinges on bodies. Agamben, *Homo Sacer*, p. 5.

15. D. Smith, *The Conceptual Practices of Power: A Feminist Sociology of Knowledge* (Toronto: University of Toronto Press, 1990), pp. 144–45.

16. Ibid., p. 145.

17. Bayatrizi, *Life Sentences*, p. 74.

18. D. LaCapra, *History, Politics, and the Novel* (Ithaca, NY: Cornell University Press, 1987), p. 4.

19. T. Bennett, 'Sociology, Aesthetics, Expertise', *New Literary History*, 41:2 (2010), pp. 253–76, on p. 3.

20. This is a common critique of Foucault, offered by theorists Judith Butler and Elizabeth Grosz, among others.

21. J. Locke, *Second Treatise of Government*, ed. C. B. Macpherson (Indianapolis, IN: Hackett Press, 1980), p. 83. Lester Crocker and Gary Glenn have offered cogent readings of the question of suicide in relation to Lockean property theory.

22. D. Andrew, 'Debate: The Secularization of Suicide in England 1660–1800', *Past and Present*, 119 (1988), pp. 158–65, on p. 159.

23. According to traditional practice, property reverted to the crown when suicides were found *felo de se* (a law that was not overturned until 1823, notwithstanding the supposed spread of tolerance for the deed.). As historian R. Houlbrooke observes, the act was 'largely decriminalized *de facto* if not *de jure*'. R. Houlbrooke, *Death, Religion, and the Family in England, 1480–1750* (Oxford: Clarendon Press, 1998), on p. 219.

24. I. Hacking, *The Taming of Chance* (Cambridge: Cambridge University Press, 1990), p. 3.

25. T. Hobbes, *Leviathan*, ed. C. B. Macpherson (London: Penguin, 1968), p. 189.

26. T. Aquinas, *Summa Theologica* (New York: Benziger, Bruce, and Glencoe, 1948), part 2, 2ae, p. 64.

27. Wendeborn, Mr, 'On the Character of the English', *The Literary Magazine and British Review* (London: C. Forster, 1791), pp. 193–97, on p. 196.

28. Josephus offers an early conflation of the 'law of nature' with 'natural law' in his assertion that 'among the animals there is not one that deliberately seeks death or kills itself; so firmly rooted is all nature's law – the will to live'. Cited in A. J. L. van Hoof, *From Autothanasia to Suicide: Self-Killing in Classical Antiquity* (London: Routledge, 1990), p. 120.

29. According to Colin Pritchard, 'Donne started the essential and necessary work of dissecting out from canonical and secular law the prohibitions and some of the stigma and terrors of suicide', and this is why he figures so largely in this account of the intellectual historical background to the suicide debate. C. Pritchard, *Suicide – The Ultimate Rejection? A Psycho-Social Study* (Buckingham: Open University Press, 1995), p. 15.

30. As John Donne writes, 'Another reason, which prevails much with me and delivers it from being against the law of nature, is this, that in all ages, in all places, upon all occasions, men of all conditions have affected it and inclined to do it'. Donne, *Biathanatos*, eds. M. Rudick and M. Pabst Battin (New York: Garland Press, 1982), p. 64.

31. B. Mandeville, *The Fable of the Bees: Or, Private Vices, Publick Benefits*, ed. P. Harth (New York: Penguin, 1970), p. 151.

32. J. Bentham notoriously dismisses natural law as 'nonsense upon stilts'.

33. D. Hume, *Essays on Suicide and the Immortality of the Soul* (Bristol: Thoemmes Press, 1992), p. 11.

34. Hume's elaboration of a form of civic suicide that relieves impediments to the public interest expresses a sentiment in circulation at the time appealing to the social benefit of voluntary death.

35. J. Cockburn, *A Discourse of Self-Murder: In Which the Heinousness of the Sin Is Expos'd* (London, 1716), p. 8.

36. P. Booth, *A Discourse On Self-Murder: Or The Cause, the Nature, and Immediate Consequences of Self-Murder, Fully Examined and Truly Stated* (London: Tho. Green, 1732), p. 13.

37. I. Kant, 'Duties towards the Body in Regard to Life', in J. Donnelly (ed.), *Suicide: Right or Wrong?* (Amherst, NY: Prometheus Books, 1998), pp. 50–7, on p. 55.

38. D. Gracia, 'Ownership of the Human Body: Some Historical Remarks', in A. M. J. Henk, T. Have, and J. V. M. Welie (eds), *Ownership of the Human Body: Philosophical Considerations on the Use of the Human Body and Its Parts in Healthcare* (Boston, MA: Kluwer Academic Publishers, 1998), pp. 67–80, on p. 72.

39. Abbé C. F. X. Millot, *Elements of the History of England, from the Invasion of the Romans to the Reign of George II* (London: J. Dodsley, 1771), p. 362.

40. J. G. A. Pocock dwells at length upon the customary association of British virtue with liberty in this period. Margaret Healy notes that 'The Whigs appear to have promoted the disease, citing it as evidence of Britain's economic success (a healthy constitution allowed more resources and time for self-indulgence), whereas, conversely, the Tories represented it as evidence of the country's decline and political failure'. M. Healy, *Fictions of Disease in Early Modern England: Bodies, Plagues and Politics* (New York: Palgrave, 2001), pp. 8–9.

41. E. Gidal, 'Civic Melancholy: English Gloom and French Enlightenment', *ECS*, 37:1 (2003), pp. 23–45, on p. 34.

42. M. Higonnet, 'Suicide: Representations of the Feminine in the Nineteenth Century', *Poetics Today*, 6 (1985), pp. 103–18, p. 104.

43. P. J. Grosley, *A Tour to London: Or, New Observations on England and Its Inhabitants*, trans. T. Nuge (Dublin, 1772), p. 237.

44. J. Prince, *Self-Murder Asserted to Be a Very Heinous Crime; in Opposition to All Arguments Brought by the Deists, to the Contrary* (London: B. Bragge, 1709), p. 7.

45. M. E. Novak, 'Boundaries of the Self: Crises of Mind and Body' (Review), *Eighteenth-Century Studies*, 37:4 (2004), pp. 683–6, on p. 686.

46. C. Gildon, *The Deist's Manual: Or, A Rational Enquiry into the Christian Religion* (London: A. Roper, 1705), p. i.

47. Ibid., p. ii.

48. Ibid., p. iii.

49. C. de Beccaria, *On Crimes and Punishments* (1764) (New York: Bobbs-Merrill, 1963).

50. Gildon, *The Deist's Manual*, p. iii.

51. Ibid., p. iv.

52. N. Hudson, *Samuel Johnson and the Making of Modern England* (Cambridge: Cambridge University Press, 2003), p. 131.

53. 'A Receptacle for Suicides', *The World*, 9 September 1756, p. 170.

54. Ibid., p. 431.
55. With the exception of J. Adams, *An Essay Concerning Self-Murther* (London: Tho. Bennett, 1700), which repeatedly represents suicide as the folly of women; looking back to ancient Rome, Adams argues that the majority of suicides in the golden era of Roman republicanism were in fact committed by women.
56. E. Grosz, *Volatile Bodies: Toward a Corporeal Feminism* (Bloomington, IN: Indiana University Press, 1994), pp. 35–6.
57. M. Douglas, *Purity and Danger: An Analysis of Concepts of Pollution and Taboo* (New York: Praeger, 1966), p. 215.
58. E. Durkheim, *Suicide: A Study in Sociology*, trans. John A. Spaulding (New York: Mac-Millan Press, 1951), p. 166. H. Kushner observes that 'suicidal behaviour among men has generally been portrayed as originating from economic and social conditions, whereas suicidal behaviour in women has typically been attributed to interpersonal, familial relations, or, less frequently, to women adopting male roles. Thus, experts have concluded that men's suicidal behaviour, especially suicide mortality rates, can serve as a barometer of social and economic well-being, but women's suicidal behaviour is a private issue requiring less public concern'. H. Kushner, 'Women and Suicidal Behaviour: Epidemiology, Gender and Lethality in Historical Perspective', in S. Canetto and D. Lester (eds), *Women and Suicidal Behaviour* (New York: Springer Press, 1995), pp. 11–35, on p. 26.
59. H. R. Fedden, *Suicide: A Social and Historical Study* (New York: Benjamin Blom, 1972), p. 326.
60. Kushner, 'Women and Suicidal Behaviour', p. 13.
61. Ibid., p. 13.
62. S. Chapone, *The Hardships of the English Laws in Relation to Wives* (London: W. Bowyer, 1735), p. 24. R. and B. Smith were the husband and wife who in 1732 notoriously took their child's life before taking their own, leaving behind an exhaustive philosophical defence of suicide along with a note enjoining their landlady to take care of their pets. Their note was published in the *Gentleman's Magazine* (1732, vol. 2).
63. Ibid., p. 24.
64. S. During has argued that 'part of the modern domination of the life-world by style and civility ... is a process of the feminization of society'. S. During, 'Literature – Nationalism's Other? The Case for Revision', in H. K. Bhabha (ed.) *Nation and Narration* (London: Routledge, 1990), pp. 138–53, on p. 143.
65. R. Brown, *The Art of Suicide* (London: Reaktion, 2001), p. 3. Brown's *The Art of Suicide* focuses specifically on visual culture and 'the historical production and relations of meanings of suicide as they interrelate with gender and nation', p. 9.
66. M. Higonnet, 'Speaking Silences: Women's Suicide', in S. R. Suleiman (ed.), *The Female Body in Western Culture: Contemporary Perspectives* (Cambridge, MA: Harvard University Press, 1986), pp. 68–83, on p. 69.
67. Moreover, in her illuminating articles on suicide, Higonnet's concern is largely with non-English writings.
68. A. Gilroy, '"Candid Advice to the Fair Sex" or, The Politics of Maternity in Late Eighteenth-Century Britain', in Hornver and Keane (eds), *Body Matters*, pp. 17–28, on p. 17.
69. J. Butler argues that construction functions as 'a constitutive constraint' producing 'unthinkable, abject, unlivable bodies' that haunt the domain of intelligibility. See J. Butler, *Bodies That Matter: On the Discursive Limits of 'Sex'* (New York: Routledge, 1993), p. xi. In many respects the female suicidal body 'abjected' from the social order corresponds to this 'unlivable body'.

70. For a particularly incisive treatment of modern medicine's 'ontology of death', see D. Leder, 'A Tale of Two Bodies: the Cartesian Corpse and the Lived Body', in D. Welton (ed.), *Body and Flesh: A Philosophical Reader* (Malden, MA: Blackwell Press, 1998), pp. 54–78.

71. For an objections to Butler's early theory of a discourse without bodies see Grosz, *Volatile Bodies*.

72. C. L. Johnson, *Equivocal Beings: Politics, Gender, and Sentimentality in the 1790s: Wollstonecraft, Radcliffe, Burney, Austen* (Chicago, IL: University of Chicago Press, 1995), p. 14.

73. G. Vaughn, 'Mother, Co-muni-cation, and the Gifts of Language', in E. Wyschogrod (ed.), *The Enigma of Gift and Sacrifice* (New York: Fordham University Press, 2002), pp. 91–116, on p. 94.

74. L. Brown, *Ends of Empire: Women and Ideology in Early Eighteenth-Century English Literature* (Ithaca, NY: Cornell University Press, 1993), p. 3.

75. Kushner, 'Women and Suicidal Behaviour, on p. 27.

76. S. Aravamudan, *Tropicopolitans: Colonialism and Agency, 1688–1804* (Durham, NC: Duke University Press, 1999), p. 122. Aravamudan argues this point in the context of an examination of the suicide of 'classical African queens'.

77. S. Sontag, *Illness as Metaphor* (New York: Farrar, Strauss and Giroux, 1978), p. 11.

78. M. McKeon, *Theory of the Novel* (Baltimore, MD: Johns Hopkins Press, 2000), p. 397. Echoing McKeon, N. Johnson affirms that 'destabilizing hegemonic categories and mediating historical events has long been a function of the novel'. N. Johnson, *The English Jacobin Novel on Rights, Property and the Law: Critiquing the Contract* (London: Palgrave, 2004), p. 13.

79. V. Knox, *Essays Moral and Literary* (Dublin, R. Marchbank, 1783), p. 123. Voluntary death was already established as a common subject of theatre during this period. The perception of suicide as a fundamentally tragic act led to its frequent representation upon the stage, and eighteenth-century drama resurrected the notion of the 'heroic suicide' in its affinity for the biographies of Cato and Seneca. As playwrights in their other literary capacities, many eighteenth-century writers, such as E. Haywood and F. Burney, draw upon the stock of tragedy in their novelistic representations of both the deed and the perpetrator, although they temper its dramatic materials with prolonged debate regarding the issue of voluntary death and its relevance to the construction of female identity. As a result, many of their narratives adhere to what N. Loraux has termed the 'law of femininity' in respect to classical tragedy, dictating that 'in the existence of misery a knotted rope should provide the way out'. N. Loraux, *Tragic Ways of Killing a Woman*, trans, A. Forster (Cambridge, MA: Harvard University Press, 1987), p. 8.

80. J. R. Timmons, 'A 'Fatal Remedy': Melancholy and Self-Murder in Eighteenth-Century England', in P. Korshin (ed.), *The Age of Johnson* (New York: AMS Press, 1990), vol. 10, pp. 259–84, on p. 279.

81. Ibid., p. 279.

82. M. MacDonald and T. R. Murphy, *Sleepless Souls: Suicide in Early Modern England* (Oxford: Clarendon Press, 1990), p. 5. As MacDonald and Murphy observe 'older, ritual kinds of communication based on the local community were gradually eclipsed by the new forms of print media, notably newspapers and magazines, that spread news throughout the whole nation'. Ibid., p. 9. Neither Murphy nor MacDonald subscribe to the 'positivist' Durkheimian sociological study dependent on statistics in the manner

of studies of nineteenth-century suicide, such as Olive Anderson's study of nineteenth-century suicide.

83. As MacDonald and Murphy observe, '[J]urors had become cultural amphibians, equipped to inhabit both the literate realm of the educated elite and the oral domain of folk tradition'. Ibid., p. 142.

84. Just one of many historiographies of suicide published in the 1990s, their survey supplies much of the material for the treatment of English suicide in G. Minois, in his *History of Suicide: Voluntary Death in Western Culture*, trans. Lydia G. Cochrane (Baltimore, MD: Johns Hopkins Press, 1999), which supports the standard thesis that attitudes towards suicide became more tolerant over time, even while it highlights the relevance of class difference to the eighteenth-century experience of suicide.

85. R. Healy, 'Suicide in Early Modern and Modern Europe' *Historical Journal*, 49 (2006), pp. 903–19, on p. 903.

86. J. Shaw, *Miracles in Enlightenment England* (New Haven, CT: Yale University Press, 2006), p. 18.

87. J. C. W Truman, 'John Foxe and the Desires of Reformation Martyrology', *ELH*, 70:1 (2003), pp. 35–66, on p. 36.

88. E. A. Castelli, *Martyrdom and Memory: Early Christian Culture Making* (New York: Columbia University Press, 2004), on p. 61.

89. Ibid., p. 63.

90. Ibid., p. 61. As Monta observes, 'the gendering of martyrdom as a form of masculinized heroism has a long history'. S. B. Monta, *Martyrdom and Literature in Early Modern England* (Cambridge: Cambridge University Press, 2005), p. 211. John Foxe's euphemism for suicide – 'play the man' – indicates the rhetorical moves that contribute to this process of gendering.

91. J. Derrida, *The Gift of Death*, trans. D. Willis (Chicago, IL: University of Chicago Press, 1995), p. 76.

92. M. Astell, *A Serious Proposal to the Ladies* (New York: Source Book Press, 1970), p. 123.

93. M. Joy insists that 'the symbolic economy of the western tradition and partriarchal religion is underwritten and mediated by the sacrifice of women'. M. Joy, 'Beyond the Given and the All-Giving: Reflections on Women and the Gift' *Australian Feminist Studies*, 14:30 (1999), pp. 315–32, on pp. 328–9. J. Butler suggests that identity occurs only through repression and exclusion in Butler, *Bodies That Matter*, pp. 3 and 52. J. Lacan and J. Derrida both identify Western culture as sacrificial; indeed, as J. MacCannell observes, psychoanalytical models are 'dangerously sacrificial and death-oriented'. J. MacCannell, *The Regime of the Brother: After the Patriarchy* (London: Routledge, 1991), p. 20. The idea of sacrifice has acquired such a centrality that theorists such as A. Caldwell can justly observe contemporary theory's 'growing consensus that order and identity are necessarily sacrificial'. A. Caldwell, 'Transforming Sacrifice: Irigaray and the Politics of Sexual Difference' *Hypatia*, 17:4 (2002), pp. 16–39, on p. 16. Caldwell goes so far as to argue for a 'sacrificial matrix' located at the heart of Western culture. Ibid., p. 20.

94. S. M. Wolf, 'Gender, Feminism, and Death: Physician-Assisted Suicide and Euthanasia', in S. M. Wolf (ed.), *Feminism and Bioethics: Beyond Reproduction* (Oxford: Oxford University Press, 1996), p. 282–317.

95. D. Raymond, '"Fatal Practices": A Feminist Analysis of Physician-Assisted Suicide and Euthanasia', *Hypatia*, 14:2 (1999): pp. 1–25, p. 10. D. Davis argues that 'those who oppose rational suicide are asking women to shoulder yet another traditional female burden: the preservation of society's moral and religious values. The stereotypical virtues

assigned to Victorian women of "piety, purity, submissiveness, and domesticity" ... can as easily be harnessed by traditionalists to argue against suicide as for it'. D. Davis, 'Why Suicide Is Like Contraception', in M. P. Battin, R. Rhodes, and A. Silvers (eds), *Physician Assisted Suicide* (New York: Routledge, 1998), p. 110.

96. This argument might seem to contradict my earlier argument regarding the effect of the socio-linguistic phenomenon of the 'invention' of suicide; however, while the introduction of the term both reflects and produces a narrow, or at least more homogenizing understanding of voluntary death, at the same time, later political and social developments inevitably assert an impact upon the definition of the concept of suicide.

97. Durkheim, *Suicide*, p. 239. As evidence, Durkheim invokes the deaths of Cato and the Girondins which were not deemed suicides by two prominent nineteenth-century French doctors, Esquirol and Falret.

98. Durkheim, *Suicide*, p. 240.

99. R. Walz, *Pulp Surrealism: Insolent Popular Culture in Early Twentieth-Century Paris* (Berkeley, CA: University of California Press, 2000), p. 127.

100. I. Strenski, *Contesting Sacrifice: Religion, Nationalism, and Social Thought in France* (Chicago, IL: University of Chicago Press, 2002), p. 153.

101. J. Mostov, 'Sexing the Nation/Desexing the Body', in T. Meyer (ed.), *Gender Ironies of Nationalism: Sexing the Nation* (London: Routledge, 2000), pp. 89–112, on p. 91.

102. In her introduction to *Gender Ironies of Nationalism*, Meyer argues that 'Because nationalism, gender and sexuality are all socially and culturally constructed, they frequently play an important role in constructing one another – by invoking and helping to construct the "us" versus "them" distinction and the exclusion of another'. T. Meyer, 'Gender Ironies of Nationalism. Setting the Stage', in Meyer (ed.), *Gender Ironies of Nationalism*, pp. 1–24, on p. 1.

103. Recent treatments of Anderson have critiqued the totalizing aspect of his salutary attitude towards the nation. In reference to Anderson's passing gender-related remarks, E. Probyn observes, 'it is hard not to feel that once again women in the guise of gender are being wheeled in as evidence of a universal materiality while the nation floats off as the abstract. In fact, it would be really paradoxical that the concrete social category of gender is taken as a universal condition if it were not for the way in which nations seem to inevitably come draped in feminine metaphors'. E. Probyn, 'Bloody Metaphors and Other Allegories of the Ordinary', in N. Alarcón, C. Kaplan, and M. Moallem (eds), *Between Woman and Nation: Nationalisms, Transnational Feminisms, and the State* (Durham, NC: Duke University Press, 1999), pp. 47–62, on p. 49. Although I agree that Anderson's exaltation of the nation is extreme, his study continues to shed illumination upon the constructedness of an idea of the nation.

104. J. P. Hunter, *Before Novels: The Cultural Contexts of Eighteenth-Century English Fiction* (New York, W.W. Norton & Co., 1990), p.144.

105. Ibid., p. 144.

106. Yet at the same time I do not altogether agree with James Thompson's claim that 'The cultural work of the novel ... despite its content of fragmentation, isolation, and alienation, is to construct or suture a historically specific (and ... severely limited.) wholeness'. J. Thompson, *Models of Value: Eighteenth-Century Political Economy and the Novel* (Durham, NC: Duke University Press, 1996), p. 194.

107. C. Routledge and J. Arndt, 'Self-sacrifice as Self-Defence: Mortality Salience Increases Efforts to Affirm a Symbolic Immortal Self at the Expense of the Physical Self', *European Journal of Social Psychology* 38:3 (2008), pp. 531–41, on p. 532.

108. Ibid., p. 539.
109. Strenski, *Contesting Sacrifice*.
110. I. Strenski, *Theology and the First Theory of Sacrifice* (Leiden: Brill, 2003), p. 8. As Strenski observes, Girard views sacrifice as a kind of moral fault, whereas for Levi-Strauss, it is a kind of 'illusion' like totemism. Strenski reserves his harshest criticism for Mizruchi, whose argument that the language of sacrifice in the nineteenth century takes on a 'social scientific dimension' he finds to be utterly untenable given the residual traces of religiosity in any public discourse of sacrifice.
111. Ibid., p. 8.
112. F. Jameson, *Fables of Aggression: Wyndham Lewis, the Modernist as Fascist* (Berkeley, CA: University of California Press, 1979), on p. 12.

1 Suicide and Spectrality in Eliza Haywood's Amatory Fiction

1.   H. Arendt, *The Human Condition* (Chicago, IL: The University of Chicago Press, 1989), p. 34.
2.   Ibid., p. 35.
3.   Ibid., p. 7.
4.   A. Ferguson, *Essay on the History of Civil Society* (1767), ed. L. Schneider (New Brunswick, NJ: Transaction, 1980), p. 183.
5.   According to Habermas's now definitive but embattled account, the eighteenth century saw the formation of a public sphere. See J. Habermas, *The Structural Transformation of the Public Sphere: An Inquiry into a Category of Bourgeois Society*, trans. T. Burger (Cambridge, MA: MIT Press, 1996).
6.   M. McKeon, *The Secret History of Domesticity* (Baltimore, MD: Johns Hopkins University Press, 2007), p. 3.
7.   L. Berlant, *The Female Complaint: the Unfinished Business of Sentimentality in Contemporary American Culture* (Durham, NC: Duke University Press, 2008), p. 110.
8.   J. Derrida, *Specters of Marx*, trans. P. Kamuf (New York: Routledge, 1994), p. 46.
9.   McKeon, *The Secret History of Domesticity*, p. 639.
10. Berlant, *The Female Complaint*, p. 2.
11. In *Acts of Religion*, J. Derrida characterizes spectrality as an 'excess above and beyond the living, whose life only has absolute value by being worth more than life'. See J. Derrida, *Acts of Religion* (New York: Routledge, 2002), p. 87.
12. In a sense, Haywood's protagonists are endowed with the 'phantasmatic investment and phantasmatic promise' that, according to Judith Butler, is typically associated with women's experience. See Butler, *Bodies That Matter*, p. 191.
13. V. Coopan, *Worlds Within: National Narratives and Global Connections in Postcolonial Writing* (Palo Alto, CA: Stanford University Press, 2009), p. 32.
14. E. Haywood, *Reflections on the Various Effects of Love, According to the Contrary Dispositions of the Person on Whom It Operates* (London: N. Dobb, 1726), p. 11.
15. As R. Ballaster observes, in Haywood's novels 'Male desire is, with rare exceptions, short-lived and end-directed, constituting a series of metonymical displacements of woman for woman in search of an impossible and unattainable satisfaction. Female desire is masochistic, self-destructive and hysterical.' See R. Ballaster, *Seductive Forms: Women's Amatory Fiction from 1684 to 1740* (Oxford: Clarendon Press, 1992), p. 175.
16. E. Haywood, *Three Novellas: The Distress'd Orphan; The Double Marriage; The City Jilt*, ed. E. A. Wilputte (East Lansing: Colleagues Press, 1995), p. 76.

17. In this sense, Freud's thesis, first articulated in *Mourning and Melancholia*, holds some relevance; according to Freud, suicide represents a redirection inwards of anger harboured toward an exterior object.

18. E. Haywood, *The British Recluse*, in P. Backscheider and J. Richetti (eds), *Popular Fiction by Women, 1660–1730* (Oxford: Oxford University Press, 1996), p. 160.

19. Ibid., p. 160.

20. Haywood, *Reflections on the Various Effects of Love*, pp. 55–6.

21. Berlant, *The Female Complaint*, p. 15.

22. Both M. Williamson and A. Messenger read Haywood as a 'survivalist' determined to assist her female readers in adapting to 'existing social structure'. See M. Williamson, *Raising Their Voices: British Women Writers, 1650–1750* (Detroit, MI: Wayne State University Press, 1990), p. 11. For a comparable argument, see A. Messenger, *His and Hers: Essays in Restoration and Eighteenth-Century Literature* (Lexington, KY: University Press of Kentucky, 1986). J. Merritt similarly reads Haywood as a 'strategist' who 'as a writer seeking discursive authority and as a feminist seeking methods for women to increase their cultural, sexual and economic power, emphasized prudence, discernment, and self-awareness'. See J. Merritt, *Beyond Spectacle: Eliza Haywood's Female Spectators* (Toronto: University of Toronto Press, 2004), p. 8. Merritt emphatically rejects the common interpretation of Haywood's work (especially her early fiction) as an endorsement of female victimhood, and instead argues for the 'strong will to power' demonstrated by many of Haywood's female protagonists. Ibid., p. 23. I find this position more appealing, although slightly more difficult to negotiate than the standard view.

23. E. Haywood, *The Female Spectator* (1744–6), p. 172.

24. G. Fairbairn critiques the 'impoverished language and conceptual apparatus available for discussing suicide and related acts' in today's society. G. Fairbairn, 'Suicide, Language, and Clinical Practice', *Philosophy, Psychiatry, & Psychology*, 5:2 (1998), pp. 157–69, on p. 157. However, as Haywood demonstrates, the eighteenth century afforded a much broader range of terms prior to the common acceptance of the word 'suicide'.

25. Fairbairn, 'Suicide, Language, and Clinical Practice', p. 157.

26. *The Invisible Spy* (1755) is the first of Haywood's works to employ the word 'suicide'.

27. Haywood, *Three Novellas*, p. 19.

28. Haywood, *Idalia: or, The Unfortunate Mistress* (London: D. Browne, 1723), p. 39. In *Love in Excess*, Alovisa contemplates laying violent hands on her own life. In *Memoirs of a certain island adjacent to the Kingdom of Utopia* (1725) 'the miser was ready to lay violent hands on his own life'. In *The Untimely Discovery* 'nothing was every more deserving wonder than that this unfortunate lady did not lay violent hands upon herself'.

29. J. Richetti, 'Histories by Eliza Haywood and Henry Fielding: Imitation and Adaptation', in K. T. Saxton and R. P. Bocchiccio (eds), *The Passionate Fictions of Eliza Haywood: Essays on her Life and Work* (Lexington, KY: University Press of Kentucky, 2000), pp. 240–58, on p. 241. Another favourite expression of Haywood's for referring to suicide is 'act of horror'.

30. K. T. Saxton, 'Telling Tales: Eliza Haywood and the Crimes of Seduction in *The City Jilt, or, The Alderman turn'd Beau*', in Saxton and Bocchicchio (eds), *The Passionate Fictions of Eliza Haywood*, pp. 115–42, on p. 116.

31. E. Haywood, 'The Fruitless Enquiry', in *Secret Histories, Novels, and Poems. Written by Mrs. Eliza Haywood* (London: S. Richardson, 1732), p. 252.

32. E. Haywood, 'The Rash Resolve', in *Secret Histories, Novels, and Poems*, p. 86.

33. To clarify, I do not refer to a death drive in the Freudian or Lacanian sense of the term. As S. Zizek has demonstrated, the will to die and the death drive are radically distinct and by no means reducible to each other. Zizek argues in his discussion of Lacan that the subject can never possess the act since there is always a disjunction between the will and the act. The death drive functions independently of the will. See S. Zizek, *The Plague of Fantasies* (London: Verso, 1997), p. 224.

34. Ballaster, *Seductive Forms*, p. 12.

35. Haywood, *Love in Excess*, ed. D. Oakleaf (Peterborough, ON: Broadview, 1994), p.173.

36. Ibid., p. 176.

37. From the twentieth-century perspective of Freudian psychopathology, Alovisa's 'accident' would be interpreted as merely her body's actualization of her unconscious desires.

38. Haywood, *Love in Excess*, p. 261.

39. Ibid., p. 273.

40. S. Black describes this as 'the standard inexpressibility topos that belongs to the discourse of love'. S. Black, 'Trading Sex for Secrets in Haywood's *Love in Excess*', *Eighteenth-Century Fiction*, 15:2 (2003), pp. 207–26, on p. 212.

41. L. Grainger, *Modern Amours* (London, 1733), p. 68.

42. According to Shebbeare's pseudonym, B. Angeloni, 'Catholics have a "cure" that Protestants do not' and 'it is to the want of this resource in England that this horrid crime of suicide is chiefly to be attributed'. [J. Shebbeare], *Letters on the English Nation: by Batista Angeloni, a Jesuit, Who Resided Many Years in London* (London: 1755), p. 32.

43. Haywood, *Love in Excess*, p. 296.

44. In her final speech, Violetta enjoins the gathered company that 'they all may be witnesses with what pleasure [she] welcome[s] [death]'. Ibid., p. 295.

45. T. Bowers, 'Collusive Resistance: Sexual Agency and Partisan Politics in *Love and Excess*', in Saxton and Bocchicchio (eds), *The Passionate Fictions of Eliza Haywood*, pp. 48–68, on p. 50.

46. Although, notably, this is not the husband of the title.

47. This at least represents the view of J. Beasley, who remarks of the Baroness of *The Injur'd Husband* that 'such a woman, no matter what the fascination with her power, is beyond redemption; Haywood ends the story by causing her to die horribly from a suicidal dose of poison, following her exposure'. J. Beasley, '*Clarissa* and Early Female Fiction', in C. Houlihan Flynn and E. Copeland (eds), *Clarissa and her Readers: New Essays for the Clarissa Project* (New York: AMS Press, 1999), pp. 69–96, on p. 77.

48. Haywood, *The Injur'd Husband, or, The Mistaken Resentment* (London: D. Browne, 1723), p. 100.

49. Haywood, *Love in Excess*, p. 144.

50. In Bowers's estimation, 'Haywood (in Melliora) imagines a heroine whose active, transgressive sexual desire operates in concert with her virtue by means of a paradox that we might call "collusive resistance", a kind of submission that is itself ultimately a form of agency'. Bowers, 'Collusive Resistance: Sexual Agency and Partisan Politics in *Love and Excess*', p. 58.

51. *Hunter, Before Novels*.

52. Cited in MacDonald and Murphy, *Sleepless Souls*, p. 282.

53. Haywood, *The Double Marriage, or, The Fatal Release* (London: J. Roberts, 1726), p. 107.

54. N. Miller, *The Heroine's Plot* (New York: Columbia University Press, 1980), p. 12. The chastity-suicide (which will be addressed in the following chapter) does not figure extensively in Haywood's short fiction (if at all).

55. Ibid., p. 140.
56. Ibid., p. 141.
57. Merritt notes in respect to *Fantomina* that 'to link theatricality to subjectivity is to reveal the constructed nature of human identity'. Merritt, *Beyond Spectacle*, p. 23. Alathia, released from her gender, can perform the act that might otherwise remain unavailable to her.
58. As N. Loraux observes 'The death of a man inevitably calls for the suicide of a woman, his wife'. Loraux, *Tragic Ways of Killing a Woman*, p. 7.
59. This is a short story that appears in the collection Haywood, *Secret Histories, Novels and Poems* (1725).
60. Ibid., p. 253.
61. Ibid., p. 254.
62. Ibid., p. 254.
63. Ibid., p. 253.
64. E. Grosz, *Space, Time, and Perversion: Essays on the Politics of the Bodies* (New York: Routledge, 1995), p. 204.
65. Merritt, *Beyond Spectacle*, p. 28.
66. N. Armstrong, *Desire and Domestic Fiction: A Political History of the Novel* (New York: Oxford University Press, 1987).
67. Haywood, *The British Recluse*, pp. 153–226, on p. 155.
68. Ibid., p.155.
69. Ibid., p.156.
70. R. P. Bocchicchio notes that 'unlike most romances – including many of Haywood's own – which are built upon a model of female rivalry over the attention of men, this story is based on female companionship bolstered by the friends' anger at the perfidy of their mutual lover'. See R. P. Bocchicchio, '"Blushing, Trembling, and Incapable of Defense": The Hysterics of *The British Recluse*', in Saxton and Bocchicchio (eds), *The Passionate Fictions of Eliza Haywood*, pp. 95–114, on p. 103.
71. This villain, as protean as Fantomina but as fickle as she is constant, is identified alternately as Lysander, Courtal, and Bellamy. Since the text appears to indicate the last of the surnames as the least specious of all that he assumes, I will refer to this character for the most part by the name of Bellamy.
72. Haywood, *The British Recluse*, p. 155.
73. Ibid., p. 155.
74. A. H. Pasco observes that 'The cumulative insights of theatrical and novelistic 'fiction' into attitudes, habits of thought, customs, and the details of ordinary life are often not just verisimilar but true, or, at least, believed true by the people of the time'. See A. H. Pasco, *Revolutionary Love in Eighteenth- and Early Nineteenth-Century France* (Burlington, VT: Ashgate, 2009), p. 22.
75. Haywood, *The British Recluse*, p. 225.
76. Ibid., p. 222.
77. Ibid., p. 195.
78. Ibid., p. 199.
79. Belinda's own story by comparison is quite bland, representing perhaps the realist corrective to Cleomira's tragic adventure. At the same time, however, the circumstances surrounding Cleomira's story of her pregnancy, miscarriage and abject poverty place it too in a realist context. In this respect, Haywood satisfies the demands both of amatory fiction and of the emergent novel genre, for Cleomira's character vexes both categories: on the one hand she represents the character of romance (or even looks ahead to later

gothic fiction), and yet, on the other hand, she finds herself ensconced in a fairly conventional suburban boarding-house. In this and other texts, Haywood provides a prosaic, ordinary backdrop for the relatively sensational events that she narrates.

80. S. Black makes this claim as well in 'Trading Secrets', p. 221.

81. Haywood, *The British Recluse*, p. 160.

82. Ibid., p. 219.

83. Interestingly enough, it is Belinda, whose summation of her woes most closely approximates the putative moral of the novella. Belinda describes herself as 'Forever lost to peace by Love and [her] own fond belief'. Ibid., p. 160. In this way, she at least partially assumes accountability for her actions and acknowledges her excessive credulity. Cleomira, on the other hand, appears to resign all agency in her own affair, since she characterizes herself as 'Undone by Love and the Ingratitude of Faithless Man'. Ibid., p. 160. But the passive-voice construction of each statement underscores the victim position that each woman readily occupies.

84. E. Bronfen, 'Fatal Conjunctions: Gendering Representations of Death', in W. Apollon and R. Feldstein (eds), *Lacan, Politics, Aesthetics* (Albany, NY: State University of New York Press, 1996), pp. 237–62, on p. 142.

85. Merritt, *Beyond Spectacle*, p. 88.

86. MacDonald and Murphy, *Sleepless Souls*, p. 327.

87. Haywood, *The British Recluse*, p. 185.

88. See M. de Montaigne, *Essays* (1580).

89. Haywood, *The British Recluse*, p. 197.

90. A. Alvarez, *The Savage God: A Study of Suicide* (New York: Random House, 1972), p. 215. Cleomira's desperation also counters the notion that method affords a clue to motive in respect to suicide.

91. As MacDonald and Murphy observe, poison was viewed as a woman's crime. See *Sleepless Souls*, p. 226. In classical tragedy, hanging oneself by one's garter was a common form of female suicide. In a perverse sense, the text almost constructs Cleomira's sheer determination to die as grimly comic, a detail that perhaps supports George Minois's claim that 'the social and intellectual elites no longer found the idea of voluntary self-homicide shocking' in this period. See Minois, *History of Suicide*, p. 198.

92. Brown, *The Art of Suicide*, p. 125.

93. Haywood, *The British Recluse*, p.187.

94. Ibid., p.185.

95. Ibid., p.188.

96. Ibid., p. 194.

97. G. Fairbairn, 'Suicide, Language, and Clinical Practice', p. 158.

98. Haywood, *The British Recluse*, p. 159.

99. Ibid., p. 155.

100. R. Ballaster, *Seductive Forms*, p. 169. Ballaster in this sense offers a qualification of her perception of 'The profound melancholia and pessimism of Haywood's depiction of female possibilities'. Ibid., p. 168.

101. R. P. Bocchicchio, '"Blushing, Trembling, and Incapable of Defense": The Hysterics of *The British Recluse*', p. 111.

102. The German psychiatrist and philosopher, K. Jaspers, exemplifies this view in his description of the hysterics, in whom 'the place of genuine experience and natural expression is usurped by a contrived stage-act, a forced kind of experience. This is not contrived "consciously" but reflects the ability of the hysteric to live entirely in his own drama,

be caught entirely in the moment and succeed in seeming genuine'. K. Jaspers, *General Psychopathology*, trans. J. Hoenig and M. Hamilton (Manchester: Manchester University Press, 1913/1963), p. 439.

103. Kushner, 'Women and Suicidal Behaviour', p. 28. Similarly, G. Fairbairn notes, the term 'attempted suicide' is 'not just meaningless but positively wrong'. See Fairbairn, 'Suicide, Language, and Clinical Practice', p. 163.

104. This is my extrapolation from L. Vandekerckhove, *On Punishment: The Confrontation of Suicide in Old-Europe* (Leuven, Belgium: Leuven University Press, 2000).

105. Ibid., p. 195.

106. Ibid., p. 197.

107. J. Baudrillard, *Seduction*, trans. B. Singer (Montreal: New World Perspectives, 1990), p. 3.

108. R. Porter, 'Introduction', in G. Cheyne, *The English Malady* (1733) ed. R. Porter (London: Tavistock/Routledge, 1991), pp. i–xviii, on p. xxxvi.

109. J. Collier, *Essays upon Several Moral Subjects* (London, 1709), p. 82.

110. R. Bowlby (ed.), 'Introduction', in S. Freud, *Studies in Hysteria* (London: Penguin, 2004), pp. i–xlii, p. xxxix.

111. A prominent late eighteenth-century poet who, afflicted by melancholia throughout his life, attempted suicide on more than one occasion.

112. Haywood, *The British Recluse*, p. 157.

113. Grainger, *Modern Amours*, p. 76.

114. Ibid.

115. Ibid., p. 2.

116. The 'placebo poison' becomes a favourite device of both dramatic and prose treatments of suicides in this century. In the 1778 comedy *The Suicide*, a gentleman bent on suicide takes a placebo administered by one of his friends, and the subsequent failure of his attempt predictably reconciles him to life.

117. Grainger, *Modern Amours*, p. 78.

118. Haywood, *The British Recluse*, p. 26.

119. J. E. D. Esquirol, *Mental Maladies: A Treatise on Insanity*, trans. R. de Saussure (New York: Hafner Press, 1965), on p. 585.

120. S. S. Canetto, 'Gender Roles, Suicide Attempts, and Substance Abuse', *Journal of Psychology*, 125 (1991): pp. 605–20, on p. 618. As A. K. Clifton and D. E. Lee point out, 'in Western cultures nonfatal suicidal acts are considered more 'feminine' than fatal suicidal acts'. See A. Clifton and D. Lee, 'Self-Destructive Consequences of Sex-Role Socialization', *Suicide and Life-Threatening Behaviour*, 6:1 (1976), pp. 11–22, on p. 15.

121. A. D. Weisman, 'Self-Destruction and Sexual Perversion', in E. S. Schneidman (ed.), *Essays in Self-Destruction* (New York: Science House, 1967), pp. 265–99, on p. 273.

122. With the exception of Adams, *An Essay Concerning Self-Murther*, which presents suicide as the recourse predominantly of women and effeminate men.

123. Haywood's romance *Love in a Madhouse* dwells at length on this subject, drawing parallels between a single woman under the authority of a tyrannical guardian and an incarcerated female 'lunatic'.

124. J. Suglia, *Hölderlin and Blanchot on Self-Sacrifice* (New York: Peter Lang, 2004), p. 147.

125. Berlant, *The Female Complaint*, p. 15. As Berlant writes, 'The position of the depressive realist who sees that love is nonetheless the gift that keeps on taking is the source of complaint epistemology'. Ibid., p. 15.

126. Zizek, *The Plague of Fantasies*, pp. 8–9.

127. This is in marked contrast to real-life suicide notes, which, according to suicidologist A. Leenaars, are consistently present-oriented and resistant to reference to future occurrences. See A. Leenaars, 'Suicide Notes and Predictive Patterns', *Bulletin of the Menninger Clinic*, 55:1 (1991), pp. 123–4.

128. Haywood, *The British Recluse*, p. 85.

129. MacDonald and Murphy, *Sleepless Souls*, p. 333.

130. Haywood, *Love in Excess*, p. 242.

131. In this respect, I agree with J. Merritt's argument that 'there is more than a hint of masochism in how female desire operates in Haywood'. See Merritt, *Beyond Spectacle*, p. 87.

132. Haywood, *Reflections on the Various Effects of Love*, p. 35.

133. Haywood, *The British Recluse*, p. 198.

134. As K. Menninger writes, eroticism is an integral component of the psychology of martyrdom. See K. Menninger, *Man against Himself* (New York: Harcourt Brace, 1938), pp. 118–25.

135. J. Lacan, *Le seminaire, Livre VIII, Le transfert, 1960–1961*, ed. J.-A. Miller (Paris: Seul, 2000), p. 23.

136. Berlant, *The Female Complaint*, p. 14.

137. Haywood, *The British Recluse*, p. 170.

138. Haywood, *The British Recluse*, p. 194. In a similar manner, Placentia of *Philidore and Placentia* (1727), rejects the possibility of religion thwarting her suicide attempt: 'I endur'd a thousand times a day all the pangs of Death; all the Principles of Christianity were scarce of force to withhold me from laying Violent Hands on my own life; and had not that faithful Girl, whom I alone made the Confident of my Passion, kept a continual watch about me, I had certainly in some abandon'd moments, put an end to the miseries I had sustain'd, by the most unwarrantable means'. Haywood, *Philidore and Placentia* (London, 1727), p. 27. The narrator of *Reflections* similarly remarks, 'where such furious wishes are suffer'd to preside, neither the dictates of religion, morality, or even nature, are of any force'. Haywood, *Reflections on the Various Effects of Love*, p. 7.

139. Haywood, *The British Recluse*, p. 197.

140. Ibid.

141. Ibid., p. 194.

142. M. Gardiner, *Critiques of Everyday Life* (London: Routledge, 2003), p. 81.

143. A considerable number of broadsides on the subjects of suicide, seduction and abandonment have been preserved from the period. A ballad printed between 1736 and 1763 takes as its subject 'The Oxfordshire tragedy; or, The death of four lovers'. Another, entitled 'The Fatal Disappointment', chronicles the seduction, impregnation, abandonment and eventual suicide of a young woman named Anne Grey. The ballad concludes with the death of a heart-broken father, and in this respect also resembles the plot of *The British Recluse* in which Cleomira's mother eventually dies of grief owing to her daughter's defection.

144. Haywood, *The British Recluse*, p. 198.

145. Ibid.

146. A. Wolfe, *Suicidal Narrative in Modern Japan* (Princeton, NJ: Princeton University Press, 1990), p. 15.

147. In their reading of the 'semiotics of suicide', M. MacDonald and T. Murphy point out that 'The signs of suicide in early modern England were expressions, gestures, and actions, that tend to imply a foreshortening of time and discontinuity of identity'. See MacDonald and Murphy, *Sleepless Souls*, p. 236.

148. Haywood, *The British Recluse*, p. 198.
149. Ibid., p. 199.
150. The title of *The British Recluse; or, The Secret History of Cleomira, Suppos'd Dead* also assumes the perspective of the male (by whom Cleomira is deemed deceased), notwithstanding the fact that much of the narrative is delivered in the first-person by Cleomira herself, and the text itself grants no interiority to Bellamy, the male rake.
151. Haywood, *The British Recluse*, p. 175.
152. Ibid., p. 224.
153. In this early feminist text, Astell had elaborated a scheme of retirement for women 'convinced of the emptiness of early enjoyments, who are sick of the vanity of the world and its impertinencies'. Astell, *A Serious Proposal to the Ladies*, p. 150.
154. Haywood, *The British Recluse*, p. 224.
155. J. Sym, *Life's Preservative against Self-Killing* (London: M. Flesher, for R. Dawlman, and L. Fawne, 1637), p. 319.
156. Haywood, *The British Recluse*, p. 185.
157. Ibid., p. 157.
158. Both Cleomira and Fantomina suggest that women's deliverance depends upon their ability to assume a shadow identity.
159. M. MacDonald and T. Murphy in part derive the title of their study of early modern suicide, *Sleepless Souls*, from the superstitious belief that suicides became ghostly beings: 'The suicide [...] never escapes the liminal stage between death and arrival in the land of the dead'. MacDonald and Murphy, *Sleepless Souls*, p. 47.
160. Not a 'nightgown' in the modern sense, but rather a state of dishabille.
161. Hudson, *Samuel Johnson and the Making of Modern England*, p. 131.
162. J. G. A. Pocock, *Virtue, Commerce, History: Essays on Political Thought and History, Chiefly in the Eighteenth Century* (Cambridge: Cambridge University Press, 1985), p. 118.
163. The term 'imagined communities' derives from C. T. Mohanty's adaptation of B. Anderson's well-known description of the nation. See C. T. Mohanty, 'Cartographies of Struggle: Third World Women and the Politics of Feminism', in C. T. Mohanty, Lourdes Russo and Ann Russo (eds), *Third World Women and the Politics of Feminism* (Bloomington, IN: Indiana University Press, 1991), pp. 1–47, on p. 4.
164. K. Kumar, *The Making of English National Identity* (Cambridge: Cambridge University Press, 2003), p. 3.
165. K. Trumpener, *Bardic Nationalism: The Romantic Novel and the British Empire* (Princeton, NJ: Princeton University Press, 1997), p. 300.
166. Kumar, *The Making of English National Identity*, p. 43.
167. See especially the introduction in T. Claydon and I. McBride, *Protestantism and National Identity Britain and Ireland, c.1650–c.1850* (Cambridge: Cambridge University Press, 1998), pp. 3–32.
168. Although Colley argues that the union fostered a genuine sense of Britishness among the inhabitants of Britain, she does not in fact argue that an emergent notion of British identification erased or elided other pre-existing identities. L. Colley, *Britons: Forging the Nation, 1707–1837* (New Haven, CT: Yale University Press, 1992). See Kumar for a defence of the embattled Colley thesis.
169. This at least, is suggested by the title's use of the word 'recluse', which, from the thirteenth century onwards, had signified 'a person shut up from the world for the purpose of religious meditation'. As a 'British Recluse', the reasons for Cleomira's sequestration are

secular rather than spiritual. See R. Allestree, *The Causes of the Decay of Christian Piety* (1704) and F. Atterbury, *Of Religious Retirement: A Sermon Preach'd before the Queen, at St. James Chappel* (1705) for identifications of the recluse with 'religious retirement'.

170. J. Harris, *Lexicon Technicum: Or, An Universal English Dictionary of Arts and Sciences* (London: 1708), p. 541.

171. A. Butler, *The Lives of the Fathers, Martyrs, and Other Principal Saints: Compiled from Original Monuments and Other Authentic Records* (1756–9), p. 439.

172. Gildon, *The Deist's Manual*, p.137.

173. Haywood, *The British Recluse*, p. 224.

174. Astell, *A Serious Proposal to the Ladies*, p. 150.

175. The distinction is important here: if Cleomira's death were to be given out as a *felo de se*, the inheritance that she leaves to her nurse (to be refunded back to herself) would be claimed by the crown as forfeited property.

176. Haywood, *The British Recluse*, p. 224.

177. Haywood represents male desire as a protean thing that consistently imposes a 'seeming good' for a 'real evil'. Haywood, *The British Recluse*, p. 155. Haywood's configuration is not quite so simplistic as this, however, since both sexes afford instances of mutual harm, as evidenced by Bellamy's mistress and Belinda's fiancé, Worthley.

178. Ibid., p. 223.

179. S. Lanser, 'Befriending the Body: Female Intimacies as Class Acts', *Eighteenth Century Studies* 32.2 (1998–9), pp. 179–98, p. 180. According to Lanser, the progressiveness of a text like *The British Recluse* in its representation of self-sufficient female friendship is undermined by later novels like *Clarissa*, which presents this bond as a supplement to heterosexuality. Ibid., pp. 187–8.

180. Haywood, *The British Recluse*, p. 222.

181. S. Spearey, 'Substantiating Discourses of Emergence', in A. Keane and A. Horner (eds), *Body Matters: Feminism, Textuality, Corporeality* (New York: St Martin's Press, 2000), pp. 170–84, on p. 173.

182. Z. Eisenstein, 'Writing Bodies on the Nation for the Globe', in S. Ranchod-Nilsson and M. A. Tetreault (eds), *Women, States, and Nationalism: At Home in the Nation?* (London: Routledge, 2000), pp. 35–53, on p. 35.

183. G. Heng and J. Devan, 'State Fatherhood: The Politics of Nationalism, Sexuality, and Race in Singapore', in A. Parker (ed.), *Nationalisms and Sexualities* (New York: Routledge, 1992), pp. 328–51, on p. 349.

184. Eisenstein, 'Writing Bodies on the Nation for the Globe', p. 43.

185. Haywood, *The British Recluse*, p. 188. The still-born child is identified as a boy.

186. Haywood's mid-century novel, *The History of Miss Betsy Thoughtless* (Peterborough, ON: Broadview, 1998 [1751]), will also engage with this problem of English melancholy, although interestingly enough, this 'history' makes of suicide a secret whereas her earlier texts, including her secret histories, deal with the subject explicitly.

187. Derrida, *Specters of Marx*, p. 4.

188. Haywood, *The British Recluse*, p. 155.

189. Ibid., p. 224.

190. K. King, 'Spying on the Conjurer: Haywood, Curiosity and the Novel in the 1720s', *Studies in the Novel* 30:2 (1998): pp. 178–93, on p. 179.

191. R. Berman, *Coming to Our Senses: Body and Spirit in the Hidden History of the West* (Toronto: Simon and Schuster, 1989), p. 150.

192. M. Fissell, *Vernacular Bodies: The Politics of Reproduction in Early Modern England* (Oxford: Oxford University Press, 2004), p. 1.
193. Richardson continues E. Haywood's work by foregrounding the prominence of the suicide debate in the eighteenth-century novel, notwithstanding the argument, recently reaffirmed by W. B. Warner, that Richardson and his successors 'overwrite' the literary output of E. Haywood.

2 *Mors Voluntaria*

1. S. Fielding, *Remarks on Clarissa* (1749) (Los Angeles: Augustan Reprint Society, 1985), p. 48.
2. C. Macaulay, *Letters on Education* (London: William Pickering, 1996), on p. 145.
3. Ibid., p. 146.
4. S. Fielding, *Remarks on Clarissa*, p. 50.
5. P. Thompson insists upon 'Clarissa's identity as a passive woman who derives meaning and importance only from her victimization by men', in P. Thompson, 'Abuse and Atonement: The Passion of Clarissa Harlowe', in D. Blewett (ed.) *Passion and Virtue: Essays on the Novels of Samuel Richardson* (Toronto: University of Toronto Press, 2001), pp. 170–209, on p. 171. Elizabeth Bergen Brophy, meanwhile, justifiably objects to the celebration of the passive woman in Richardson's novels. However, the text arguably takes us beyond this position, and in this respect I agree with L. Fasick's argument that 'The self-destructive element in Clarissa's abstinence is easy to see: indeed, it is overwhelmingly important. But it need not necessarily lead us to interpret Clarissa's death as simple victimization'. L. Fasick, *Vessels of Meaning: Women's Bodies, Gender Norms, and Class Bias from Richardson to Lawrence* (Dekalb, IL: Northern Illinois Press, 1997), on p. 44.
6. M. A. Doody, *A Natural Passion: A Study of the Novels of Samuel Richardson* (Oxford: Clarendon Press, 1974), p. 101.
7. This is Edward Young's assessment, which he adheres to throughout his correspondence with Richardson. S, Richardson, *The Correspondence of Samuel Richardson in Six Volumes*, ed. P. Sabor (New York: AMS Press, 1966), vol. 2, p. 5.
8. Furthermore, as a member of the working class, Pamela's suicide would be subject to both civil and church reprisal, whereas Clarissa's upper-class status ostensibly insulates her from reproach.
9. S. P. Gordon, *The Power of the Passive Self in English Literature, 1640–1770* (Cambridge: Cambridge University Press, 2002), p.17. H. Zias ventures still further in her claim that 'Both the assertion of autonomy and the abdication of personal power in the sentimental construction of a passively reacting self were interconnected means a culture employed to keep itself unaware of its own internal mechanisms'. H. Zias, 'Who Can Believe? Sentiment versus Cynicism in Richardson's *Clarissa*', *Eighteenth-Century Life*, 27:3 (2003), pp. 99–122, on p. 101.
10. Gordon, *The Power of the Passive Self*, p. 5.
11. Ibid., p. 17.
12. Ibid., p. 341.
13. Ibid.
14. Ibid., p. 891.
15. Ibid., p. 1013.
16. S. Richardson, *Clarissa; or, The History of a Young Lady*, ed. A. Ross (New York: Penguin, 1985), p. 10.

17. Ibid., p. 346.
18. Kushner, 'Women and Suicidal Behaviour', p. 25.
19. Richardson, *Clarissa*, p. 341.
20. J. Shaw, 'Religious Experience and the Formation of the Early Enlightenment Self', in R. Porter (ed.), *Rewriting the Self: Histories from the Renaissance to the Present* (London: Routledge, 1997), pp. 61–71, on p. 66.
21. Donnalee Frege and Maud Ellman have both presented fascinating studies of this phenomenon, although neither explore the suicidal implications of Clarissa's dogged fasting. Ellman insists that Clarissa does not in fact 'opt for suicide'. M. Ellman, *The Hunger Artists: Starving, Writing and Imprisonment* (Cambridge, MA: Harvard University Press, 1993), p. 77.
22. Menninger, *Man against Himself*, p. 77.
23. Ibid., p. 77.
24. Ibid., p. 88.
25. Richardson, *Clarissa*, p. 1265.
26. Ibid., p. 1127.
27. Ibid., p. 1129.
28. Ibid., p. 1129.
29. Although R. Goldberg contends that 'however Clarissa may protest on the subject, it is quite clear that the *physical* cause of her death is starvation' (italics in text). R. Goldberg, *Sex and the Enlightenment: Women in Richardson and Diderot* (Cambridge: Cambrige University Press, 1984), on p. 124.
30. Richardson, *Clarissa*, p. 1084.
31. Ibid., p. 1059.
32. A. Giddens, *Modernity and Self-Identity* (Cambridge: Polity Press, 1991), p. 170.
33. Although, as both Frege and Ellman observe, her abstinence begins much earlier.
34. Richardson, *Clarissa*, p. 1058.
35. This is Ellman's term. Ellman, *The Hunger Artists*, p.71.
36. D. Hartley, *Hartley's Theory of the Human Mind, on the Principle of the Association of Ideas*, ed. J. Priestley (New York: AMS Press, 1973), p. 35.
37. Richardson, *Clarissa*, p. 1127.
38. Ibid., p. 1113.
39. Ibid., p. 1098. The notable difference between the two remarks, namely Lovelace's use of the personal pronoun 'him' as opposed to Anna Howe's impersonal 'it' in reference to death stems, of course, from Lovelace's fanciful allegorical reading of Clarissa's 'courtship' of death. Moreover, Lovelace's affinity for personifying death suggests the morbid aspect of the libertine psychology.
40. This, at least, represents the 'reasonable' position that is never quite effectively overcome by Richardson.
41. G. Cheyne, *An Essay on Health and Long Life* (London: 1745), p. 5.
42. In Knaggs's opinion, Moses, Elijah, Job and Jonah are culpable because they fail to exhibit sufficient patience and forbearance. For Knaggs, the prophets' strongly articulate desire for death is not only unlawful and contrary to religion and nature, but also 'unmannerly'. See Knaggs, *A Sermon against Self-Murder* (London, H. Hill, 1708).
43. Butler, *Bodies That Matter*, p. 124.
44. According to V. Vasterling, 'Every citation implies, by itself, a shift: the words I am citing here and now are cited in a temporal and spatial setting that is necessarily different from

former or later citations elsewhere of the same word'. V. Vasterling, 'Butler's Sophisticated Constructivism: A Critical Assessment' *Hypatia*, 14:3 (1999): pp. 17–38, on p. 26.

45. Or even, as Richardson hints, discover the very fetus Clarissa's relations suspect her to be carrying.

46. Indeed, Clarissa's character might be considered what theorist Susan Hekman terms 'the discursive subject' whose constitution by language does not preclude her agency since 'agency itself is a product of discourse, a capacity that flows from discursive formations'. S. Hekman, 'Subjects and Agents: The Question for Feminism', in J. K. Gardiner (ed.), *Provoking Agents: Gender and Agency in Theory and Practice* (Urbana, IL: University of Illinois Press, 1995), pp. 194–207, on p. 202. Clarissa exists as a discursive being, defining herself through her letters, conversations, her last will, and any other communicative modes available to her. Hekman's redefinition of agency circumvents the problem raised by a Foucauldian view of the self as a constructed entity by locating the agency of subjects 'within the discursive spaces open to them in their particular historical period'. Ibid., p. 202.

47. Cheyne, *An Essay on Health and Long Life*, p. 5.

48. E. Hervey, *Melissa and Marcia; or, the Sisters, a Novel* (London: 1788), p. 302.

49. Anon., *Adeline; or the Orphan* (London: 1790), p. 75.

50. Of course, this narrative had its antecedents in earlier eighteenth-century works. A similar scenario unfolds in the anonymous work (which some attribute to Elizabeth Montagu), 'The Fair Suicide, being an Epistle from a Young Lady, to the Person who was the cause of her death' (1733), wherein a woman suffers bodily decay subsequent to her assault and meditates at length upon suicide.

51. Richardson, *Clarissa*, p.1161.

52. Durkheim, *Suicide*, p. 42.

53. S. S. Canetto, 'Introduction', in Canetto and Lester (eds), *Women and Suicidal Behaviour*, p. 17.

54. A. Guerrini, *Obesity and Depression in the Enlightenment: The Life and Times of George Cheyne* (Norman, OK: University of Oklahoma Press, 2000), p. 17.

55. S. Bordo, *Unbearable Weight: Feminism, Western Culture, and the Body* (Berkeley, CA: University of California Press, 1993), p. 69.

56. Bordo, *Unbearable Weight*, p. 69.

57. Richardson, *Clarissa*, p. 974.

58. M. P. Battin (ed.), *The Death Debate: Ethical Issues in Suicide* (Saddle River, NJ: Prentice-Hall, 1995), pp. 278–9.

59. E. Bronfen, *Over Her Dead Body: Death, Femininity, and the Aesthetic* (Manchester: Manchester University Press, 1992), p. 153.

60. Blanchot, M., *The Space of Literature*, trans. A. Smock (Lincoln, NE: University of Nebraska Press, 1982), p. 103.

61. S. Critchley, *Very Little ... Almost Nothing: Death, Philosophy, Literature* (London: Routledge, 1997), p. 81.

62. Donne, *Biathanatos*, p.14.

63. E. Messer-Davidow, 'Acting Otherwise', in Gardiner (ed.), *Provoking Agents*, pp. 23–51, on p. 27.

64. C. Walker Bynum, *Fragmentation and Redemption: Essays on Gender and the Human Body in Medieval Religion* (New York: Zone, 1991), p. 56.

65. C. G. Wolff, *Samuel Richardson and the Eighteenth-Century Puritan Character* (Hamden, CT: Shoestring Press, 1972). To a large extent, Richardson scholarship either

assumes that Clarissa's death is a suicide, or overlooks the issue altogether. Critical engagement chronically wards off but never entirely exorcises the spectre of suicide. Critics acknowledging the suspicious nature of Clarissa's death include T. Castle, who alludes to Clarissa's 'curious acts of physical self-abnegation ... and quasi-anorexic refusal to eat' in T. Castle, *Clarissa's Ciphers: Meaning and Disruption in Richardson's* Clarissa (Ithaca, NY: Cornell University Press, 1982), p. 124. Castle, however, deflects the discussion of suicide into a consideration of the intersections between writing and death, while E. Bronfen, reads the narrative as 'an aesthetically staged performance of death' but concerns herself more with the metaphorical significance of Clarissa's fetishized corpse as opposed to the social and literary implications of the character's death in Bronfen, *Over Her Dead Body*, p. 147. Doody observes that 'Richardson ... carefully attempts to repudiate any suggestion that she is responsible for shortening her own life', and subsequent acknowledges that 'Clarissa's illness (probably galloping consumption) is certainly a trifle mysterious' in Doody, *A Natural Passion*, p. 172.

66. Wolff, *Samuel Richardson and the Eighteenth-Century Puritan Character*, p. 172.
67. T. Hill, *Ambitiosa Mors: Suicide and Self in Roman Thought and Literature* (New York: Routledge, 2004), p. 13. David Daube observes that the Latin *mors voluntaria* 'stresses the voluntary nature of such dying, English 'suicide', 'self-killing', the fact that oneself is the object'. Daube, *The Linguistics of Suicide*, p. 64.
68. Richardson, *The Correspondence*, vol. 2, p. 91.
69. Ibid., vol. 2, p. 95.
70. J. Stachniewski, *The Persecutory Imagination: English Puritanism and the Literature of Religious Despair* (Oxford: Clarendon Press, 1991), p. 46. John Sym's *Life's Preservative against Self-Killing* (1637), which Stachniewski identifies as the first published book solely on suicide, treats religious despair as the major inducement to voluntary death in the period.
71. Richardson, *The Correspondence*, vol. 2, p. 91.
72. Interestingly enough, in the same body of correspondence, Richardson cautions Collier 'neither to covet life, nor to wish for death, but to wait the appointed time with chearfulness'. Richardson, *The Correspondence*, vol. 2, p. 83.
73. Richardson, *Clarissa*, p. 950.
74. Particularly, St Jerome and St Pelagia. Louis Dubin writes, 'The early Christians apparently accepted the prevailing attitudes of their time on suicide, particularly when persecution made life unbearable for them. The Apostles did not denounce suicide; the New Testament touched on the question only indirectly, and for several centuries the leaders of the Church did not condemn the practice, which apparently was rather common'. L. Dublin, *Suicide: A Sociological and Statistical Study* (New York: Ronald Press Co., 1963), p. 137.
75. Pufendorf, S., *The Duty of Man and Citizen According to Natural Law* (1673), p. 47.
76. See L. Hinton, 'The Heroine's Subjection: Clarissa, Sadomasochism, and Natural Law', *Eighteenth-Century Studies*, 32:3 (1999): pp. 293–308; and Zias, 'Who Can Believe?'.
77. Zias, 'Who Can Believe?', p. 104.
78. Richardson, *Clarissa*, p. 1119.
79. Ibid., 1143.
80. J. Finnis, *Natural Law and Natural Rights* (Oxford: Clarendon Press, 1979), p. 18.
81. E. Bloch, *Natural Law and Human Dignity*, trans. D. Schmidt (Cambridge, MA: MIT Press, 1980), p. 113.
82. This is Laura Hinton's term.

83. J. Zomchick, *Family and the Law in Eighteenth-Century Fiction: The Public Conscience in the Private Sphere* (Cambridge: Cambridge University Press, 1993).

84. T. Keymer, *Richardson's* Clarissa *and the Eighteenth-Century Reader* (Cambridge: Cambridge University Press, 1992), p. 164.

85. D. S. Lynch, 'The (Dis)locations of Romantic Nationalism: Shelley, Staël, and the Home-Schooling of Monsters', in M. Cohen and C. Dever (eds.) *The Literary Channel: The Inter-National Invention of the Novel* (Princeton, NJ: Princeton University Press, 2002), pp. 194–224, on p. 121.

86. Richardson, *Clarissa*, p. 1202.

87. As G. Minois observes, 'In practice, the aristocratic code offered dueling as an effective substitute for killing oneself. Theologians and moralists were not fooled, and they included the practice in their anathemas on suicide'. Minois, *History of Suicide*, p. 153. Minois alludes to the proliferation of manuals on duelling circulating in the seventeenth century, which explicitly compare the act to suicide.

88. Durkheim, *Suicide*, p. 42.

89. W. Jones, *Consensual Fictions: Women, Liberalism, and the English Novel* (Toronto: University of Toronto Press, 2005), p. 62. Steele's *The Christian Hero* (1701) and Thomas Hughes's *The Manliness of Christ* (1880) are works on either end of this period intent on establishing a version of 'muscular Christianity'.

90. Castelli, *Martyrdom and Memory*, p. 62.

91. Thompson, 'Abuse and Atonement', p. 155.

92. Ibid., p. 168.

93. The story is also recounted by Ovid, Chaucer and Shakespeare, among others.

94. S. H. Jed, *Chaste Thinking: The Rape of Lucretia and the Birth of Humanism* (Bloomington, IN: Indiana University Press, 1989), p. 12. As Lucretia affirms in Livy's account, '*Mors testis erit*.'

95. B. J. Baines, *Representing Rape in the English Early Modern Period* (Lewiston, NY: Edwin Mellen Press, 2003), p. 158.

96. Richardson, *Clarissa*, p. 901. Take, for example, her caution, 'Take care, Lovelace...If I fall, though by my own hand, inquisition will be made for my blood'. Richardson, *Clarissa*, p. 911.

97. Ibid., p. 953.

98. Ibid., p. 867.

99. Ibid., p. 895.

100. Baines, *Representing Rape in the English Early Modern Period*, p. 88.

101. Hill, *Ambitiosa Mors*, p. 4.

102. Castelli, *Martyrdom and Memory*, p. 54.

103. Matthes, *The Rape of Lucretia and the Founding of Republics* (University Park, PA: Penn State University Press, 2000), p. 42. In *The Rapes of Clarissa*, Terry Eagleton also reads Clarissa as a 'scapegoat, who though innocent, assumes the sins of the community'. See T. Eagleton, *The Rapes of Clarissa* (Minneapolis, MN: University of Minnesota Press, 1982), p. 91.

104. Richardson, *Clarissa*, p. 913. Elizabeth Castelli observes in her study of the Christian martyrology's absorption of pagan sacrificial practices that 'Christians inverted the expected social framework by embracing the characteristics of the sacrificial victim – willingness, passivity, and submission – and, indeed, using gender to inflect their appropriation of the sacrificial economy'. Castelli, *Martyrdom and Memory*, p. 54.

105. J. Kristeva, *The Powers of Horror: An Essay on Abjection*, trans. L. S. Roudiez (New York: Columbia University Press, 1982), p. 111.

106. Richardson, *Clarissa*, p. 1439.

107. Augustine, *The City of God*, ed. M. Dods (Edinburgh: T. & T. Clark, 1888), vol. 1, p. 29.

108. Ibid., p. 29.

109. In his compendious study of the *Rapes of Lucretia* (1982), Ian Donaldson affirms that the story acted 'as a creative stimulant' to others. See I. Donaldson, *The Rapes of Lucretia: A Myth and Its Transformations* (Oxford: Clarendon Press, 1982), p. 83.

110. Fedden, *Suicide*, p. 81.

111. Richardson, *Meditations Collected from the Sacred Books* (1750) (New York: Garland Press, 1976), p. v.

112. Although D. Amundsen insists that Augustine did not formulate Church doctrine on suicide but merely clarified it, Augustine's denunciation of virgin suicides departed from earlier patristic positions that sought to promote chastity even unto death. D. A. Amundsen, 'Suicide and Early Christian Values', in B. A. Brody (ed.), *Suicide and Euthanasia: Historical and Contemporary Themes* (Boston, MA: Kluwer Academic Press, 1989), pp. 77–154. As Alexander Murray notes, 'most of Augustine's anti-suicide arguments ... are not even Christian', and I argue that many of them responded to critical historical events. A. Murray, *Suicide in the Middle Ages*, 2 vols (Oxford: Oxford University Press, 1998), p. 121.

113. Minois, *History of Suicide*, p. 163.

114. St Jerome, *Commentarii in Jonam*, i.12.

115. The instrumentality of time in distinguishing between Lucretia's suicide and Clarissa's death is observed by Isobel Grundy who notes that 'unlike Lucretia, she lives long enough to work her way out of the victim mentality that it is the aim of rape to produce. Through her escape from control she becomes – paradoxically – what the feminist discourse of rape terms a survivor'. See I. Grundy, 'Seduction Pursued by Other Means? The Rape in *Clarissa*', in Houlihan Flynn and Copeland (eds.), *Clarissa and Her Readers*, pp. 214–55, on p. 255.

116. Augustine, *The City of God*, I.xxii.

117. Colley, *Britons*, pp. 25–6.

118. In his notes to *Pamela*, Peter Sabor identifies *The Book of Martyrs* as the text alluded to in this passage. Richardson, *Pamela*, ed. Peter Sabor, p. 523.

119. W. Haller, *The Elect Nation: The Meaning and Relevance of Foxe's Book of Martyrs* (New York: Harper & Row, 1963), p. 77.

120. J. Foxe, *Book of Martyrs (Abridged.)*, ed., G. A. Williamson (London: Secker and Warburg, 1965), p. 175.

121. Ibid., p. 175.

122. Augustine, *The City of God*, vol. 1, p. 28.

123. Truman, 'John Foxe and the Desires of Reformation Martyrology', p. 35.

124. Foxe, *Book of Martyrs*, p. 384.

125. Ibid., p. 280.

126. L. Greenfeld, *Nationalism: Five Roads to Modernity* (Cambridge, MA: Harvard University Press, 1992).

127. Kumar, *The Making of English National Identity*, p. 112.

128. Foxe, *Book of Martyrs*, p. 488.

129. G. G. Starr, *Lyric Generations: Poetry and the Novel in the Long Eighteenth Century* (Baltimore, MD: Johns Hopkins University Press, 2004).

130. Donne, *Biathanatos*, I.ii.2.
131. Ibid., II.vi.5.
132. Monta, *Martyrdom and Literature in Early Modern England*, p. 132.
133. Augustine, *Contra Gaudentium Donatistarum*, I.14.15. Lieven Vandekerckhove writes that 'In his letters against Gaudentius, the rejection of suicide is almost a primary theme, continually present in the background and regularly brought to the fore when accompanying argumentation'. Vandekerckhove, *On Punishment*, p. 34.
134. 'England's New Religion', *The Daily Gazetteer*, 17 November 1738, No. 1053. The literary critic John Dussinger speculates that 'Richardson might very well have written [the essay] in [its] entirety'. See J. A. Dussinger, '"*Ciceronian* Eloquence": The Politics of Virtue in Richardson's *Pamela*', in Blewett (ed.), *Passion and Virtue*, pp. 27–51, on p. 42. Although Courtville emphasizes that suicide is 'a failure of circumspection, an act of madness', the essay avoids reference to the orthodox Christian view against suicide. See J. A. Dussinger, '*Ciceronian* Eloquence', p. 44.
135. 'To Mr. Fitz Adam', *The World*, 23 September 1756, pp. 190–200, on p. 192.
136. Ibid., p. 193.
137. A. McClintock, '"No Longer in a Future Heaven": Nationalism, Gender, and Race', in G. Eley and R. G. Suny (eds.), *Becoming National: A Reader* (New York: Oxford University Press, 1996), pp. 260–83, on p. 264.
138. Ibid., p. 264.
139. Matthes, *The Rape of Lucretia and the Founding of Republics*, p. 7.
140. Ibid.
141. I. Donaldson provides a thorough survey of the Lucretia intertext's relevance yet overlooks the nationalist subtext.
142. Richardson, *Clarissa*, p. 1148. J. P. Wilson observes that 'By separating the personal from the political in his own case, Lovelace ignores any duties he may owe to his community as its most privileged member. While he formerly fantasized about seizing absolute political power, Lovelace now uses his lack of it to abjure any reflection of national standards in his behaviour'. See J. P. Wilson, '*Clarissa*: The Nation Misrul'd', in A. J. Rivero, G. Justice and M. Collins (eds.), *The Eighteenth-Century Novel* (AMS Press, 2003), vol. 3, pp. 65–96, on p. 90.
143. S. Kierkegaard, *Papers and Journals: A Selection*, trans. A. Hannay (London: Penguin, 1996), p. 352.
144. A. E. MacLeod, 'Hegemonic Relations and Gender Resistance: The New Veiling as Accommodating Protest in Cairo', *Signs*, 17:3 (1992): pp. 533–51, on p. 533.
145. Castelli, *Martyrdom and Memory*, p. 4.
146. Richardson, *Clarissa*, p. 1143.
147. Ibid., p. 1142.
148. Pettman, 'Boundary Politics: Women, Nationalism and Danger', in M. Maynard and J. Purvis (eds), *New Frontiers in Women's Studies: Knowledge, Identity, and Nationalism* (London: Taylor & Francis, 1996), pp. 187–202, on pp. 188–9.
149. K. J. Kaplan and M. Schwartz, 'To Be or Not to Be? The Question of Suicide', *Journal of Psychology and Judaism*, 24:1 (2000), pp. 17–25, p. 3.
150. Donaldson, *The Rapes of Lucretia*, p. 74.
151. D. Marshall makes a similar point, describing Clarissa's fantasy as 'a Gothic or even a Jacobean scenario of revenge'. See D. Marshall, 'Fatal Letters: Clarissa and the Death of Julie', in Houlihan Flynn and Copeland (eds.), Clarissa *and her Readers: New Essays for the* Clarissa *Project*, pp. 213–54, on p. 216.

214 *Notes to pages 80–3*

152. Chung's reading endorses both B. Anderson's construct of the 'imagined community' and L. Colley's conception of antagonistic Protestantism as the basis for national identification and is accordingly straitened by the limitations of both readings. See E. Chung, *Samuel Richardson's New Nation: Paragons of the Domestic Sphere and 'Native' Virtue* (New York: Peter Lang, 1998). In '*Clarissa:* The Nation Misrul'd', J. P. Wilson argues that the tragedies of Lovelace and Clarissa represent 'dangers for England' that the narrative never entirely resolves.

153. As M. Redfield observes, nationalist ideology insists that 'all a woman will ever be able to do is mourn. She mourns, furthermore, above all as a mother ...'. See M. Redfield, 'Imagi-Nation: The Imagined Community and the Aesthetics of Mourning', in P. Cheah and J. Culler (eds.), *Grounds of Comparison: Around the Work of Benedict Anderson* (New York: Routledge, 2003), pp. 75–106, on pp. 86–7.

154. M. Domish and Joni Seager, *Putting Women in Place: Feminist Geographers Make Sense of the World* (New York: Guilford P, 2001), p. 535. Kathryn Temple reads *Charles Grandison* as a 'national allegory', albeit one constructed within a transnational context.

155. Richardson, *Clarissa*, p. 41.

156. E. Renan, 'What Is a Nation?', in Bhabha (ed.), *Nation and Narration*, pp. 8–22.

157. Richardson, *Clarissa*, p. 313.

158. Chung, *Samuel Richardson's New Nation: Paragons of the Domestic Sphere and 'Native' Virtue*, p. 76.

159. Ibid., p. 288.

160. Richardson, *Meditations*, p. 4.

161. Ibid., p. 2.

162. Ibid., p. 17.

163. An instance of this identification is afforded by her affirmation, 'But I am sure, if I may say it with as little presumption as grief, in the words of Job, That God will soon *dissolve my substance; and bring me to death, and to the house appointed for all living*' (italics in text). Richardson, *Clarissa*, p. 1118.

164. J. Lamb, *The Rhetoric of Suffering: Reading the Book of Job in the Eighteenth Century* (Oxford: Clarendon Press, 1995), p. 245.

165. Donne, *Biathanatos*, III.ii.4–5.

166. S. Zizek, 'The Act and its Vicissitudes', *The Symptom*, 6 (2005), pp. 1–3, on p. 1.

167. Castle describes this process as committing a sort of 'editorial violence'. See Castle, *Clarissa's Ciphers*, p. 130. Keymer observes that 'As the fragmentation and rearrangement of sacred texts takes over as her chosen means of signification, Clarissa effectively reconstitutes herself in the image of her exemplar, so that her own experience appears simply as a recapitulation of his, radiant with the same meanings'. See T. Keymer, 'Richardson's *Meditations:* Clarissa's *Clarissa*', in M. A. Doody and P. Sabor (eds.), *Samuel Richardson: Tercentenary* (Cambridge: Cambridge University Press, 1989), pp. 89–109, on p. 100.

168. Castle, *Clarissa's Ciphers*, p. 21.

169. In general reference to the act of suicide itself, L. Crocker claims that it is without absolute, determinate value. See L. Crocker, 'Interpreting the Enlightenment: A Political Approach', *Journal of the History of Ideas*, 46:2 (1985), pp. 211–31.

170. H. C. Shelley (ed.), *The Life and Letters of Edward Young*, 3 vols (Boston, MA: Little, Brown, & Co., 1914), vol. 2, pp. 5–6.

171. Richardson, *Clarissa*, p. 1148.

172. Monta, *Martyrdom and Literature in Early Modern England*, p. 35.

173. Richardson, *The Correspondence*, vol. 6, p. 230.

174. G. Flaubert, *Madame Bovary*, trans. Paul de Man (New York: W.W. Norton and Co., 1965), p. 242.
175. Castelli, *Martyrdom and Memory*, p. 133.
176. J. Zigarovich, 'Courting Death: Necrophilia in Samuel Richardson's *Clarissa*', *Studies in the Novel*, 32:2 (2000), pp. 12–28, on p. 14.
177. Menninger, *Man against Himself*, p. 118.
178. Richardson, *Clarissa*, p. 1117.
179. Critchley, *Very Little ... Almost Nothing*, p. 82.
180. Richardson, *Clarissa*, p. 1117.
181. In her subsequent retrospective explication of her post-rape mentality, Clarissa downplays the severity of suicide attemptedin a state of distress: 'More than once, indeed, was I urged by thoughts so sinful: but then it was in the height of my distress ... As I am of opinion, that it would have manifested more of revenge and despair, than of principle, had I committed a violence upon myself when the villainy was *perpetrated*; so I should think it equally criminal, were I now *willfully* to neglect myself; were I *purposely* to run into the arms of death (as that man supposes I shall do) when I might avoid it'. Richardson, *Clarissa*, p. 1117.
182. See J. Altman, *Epistolarity: Approaches to a Form* (Columbus, OH: Ohio State University Press, 1982); and E. J. MacArthur, *Extravagant Narratives: Closure and Dynamics in the Epistolary Form* (Princeton, NJ: Princeton University Press, 1990).
183. J. Bray, *The Epistolary Novel: Representations of Consciousness* (London: Routledge, 2003), on p. 43.
184. Renan, 'What Is a Nation?', p. 19.
185. H. K. Bhabha, 'DissemiNation: Time, Narrative, and the Margins of the Modern Nation', in Bhabha (ed.), *Nation and Narration*, pp. 291–323, on p. 310.
186. In this respect I agree with the literary critic, T. O. Beebee, who insists that death in Clarissa 'is not a plot device; plot serves as an excuse for the observation and description of death'. See T. O. Beebee, *Epistolary Fiction in Europe, 1500–1850* (Cambridge: Cambridge University Press, 1999), p. 83.
187. Baudrillard's comments on the anti-progressive strain in modern culture lead him to state that 'the cult of the body no longer stands in contradiction to the cult of the soul: it is the successor to that cult and heir to its ideological function'. See J. Baudrillard, 'The Finest Consumer Object: The Body', in M. Fraser and M. Greco (eds.), *The Body, a Reader* (London: Routledge, 2005), pp. 277–82, on p. 282.

3 English Maladies and Material Culture at Mid-Century

1. As discussed in previous chapters, R. Bartel effectively exploded the myth of the English suicidal temperament in 1967. See R. Bartel, 'Suicide in Eighteenth-Century England: The Myth of a Reputation', *Huntington Library Quarterly* (1967), pp. 145–58. However, the fallacy of this belief does not negate the fact of its existence, as M. Novak insists in his review of G. Minois's *History of Suicide*, which follows Bartel in its survey of English suicide. See Novak, 'Boundaries of the Self'.
2. Cowper recorded this sentiment in a letter to Mrs King, 4 August 1791. See W. Cowper, *Correspondence of William Cowper*, ed. T. Wright, 4 vols (New York: Dodd Mead, 1904), vol. 4, on p. 104.
3. H. Kushner argues that, with the beginning of modernity, 'self-destructive behaviour became a prima facie example of the corrupting effects of urbanization and the incidence

of suicide developed into a barometer for social health'. See H. Kushner, 'Suicide, Gender, and the Fear of Modernity', in J. Weaver and D. Wright (eds.), *Histories of Suicide: International Perspectives on Self-Destruction in the Modern World* (Toronto: University of Toronto Press, 2009), pp. 19–52, on p. 19.

4.   The transformation of melancholy into a desirable index of reflective and restrained behaviour has been the subject of recent scholarship by literary historians, for example, see Gidal, 'Civic Melancholy'.

5.   Healy, *Fictions of Disease in Early Modern England.*

6.   J. Shebbeare, *Lydia, or, Filial Piety,* 4 vols (New York: Garland Press, 1974).

7.   It should be noted, however, that Shebbeare conveniently transferred his allegiance to the Whigs when they purchased his silence by granting him a pension towards the end of his career.

8.   R. Cobb, *Death in Paris, 1795–1801* (Oxford, Oxford University Press, 1978).

9.   In this sense, Shebbeare anticipates Durkheim's 1897 sociology of suicide, *Le Suicide.*

10. J. Hutchinson, 'Moral Innovators and the Politics of Regeneration: The Distinctive role of Cultural Nationalists in Nation-Building', *International Journal of Comparative Sociology,* 33 (1992), pp. 101–17, on p. 110.

11. J. Shebbeare, *The Practice of Physick, Founded on Principles of Pathology Hitherto Unapplied in Physical Enquiries* (London: Hodges, 1755), p. 50.

12. Shebbeare, *Lydia,* Chapter 2.

13. O. Doughty, 'The English Malady of the Eighteenth Century', *The Review of English Studies,* 2:7 (1926), pp. 257–69, on p. 262.

14. Canasetego (c. 1684–1750) exhorted the British colonies to form a united front modelled on the example of the Iroquois confederacy. After brokering significant land treaties with the Pennsylvania colony, he became disenchanted with the colonists when they took more land than the treaty allowed. He is believed to have been poisoned by Iroquois who were either pro-French or incensed at what may have been questionable dealings with the Pennsylvanians. For a fuller account of Canasetego's political career, see W. A. Starna, 'The Diplomatic Career of Canasatego', in W. A. Pencak and D. K. Richter (eds.), *Friends and Enemies in Penn's Woods: Indians, Colonists, and the Racial Construction of Pennsylvania* (University Park, PA: Pennsylvania State University Press, 2004), pp. 144–63.

15. Shebbeare, *Lydia,* p. 11.

16. Ibid., vol. 1, p. 2.

17. Ibid., vol. 1, p. 2.

18. B. A. Mann, *Native American speakers of the Eastern Woodlands: Selected Speeches and Critical Analyses* (Westport, CT: Greenwood Publishing, 2001), p. 92.

19. Shebbeare, *Lydia,* vol. 1, p. 10.

20. G. Cheyne, *The English Malady,* p. xxi.

21. W. B. Ober describes *The English Malady* as 'the most popular and influential book on melancholy in the eighteenth century'. See W. B. Ober, 'Eighteenth-Century Spleen', *Psychology and Literature in the Eighteenth Century,* ed., C. Fox (New York: AMS Press, 1987), pp. 225–58, on p. 243. Written for a lay audience in an accessible style devoid of specialist medical terminology, Cheyne's work asserted a tremendous impact on discourses of sensibility and attitudes towards voluntary death. Many more recent studies have unquestioningly accepted statistical data; as Murphy and MacDonald observe, the pioneering S. E. Sprott consulted the London Bills of Mortality in his attempt to attribute the suicide 'epidemic' to the rise of urban Puritanism. As Murphy and MacDonald

point out, 'Taken at face value, the figures in the bills told a simple and striking tale. In almost any year from 1660 to 1735, the number of suicides increased'. See MacDonald and Murphy, *Sleepless Souls*, p. 244.

22. Haywood, *The Female Spectator*, pp. 147–8.
23. 'Reflections on Suicide', *London Magazine*, March 1762, pp. 144–6, on p. 144.
24. Grosley, *A Tour to London*, p. 123.
25. Brown, *The Art of Suicide*, p. 145.
26. G. Colman, *The Connoisseur* (Dublin, 1756), p. 290.
27. W. Chaigneau, *The History of Jack Connor* (1752), p. 208.
28. 'Reflections on Suicide', *The London Magazine*, March 1762, pp. 144–6, on p. 144.
29. Ibid., p. 145.
30. Cheyne, *The English Malady*, pp. ii–iii. Interestingly enough, the words self-murder and suicide do not appear in the treatise itself.
31. Ibid., p. 2.
32. Porter, 'Introduction' , p. ii.
33. Cheyne, *The English Malady*, p. 2. .
34. 'To Mr. Fitz-Adam', *World*, 23 September 1756, p. 185.
35. Ibid., p. 105.
36. 'Some Observations on the Causes of Suicide', *Gentleman's Magazine*, vol. 26 (1756), p. 28.
37. Minois, *History of Suicide*, p. 194.
38. S. Freud, 'Mourning and Melancholia', in *On Metapsychology: The Theory of Psychoanalysis*, ed., J. Strachey, (New York: Viking Penguin, 1984), pp. 245–68, on p. 247.
39. Owing largely to his *Letters to the People of England*, Shebbeare succeeded in this aim, and on 5 December 1758, was obliged to spend one hour imprisoned in (actually beside, owing to his social status) a pillory, as a servant held an umbrella over his head to shelter him from the rain; given his critique of upper-class privilege, this account seems somewhat ironic.
40. J. Shebbeare, *Second Letter to the People of England* (London, 1755), p. 8.
41. Ibid., p. 1.
42. Ibid., p. 18.
43. [Shebbeare], *Letters on the English Nation*. Shebbeare's strategy of employing the Angeloni pseudonym as a distancing device to air his grievances with the country from a relatively protected vantage point, did not, of course, save Shebbeare from the pillory. The earliest English reviewers of the work deduced that no such person as B. Angeloni historically existed and accordingly dismissed it as no more than an imitation of Voltaire's earlier letters on the English nation. 'Letters on the English Nation', *Monthly Review* XII, April and May 1755, pp. 387–8).
44. [Shebbeare], *Letters on the English nation*, p. 27.
45. Ibid., p. 27.
46. Ibid., p. 92.
47. Ibid., p. 31. This argument, although somewhat uncommon in its time, finds support in a 1762 letter to the *London Magazine*, which affirms that 'They, whom Providence has favoured with the conveniences of life, have the most probable means of recovery in their own hands. But shall the poor be suffered to languish unpitied, and be exposed, when breathless, to the gibes and reproaches of fools and savages?', 'Reflections on Suicide', *The London Magazine* March 1762, pp. 144–6, on p. 144. Only of secondary import is the

'religious melancholy' that, according to Angeloni, the Church of England instills in its subjects by denying them the emotional outlet of confession.

48. J. Shebbeare, *The Marriage Act* (New York: Garland, 1974), p. 266.
49. Please see Chapter 2 for a discussion of this concept/practice.
50. Shebbeare, *Second Letter to the People of England*, p. 3.
51. Guerrini, *Obesity and Depression in the Enlightenment*, p. 147.
52. S. Gregg identifies 'the links forged between effeminacy and other demons of manliness – such as luxury, sexuality and irrationality' as 'commonplaces of civic humanism'. See S. Gregg, '"A Truly Christian Hero": Religion, Effeminacy and Nation in the Writings of the Societies for Reformation of Manners', *Eighteenth-Century Life*, 25:1 (2001), pp. 17–28, on p. 28.
53. Shebbeare, *Lydia*, vol. 2, p. 8. The case of the colonel's wife who drowned herself in the St James Park canal in 1765 is taken by P. J. Grosley in his *A Tour to London* (1772) as paradigmatic of female suicidal behaviour.
54. Shebbeare, *Lydia*, vol. 2, p. 11.
55. Ibid., vol. 1, p. 257.
56. Ibid., vol. 1, p. 271.
57. Ibid., vol. 2, p. 23.
58. Ibid., vol. 2, p. 19.
59. See MacDonald and Murphy, *Sleepless Souls*, pp. 260–74 for a discussion of poverty in relation to eighteenth-century cases of suicide.
60. K. Siena, 'Suicide as an Illness Strategy in the Long Eighteenth Century', in Weaver and Wright (eds), *Histories of Suicide*, pp. 53–72, on p. 66.
61. This is F. Burney's term that recurs throughout her final novel, *The Wanderer, or, Female Difficulties* (Oxford: Oxford University Press, 1991 [1814]).
62. Shebbeare, *Lydia*, vol. 1, p. 270.
63. Ibid., vol.1, p. 283.
64. Ibid., vol. 1, p. 283.
65. Ibid., vol. 1, p. 284.
66. Quoted in M. Craske, *Art in Europe, 1700–1830* (Oxford: Oxford University Press, 1997), p. 33.
67. See H. Walpole, *Anecdotes of Painting* (London, 1786), p. 375.
68. D. Bindman and M. Baker, *Roubiliac and the Eighteenth-Century Monument* (New Haven, CT: Yale University Press, 1995), p. 3.
69. T. Gray's magisterial *Elegy Written in a Country Churchyard* (1751) rebukes the elitist pretensions of monument culture in the strongest of terms:

> Nor you, ye Proud, impute to these the fault. If Memory o'er their tomb no trophies raise, Where through the long-drawn aisle and fretted vault. The pealing anthem swells the note of praise. Can storied urn or animated bust Back to its mansion call the fleeting breath? Can Honour's voice provoke the silent dust, Or Flattery soothe the dull cold ear of Death?

70. 'The Last Guinea Club', *Connoisseur 9 January 1755*, p. 297. While in *Hamlet* the controversy stems from the fact that Ophelia receives a Christian burial, in the eighteenth century it was the lavishness and grand scale of the burials that attracted censure.
71. Shebbeare, *Lydia*, vol. 1, p. 220.
72. Ibid., vol. 1, p. 220.
73. Ibid., vol. 1, p. 224.

74. Ibid., vol. 1, p. 223.

75. Ibid., vol. 2, p. 231.

76. Ibid., vol. 2, p. 235.

77. Ibid., vol. 2, p. 50.

78. See P. Connell, 'Death and the Author: Westminster Abbey and the Meanings of the Literary Monument', *Eighteenth-Century Studies*, 38:4 (2005), pp. 557–85, on p. 564.

79. Shebbeare, *Lydia*, vol. 2, p. 147.

80. Ibid., vol. 2, p. 249.

81. Ibid., vol. 2 , p. 249.

82. Ibid., vol. 2, p. 247.

83. Ibid., vol. 2, p. 10.

84. Ibid., vol. 1, p.15.

85. Ibid., vol. 1, pp. 3–4.

86. Ibid., vol. 1, p. 138.

87. Ibid., vol. 1, p. 137.

88. J. Barrell observes an increasing division between 'virtue and vertu, between manly politeness and luxurious effeminacy' during this period. J. Barrell, '"The Dangerous Goddess": Masculinity, Prestige, and the Aesthetic in Early Eighteenth-Century Britain', *Cultural Critique,* 12 (1989), pp. 101–31, on p. 104.

89. Shebbeare, *Lydia*, vol. 4, p. 257. Shebbeare likely has in mind one of Eliza Haywood's many works as discussed in chapter one.

90. Ibid., vol. 2, p. 260.

91. D. Andrew, 'The Suicide of Sir Samuel Romilly: Apotheosis or Outrage?', in J. Weaver (ed.), *From Sin to Insanity* (New York: Cornell University Press, 2004), pp. 175–88, on p. 176.

92. T. Edensor, *National Identity, Popular Culture and Everyday Life* (Oxford: Berg, 2002), p. vii.

93. D. Sibley, 'Survey 13: Purification of Space', *Environment and Planning D: Society and Space*, 6 (1988), pp. 409–21, on p. 409.

94. Edensor, *National Identity, Popular Culture and Everyday Life*, p. 39.

95. Shebbeare, *Lydia*, vol. 4, p. 139.

96. [Shebbeare], *Letters on the English Nation*, p. 10.

97. Kushner, 'Suicide, Gender, and the Fear of Modernity', p. 33.

98. M. D. Faber, 'Shakespeare's Suicides: Some Historic, Dramatic and Psychological Reflections', in Schneidman (ed.), *Essays in Self-Destruction*, pp. 30–58, on p. 52.

99. Shebbeare, *Lydia*, vol. 1, p. 24.

100. Ibid., vol. 1, p. 22.

101. Wendeborn, 'On the Character of the English', p. 196.

102. Shebbeare, *Lydia*, vol. 1, p. 194.

103. Ibid., vol. 1, p. 138. .

104. Ibid., vol. 1, p. 193.

105. Ibid., vol. 1, p. 192.

106. Ibid., vol. 1, p. 160.

107. Porter, 'Introduction', p. xxxii.

108. As M. A. Cutter observes, 'the diagnosis of disease is an aesthetic event' involving 'aesthetic judgments'. M. A. Cutter, *Reframing Disease Contextually* (Boston, MA: Kluwer Academic Press, 2003), p. 98.

109. Shebbeare, *Lydia*, vol. 1, p. 138. The wry description is replete with innuendo.

110. M. E. McAllister observes that 'Criticism of the Grand Tour ... often hinted at the risk of contracting venereal disease abroad – one of the unspoken purposes of the tour being to sow one's wild oats'. M. E. McAllister, 'Stories of the Origin of Syphilis in Eighteenth-Century England: Science, Myth and Prejudice', *Eighteenth-Century Life*, 24:1 (2000), pp. 22–44, on p. 25. In *The Female Spectator*, E. Haywood notes that 'those who are at an infinite Expense in traveling for Improvement, yet bring Home little besides the worst Part of the Nations where they have been'. Haywood, *The Female Spectator*, p. 51.

111. McAllister provides considerable evidence for this position. McAllister, 'Stories of the Origin of Syphilis in Eighteenth-Century England', p. 26.

112. A. Guerrini affirms that Cheyne 'hoped to redefine the English malady as a legitimate disease, distinct from a 'lower Degree of Lunacy'. Guerrini, *Obesity and Depression in the Enlightenment*, p. 149. At the same time, however, as a Scot, Cheyne is somewhat insulated from the stigma of English melancholia.

113. In his *Treatise of the Hypochondriack and Hysterick Passions* (1711), B. Mandeville attributes the onset of his acute melancholia to his apprehension that he 'has contracted syphilis, even ... believing his nose and palate had been destroyed', as W. Ober observes. Ober, 'Eighteenth-Century Spleen', p. 237.

114. Cheyne, *The English Malady*, p. 151.

115. Literally, 'men of mercury', a euphemism for a man afflicted with venereal disease.

116. McAllister, 'Stories of the Origin of Syphilis in Eighteenth-Century England', 22–44, on p. 33.

117. Please see McAllister for the relevance of eighteenth-century medical beliefs to contemporary attitudes towards the origin and transmission of communicable disease.

118. J. Sena, 'Melancholic Madness and the Puritans', *The Harvard Theological Review*, 66:3 (1973), pp. 293–309, on p. 294.

119. J. Purcell, *A Treatise of Vapours and Hysteric Fits* (London, 1702), pp. 1–2.

120. McAllister confirms 'a connection between nervous condition and venereal disease' in the eighteenth-century popular imagination. See McAllister, 'Stories of the Origin of Syphilis in Eighteenth-Century England', p. 33.

121. Shebbeare, *Lydia*, vol. 1, p. 184.

122. See Haywood, *The History of Miss Betsy Thoughtless* for a treatment of Westminster Abbey as an eroticized space.

123. M. Springborg argues that 'The idea of women as carriers of venereal disease was derived from more general views about the inferiority of the female body ... that men acquired venereal disease from women is taken for granted throughout the medical literature on the subject'. See M. Springborg, *Feminizing Venereal Disease: The Body of the Prostitute in Nineteenth-Century Medical Discourse* (London: MacMillan Press, 1997), pp. 2–3.

124. Shebbeare, *Lydia*, vol. 1, p. 193.

125. Ibid., vol. 1, p. 193.

126. M. Springborg, *Feminizing Venereal Disease*, p. 5. April London similarly notes the tendency of the mid-century novel to depict 'women as agents of contamination rather than, equally with men, victims of venereal disease'. A. London, 'Avoiding the Subject: The Presence and Absence of Venereal Disease in the Eighteenth-Century Novel', in L. Merians (ed.), *The Secret Malady: Venereal Disease in Eighteenth Century Britain and France* (Lexington, KY: University Press of Kentucky, 1996), pp. 213–27, on p. 218. As comprehensive as her discussion is, however, it does not extend to Shebbeare's work, which concerns itself inordinately with the problem. In his earlier novel, *The Marriage Act* (1754), Shebbeare places the blame squarely on English lawmakers whose prohibi-

tion of the marriage of minors in the absence of parental consent encourages non-marital sexual relations and by extension, suicide, according to Shebbeare.

127. Cheyne, *The English Malady*, p. 5.

128. Shebbeare's hostility towards the Scottish runs particularly deep, as reflected in his unflattering depiction of *Lydia*'s Dr Macpherson as a quack more concerned with writing treatises on gunshot wounds than actually treating his patients. Shebbeare possibly models MacPherson on popular Scottish physicians like Cheyne.

129. R. Sweet, 'Antiquaries and Antiquities in Eighteenth-Century England', *Eighteenth Century Studies*, 34:2 (2001), pp. 181–206.

130. E. Hobsbawm, 'Introduction: Inventing Tradition', in E. Hobsbawm and T. Ranger (eds), *The Invention of Tradition* (Oxford: Blackwell, 1983), pp. 1–15, on p. 1.

131. Edensor, *National Identity, Popular Culture and Everyday Life*, p. 4. In Edensor's opinion, Hobsbawm's work particularly reveals a Frankfurtian understanding that the masses are drawn together by such ceremonies, and are powerless to resist the overwhelming appeal that they impart, passively ingesting ideological messages. Rather than the culture industries, it is the cultural elite who bewitch them with their designs'. Ibid., p. 5. As Edensor points out, both historians view the nation as a wholly modern construct, rather than having a pre-modern, ethnic basis, which is the contention of Anthony Smith and John Hutchinson.

132. R. Radhakrishnan would argue that paradox is a distinguishing feature of the 'contradictory discourse of nationalism'. Radhakrishnan, *Diasporic Mediations: Between Home and Location* (Minneapolis, MN: University of Minnesota Press, 1996), p. 195.

133. Adams, *An Essay Concerning Self-Murther*, p. 2.

134. In other words, although Christian moralists and legal authorities were inclined to punish suicide more severely in the absence of extenuating circumstances such as lunacy or acute despair, an alternative strand of thought concentrated on the deleterious effects of a suicidal mentality left at large in the world.

4 The Pathology of Sentiment

1.   J. W. von Goethe, *The Autobiography of Goethe: Truth and Fiction Relating to My Life*, trans. John Oxenford (London: G. Bell & Sons, 1874), vol. 1, p. 163.

2.   C. Moore, *A Full Inquiry into the Subject of Suicide*, 2 vols (London, J. F. and C. Rivington, 1790), vol. 1, p. 360.

3.   Ibid.

4.   B. Duncan remarks that the idea that 'the book inspired numerous people to take their own lives, is largely a fiction invented by overly zealous social guardians, but one that still adds stability to the novel's history and underscores its cultural significance'. See B. Duncan, *Goethe's* Werther *and the Critics* (Rochester, NY: Camden House, 2005), p. 1. Later in life, Goethe retrospectively remarked, 'My ... friends thought that they must transform poetry into reality, imitate a novel like this in real life and, in any case, shoot themselves; and what occurred at first among a few took place later among the general public.' ... Goethe is quoted in D. Phillips, 'The Influence of Suggestion on Suicide: Substantive and Theoretical Implications of the Werther Effect', in *The American Sociological Review*, 39:3 (1974), pp. 340–54, on p. 340.

5.   G. Minois reports that in 1784 a young Englishwoman killed herself in her bed with a copy of Werther under her pillow, while a 'young Swede' similarly shot himself with a

copy of Werther by his side, and another individual cast himself out of the window with the novel on his person. Minnois, *History of Suicide*, p. 267.

6. P. Mortensen, *British Romanticism and Continental Influences: Writing in an Age of Europhobia* (New York: Palgrave, 2004), p. 32.

7. As R. Bell observes, *Werther* was based loosely on Rousseau's *Nouvelle Heloise*. R. Bell, 'In Werther's Thrall: Suicide and the Power of Sentimental Reading in Early National America', *Early American Literature*, 46:1 (2011), pp. 93–120, on p. 94.

8. The mass anxiety aroused by the publication of *The Sorrows of Werther* did not prevent the book from being repackaged as tragedy and performed on stage. On March 2, 1786, the *Times* announced the benefit performance of *Werter*, a tragedy based on the Goethe novel, which, perhaps owing to the 'very elegant and very full audience' it attracted to its 'second representation', led to its subsequent appearance at the Covent Garden Theatre, featuring Sarah Siddons in the role of Lotte. The aesthetic double standard according to which Werther cannot find accommodation within the novel but may appear without repercussions on the stage, provided he renounce his suicide belatedly, meets with protest in *Desmond* in the form of Geraldine's complaint that 'while novels have been condemned as being injurious to the interest of virtue, the play-house has been called the school of morality'. C. Smith, *Desmond*, eds. A. Blank and J. Todd (Peterborough, ON: Broadview, 2001), p. 224. The Werther effect was, according to this logic, strictly a text-borne epidemic.

9. Although clearly a notion of suicide contagion was in currency during this period, the term 'Werther effect' was not coined until the early 1970's sociological research of D. Phillips who, having detected a correlation between newspaper headlines reporting suicide and the rate of suicide, suggested that 'behavioural patterns in society can in fact operate as "contagions"'. See D. Phillips, 'The Influence of Suggestion on Suicide', p. 340.

10. M. MacDonald has written extensively on the subject of how 'The rapid growth of the newspaper and periodical industry after 1700 transformed the social context within which suicide was understood. The press made suicide a much more public event than it had been before'. See M. MacDonald, 'Suicide and the Rise of the Popular Press in England', *Representations*, 22 (1988), pp. 36–59, on p. 41.

11. Minois affirms that 'Werther did not create a fashion; it expressed a climate to which it gave form'. See Minois, *History of Suicide*, p. 267.

12. F. J. Lampert remarks that the 'blue coat is an interesting if perhaps rather trivial illustration of the complexity of Anglo- or [...] British-German literary relations at the time: the blue coat habitually worn by K. W. Jerusalem, the real-life or real-death model for Goethe's Werther, was, as Goethe tells us in his autobiography, an "English fashion"'. See F. J. Lampert, 'Goethe, Ossian and Werther', in F. Stafford and H. Gaskill (eds.), *From Gaelic to Romantic: Ossianic Translation* (Amsterdam: Rodopi, 1998), pp. 97–106, on p. 97. Moreover, as R. Schiffman notes in her recent survey of Wertherism in Britain, 'Werther had ceased to be German in the minds of the reading and publishing public; instead, he became an English sentimental and Romantic character. There were many English Werthers; something about his character uniquely suited the British, and he fit very comfortably into the century's taxonomy of men of feeling, Mackenzie's *Man of Feeling* having appeared just three years before *Werther*'s original German publication'. R. Schiffman, 'A Concert of Werthers', *Eighteenth-Century Studies*, 43:2 (2010), pp. 207–22, on p. 211. Schiffman mentions R. Croft, *Love and Madness* (London: G. Kearsly, 1780) in passing, but is more concerned with the Anglicicization of Werther than with the contagion of suicide, which is the focus of this discussion.

13. M. Novak, 'The Sensibility of Sir Herbert Croft in *Love and Madness* and the *Life of Edward Young*', in P. Korshin (ed.), *The Age of Johnson* (New York: AMS Press, 1987), p. 193. As Novak notes, the introduction to the first English translation of *Werther* indicated that 'the design ... is to exhibit a picture of that disordered state of mind, too common in our own country'.

14. See the portrayal of the suicidal Orlando Faulkland in Frances Sheridan's *Memoirs of Miss Sidney Bidulph* (Oxford: Oxford University Press, 1995).

15. Moore, *A Full Inquiry into the Subject of Suicide*, vol. 2, p. 125.

16. W. Rowley, *A Treatise on Female, Nervous, Hysterical, Hypochondriacal, Bilious, Convulsive Diseases; Apoplexy and Palsy; with Thoughts on Madness, Suicide* (London: C. Nourse, 1788), p. 401. According to Rowley, 'Religious and civil toleration are productive of political and religious madness; but where no such toleration exists, no such insanity appears'.

17. Ibid., p. 400.

18. Ibid., p. 94.

19. Cubitt, 'Introduction', in G. Cubitt (ed.), *Imagining Nations* (Manchester: Manchester University Press, 1998), pp. 1–18, on p. 3.

20. Rowley, *A Treatise on Female*, p. 334.

21. R. Huston, 'The Medicalization of Suicide: Medicine and the Law in Scotland and England, circa 1750–1850', in Weaver and Wright (eds), *Histories of Suicide*, pp. 91–118, on p. 109. As Huston writes, the 'discourse of suicide' engaged in by English doctors 'clashed with that of the public'. Ibid., p. 109.

22. Ibid., p. 93.

23. See G. de Staël, *Refléxions sur le suicide* (Paris: Editions de l'Opale, 1983), p. 184.

24. Ibid., p. 183.

25. See Durkheim, *Suicide*, p. 147.

26. D. Hume, *Treatise of Human Nature* (New York: Dover, 2003), 2.1.11, p. 317.

27. Spinoza's concept of 'the imitation of affects' holds that 'the images of things are affections of the human body whose ideas represent external bodies as present to us, that is, whose ideas involve the nature of our body and at the same time the present nature of the external body'. Spinoza, *Ethics* (New York: Dover, 1955), p. 27.

28. A. Smith, *The Theory of Moral Sentiments* (Cambridge: Cambridge University Press, 1997), p. 345.

29. B. Lowe, *Victorian Fiction and the Insights of Sympathy* (London and New York: Anthem Press, 2007), p. 32.

30. M. Robert, *The Origins of The Novel* (Brighton: Harvester Press, 1980), p. 170.

31. Moore, *A Full Inquiry into the Subject of Suicide*, vol. 2, p. 126.

32. See *The Autobiography of Goethe: Truth and Fiction* for Goethe's account of the inspiration that Jerusalem's death gave him for *Werther*.

33. McKeon (ed.), *Theory of the Novel*, p. 607.

34. In this one regard I disagree with R. Miles's compelling reading of print culture in 'Forging a Romantic Identity: Herbert Croft's *Love and Madness* and W. H. Ireland's Shakespeare MS', *Eighteenth-Century Fiction*, 17:4 (2005), pp. 600–27, p. 624. Miles offers a detailed and provocative account of Croft's manipulation of celebrity culture in reconstructing Hackman's interiority, arguing that the 'fictive' is not itself contagious, but it is really the manipulation of the image in certain contexts that promotes contagion.

35. J. M. R. Lenz, 'Letters on the Morality of *The Sorrows of Young Werther*', in T. J. Chamberlain (ed.), *Eighteenth-Century German Criticism* (New York: Continuum, 1992), pp. 197–203, on p. 202.

36. C. Wellbery, 'From Mirrors to Images: The Transformation of Sentimental Paradigms in Goethe's *The Sorrows of Young Werther*', *Studies in Romanticism*, 25:2 (1986), pp. 231–49, on p. 246. Literary critic T. Siebers similarly attributes Werther's appeal to 'the superior power of esthetics to organize our sentiments'. T. Siebers, 'The Werther Effect: The Esthetics of Suicide', *Mosaic*, 26:1 (1993), pp. 15–34, on p. 33.

37. Lowe, *Victorian Fiction and the Insights of Sympathy*.

38. C. Pateman, *The Sexual Contract* (Palo Alto, CA: Stanford University Press, 1988), p. 96.

39. Moore, *A Full Inquiry into the Subject of Suicide*, vol. 2, p. 147.

40. Ibid., vol. 2, p. 129.

41. Quoted in M. O. Grenby, The *Anti-Jacobin Novel: British Conservatism and the French Revolution* (Cambridge: Cambridge University Press, 2001), p. 10.

42. Johnson, *Equivocal Beings*, p. 13.

43. Rowley, *A Treatise on Female*, p. 56.

44. J. W. von Goethe, *The Sufferings of Young Werther*, trans. H. Steinhauer (New York: Norton, 1970), p. 80.

45. Brown, *The Art of Suicide*, pp. 134–5. Brown argues that these thinkers were more concerned with 'protecting English masculinity from romantic and daring notions of suicide than with a deliberate resignification of suicide as masculine or masculinity itself'.

46. R. Miles ironically but appropriately describes the sensation provoked by the event as 'Hackmania'. Miles, 'Forging a Romantic Identity', p. 614.

47. In his compelling treatment of the implications of Croft's initially anonymous publication of *Love and Madness*, R. Griffin represents the author as a savvy and shrewd businessman eager to capitalize on public interest in the scandal. As he notes, in part because some readers initially believed in the correspondence's authenticity, the book was enormously successful, 'went to a second edition after one month, and a third and a fourth within one year'. See R. J. Griffin, 'Fact, Fiction, and Anonymity: Reading *Love and Madness: A Story Too True* (1780)', *Eighteenth-Century Fiction*, 16:4 (2004), pp. 619–48, on p. 624.

48. Whether M. Ray did in fact enter into an affair with Hackman has never been established. The historical record paints Hackman as a sensitive youth unable to overcome his fatal infatuation with Sandwich's mistress, but Croft's and other accounts are based largely on speculation. For a detailed treatment of the case, see J. Brewer, *A Sentimental Murder: Love and Madness in the Eighteenth Century* (New York: Farrar, Straus, and Giroux, 2004).

49. Croft, *Love and Madness*, p. 21. The ominous use of the adverb 'yet' suggests that Hackman's metamorphosis into the archetypal figure of jealousy has already begun. Despite his identification of Othello as one of his personal heroes, Hackman insists that Othello 'should have put himself to death in his wife's sight, not his wife' (on p. 26). Hackman maintained until his execution that his intention had been only to kill himself in Ray's presence, and it's plausible that Croft inserts this detail to bolster the case that Hackman's shooting of Ray was not premeditated.

50. Croft, *Love and Madness*, p. 22.

51. As D. Rabin has shown, juries at this time may have been sympathetic to the temporary insanity plea, but on the whole failed to be persuaded by this sort of defence. D. Rabin,

'Searching for the Self in Eighteenth-Century English Criminal Trials, 1730–1800',
Eighteenth-Century Life, 27:3 (2003), pp. 85–106.

52. Croft, *Love and Madness*, p. 16.
53. Nowhere is this compulsion to write more evident than in Hackman's digression on T.
    Chatterton's life in Letter 51, which exceeds one hundred and twenty pages.
54. The trial that followed was so public as to render its representation in *Love and Mad-
    ness* altogether unnecessary. Significantly, the judge who presided over the case was none
    other than W. Blackstone, the formidable legal mind of the eighteenth century who had
    long since declared suicide an offense to both 'God and King'.
55. 'Review: Herbert Croft's *Love and Madness*', *The London Magazine* 1780, vol. 50, p. 179.
56. Croft, *Love and Madness*, p. 252.
57. Ibid., p. 252.
58. Ibid.
59. Ibid., p. 253.
60. R. Schiffman observes, 'The novel's many editions (both authorized and pirated.) and
    translations flooded the German, French, British, and American literary markets into
    the nineteenth century. Thirty separate British and American editions and translations
    of *Werther* appeared in 1779, when it was first translated into English, until 1886; there
    were over fifty in French'. 'A Concert of Werthers', p. 208.
61. Moore, *A Full Inquiry into the Subject of Suicide*, vol. 2, p. 123.
62. In his book-length study of the case, J. Brewer notes that Croft's name was included on
    the subscription list to Moore's work. Brewer, *A Sentimental Murder*, p. 172.
63. *London Magazine* 1779; vol. 49.230.
64. What is interesting to note here is that, as the amatory correspondence in *Love and Mad-
    ness* reaffirms, a French translation of Goethe's work had already been in circulation in
    Britain by 1775.
65. Croft's own representation of the fictionalized correspondence between M. Ray and J.
    Hackman as authentic, as well as his purloined Chatterton letter, requires this justifi-
    cation. See B. Goldberg's article, 'Romantic Professionalism in 1800: Robert Southey,
    Herbert Croft, and the Letters and Legacy of Thomas Chatterton', *ELH*, 63:3 (1996),
    pp. 681–706.
66. S. A. D. Tissot, 'Essay on the Diseases Incident to Literary Persons' (Dublin: James Wil-
    liams, 1769), p. 254.
67. MacDonald and Murphy, *Sleepless Souls*, p. 194.
68. Perhaps as a result of a growing concern over adolescent suicide, the first English transla-
    tion omitted the adjectival reference to youth.
69. Novak, 'The Sensibility of Sir Herbert Croft in *Love and Madness* and the *Life of Edward
    Young*', p. 193.
70. Croft's suspicion of the contaminating influence of the novel has its roots in seventeenth-
    century thought. As M. Fournier observes in respect to seventeenth-century French
    atttitudes towards the novel, 'Early modern critics who attack bad reading habits make
    the novel into the contagious genre *par excellence*, as it propagates vice and illegitimate
    passions'. See M. Fournier, 'The Pathology of Reading: The Novel as an Agent of Con-
    tagion', in C. L. Carlin (ed.), *Imagining Contagion in Early Modern Europe* (New York:
    Palgrave, 2005), pp. 195–211, on p. 195.
71. Croft, *Love and Madness*, p. 297.
72. However, as R. Miles observes, the fear of contagion was exactly what 'subsequent news-
    paper reports reveal ... for some time after (the Hackman scandal), the press reported

various copycat incidences from around the country'. Miles, 'Forging a Romantic Identity', p. 616.

73. Croft, *Love and Madness*, p. 286.

74. Ibid., p. 33. Croft also avers in a footnote that 'Had [Werther] not died by his own hand, he had not deserved to live' before making the unqualified anti-Goethe remark that 'the writer is not a much better man'. Ibid., p. 286. Croft's conflation of Werther with Goethe suggests the autobiographical reading of his novel that was so common in the period.

75. Croft, *Love and Madness*, p. 73.

76. Moore, *A Full Inquiry into the Subject of Suicide*, vol. 2, p. 124.

77. According to McKeon, example is bound up with the social exercise of virtue whereas precept might be aligned with the epistemological category of the truth. See McKeon's chapter in McKeon (ed.), *Theory of the Novel*.

78. Moore, *A Full Inquiry into the Subject of Suicide*, vol. 2, p. 156.

79. Ibid., vol. 2, p. 157.

80. Ibid., vol. 2, p.157.

81. Croft, *Love and Madness*, p. 75.

82. Ibid., p. 146.

83. Communities of individuals all united by their shared suicidal tendencies, English organizations such as the 'Last Guinea Club' were arguably products of this mentality. Paradoxically, in presenting suicide as a group activity, the club masculinizes suicide, placing it on a par with the group sacrifices of revolutionary events.

84. Brewer, *A Sentimental Murder*, p. 70.

85. Croft, *Love and Madness*, p. 297.

86. Ibid., unnumbered page.

87. Hackman's execution suggests the transition to the 'ceremony of mourning' that, as Foucault points out, replaced the older spectacular rite of execution. In the late eighteenth century, public punishment manifested a 'double affliction: that a citizen should have been capable of ignoring the law and that one should have been obliged to separate oneself from a citizen'. M. Foucault, *Discipline and Punish: The Birth of the Prison*, trans. A. Sheridan (New York: Vintage, 1995), p. 110. The atmosphere of mourning that attended Hackman's demise illustrates the extent to which a scene of execution could galvanize public sentiment by instituting the victim as a martyr figure. Hackman's execution scene actualizes his death wish and becomes the centre of a 'community of sentiment' defined by national mourning of voluntary death.

88. W. Dawes, *The Case and Memoirs of the Late Reverend James Hackman* (London: G. Kearsley, 1779), unnumbered postscript. This work claimed to derive firsthand from Hackman during visits to his cell. This account was challenged by *The Case and Memoirs of Mrs. Martha Reay* that appeared shortly after this work.

89. Dawes, *The Case and Memoirs of the Late Reverend James Hackman*, p. 28. Hackman was merely nineteen upon their first meeting and eleven years Ray's junior.

90. Although Croft distances himself from the work through the mouthpiece of Hackman's friend Charles, who claims that 'the pamphlet called "Case and Memoirs" is a miserable business, and may do that very mischief of which Hackman was afraid' (Croft, *Love and Madness*, p. 296), it was, as J. Brewer points out, published by G. Kearsley as part of 'an elaborate publicity campaign to promote *Love and Madness*' (Brewer, *A Sentimental Murder*, p. 152), which was also published by the Kearsley printing house. The 'mischief' that Croft alludes to concerns the painting of Ray as a 'capricious and ungrateful woman',

which could not have pleased her lover, the Earl of Sandwich, to whom Croft sent a copy of a later edition of the work in 1786 in an effort to placate him.

91. Dawes, *The Case and Memoirs of the Late Reverend James Hackman*, p. 27.
92. Ibid., p. 21.
93. Brewer, *A Sentimental Murder*, p. 181.
94. Croft, *Love and Madness*, p. 284.
95. Moore, *A Full Inquiry into the Subject of Suicide*, vol. 2, p. 163.
96. B. Goldberg observes that 'Hackman thus emerges, in Croft's terms, as more honorable than Othello, whose final speech provides the introduction to this fictional correspondence. He also proves in this way to be more honorable than the poor sexton's son, T. Chatterton, whose life takes up nearly a third of the novel, and whose own suicide makes him the thematic foil to the "virtuous" Hackman'. Goldberg, 'Romantic Professionalism in 1800', p. 682.
97. *Inventaire de la Correspondance litteraire de Grimm et Meister/Ulla Kolving et Jeanne Carriat*, ed. U. Kolving and J. Carriat (Oxford: Voltaire Foundation at the Taylor Institution, 1984), p. 210. On the other side of the debate, the physician W. Rowley attributes Cato's death to 'his pride and timidity'. Rowley, *A Treatise on Female*, p. 339.
98. Siebers, 'The Werther Effect: The Esthetics of Suicide', p. 31.
99. Goethe, *The Sufferings of Young Werther*, p. 81. As countless critics have pointed out, the translation of Goethe's title as *The Sufferings of Werther* more closely approximates the German title with its emphasis on the almost Job-like, paschal ordeals that the character endures. The English translation, *The Sorrows of Werther*, in a sense downplays the character's sufferings by rendering them as purely an emotional affliction.
100. See John, 10:17–18, 'For this reason the Father loves Me, because I lay down My life so that I may take it again. No one has taken it away from Me, but I lay it down on My own initiative. I have authority to lay it down, and I have authority to take it up again. This commandment I received from My Father'.
101. R. Barthes, *A Lover's Discourse: Fragments*, trans. R. Howard (New York: Hill & Wang, 1978), p. 210.
102. Goethe, *The Sufferings of Young Werther*, p. 30.
103. Croft, *Love and Madness*, p. lix.
104. Ibid., p. 275.
105. Moore, *A Full Inquiry into the Subject of Suicide*, vol. 2, p. 161.
106. V. Lind's category for this phenomenon is that of the 'suicidal murder', which she reads as an extreme case in which the knowledge of the religious consequences of suicide still current in the early modern period led to a 'coldly calculated, active strategy by people who were fully conscious of their actions'. V. Lind, 'The Suicidal Mind and Body: Examples from Northern Germany', in J. Watt (ed.), *From Sin to Insanity: Suicide in Early Modern Europe* (Ithaca, NY: Cornell University Press, 2004), pp. 64–80, on p. 78.
107. Goethe, *The Sufferings of Young Werther*, p. 54.
108. R. Bage, *Hermsprong; or, Man as He Is Not*, ed. P. Perkins (Peterborough, ON: Broadview, 2002), p. 105. Hermsprong takes 'suicide as a proof compleat' that 'man can get above the fear of death' (p. 105) and insists that it need not be interpreted as a mark of insanity. Even though Hermsprong does not explicitly countenance suicide, his interlocutor accuses him of disseminating 'the abominable doctrines of the French philosophers' (p. 185).
109. Moore, *A Full Inquiry into the Subject of Suicide*, vol. 2, p. 151.

110. E. J. Clery, *The Feminization Debate in Eighteenth-Century England. Literature, Commerce, and Luxury* (London: Palgrave, 2004), p. 172. In *Desmond*, the protagonist's French reformist friend, Montfleuri, complains that 'throughout the revolution, every circumstance has, on [the English] side of the water, been exaggerated, falsified, distorted, and misrepresented, to serve the purposes of Party'. C. Smith, *Desmond*, p. 412.

111. Grenby, *The Anti-Jacobin Novel*, p. 18.

112. Quoted in ibid., p. 11.

113. *The London Corresponding Society* 1796, vol. 1, p. 201.

114. Indeed, the impression of many that Rousseau advocated suicide probably resulted in the mistaken belief that he had taken his life when in 1778 he died of a sudden attack of thrombosis.

115. *The Anti-Jacobin Examiner* (1799), p. 167. As M. O. Grenby writes, 'Jacobinism [...] was a gestalt with no set definition [...] a label for all that conservatives found detestable in society'. Grenby, *The Anti-Jacobin Novel*, p. 7.

116. *The London Corresponding Society*, 1796, vol. 1, p. 201.

117. Goethe, *The Sufferings of Young Werther*, p. 7.

118. P. Higonnet, *Goodness beyond Virtue: Jacobins during the French Revolution* (Cambridge, MA: Harvard University Press, 1998), p. 205.

119. To this end, the perennially suicidal Coke Clifton of Holcroft's *Anna St. Ives* (1791) is restored to life numerous times and ultimately persuaded that his life is indeed 'survivable'. The narrator of Bage's *Hermsprong* fails even in his attempt at a suicide, while Frederick Seymour in Williams's *Julia* conveniently meets a 'natural' death before he can realize the fate of Werther.

120. D. L. Hoeveler identifies *Emmeline* as 'a sentimental novel with a gothic novel buried within it', the 'forgotten urtext for the female gothic novel tradition'. D. L. Hoeveler, *Gothic Feminism: The Professionalization of Gender from Charlotte Smith to the Brontes* (University Park, PA: Pennsylvania State University Press, 1998), pp. 37–8. Arguably, this novel introduces Werther to the gothic plot.

121. C. Smith, *Emmeline*, ed. Loraine Fletcher (Peterborough, ON: Broadview, 2003), p. 187.

122. Ibid., p. 209.

123. Ibid., p. 186.

124. Ibid.

125. Ibid., p. 187.

126. Ibid.

127. C. Moore identifies duelling as 'another kind of suicide [...] its danger being promoted or at least voluntarily submitted to by the person himself'. Moore, *A Full Inquiry into the Subject of Suicide*, vol. 1, p. 3.

128. Werther's mentality is so permeated from the beginning by the idea of suicide that even a figurative allusion to being pierced as with a sword by Lotte's words elicits his wish to 'run a sword through his body' or 'seize a knife [...] to ease this oppressed heart of mine'. Goethe, *The Sufferings of Young Werther*, p. 54.

129. Hoeveler, *Gothic Feminism*, p. 42.

130. Delamere resembles the aptly named Orlando Somerive, the romantic hero of Smith's slightly later novel, *The Old Manor House* (1794), who fights against his conscience on the British side of the American War of Independence.

131. As Thorold assures Celestina, 'If the sacrifice I make has any merit in your eyes, how cheaply would your approbation be purchased even by the loss of existence'. Smith, *Celestina*, ed. L. Fletcher (Peterborough, ON: Broadview, 2004), p. 341.

132. Ibid., p. 116.

133. Ibid., p. 117.

134. The prosthetic object of the book reminds us of the etymological import of contagion, which literally derives from the Latin word for 'touch'. The fact that the book is denounced by Cathcart's insensible and mean-spirited employers suggests the text's tacit affirmation of *Werther*.

135. Smith, *Celestina*, p. 571 (appendix).

136. J. Todd attributes Smith's resignation to the plot of the sentimental courtship novel to the demands of both her public and her publisher. The fact that the tragedy version of *Werther* enjoyed so much success seems to dispute Smith's assessment of the public taste. J. Todd, 'Introduction', in Smith, *Desmond*, pp. v–vii.

137. Smith, *Desmond*, p. 45.

138. Ibid., p. 299.

139. As Bethel informs Desmond, 'I expect to have you enacting very soon the part of an English Werter; for you seem far gone in his species of insanity'. Smith, *Desmond*, p. 299.

140. Smith, *Desmond*, p. 147.

141. Rowley, *A Treatise on Female*, p. 345.

142. Smith, *Desmond*, p. 299.

143. Ibid., p. 57.

144. Even Croft's Hackman critiques Werther's passivity for 'quietly seeing Charlotte marry another man, without so much as offering to marry her [him]self'. Croft, *Love and Madness*, p. 284.

145. Smith, *Desmond*, p. 178.

146. Ibid., p. 378.

147. Ibid.

148. Ibid., p. 378.

149. Ibid., p. 374.

150. J. Goldhammer, *The Headless Republic: Sacrificial Violence in Modern French Thought* (Ithaca, NY: Cornell University Press, 2005), p. 21.

151. Smith, *Desmond*, p. 389.

152. Ibid., p. 161.

153. Lind, 'The Suicidal Mind and Body', p. 67.

154. Smith, *Desmond*, p. 412. In his dissertation on suicide, Charles Moore exempts those 'who sacrifice themselves for the good of their country' from the charge of suicide. Claiming that 'The performance of the duties being [the soldier's] just point in view, he is not answerable for consequences that he cannot obviate, even though they should bring death and destruction upon himself', Moore insists that 'death comes as an uninvited guest, attendant on some just or noble action [...] through the medium of external causes'. *A Full Inquiry into the Subject of Suicide*, vol. 1, pp. 37–8.

155. Sympathy for citizens of other countries was intrinsic to this sense of cosmopolitanism. Celestina, in Smith's novel of the same name, declares that 'the whole world was her country', in keeping with this spirit of internationalism. Smith, *Celestina*, p. 460.

156. E. Wikborg, 'Political Discourse versus Sentimental Romance: Ideology and Genre in Charlotte Smith's *Desmond*', *English Studies: A Journal of English Language and Literature*, 78 (1997), pp. 522–31, on p. 531.

157. In this respect I agree with A. Conway's position that the novel 'articulates most forcefully the way that desire informs politics'. See A. M. Conway, 'Nationalism, Revolution, and the Female Body: Charlotte Smith's *Desmond*', *Women's Studies*, 24:5 (1995), pp. 395–409, on p. 396.

158. In her introduction to the Broadview edition of *Celestina*, L. Fletcher persuasively argues that English sympathizers with the French revolutionaries' cause identified more explicitly with the Girondins' position than with the more radical politics of the French Jacobins. Fletcher, 'Introduction', in Smith, *Celestina*, p. 31. If the English Jacobins sympathized primarily with the Girondins, the revolutionaries' collective suicides (a choice many apparently preferred to execution at the hands of Robespierre, who had declared them enemies to the state in 1793) must have registered as an extreme shock to their sympathizers' sensibility, notwithstanding the fact, as Durkheim notes, that the Girondins' deaths were not considered suicides by prominent early nineteenth-century French thinkers such as Esquirol and Falret. Durkheim, *Suicide*, p. 239.

159. N. J. Watson, *Revolution and the Form of the British Novel 1790–1825* (Oxford: Clarendon Press, 1994), p. 38.

160. Geraldine is also modelled on the character of Julie, who in Rousseau's *La Nouvelle Heloise* (1764) redeems herself for previous indiscretions by remaining faithful to her husband notwithstanding the continued devotion of her former lover, St Preux.

161. The second English translation of the work reveals the interest British readers took in Charlotte's character in its revised title, *Werter and Charlotte*, while editions of Charlotte's letters to Werther and poems composed on the 'Sorrows of Charlotte', all work to illuminate her perspective.

162. As D. Bowstead observes, Geraldine is driven 'by the emotional impetus of suicidal despair'. D. Bowstead, 'Charlotte Smith's *Desmond:* The Epistolary Novel as Ideological Argument', in M. A. Schofield and C. Macheski (eds), *Fetter'd or Free? British Women Novelists, 1670–1815* (Athens, OH: Ohio University Press, 1986), pp. 237–63, on p. 260.

163. Smith, *Desmond*, p. 284.

164. Ibid., p. 220. R. Brown's observation (in reference to views expressed in Lombroso's nineteenth-century text, *The Female Offender)* that 'female suicide is described as lacking virtue and maternal instinct' might as readily be applied generally to attitudes towards the suicide of mothers in this period. See Brown, *The Art of Suicide*, p. 189.

165. N. Alarcón, C. Kaplan and M. Moallem, 'Introduction: Between Woman and Nation', in Alarcón et al. (eds) *Between Woman and Nation*, pp. 1–18, on p. 13.

166. Smith, *Desmond*, p. 303.

167. Ibid., p. 172.

168. For a discussion of the construction of femininity in revolutionary iconography, see Higonnet, *Goodness beyond Virtue*.

169. The real-life precedent for this figure is provided by M. Wollstonecraft; Godwin's *Memoirs of the Author of a Vindication of the Rights of Women* identifies Mary Wollstonecraft as 'a female Werther' on account of the 'refined and exquisite sensibility' she shared with the Germanic literary figure.

170. Smith, *Desmond*, p. 226.

171. Ibid., p. 334.

172. Ibid., p. 159.

173. The irony of her statement is revealed to her only at the end of the narrative, when Geraldine recognizes that Desmond has enacted the 'saviour' role of Faulkland throughout.

174. K. M. Rogers, *Feminism in Eighteenth-Century England* (Brighton: Harvester, 1982), p. 125.

175. Geraldine does express an interest in political developments across the Channel and identifies herself explicitly as a democrat, although she confesses that the chief reason for her politics is the fact that they differ from her husband's own aristocratic leanings. N. Watson observes that Smith 'depicts [Geraldine] emphasizing their fellowship in suffering rather than exploring the possibility of analogous rebellion', in Watson, *Revolution and the Form of the British Novel 1790–1825*, p. 37. The political is not altogether foreclosed to Geraldine, but it is translated into the feminine idiom of passive empathy. Wikborg notes that 'Geraldine's submission to martyrdom is actually less passive than it may seem, for she is shown as actively seeking it as a form of self-justification'. Wikborg, 'Political Discourse versus Sentimental Romance', p. 529.

176. W. Donoghue, *Enlightenment Fiction in England, France, and America* (Gainesville, FL: University Press of Florida, 2002).

177. Johnson, *Equivocal Beings*, p. 12. In this book Johnson emphatically rejects the notion that the feminization of eighteenth-century culture via the endorsement of sensibility actually served to empower women, an argument suggested in G. J. Barker-Benfield, *The Culture of Sensibility: Sex and Society in Eighteenth-Century Britain* (Chicago, IL: University of Chicago Press, 1992).

178. This is the claim that Blanchot makes in his discourse on suicide, which argues that an individual strong enough to commit suicide is strong enough to live in the world and indeed lead it. Blanchot, *The Space of Literature*, p. 99.

179. In his recent study of J. Austen's writing, D. A. Miller argues that the hypochondriac theme that dominates her last work enacts a morbidity drive of sorts, which, like Freud's death drive, involves 'the insistent push of all things ... toward their undoing' but, unlike Freud's reality principle, stops at the point of death, given the constraints of the novel and its need for the consummation of the marriage plot. D. A. Miller, *Jane Austen, or the Secret of Style* (Princeton, NJ: Princeton University Press, 2003), p. 77.

180. Smith, *Desmond*, p. 330.

181. Bethel's demand, 'Why is it that such a cruel sacrifice was ever made?' (Smith, *Desmond*, p. 180), recurs in various forms throughout the narrative. In his *Thoughts on the Frequency of Divorce in the Modern Times, and on the necessity of legislative exertion to prevent their continued prevalence* (1800), A. Sibbit blames the rising divorce rate on female reading habits, protesting that 'The voluptuous pages of the distinguished citizen of Geneva, the ravings of *Werter*, the profane *Monk*, and all that horde of licentious miscreants, whose writings can only tend to dethrone reason and set fire to the passions, are all devoured by *Miss* in her teens'. A. Sibbit, *Thoughts on the Frequency of Divorce in the Modern Times* (London: 1800), pp. 10–11. C. Moore similarly complained that Goethe's work fostered conjugal disaffection by representing the 'unrestrained intercourse' between Lotte and Werther. Moore, *A Full Inquiry into the Subject of Suicide*, vol. 2, p. 147. Reluctant to follow T. Holcroft's example in *Anna St. Ives* (1792) of rejecting marriage as a moribund institution, Smith treads delicately in her Werther plots, and in *Desmond* offers an affirmation of marriage through the union of Desmond and Geraldine at the narrative's end.

182. Watson, *Revolution and the Form of the British Novel 1790–1825*, p. 16.

183. Bowstead, 'Charlotte Smith's *Desmond*', p. 238.

184. Quoted in ibid., p. 239.

185. Smith, *Desmond*, p. 324.

186. Ibid., p. 325.

187. Ibid., p. 325.

188. Ibid., p. 330.

189. Ibid., p. 223.

190. Ibid., p. 225.

191. Ibid.

192. Ibid., p. 226.

193. Donoghue, *Enlightenment Fiction in England, France, and America*, p. 14.

194. Smith, *Desmond*, p. 215.

195. As Mortensen notes, the malady metaphor 'severs textual affects from personal agency and authorial subjectivity, erasing the distinctions between victim and perpetrator'. Mortensen, *British Romanticism and Continental Influences*, p. 42.

196. S. Currie observes that in Roman culture poison and women were historically associated. S. Currie, 'Poisonous Women and Unnatural History in Roman Culture', in M. Wyke (ed.), *Parchments of Gender: Deciphering the Bodies of Antiquity* (Oxford: Clarendon Press, 1998), pp. 147–67.

197. Smith, *Desmond*, p. 215.

198. McKeon (ed.), *Theory of the Novel*, p. 601.

199. Smith, *Desmond*, p. 223.

200. Yet even while Geraldine claims to have been impervious to the novel's influence and obliquely suggests that she might have been better advised to learn filial 'disobedience' from those novels that she did read, she acknowledges her similarity to S. Bidulph, as mentioned already.

201. Smith, *Desmond*, p. 216.

202. Ibid.

203. M. McKeon states that 'one effect of the cult of sensibility was to sensitize commentators to the way the circuit between feeling and thought, example and precept, fictional distress and active moral response, could be shorted out by the very textual pleasures that were supposed to complete it'. McKeon (ed.), *Theory of the Novel*, p. 606. Given that detractors of *Werther* inevitably endorsed this notion that aesthetic pleasure could neutralize a work's didactic import, it is not surprising that Smith would identify the novel's function as the soothing of the anxieties produced by everyday life. Smith insists upon the novel's neutrality, perhaps even amorality, even as she employs it as a vehicle to promote a reformist agenda. T. Castle has addressed the growing sense in the late eighteenth and early nineteenth century that reading was a 'phantasmagorical process': 'Medical writers [...] frequently warned that excessive reading – and especially reading books of a romantic or visionary nature – could send one into morbid hallucinatory states'. T. Castle, *The Female Thermometer: Eighteenth-Century Culture and the Invention of the Uncanny* (Oxford: Oxford University Press, 1995), p. 56.

204. M. Hays, *Letters and Moral Essays* (London: T. Knot, 1793), p. 94.

205. Hays, *Letters and Moral Essays*, p. 94.

206. E. P. Thompson, *The Making of the English Working Class* (New York: Vintage, 1966), p. 83.

207. H. M. Williams, *Julia: A Novel* (New York: Garland Press, 1974), p. 202. C. Moore condemned the 'woe-worn print on the grounds that it was 'ill-calculated to promote the cause of conjugal felicity'. Moore, *A Full Inquiry into the Subject of Suicide*, vol. 2, p. 124. More recently, M. Ellis reads the engraving as 'an overdetermined sign [...] whose citation implicitly repudiates the resolution of the narrative dilemma by suicide'. See M. Ellis, *The Politics of Sensibility: Race, Gender and Commerce in the Sentimental Novel*

(Cambridge: Cambridge University Press, 1996), p. 219. Notably, the print foregrounds female sensibility, focusing on Lotte's mourning and the afterlife of Werther that was celebrated in English culture.

208. Williams, *Julia*, vol. 2, p. 202. W. Stafford calls *Julia* 'a rewriting, a cleaning-up of Goethe's *Werther* and perhaps of Rousseau's *Julie*'. See W. Stafford, *English Feminists and Their Opponents in the 1790s: Unsex'd and Proper Females* (Manchester: Manchester University Press, 2002), p. 106.

209. Williams, *Julia*, p. 203.

210. Ibid.

211. C. E. Forth, 'Moral Contagion and the Will', in A. Bashford and C. Hooker (eds), *Contagion: Epidemics, History and Culture from Smallpox to Anthrax* (Australia: Pluto Press, 2002), pp. 61–75, on p. 63.

212. For women, this model is particularly problematic and indicative of the sort of thinking attributed to Martha Ray in *Love and Madness*, which suggests that she derives sadomasochistic pleasure from the thought of dying at Hackman's hands.

213. See J. Goldhammer for a discussion of the French Revolution's recuperation of 'ancient concepts of sacrificial virtue'. Goldhammer, *The Headless Republic*, p. 2.

214. As B. Noys points out, 'the "medicalisation of death" is another sign of the "politicisation of death"'. B. Noys, *The Culture of Death* (Oxford: Berg, 2005), p. 72.

215. J. Fliegelman, *Prodigals and Pilgrims: The American Revolution against Patriarchal Authority, 1750–1800* (Cambridge: Cambridge University Press, 1982), p. 151.

216. 'When the doctor came to the unhappy man, he found him on the floor beyond help, his pulse beating but all his limbs paralyzed. He had shot himself through the head above the right eye; his brains were protruding'. Goethe, *The Sufferings of Werther*, p. 95.

5 'The Death of Reason'

1. X. Bichat, *Physiological Researches on Life and Death*, trans. F. Gold (Boston, MA: Richardson and Lord, 1827), p. 9.

2. F. Broussais, *De l'irritation et de la folie: ouvrage dans lequel les rapports du physique et du moral sont etablis sure les bases de la medicine physiologique* (Paris, 1828), p. 12. I. Hacking observes that 'no one one did find any defective stay-alive organs, but the idea lasted a long time'. Hacking, *The Taming of Chance*, p. 70.

3. Although as E. Williams observes, Broussais 'railed against Montpellier doctrine and vitalism generally' he nonetheless 'employed terms and concepts that were recognizably vitalist in origin'. E. Williams, *The Physical and the Moral: Anthropology, Physiology and Philosophical Medicine in France* (Cambridge: Cambridge University Press, 1994), p. 196.

4. In 'Beyond the Pleasure Principle', Freud avers, 'The hypothesis of self-preservative instincts, such as we attribute to all living beings, stands in marked opposition to the idea that instinctual life as a whole serves to bring about death. Seen in this light, the theoretical importance of the instincts of self-preservation, of self-assertion and of mastery greatly diminished'. Freud, 'Beyond the Pleasure Principle', in *On Metapsychology: The Theory of Psychoanalysis*, trans. J. Strachey (New York: Viking Penguin, 1984), pp. 269–338, on p. 311.

5. Although vitalism was in the ascendancy in the final decades of the eighteenth century, it actually predated the Enlightenment and owed its genesis in large part to the work of G. E. Stahl (1660–1734).

6. Although, as R. Rey points out, this theory does not altogether 'exclude mechanistic or chemical explanations but it subordinates them to a powerful order, the order of life and teleology'. See Rey, 'Vitalism, Medicine and Society', in R. Porter (ed.), *Medicine in the Enlightenment* (Amsterdam: Rodopi Press, 1995), pp. 274–88, on p. 274.
7. The 'cult of sensibility' was also congenial to the 'medico-philosophy' of vitalists like T. de Bordeu who enthused, 'to live is only to feel, and to move, in virtue of feeling'. Quoted in E. Williams, *The Physical and the Moral*, p. 33.
8. R. Rey, 'Vitalism, Medicine and Society', p. 276.
9. P. Cheah succinctly defines vitalism in the following manner: 'Vitalism is the view that organic matter contains a special nonmaterial property, a vital force (i.e., life) that gives it a purposive dyanamism and distinguishes it from matter in general, which is inanimate, unorganized, and governed by mechanical laws. In biological theory, vitalism is associated with the position that life cannot be explained in physicochemical terms'. P. Cheah, *Spectral Nationality: Passages of Freedom from Kant to Postcolonial Literatures of Liberation* (New York: Columbia University Press, 2003), p. 84.
10. For an abbreviated account of this controversy and its relevance to the background for Shelley's *Frankenstein*, see J. M. Caldwell, *Literature and Medicine in Nineteenth-Century Britain: From Mary Shelley to George Eliot* (Cambridge: Cambridge University Press, 2004), p. 26.
11. Marsh, *Suicide: Foucault, History, and Truth*, pp. 98–9.
12. An argument that D. Jones makes in 'Radical Ambivalence: Frances Burney, Jacobinism, and the Politics of Romantic Fiction', *Women's Writing*, 10:1 (2003), pp. 3–25, on p. 3.
13. F. Burney, *Camilla* (Oxford: Oxford University Press, 1999), p. 839.
14. Burney, *The Wanderer*, p. 596.
15. As early as her first novel, Burney reveals ambivalence towards all things automated. Evelina's reaction to the mechanical spectacles on display at Cox's museum aligns automata with lack, as intimated by her admission that 'she seems to miss something'. Despite Burney's appreciation for the 'ingenious creations' of John Joseph Merlin, Cox's chief mechanic, her second novel refers to the term 'automaton' as a 'degraded epithet', while her third novel likewise dismisses the cousin of and foil to *Camilla* as a 'beautiful automaton'.
16. Burney, *Camilla*, p. 820.
17. Ibid., p.825.
18. Ibid., p. 824.
19. Ibid., p. 828.
20. Ibid., p 838.
21. Ibid., p 889.
22. Bichat affirms, 'To create the universe God endowed matter with gravity, elasticity, affinity ... and furthermore one portion received as its share sensibility and contractility'. Quoted in W. Bechtel's and R. C. Richardson's entry on vitalism in the *Routledge Encyclopedia of Philosophy*, ed. E. Craig (London: Routledge, 1998).
23. Claudia Johnson affirms that Burney betrays 'a wish to protest the effects of social injustice while making sure that the social structures, customs, and attitudes that produced them remain intact'. Johnson, *Equivocal Beings*, p. 173.
24. Burney, *The Wanderer*, p. 862.
25. Burney, *Camilla*, p. 872.
26. Burney may have had in mind here Blaise Pascal's infamous wager on eternity in his *Pensées* (1670).

27. G. de Staël, 'Reflections on Suicide', in V. Folfenflik (ed.), *Major Writings of Germaine de Staël* (New York: Columbia University Press, 1987), pp. 349–58, on p. 355.
28. Burney, *Camilla*, p. 839.
29. Ibid., p. 839.
30. Ibid., p. 875.
31. Ibid., p. 871.
32. Ibid., p. 874.
33. Castle, *The Female Thermometer*, p.129.
34. Burney, *Camilla*, p. 875.
35. Ibid., p. 875.
36. Ibid., p. 875.
37. Camilla's vision suggests her total alienation not only from the means of written communication but also from oral expression. With its countless allusions to physical and vocal 'vibrations' and its highly mechanized representations of bodily movement, Burney's text employs the terminology that D. Hartley so completely appropriated to describe the mechanics of bodily movement just a couple of decades prior. Hartley's mid-century text, *Observations on Man*, attempts to explain automatic motions and prove that 'every mental process is a mechanical effect and therefore ... derivable from vibratory motions'. Hartley, *Hartley's Theory of the Human Mind*, p. 72. As J. Yolton has observed, 'Hartley admitted the reference to automata: the automatic motions are called automatic, from their resemblance to the motions of automata, or machines, whose principles of motion is within themselves'. J. Yolton, *Thinking Matter: Materialism in the Eighteenth Century* (Minneapolis, MN: University of Minnesota Press, 1983), p. 195. Camilla has become a self-regulating, self-scrutinizing machine. Even writing, by becoming automatic, has turned against her and accuses her with 'its guilty characters'.
38. In *Evelina*, the heroine and her entourage's famous visit to Cox's Museum conveys distaste for the fashionability of the automata featured as the museum's chief attractions.
39. Numerous critics, including M. A. Doody, M. Jerinic and R. M. Cutting have argued that the novel would have inevitably met with a warmer reception from the English public had it been published while history was playing itself out against the backdrop of the French Revolution.
40. Burney, *The Wanderer*, p. 1.
41. The Wanderer is alternately styled the 'incognita', Juliet (an acronym from the initials L. S.), and finally Juliet Granville.
42. Henceforth I will employ 'Juliet' or 'the Wanderer' for the sake of expedience.
43. Burney, *The Wanderer*, p. 782. The act of suicide as Camilla prepares to undertake it is wholly passive, and the result of self-neglect.
44. Ibid., p. 177.
45. It also echoes J. J. Rousseau's *Emile ou de l'education* (1762), which, as M. A. Doody observes in the notes to *The Wanderer*, laments 'that women should be raised as thoughtless and unknowing automata'. Doody, 'Notes', in F. Burney, *The Wanderer*, p. 921.
46. M. Wollstonecraft, *Letters on Norway, Denmark, and Sweden* (New York: Kessinger Publishing, 2004), p. 68. Wollstonecraft muses '[W]ithout hope, what is to sustain life, but the fear of annihilation – the only thing of which I have ever felt a dread – I cannot bear to think of being no more ... though existence is often but a painful consciousness of misery; nay, it appears to me impossible that I should cease to exist, or that this active, restless spirit, equally alive to joy and sorrow, should only be organized dust – ready to

fly abroad the moment the spring snaps, or the spark goes out, which kept it together'. Ibid., p. 68.

47. Staël, 'Reflections on Suicide', in *Major Writings*, p. 348.

48. Unless otherwise indicated, all citations of Staël's works refer to V. Folfenflik's translated compilation of *The Major Writings of Germaine de Staël* (New York: Columbia University Press, 1987).

49. G. de Staël, 'The Influence of the Passions on the Happiness of Individuals and Nations', *Major Writings of Germaine de Staël*, pp. 151–71, on p. 167.

50. G. de Staël, 'On Literature', *Major Writings of Germaine de Staël*, pp. 172–208, on p. 184.

51. As G. May asserts, Staël's opinions 'flow in two different riverbeds'. May, 'The Fascination of Suicide', in M. Gutwirth, A. Goldberger, and K. Szmurlo (eds), *Germaine de Staël: Crossing the Borders* (New Brunswick, NJ: Rutgers University Press, 1991), pp. 174–80, on p. 176.

52. L'Hôpital Necker was run by Dr Fouquet, a Montpellier vitalist. W. R. Albury affirms that 'although never fully accepted by the Parisian Medical community, [Montpellier vitalism] was embraced by persons of influence both at the court and in the salons'. W. R. Albury, 'A Cultural History of Medical Vitalism in Enlightenment Montpellier [Review]', *Bulletin of the History of Medicine*, 78:2 (2004), pp. 477–9, on p. 478. As E. Williams points out, L'Hôpital Necker was opened in 1785 by Mme Necker with a mandate to tend to the Protestant poor. Williams, *The Physical and the Moral*, p. 222.

53. Staël, 'The Influence of the Passions', p. 167.

54. Her own connection with D. J. Larrey, Napoleon's surgeon who amputated her breast in the operation described so famously in her journals, also suggests another Montpellier vitalist connection. Larrey spent time at Montpellier and published his book on aphasia there.

55. C. Hannaway and A. La Berge, 'Introduction: Paris Medicine: Perspectives Past and Present', in *Constructing Paris Medicine* (Atlanta, GA: Rodopi, 1998), pp. 1–70, on p. 29.

56. Stahl insisted upon the existence of 'a rational agent presiding over the fabric of the body, and producing effects that are not subject to the laws of mechanism'. Quoted in R. Porter, *Flesh in the Age of Reason* (London: Allen Lane, 2003), p. 184. R. Fulhop-Miller characterizes this doctrine as a form of 'healing vitalism'. R. Fulhop-Miller, *The Triumph over Pain* (New York: Literary Guild of America, 1938), p. 28.

57. L. Birke, 'Bodies and Biology', in M. Shildrick and J. Price (eds), *Feminist Theory and the Body* (Edinburgh: Edinburgh University Press, 1999), pp. 42–9, on p. 47.

58. Leder ascribes the dead body's centrality to the regulation of modern medicine to the work of R. Descartes, whom he views as positioning the corpse at 'heart of his metaphysics' and 'investigative methodology'. Leder, 'A Tale of Two Bodies', p. 17.

59. Grosz, *Volatile Bodies*, p. 9.

60. Burney, *The Wanderer*, p. 862. If Elinor is figured as masculine, Juliet occupies a much more ambiguous position, for as Claudia Johnson observes, 'Rather than establishing Juliet/Juliet as representatively 'FEMALE', it unsexes her, insisting with respect to her feelings, as well as to virtually everything else, that she is extraordinary'. Johnson, *Equivocal Beings*, p. 175.

61. Burney, *The Wanderer*, p. 359.

62. Ibid., p. 358.

63. At the same time, this scene harks back to Haywood's amatory fiction in which the stance of masculinity facilitates masculine action.

64. Johnson, *Equivocal Beings*, p.182.

65. V. Jones, *Women in the Eighteenth Century: Constructions of Femininity* (London and New York: Routledge, 1990), p. 8. According to Julia Epstein, Burney exaggerates Elinor's role to lampoon society's conventions. See J. Epstein, *The Iron Pen: Frances Burney and the Politics of Women's Writing* (Madison, WI: University of Wisconsin Press, 1989). In contrast, Barbara Zonitch insists that Elinor 'hyperbolically plays the role her society might expect that of a woman swept away by her emotions'. B. Zonitch, *Familiar Violence: Gender and Social Upheaval in the Novels of Frances Burney* (Newark: University of Delaware Press, 1997), p. 78.

66. K. Straub 'The Guilty Pleasures of Female Theatrical Cross-Dressing and the Autobiography of Charlotte Charke' in J. Epstein and K. Straub (eds), *Body Guards: The Cultural Politics of Gender Ambiguity* (New York: Routledge, 1991), p.150.

67. K. M. Rogers, *Frances Burney: The World of 'Female Difficulties'* (New York: Harvester Wheatsheaf, 1990), p. 161.

68. Burney, *The Wanderer*, p. 586.

69. Delphine's self-sacrificial suicide is decidedly public, occurring prior to a public execution scene at the end of Staël's first novel, whereas Corinne meets a voluntary death publicly at the Capitol.

70. According to Hume, 'It is observed by such as have been reduced by the calamities of life to the necessity of employing this fatal remedy, that, if the unseasonable care of their friends deprive them of that species of death, which they proposed to themselves, they seldom venture upon any other, or can summon up so much resolution a second time, as to execute their purpose'. Hume, *Essays on*, p. 98. Hume attributes this phenomenon to the 'horror of death' inherent in every individual psyche and he returns to the idea repeatedly over the course of his short essay, reiterating the phrase 'so great is our horror of death ...' both at the beginning and end of the essay.

71. Staël, 'Reflections on Suicide', in *Major Writings of Germaine de Staël*, p. 353.

72. Burney, *The Wanderer*, p. 396.

73. Hume, *Treatise of Human Nature*, p. 80.

74. Burney, *The Wanderer*, p. 360.

75. Ibid., p. 400.

76. Ibid., p. 360.

77. Ibid., p. 360.

78. Ibid., p.188.

79. M. Heyd, *Be Sober and Reasonable: The Critique of Enthusiasm in the Seventeenth and Early Eighteenth Centuries* (New York: E.J. Brill, 1995), p. 250.

80. Ibid., p. 250.

81. Burney, *The Wanderer*, p. 182.

82. Cheyne, *The English Malady*, p. 4.

83. Burney, *The Wanderer*, p. 371.

84. Ibid., p. 191.

85. Hartley, *Hartley's Theory of the Human Mind*.

86. La Mettrie, whose *L'Homme Machine* represents almost a manifesto of the mechanist outlook in its reinforcement of much of the groundwork already laid in the century prior, refers to this mechanical body as a machine so complicated 'that it is impossible to know its essence'. J. O. de la Mettrie, *Machine Man and Other Writings*, ed. A. Thomson (Cambridge: Cambridge University Press, 1996), p. 100.

87. Arguing that the notion of providence actually accommodates suicide, Hume notoriously demanded 'Where then is the crime of turning a few ounces of blood from their natural channel?' Hume, *Essays on Suicide*, p. 101.
88. Burney, *The Wanderer*, p. 783.
89. Kristina Straub's argument that 'the ideological tensions inherent in the lives of middle-class women'map themselves onto the divided selves of Burney's female characters goes far toward explaining the ambivalence that surrounds not just her treatment of suicide but every aspect of female experience as represented in her novels. K. Straub, *Divided Fictions: Fanny Burney and Feminine Strategy* (Lexington, KY: University Press of Kentucky, 1987), p. 20.
90. Burney, *The Wanderer*, p. 191.
91. Ibid., p. 783.
92. Crocker, 'Interpreting the Enlightenment', p. 54.
93. Burney, *The Wanderer*, p. 783.
94. Elinor's embrace of a 'death of reason' anticipates Nietzsche's arguments that 'natural death is death in the most contemptible conditions, a death which is not free, which does not come when it should, a coward's death. Love of life should make us wish for an altogether different death, a free and conscious death, one which is no accident and holds no surprises'. Quoted in Blanchot, *The Space of Literature*, p. 87. As Blanchot writes, 'Nietzsche's words resound like an echo of liberty. One doesn't kill oneself, but one can.' Ibid., p. 97.
95. Burney, *The Wanderer*, p. 791.
96. Ibid., p. 791.
97. C. Packham, 'The Physiology of Political Economy: Vitalism and Adam Smith's *Wealth of Nations*', *Journal of the History of Ideas*, 63:3 (2002), pp. 465–81, on p. 470. Packham's article presents an excellent survey and application of vitalist philosophy to eighteenth-century economic principles.
98. Burney, *The Wanderer*, p. 792.
99. B. Clarke, *Dora Marsden and Early Modernism: Gender, Individualism, Science* (Ann Abor, MI: University of Michigan Press, 1996), p. 30.
100. C. Williams has also commented on the implicit references to the Royal Humane Society in *The Wanderer*, but she does not make the further connection to a broader vitalist philosophical context that I argue underpins Burney's treatment of suicide in her last novel. Please see her illuminating discussion in C. Williams, '"Inhumanly Brought Back to Life and Misery": Mary Wollstonecraft, *Frankenstein*, and the Royal Humane Society', *Women's Writing*, 8:2 (2001), pp. 212–34.
101. G. Gregory, *Sermon on Suicide Presented on the Anniversary of the Royal Humane Society* (London: J. Nichols, 1797), p. 14.
102. Ibid., p. 12.
103. Ibid., p. 30.
104. Ibid., p. 29.
105. Burney, *The Wanderer*, p. 471.
106. Ibid., p. 361.
107. E. Burke, *A Philosophical Enquiry into the Origin of our Ideas of the Sublime and Beautiful* (Oxford: Oxford University Press, 1999), p. 72.
108. E. J. Clery, *The Rise of Supernatural Fiction, 1762–1800* (New York: Cambridge University Press, 1995), p. 28.
109. Burney, *The Wanderer*, p. 398.

110. Ibid., p. 380.
111. See Kristeva's description of the abjection as 'lined with the sublime' in *The Powers of Horror*. Abjection, as Kristeva observes, 'does not respect boundaries, systems, rules' and Elinor appears as a virtual spokesperson for abjection in this text. Kristeva, *The Powers of Horror*, p. 4.
112. Burney, *The Wanderer*, p. 375.
113. E. Scarry, *The Body in Pain: The Making and Unmaking of the World* (New York: Oxford University Press, 1985), p. 47.
114. Scarry, *The Body in Pain*, p. 53.
115. I. Kant, *Critique of Judgment*, trans. W. S. Pluhar (New York: Hackett Press, 1987), p. 520.
116. Ibid., p. 521.
117. Ibid., p. 521.
118. Ibid., p. 528.
119. Kant, 'Duties towards the Body in Regard to Life', p. 54. Kant also makes an interesting argument in *Fundamental Principles of The Metaphysic of Morals*: 'He who contemplates suicide should ask himself whether his action can be consistent with the idea of humanity as an end in itself'. I. Kant, *Fundamental Principles of The Metaphysic of Morals* (New York: Cosimo, 2009), p. 46. Kant connects the suicidal subject to the universal ideal and wonders if one could only wish the same destiny for humanity, thus annihilating the race. It is on these grounds that Kant opposes suicide.
120. Burney, *The Wanderer*, p. 783.
121. Hume, *Essays on Suicide*, p. 102. This notion, however, Kant explicitly rejects in articulating his position on voluntary death, which predictably enough is diametrically opposed to that of Hume, whose essay on 'suicide' appeared to considerable rancour only a decade or so prior to Kant's own writings on the subject.
122. Kant, 'Duties of the Body in Respect to Life', p. 34. L. Crocker observes that 'in only one writer is exaltation of man's cosmic importance coupled with the condemnation of suicide'. Crocker, 'Interpreting the Enlightenment', p. 62. Other writers view this as a paradox, and Hume would dismiss it as supreme arrogance, given his insistence that 'It is a kind of blasphemy to imagine that any created being can disturb the order of the world or invade the business of providence'. Hume, *Essays on Suicide*, p. 103.
123. Staël, 'On Germany', in *Major Writings of Germaine de Staël*, pp. 292–324, on p. 312.
124. Staël, *Reflêxions sur le suicide*, p. 90 (my translation).
125. Staël, "On Germany', p. 311.
126. Cheah, *Spectral Nationality*, p. 84.
127. Ibid., p. 85.
128. Kant, *Critique of Judgment*, p. 253.
129. L. Lacaze, *L'idee de l'homme physique et moral* (Paris: H. L. Guerin and L. F. Delatour, 1755), pp. 365–6.
130. Quoted in E. Williams, *The Physical and the Moral*, p. 428.
131. Staël, 'Reflections on Suicide', in *Major Writings of Germaine de Staël*, p. 356.
132. Staël, *Réflexions sur le suicide*, p. 85 (my translation).
133. Ibid., p. 84.
134. Goodden, *Madame de Staël: Dangerous Exile* (Oxford: Oxford University Press, 2008), on p.23.
135. Burney, *Camilla*, p. 872.
136. Burney, *The Wanderer*, p. 872.

137. Ibid., p. 783.
138. Ibid., p. 795.
139. Ibid., p.796.
140. Ibid., p. 796.
141. The literary critic M. Jerinic reads this novel as a rewriting of *Evelina*, Burney's first work, a convincing argument insofar as it highlights the fact of Evelina's French connections. Jerinic's discussion emphasizes Burney's use of the institutions of religion and marriage to complicate constructions of Englishness. While I accept Jerinic's argument, the central role of Elinor within Burney's representation of transnational relations also merits attention. See M. Jerinic, 'Challenging Englishness: Frances Burney's *The Wanderer*', in A. Craciun and K. E. Lokke (eds), *Rebellious Hearts: British Women Writers and the French Revolution* (Albany, NY: State University of New York Press, 2001), pp. 63–84.
142. Burney, *The Wanderer*, p. 357.
143. '*The Wanderer; or, Female Difficulties*. By the author of "Evelina," "Cecilia," and "Camilla."' *Gentleman's Magazine* June (1814), pp. 579–81, on p. 579.
144. Ibid., 580. As Higonnet observes, 'some women writers leave the outcome uncertain, possibly in an effort to write beyond the endings conventionally dictated by the social scripts for women's lives [...] the narrative circles around the protagonist's death, announcing it but not enacting it'. M. Higonnet, 'Frames of Female Suicide' *Studies in the Novel*, 32:2 (2000), pp. 229–42, on p. 236.
145. Burney, *The Wanderer*, p. 797.
146. Ibid., p. 359.
147. A. McKenna, *Violence and Difference: Girard, Derrida, and Deconstruction* (Urbana, IL: University of Illinois Press, 1992), p. 30.
148. S. During argues that this very emphasis on 'familial filiation' is central to Burke's counter-revolutionary discourse and to Wollstonecraft's 'feminized bourgeois ethic'. S. During, *Cultural Studies: A Critical Introduction* (New York: Routledge, 2005), p. 382. We also encounter this tendency in Staël.
149. Burney, *The Wanderer*, p. 4.
150. Ibid., pp. 371–2.
151. Significantly, suicide had been redesignated by French vitalists such as Sauvages as a '*melancholia anglica*' earlier in the century, as Hacking points out. Hacking, *The Taming of Chance*, p. 66.
152. The doctrine of the 'eternal sleep of death' that was associated with Jacobin secret societies and the assumption that many of the Girondins condemned by Robespierre committed suicide rather than be executed in part supports the attribution of Elinor's suicidal affinities to France; however, a crucial point to note is that Elinor departs for France already infected in body, ostensibly suffering from a disorder that is not wholly distinct from the English Malady.
153. Newman, *The Rise of English Nationalism: A Cultural History, 1740–1830* (New York: St Martin's Press, 1987).
154. For Burney, the ethnic intolerance manifested by the cross-section of society that *The Wanderer* presents is consistent with the virulent racism that these same individuals display at the outset of the novel, when confronted with 'the black insect' as they label the Wanderer in her initial disguise of 'blacks and whites'. Burney, *The Wanderer*, p. 27. The fact that Burney is not herself exempt from this racist attitude is suggested by her representation of the Wanderer's resplendent 'unveiling' scene in which she emerges in all her triumphant whiteness. S. Salih argues in respect to this scene that Burney 'made her her-

oine black only to (re)make her white'. S. Salih, 'Her Blacks, her Whites and Her Double Face! Altering Alterity in *The Wanderer*', 11:3 (1999), pp. 302–15, on p. 314. Suggesting that Gayatri Chakravorty Spivak's paradigm of the 'self-immolating colonial subject … sacrificed as an insane animal for her [white] sister's consolidation' fully applies to Burney's representation of race in *The Wanderer*, Salih argues that Juliet constructs a 'white "feminine" identity out of the debris of her discarded blackness'. Ibid., p. 314.

155. Fierce English patriots found in the French Revolution further justification for their self-righteousness, and Juliet's expatriation repeatedly comes under fire; her own uncle goes so far as to suggest that she were better off dead than an expatriat living in France. Burney, *The Wanderer*, p. 835.

156. *The Wanderer; or, Female Difficulties. By the author of* "Evelina," "Cecilia," *and* "Camilla."' *Gentleman's Magazine* June (1814), pp. 579–81, on p. 580.

157. A perceived 'epidemic' of suicides in France at mid-century had earlier raised alarm, which, as Z. G. Cahn observes, was defused by Voltaire's timely intervention. See Z. G. Cahn, *Suicide in French Thought from Montesquieu to Cioran* (New York: Peter Lang, 1998), p. 55.

158. Quoted in Hacking, *The Taming of Chance*, p. 64.

159. J.-P. Falret, *De l'hypochondrie et du suicide* (Paris, 1822).

160. T. Arnold, *Observations on the Nature, Kinds, Causes, and Prevention of Insanity, Lunacy, or Madness* (New York: Arno Press, 1976), p. 39.

161. See Hume's essay 'Of National Characters' (1748) for Hume's dismissal of an essential Englishness. This is a term that she invokes in her third novel, *Camilla*, to question the applicability of the stereotypes of Irishness as applied to Camilla's friends, the O'Lerneys.

162. Staël attributes the superior imaginative 'fertility' of Northern peoples to the fact that they 'are more concerned with pain than pleasure'. Staël, 'On Literature', p. 176.

163. In *Refléxions sur le suicide* (1813), Staël maintains that suicide is endemic to the English, although she attributes this trait not so much to climate influence or diet as to their acute sensitivity to public opinion.

164. Minois, *History of Suicide*, p. 214.

165. Maria Fairweather observes that Staël's 'discovery that individuals and nations share the same traits, albeit on a different scale is a crucial concept that permits the author to generalize about Nordic and Southern peoples'. Fairweather, *Madame de Staël* (New York: Carroll & Graf Press, 2005), p. 49. As Margaret Higonnet notes, along with earlier writers on the subject such as Montesquieu and Voltaire, Staël feels compelled to 'locate suicide at the site of the Other, as both a feminine gesture and a sign of cultural alterity […] [s]o long as suicide remains under a cloud of social or religious opprobrium'. Higonnet, 'Frames of Female Suicide', p. 232.

166. One would expect that Staël's perennial state of exile and Burney's ten-year residence in France at the beginning of the nineteenth century, only served to erode both women's senses of national affiliation as they traversed and re-traversed the English Channel. As Deirdre Lynch observes, Napoleon's civil code further served to weaken women's ties to a 'homeland' by aligning their national identities with those of their husbands. Lynch, 'The (Dis)locations of Romantic Nationalism: Shelley, Staël, and the Home-Schooling of Monsters', p. 199. In this sense, women's suicides cannot factor into larger questions of national character because their identities are contingent and their agency itself constantly contested under the law.

167. Romani, *National Character and Public Spirit in Britain and France, 1750–1914* (Cambridge: Cambridge University Press, 2002), p. 7.

168. McClintock, 'No Longer in a Future Heaven', p. 262.
169. Although both Burney and Staël recognize that women typically stood outside society and politics, neither of them in fact offers any productive strategy for moving beyond this position. Notwithstanding the validity of G. May's assertion that 'staël was no Mary Wollstonecraft' both Staël and Burney present a Wollstonecraftian solution to the problem of both suicide and women's disenfranchisement. May, 'The Fascination of Suicide', p. 296. Like Wollstonecraft, both call for the submission of the passions to the control of reason, a solution that merely reinforces the mind-body dualism that leads to women's exclusion from participation in the matters of the state in the first place.
170. In this early work, Staël insists that in the absence of the passions, government (and the individual) would function as a machine. *The Influence of the Passions*, p. 167. Yet the passions foster unhappiness and often suicide for, as Staël writes, 'anyone can enter the career of the passions if he is willing to put suicide on his list of resolutions'. Ibid., p. 167. Although Staël recommends philosophy as a curb to the passions, she nonetheless celebrates both the passions and suicide.
171. C. Schmitt argues that the Gothic as a form 'not only registered this work of nation-making but provided a glossary of figures and narrative conventions with which Englishness was defined and redefined' See C. Schmitt, 'Techniques of Terror: Technologies of Nationality: Anne Radcliffe's *The Italian*', *ELH*, 61:4 (1994), pp. 853–76, on p. 854.
172. Gothicism and vitalism are not in fact mutually exclusive in Burney's treatment of suicide. A gothic vision of the nation is necessarily a morbid one; however, a counter-strain of vitalism, which I am counterpointing with the death drive is typically aligned with the nation and with death.
173. Schmitt, 'Techniques of Terror', p. 854.
174. Rey, 'Vitalism, Medicine and Society', on p. 275.
175. Johnson, *Equivocal Beings*, p. 105.
176. Both the narrator and Juliet repeatedly refer to her marriage as a 'sacrifice'; in one sample of free indirect discourse that unites the two voices, we are told that 'Recollection, also, told her that, at the epoch when, with whatever misery, she had suffered him to take her hand, no mental reservation had prepared for future flight and disavowal: she laboured therefore, now, to plead to herself the vows which she had listened to, though she had not pronounced; and to animate her sacrifice by the terrour of perjury'. Burney, *The Wanderer*, p. 845.
177. For a discussion of the relation between national and international identity formation, see S. Reicher, N. Hopkins and S. Condor, 'The Lost Nation of Psychology', in C. C. Barfoot (ed.), *Beyond Pug's Tour: National and Ethnic Stereotyping in Theory and Literary Practice* (Atlanta, GA: Rodopi, 1997), pp. 53–84.
178. Houlbrooke, *Death, Religion, and the Family in England*, p. 212.

Conclusion

1. McClintock, 'No Longer in a Future Heaven', p. 264.
2. F. G. Stephens and M. D. George, *Catalogue of Political and Personal Satires in the Department of Prints and Drawings in the British Museum* (London, BMP, 1870), 11 vols. © Trustees of the British Museum.
3. This is McClintock's term for the phantom presence of women in Bhabha's postcolonial theory. McClintock, 'No Longer in a Future Heaven', p. 266.
4. Colley, *Britons*, p. 237.

5. R. R. Pierson, 'Nations: Gendered, Racialized, Crossed with Empire', in I. Blom, K. Hagemann and C. Hall (eds), *Gendered Nations: Nationalisms and Gender Order in the Long Nineteenth Century* (Oxford: Berg, 2000), pp. 41–62. That the nation is typically gendered as female facilitates this process of exclusion.

6. Colley, *Britons*, p. 240.

7. Leenaars, 'Suicide Notes and Predictive Patterns', p. 123.

8. T. Lacquer, *Making Sex: Body and Gender from the Greeks to Freud* (Cambridge, MA: Harvard University Press, 1999).

9. M. Domosh and J. Seager, *Putting Women in Place: Feminist Geographers make Sense of the World* (New York: Guilford P, 2001), p. 161.

10. E. Durkheim's theory that suicide was a sign of civilization and therefore inaccessible as an act to women merely consolidated a notion already present in eighteenth-century thought.

11. J. Mullan, 'Feelings and Novels', in Porter (ed.), *Rewriting the Self*, pp. 119–34, on p. 130.

12. Castelli, *Martyrdom and Memory*, p. 33.

13. Kant, 'Duties towards the Body in Regard to Life', p. 52.

BIBLIOGRAPHY

Primary Bibliography

Adams, J., *An Essay Concerning Self-Murther* (London: Tho. Bennett, 1700).

Aquinas, T., *Theologica* (New York: Benziger, Bruce, and Glencoe, 1948).

Arnold, T., *Observations on the Nature, Kinds, Causes, and Prevention of Insanity, Lunacy, or Madness* (New York: Arno Press, 1976).

Astell, M., *A Serious Proposal to the Ladies* (New York: Source Book Press, 1970).

Augustine, *The City of God*, ed. M. Dods (Edinburgh: T. & T. Clark, 1888).

Bichat, X., *Physiological Researches on Life and Death*, trans. F. Gold (Boston, MA: Richardson and Lord, 1827).

Blackstone, W., *The Sovereignty of the Law: Selections from Blackstone's Commentaries on the Laws of England*, ed. G. Jones (Toronto: University of Toronto Press, 1973).

Booth, P., *A Discourse on Self-Murder: Or The Cause, the Nature, and Immediate Consequences of Self-Murder, Fully Examined and Truly Stated* (London: Tho. Green, 1732).

Broussais, F., *De l'irritation et de la folie: ouvrage dans lequel les rapports du physique et du moral sont etablis sure les bases de la medicine physiologique* (Paris, 1828).

Burney, F., *The Wanderer, or, Female Difficulties* (Oxford: Oxford University Press, 1991).

—, *Evelina* (London: Penguin, 1994).

—, *Camilla* (Oxford: Oxford University Press, 1999).

Burton, R., *The Anatomy of Melancholy* (London: Clarendon Press, 1989).

Butler A., *The Lives of the Fathers, Martyrs, and Other Principal Saints: Compiled from Original Monuments and Other Authentic Records* (London: 1756–9).

Chapone, S., *The Hardships of the English Laws in Relation to Wives: With an Explanation of the Original Curse of Subjection Passed on the Woman* (London: W. Bowyer, 1735).

Cheyne, G., *An Essay on Health and Long Life* (London: 1745).

—, *The English Malady* (1733), ed. R. Porter (London: Tavistock Routledge, 1991).

Cockburn, J., *A Discourse of Self-Murder: In Which the Heinousness of the Sin Is Expos'd* (London, 1716).

Collier, J., *Essays on Several Moral Subjects* (London, 1709).

Cowper, W., *Correspondence of William Cowper*, ed. T. Wright, 4 vols (New York: Dodd Mead, 1904), vol. 4.

Croft, H., *Love and Madness* (London: G. Kearsly, 1780).

Dawes, W., *The Case and Memoirs of the Late Reverend James Hackman* (London: G. Kearsly, 1779).

Donne, J., *Biathanatos*, ed. M. Rudick and M. Pabst Battin (New York: Garland Press, 1982).

Esquirol, J. E. D., *Mental Maladies: A Treatise on Insanity*, trans. R. de Saussure (New York, Hafner Press, 1965).

Falret, J.-P., *De l'hypochondrie et du suicide* (Paris, 1822).

Ferguson, A., *Essay on the History of Civil Society* (1767), ed. L. Schneider (New Brunswick, NJ: Transaction, 1980), p. 183.

Fielding, S., *Remarks on Clarissa* (1749) (Los Angeles, CA: Augustan Reprint Society, 1985).

Figaro, *The Novelties of a Year and a Day* (London: J. Murray, 1783).

Foxe, J., *Book of Martyrs (Abridged)*, ed., G. A. Williamson (London: Secker and Warburg, 1965).

Gildon, C., *The Deist's Manual: Or, A Rational Enquiry into the Christian Religion* (London: A. Roper, 1705).

Goethe, J. W. von, *The Sufferings of Young Werther*, trans. H. Steinhauer (New York: Norton, 1970).

Grainger, L., *Modern Amours* (London, 1733).

Gregory, G., *Sermon on Suicide Presented on the Anniversary of the Royal Humane Society* (London: J. Nichols, 1797).

Griffith, R., *A Series of Genuine Letters between Henry and Frances* (Dublin: NP, 1760).

Grimm, F. M., *Inventaire de la Correspondance litteraire de Grimm et Meister/Ulla Kolving et Jeanne Carriat*, ed. U. Kolving and J. Carriat (Oxford: Voltaire Foundation at the Taylor Institution, 1984).

Grosley, P. J., *A Tour to London: Or, New Observations on England, and Its Inhabitants*, trans. T. Nugent (Dublin, 1772).

Harris, J., *Lexicon Technicum: Or, An Universal English Dictionary of Arts and Sciences* (London: 1708).

Hartley, D., *Hartley's Theory of the Human Mind, on the Principle of the Association of Ideas*, ed. J. Priestley (New York: AMS Press, 1973).

Haywood, E., *Idalia: or, The Unfortunate Mistress* (London: D. Browne, 1723).

—, *The Injur'd Husband, or, The Mistaken Resentment* (London: D. Browne, 1723).

—, *The Double Marriage, or, The Fatal Release* (London: J. Roberts, 1726).

—, *Reflections on the Various Effects of Love, According to the Contrary Dispositions of the Person on Whom It Operates* (London: N. Dobb, 1726).

—, *Philidore and Placentia* (London, 1727).

—, *Secret Histories, Novels, and Poems: Written by Mrs. Eliza Haywood* (London: S. Richardson, 1732).

—, *Love in Excess*, ed. D. Oakleaf (Peterborough, ON: Broadview, 1994).

—, *Three Novellas: The Distress'd Orphan; The Double Marriage; The City Jilt*, ed. E. A. Wilputte (East Lansing: Colleagues Press, 1995).

—, *The British Recluse*, in P. Backscheider and J. Richetti (eds), *Popular Fiction by Women, 1660–1730* (Oxford: Oxford University Press, 1996), pp.153–226.

—, *The History of Miss Betsy Thoughtless* (Peterborough, ON: Broadview, 1998).

Hays, M., *Letters and Moral Essays* (London: T. Knot, 1793).

Hobbes, T., *Leviathan*, ed. C. B. Macpherson (London: Penguin, 1968).

Hume, D., *Essays on Suicide and the Immortality of the Soul* (Bristol: Thoemmes Press, 1992).

—, *Treatise of Human Nature* (New York: Dover, 2003).

Hunter, J., *A Treatise on the Blood, Inflammation, and Gun-Shot Wounds, by the Late John Hunter. To Which is Prefixed, a Short Account of the Author's Life* (London: J. Richardson, 1794).

Jeffery, J., *Felo de se: Or, A Warning against the Most Horrid and Unnatural Sin of Self Murder* (Norwich: Fr. Burges, 1702).

Josephus, Flavius. *Flavius Josephus: Selections from His Works*, trans. A. Wasserstein (New York, Viking Press, 1974).

Kant, I., *Critique of Judgment*, trans. Werner S. Pluhar (New York: Hackett Press, 1987).

—, 'Duties towards the Body in Regard to Life', in J. Donnelly (ed.), *Suicide: Right or Wrong?* (Amherst, NY: Prometheus Books, 1998), pp. 50–7.

—, Kant, *Fundamental Principles of The Metaphysic of Morals* (New York: Cosimo, 2009).

Kierkegaard, S., *Papers and Journals: A Selection*, trans. A. Hannay (London: Penguin, 1996).

Knox, V., *Essays Moral and Literary* (Dublin, R. Marchbank, 1783).

Lacaze, L., *L'idee de l'homme physique et moral* (Paris: H. L. Guerin and L. F. Delatour, 1755).

Locke, J., *Second Treatise of Government*, ed. C. B. Macpherson (Indianapolis, IN: Hackett Press, 1980).

—, *An Essay Concerning Human Understanding*, ed. J. Yolton (London: Everyman, 1993).

Macaulay, C., *Letters on Education* (London: William Pickering, 1996).

Mettrie, J. O. de la, *Machine Man and Other Writings*, ed. A. Thomson (Cambridge: Cambridge University Press, 1996).

Millot, Abbé C. F. X., *Elements of the History of England, from the Invasion of the Romans to the Reign of George II* (London: J. Dodsley, 1771).

Moore, C., *A Full Inquiry into the Subject of Suicide* (London, J. F. and C. Rivington 1790).

Prince, J., *Self-Murder Asserted to Be a Very Heinous Crime; in Opposition to All Arguments Brought by the Deists, to the Contrary* (London: B. Bragge, 1709).

Pufendorf, S., *The Duty of Man and Citizen According to Natural Law* (1673).

Purcell, J. *A Treatise of Vapours and Hysteric Fits* (London, 1702), pp. 1–2.

Richardson, S., *The Correspondence of Samuel Richardson in Six Volumes*, ed. P. Sabor (New York: AMS Press, 1966).

—, *Meditations Collected from the Sacred Books* (1750) (New York: Garland Press, 1976).

—, *Pamela*, ed. P. Sabor (New York: Penguin, 1982).

—, *Clarissa; or, The History of a Young Lady*, ed. A. Ross (New York: Penguin, 1985).

Rowley, W., *A Treatise on Female, Nervous, Hysterical, Hypochondriacal, Bilious, Convulsive Diseases; Apoplexy and Palsy; with Thoughts on Madness, Suicide* (London: C. Nourse, 1788).

Shebbeare, J., *Letters on the English nation: by Batista Angeloni, a Jesuit, who resided many years in London* (London: 1755).

—, *Second Letter to the People of England* (London, 1755).

—, *The Practice of Physick, Founded on Principles of Pathology Hitherto Unapplied in Physical Enquiries* (London: Hodges, 1755).

—, *Lydia, or, Filial Piety* (New York: Garland Press, 1974).

—, *The Marriage Act* (New York: Garland Press, 1974).

Smith, A., *The Theory of Moral Sentiments* (Cambridge: Cambridge University Press, 1997).

Smith, C., *Celestina*, ed. L. Fletcher (Peterborough, ON: Broadview, 2004).

—, *Desmond*, ed. A. Blank and J. Todd (Peterborough, ON: Broadview, 2001).

—, *Emmeline*, ed. L. Fletcher (Peterborough, ON: Broadview, 2003).

de Staël, G., *Refléxions sur le suicide* (Paris: Editions de l'Opale, 1983).

—, 'The Influence of the Passions on the Happiness of Individuals and Nations', in V. Folfenflik (ed), *Major Writings of Germaine de Staël* (New York: Columbia University Press, 1987), pp. 151–71.

—, 'On Literature', in V. Folfenflik (ed.), *Major Writings of Germaine de Staël* (New York: Columbia University Press, 1987), pp. 172–208.

—, 'On Germany', in V. Folfenflik (trans.), *Major Writings of Germaine de Staël* (New York: Columbia University Press, 1987), pp. 292–324.

—, 'Reflections on Suicide', in V. Folfenflik (ed.), *Major Writings of Germaine de Staël* (New York: Columbia University Press, 1987), pp. 349–58.

Sym, J. *Life's Preservative against Self-Killing* (London: M. Flesher, for R. Dawlman, and L. Fawne, 1637).

Tissot, S. A. D., 'Diseases Incidental to Literary and Sedentary Persons', in *Three Essays* (Dublin: J. Williams, 1772).

Walpole, H. *Anecdotes of Painting* (London, 1786).

Williams, H. M., *Julia. A Novel* (New York: Garland Press, 1974).

Wollstonecraft, M., *A Vindication of the Rights of Men with A Vindication of the Rights of Woman and Hints*, ed. S. Tomaselli (Cambridge: Cambridge University Press, 1995).

—, *Letters on Norway, Denmark, and Sweden* (New York: Kessinger Publishing, 2004).

Secondary Bibliography

Agamben, G., *Homo Sacer: Sovereign Power and Bare Life*, trans. D. Heller-Roazen (Palo Alto, CA: Stanford University Press, 1998).

—, *Stanzas: Word and Phantasm in Western Culture*, trans. R. L. Martinez (Minneapolis, MN: University of Minneapolis Press, 1993).

Alarcón, N., C. Kaplan and M. Moallem, 'Introduction: Between Woman and Nation', in Alarcón, N., C. Kaplan and M. Moallem (eds), *Between Woman and Nation: Nationalisms, Transnational Feminisms, and the State* (Durham, NC: Duke University Press, 1999), pp. 1–18.

Albury, W. R., 'A Cultural History of Medical Vitalism in Enlightenment Montpellier', *Bulletin of the History of Medicine*, 78:2 (2004), pp. 477–9.

Alliston, A., *Virtue's Faults: Correspondences in Eighteenth-Century British and French Women's Fiction* (Palo Alto, CA: Stanford University Press, 1996).

Altman, J. G., *Epistolarity: Approaches to a Form* (Columbus, OH: Ohio State University Press, 1982).

Alvarez, A., *The Savage God: A Study of Suicide* (New York: Random House, 1972).

Amery, J., *Suicide: A Discourse on Voluntary Death*, trans. J. D. Barlow (Bloomington, IN: Indiana University Press, 1999).

Amundsen, D. A. 'Suicide and Early Christian Values', in B. A. Brody (ed.), *Suicide and Euthanasia: Historical and Contemporary Themes* (Boston, MA: Kluwer Academic Press, 1989), pp. 77–154.

Anderson, B., *Imagined Communities: Reflections on the Origin and Spread of Nationalism* (London: Verso, 1991).

Andrew, D., 'Debate: The Secularization of Suicide in England 1660–1800', *Past and Present* 119 (1988), pp. 158–65.

—, 'The Suicide of Sir Samuel Romilly: Apotheosis or Outrage?', in J. Weaver (ed.), *From Sin to Insanity* (New York: Cornell University Press, 2004), pp. 175–88.

Aravamudan, S., *Tropicopolitans: Colonialism and Agency, 1688–1804* (Durham, NC: Duke University Press, 1999).

Arendt, H., *The Human Condition* (Chicago, IL: University of Chicago Press, 1989).

Ariès, P., *The Hour of our Death*, trans. H. Weaver (New York: Alfred Knopf, 1981).

Armstrong, N., *Desire and Domestic Fiction: A Political History of the Novel* (New York: Oxford University Press, 1987).

Backscheider, P. R. 'The Story of Eliza Haywood's Novels: Caveats and Questions', in K. T. Saxton and R. P. Bocchicchio (eds), *The Passionate Fictions of Eliza Haywood: Essays on her Life and Work* (Lexington, KY: University Press of Kentucky, 2000), pp. 19–47.

Baines, B. J., *Representing Rape in the English Early Modern Period* (Lewiston, NY: Edwin Mellen Press, 2003).

Balibar, E., 'The Nation Form: History and Ideology', in G. Eley and R. G. Suny (eds), *Becoming National: A Reader* (New York: Oxford University Press, 1996), pp. 132–50.

Ballaster, R., 'A Gender of Opposition: Eliza Haywood's Scandal Fiction', in K. T. Saxton and R. P. Bocchicchio (eds), *The Passionate Fictions of Eliza Haywood: Essays on her Life and Work* (Lexington, KY: University Press of Kentucky, 2000), pp. 143–67.

—, *Seductive Forms: Women's Amatory Fiction from 1684 to 1740* (Oxford: Clarendon Press, 1992).

Barney, R., *Plots of Enlightenment: Education and the Novel in Eighteenth-Century England* (Palo Alto, CA: Stanford University Press, 1999).

Barraclough, B. and D. Shepard, 'A Necessary Neologism: The Origin and Uses of Suicide', *Suicide and Life-Threatening Behaviour*, 24:2 (1994), pp. 113–24.

Barrell, J., '"The Dangerous Goddess": Masculinity, Prestige, and the Aesthetic in Early Eighteenth-Century Britain', *Cultural Critique*, 12 (1989), pp. 101–31

Barry, R., *Breaking the Thread of Life: on Rational Suicide* (New Brunswick, NJ: Transaction Press, 1994).

Bartel, R., 'Suicide in Eighteenth-Century England: The Myth of a Reputation', *Huntington Library Quarterly* (1967), pp. 145–58.

Barthes, R., *A Lover's Discourse: Fragments*, trans. Richard Howard (New York: Hill & Wang, 1978).

Bartky, S. L., 'Agency: What's the Problem?', in J. K. Gardiner, *Provoking Agents: Gender and Agency in Theory and Practice* (Urbana, IL: University of Illinois Press, 1995, pp. 178–93.

Bartolomeo, J., *Matched Pairs: Gender and Intertextual Dialogue in Eighteenth-Century Fiction* (Cranbury, NJ: Rosemount Press, 2002).

Battin, M. P. (ed.), *Ethical Issues in Suicide* (New Jersey: Prentice-Hall, 1995).

—, 'Can Suicide be Rational? Yes, Sometimes', in J. L. Werth (ed.), *Contemporary Perspectives on Rational Suicide* (Ann Arbor, MI: Braun-Brumfield, 1999), pp. 13–21.

Baudrillard, J., 'The Finest Consumer Object: The Body', in M. Fraser and M. Greco (eds), *The Body, a Reader* (London: Routledge, 2005), pp. 277–82.

—, *Seduction*, trans. B. Singer (Montreal: New World Perspectives, 1990).

Bayatrizi, Z., *Life Sentences: The Ordering of Mortality* (Toronto: University of Toronto Press, 2010).

Beasley, J. C., '*Clarissa* and Early Female Fiction', in C. Houlihan Flynn and E. Copeland (eds), *Clarissa and her Readers: New Essays for the* Clarissa *Project* (New York: AMS Press, 1999), pp. 69–96.

Beauchamp, T., 'Suicide in the Age of Reason', in B. A. Brody (ed.), *Suicide and Euthanasia: Historical and Contemporary Themes* (Boston, MA: Kluwer Academic Press, 1989), pp. 183–220.

Bechler, R., '"Triall by what is contrary": Samuel Richardson and Christian Dialectic', in V. Grosvenor Myer (ed.), *Samuel Richardson: Passion and Prudence* (London: Vision Press, 1986), pp. 93–113.

Becker, L. M. *Death and the Early Modern Englishwoman* (Burlington, VT: Ashgate, 2003).

Beebee, T. O., *Epistolary Fiction in Europe, 1500–1850* (Cambridge: Cambridge University Press, 1999).

Beiner, R., 'Arendt and Nationalism', in D. Villa (ed.), *The Cambridge Companion to Hannah Arendt* (New York: Cambridge University Press, 2000), pp, 44–64.

Bell, R., 'In Werther's Thrall: Suicide and the Power of Sentimental Reading in Early National America', *Early American Literature*, 46:1 (2011), pp. 93–120.

Benedict, B., 'The Curious Genre: Female Inquiry in Amatory Fiction', *Studies in the Novel*, 30 (1998), pp. 194–210.

Benjamin, W., 'Goethe', *Walter Benjamin: Selected Writings, Volume 2. 1927–1934*, ed. M. W. Jennings, H. Eiland, and G. Smith (London: Belknap Press of Harvar University Press, 1999), pp. 161–93.

Bennett, T., 'Sociology, Aesthetics, Expertise', *New Literary History*, 41:2 (2010), pp. 253–76.

Bennington, G., 'Postal politics and the institution of the nation', in H. K. Bhabha (ed.), *Nation and Narration* (London: Routledge, 1990), pp. 121–37.

Berg, M., *Luxury and Pleasure in Eighteenth-Century Britain* (Oxford: Oxford University Press, 2005).

Berge, A. La, *French Medical Culture in the Nineteenth Century* (Atlanta, GA: Rodopi, 1994).

Berlant, L., *The Female Complaint: the Unfinished Business of Sentimentality in Contemporary American Culture* (Durham, NC: Duke University Press, 2008).

Berman, R., *Coming to Our Senses: Body and Spirit in the Hidden History of the West* (Toronto: Simon and Schuster, 1989).

Bhabha, H. K., 'Introduction: Narrating the Nation' and 'DissemiNation: time, narrative, and the margins of the modern nation', in H. K. Bhabha (ed.), *Nation and Narration* (London: Routledge, 1990), pp. 1–7, and pp. 291–323.

D. Bindman and M. Baker, *Roubiliac and the Eighteenth-Century Monument* (New Haven, CT: Yale University Press, 1995).

Binhammer, K., 'Revolutionary Domesticity in Charlotte Smith's *Desmond*', in L. Lang-Peralta, *Women, Revolution, and the Novels of the 1790s* (East Lansing, MI: Michigan State University Press, 1999), pp. 25–6.

Birke, L., 'Bodies and Biology', in M. Shildrick and J. Price (eds), *Feminist Theory and the Body* (Edinburgh: Edinburgh University Press, 1999), pp. 42–9.

Black, S., 'Trading Sex for Secrets in Haywood's Love in Excess', *Eighteenth-Century Fiction*, 15:2 (2003), pp. 207–26.

Blanchot, M., *The Space of Literature*, trans. A. Smock (Lincoln, NE: University of Nebraska Press, 1982).

Bloch, E., *Natural Law and Human Dignity*, trans. D. Schmidt (Cambridge, MA: MIT Press, 1980).

Bocchicchio, R. P. '"Blushing, Trembling, and Incapable of Defense": The Hysterics of *The British Recluse*', in K. T. Saxton and R. P. Bocchicchio (eds), *The Passionate Fictions of Eliza Haywood: Essays on her Life and Work* (Lexington, KY: University Press of Kentucky, 2000), pp. 95–114.

Boothby, R., *Death and Desire: Psychoanalysis theory in Lacan's return to Freud* (New York: Routledge, 1991).

Bordo, S., *Unbearable Weight: Feminism, Western Culture, and the Body* (Berkeley, CA: University of California Press, 1993).

Bourdieu, P., *Outline of a Theory of Practice*, trans. R. Nice (Cambridge: Cambridge University Press, 2002).

Bowers, T., *The Politics of Motherhood: British Writing and Culture, 1680–1760* (Cambridge: Cambridge University Press, 1996).

—, 'Collusive Resistance: Sexual Agency and Partisan Politics in *Love and Excess*', in K. T. Saxton and R. P. Bocchicchio (eds), *The Passionate Fictions of Eliza Haywood: Essays on her Life and Work* (Lexington, KY: University Press of Kentucky, 2000), pp. 48–68.

R. Bowlby (ed.), 'Introduction', in S. Freud, *Studies in Hysteria* (London: Penguin, 2004), pp. i–xlii.

Bowstead, D., 'Charlotte Smith's *Desmond*: The Epistolary Novel as Ideological Argument', in M. A. Schofield and C. Macheski (eds), *Fetter'd or Free? British Women Novelists, 1670–1815* (Athens, OH: Ohio University Press, 1986), pp. 237–63.

Bray, J., *The Epistolary Novel: Representations of Consciousness* (London: Routledge, 2003).

Brennan, T., 'The National Longing for Form', in H. K. Bhabha (ed.), *Nation and Narration* (London: Routledge, 1990), pp., 44–70.

Brewer, D., '"Haywood", Secret History, and the Politics of Attribution', in K. T. Saxton and R. P. Bocchicchio (eds), *The Passionate Fictions of Eliza Haywood: Essays on her Life and Work* (Lexington, KY: University Press of Kentucky, 2000), pp. 217–40.

Brewer, John. *The Birth of a Consumer Society* (London: Europa, 1982).

—, *Consumption and the World of Goods* (New York: Routledge, 1993).

—, *A Sentimental Murder: Love and Madness in the Eighteenth Century* (New York: Farrar, Straus, and Giroux, 2004).

Brockliss, L. W. B. 'Before the Clinic: French Medical Teaching in the Eighteenth Century', in C. Hannawa and A. F. La Berge (eds), *Constructing Paris Medicine* (Atlanta, GA: Rodopi, 1998), pp. 71–116.

Bronfen, E. 'Fatal Conjunctions: Gendering Representations of Death', in W. Apollon and R. Feldstein (eds), *Lacan, Politics, Aesthetics* (Albany, NY: State University of New York Press, 1996), pp. 237–62.

—, 'Introduction', *Death and Representation* (Baltimore, MD: Johns Hopkins University Press, 1993), pp. 3–25.

—, *Over Her Dead Body: Death, Femininity, and the Aesthetic* (Manchester: Manchester University Press, 1992).

Brooks, P., *Reading for the Plot: Design and Intention in Narrative* (New York: Alfred Knopf, 1984).

Brown, L., *Ends of Empire: Women and Ideology in Early Eighteenth-Century English Literature* (Ithaca, NY: Cornell University Press, 1993).

Brown, N. O., *Life against Death: The Psychoanalytic Meaning of History* (New York: Vintage, 1959).

Brown, R., *The Art of Suicide* (London: Reaktion, 2001).

Butler, J. *Bodies That Matter: On the Discursive Limits of 'Sex'* (New York: Routledge, 1993).

—, *Excitable Speech: A Politics of the Performative* (New York: Routledge, 1997).

—, *The Psychic Life of Power: Theories in Subjection* (Palo Alto, CA: Stanford University Press, 1997).

Bynum, C. W., *Fragmentation and Redemption: Essays on Gender and the Human Body in Medieval Religion* (New York: Zone, 1991).

—, *Holy Feast and Holy Fast: The Religious Significance of Food to Medieval Women* (Berkeley, CA: University of California Press, 1987).

Cahn, Z. G., *Suicide in French Thought from Montesquieu to Cioran* (New York: Peter Lang, 1998).

Caldwell, A., 'Transforming Sacrifice: Irigaray and the Politics of Sexual Difference', *Hypatia*, 17:4 (2002), pp. 16–39.

Caldwell, J. M, *Literature and Medicine in Nineteenth-Century Britain: From Mary Shelley to George Eliot* (Cambridge: Cambridge University Press, 2004).

Canetto, S. S., 'Introduction', in S. S. Canetto and D. Lester (eds), *Women and Suicidal Behaviour* (New York: Springer Press, 1995).

—, 'Gender Roles, Suicide Attempts, and Substance Abuse', *Journal of Psychology*, 125 (1991), pp. 605–20.

Canguilhem, G., *The Normal and the Pathological*, trans. C. R. Fawcett (New York: Zone, 1989).

—, *Vital Rationalist: Selected Writings from Georges Canguilhem*, ed. F. Delaporte (New York: Zone, 1994).

Castelli, E. A., *Martyrdom and Memory: Early Christian Culture Making* (New York: Columbia University Press, 2004).

Castle, T., *Clarissa's Ciphers: Meaning and Disruption in Richardson's* Clarissa (Ithaca, NY: Cornell University Press, 1982).

—, *The Female Thermometer: Eighteenth-Century Culture and the Invention of the Uncanny* (Oxford: Oxford University Press, 1995).

Chatterjee, P., 'Whose Imagined Community?', *Millennium – Journal of International Studies* 20:3 (1991), pp. 521–5.

Cheah, P., 'Spectral Nationality: The Living On [sur-vie] of the Postcolonial Nation in Neo-colonial Globalization', *Boundary*, 26:3 (1999), pp. 225–52.

—, *Spectral Nationality: Passages of Freedom from Kant to Postcolonial Literatures of Liberation* (New York: Columbia University Press, 2003).

Cholbi, M., 'Suicide Intervention and Non-Ideal Kantian Theory', *Journal of Applied Philosophy*, 19:3 (2002), pp. 245–59.

—, 'Self-ManSlaughter and the Forensic Classification of Self-Inflicted Death', *Journal of Medical Ethics*, 33:3 (2007), pp. 155–7.

Chung, E., *Samuel Richardson's New Nation: Paragons of the Domestic Sphere and 'Native' Virtue* (New York: Peter Lang, 1998).

Clarke, B., *Dora Marsden and Early Modernism: Gender, Individualism, Science* (Ann Abor, MI: University of Michigan Press, 1996).

Claydon, T. and I. McBride (eds), 'Introduction', in *Protestantism and National Identity Britain and Ireland, c.1650–c.1850* (Cambridge: Cambridge University Press, 1998), pp. 3–32.

Clery, E. J., *The Feminization Debate in Eighteenth-Century England: Literature, Commerce, and Luxury* (London: Palgrave, 2004).

—, *The Rise of Supernatural Fiction, 1762–1800* (New York: Cambridge University Press, 1995).

Clifton, K. and D. Lee, 'Self-Destructive Consequences of Sex-Role Socialization', *Suicide and Life-Threatening Behaviour*, 6:1 (1976), pp. 11–22.

Cobb, R. *Death in Paris, 1795–1801* (Oxford, Oxford University Press, 1978).

Cody, L. F., *Birthing the Nation: Sex, Science, and the Conception of Eighteenth-Century Britons* (Oxford: Oxford University Press, 2005).

Coen, M. and T. Hitchcock (eds), *English Masculinities 1660–1800* (London: Longman, 1999).

Cohen, M., 'Sentimental Communities', in M. Cohen and C. Dever (eds), *The Literary Channel: The Inter-National Invention of the Novel* (Princeton, NJ: Princeton University Press, 2002), pp. 106–32.

Cohen, J. J. and G. Weiss, *Thinking the Limits of the Body* (Albany, NY: State University of New York Press, 2003).

Colley, L., *Britons: Forging the Nation, 1707–1837* (New Haven, CT: Yale University Press, 1992).

Condon, S., N. Hopkins and S. Reicher, 'The Lost Nation of Psychology', in C. C. Barfoot (ed.), *Beyond Pug's Tour: National and Ethnic Stereotyping in Theory and Literary Practice* (Atlanta, GA: Rodopi, 1997).

Connell, P., 'Death and the Author: Westminster Abbey and the Meanings of the Literary Monument', *Eighteenth-Century Studies*, 38:4 (2005), pp. 557–85.

Conway, A., 'Nationalism, Revolution, and the Female Body: Charlotte Smith's *Desmond*', *Women's Studies*, 24:5 (1995), pp. 395–409.

Cook, E. H., *Epistolary Bodies: Gender and Genre in the Eighteenth-Century Republic of Letters* (Palo Alto, CA: Stanford University Press, 1996).

Coopan, V., *Worlds Within: National Narratives and Global Connections in Postcolonial Writing* (Palo Alto, CA: Stanford University Press, 2009).

Cracian, A. and K. E. Lokke (eds), *Rebellious Hearts: British Women Writers and the French Revolution* (Albany, NY: State University of New York Press, 2001).

Craske, M., *Art in Europe, 1700–1830* (Oxford: Oxford University Press, 1997).

Critchley, S., *Very Little ... Almost Nothing: Death, Philosophy, Literature* (London: Routledge, 1997).

Crocker, L., 'Interpreting the Enlightenment: A Political Approach', *Journal of the History of Ideas*, 46:2 (1985), pp. 211–31.

Croskery, M. C., 'Masquing Desire: The Politics of Passion in Eliza Haywood's *Fantomina*', in K. T. Saxton and R. P. Bocchicchio (eds), *The Passionate Fictions of Eliza Haywood: Essays on her Life and Work* (Lexington, KY: University Press of Kentucky, 2000), pp. 69–94.

Cubitt, G. 'Introduction', in G. Cubitt (ed.), *Imagining Nations* (Manchester: Manchester University Press, 1998), pp. 1–18.

Culler, J., 'Anderson and the Novel', *Diacritics*, 29:4 (1999), pp. 20–39.

Currie, S. 'Poisonous Women and Unnatural History in Roman Culture', in M. Wyke (ed.), *Parchments of Gender: Deciphering the Bodies of Antiquity* (Oxford: Clarendon Press, 1998), pp. 147–67.

Cutter, M. A., *Reframing Disease Contextually* (Boston, MA: Kluwer Academic Press, 2003).

Damrosch, D., *What is World Literature?* (Princeton, NJ: Princeton University Press, 2003).

Daube, D., *The Linguistics of Suicide* (Princeton, NJ: Princeton University Press, 1972).

Davis, D. S., 'Why Suicide Is Like Contraception', in M. P. Battin, R. Rhodes, and A. Silvers (eds), *Physician Assisted Suicide* (New York: Routledge, 1998), pp. 113–22.

Deleuze, G., *Foucault*, trans. S. Hand (London: Athlone Press, 1988).

Derrida, J., *Specters of Marx*, trans. P. Kamuf (New York: Routledge, 1994).

—, *The Gift of Death*, trans. D. Willis (Chicago, IL: University of Chicago Press, 1995).

—, 'The Onto-Theology of National-Humanism (Prolegomena to a Hypothesis)', trans. G. Bennington, *Oxford Literary Review*, 14:1–2 (1992), pp. 3–23.

—, *Acts of Religion* (New York: Routledge, 2002).

—, 'Autoimmunity: Real and Symbolic Suicide', in G. Borradori (ed.), *Philosophy in a Time of Terror* (Chicago, IL: The University of Chicago Press, 2003), pp. 85–136.

Dever, C. and M. Cohen (eds), 'Introduction', in *The Literary Channel: The Inter-National Invention of the Novel* (Princeton, NJ: Princeton University Press, 2002), pp. 1–34.

De Vries, H., *Religion and Violence: Philosophical Perspectives from Kant to Derrida* (Baltimore, MD: Johns Hopkins Press, 2002).

DiNola, V. F., 'Anorexia Multiforme: Self-Starvation in Historical and Cultural Context', *Transcultural Psychiatric Research Review*, 27 (1990), pp. 165–96.

Dollimore, J., *Death, Desire and Loss in Western Culture* (New York: Routledge, 1998).

Domosh, M. and J. Seager, *Putting Women in Place: Feminist Geographers Make Sense of the World* (New York: Guilford P, 2001).

Donaldson, I., *The Rapes of Lucretia: A Myth and Its Transformations* (Oxford: Clarendon Press, 1982).

Donoghue, W., *Enlightenment Fiction in England, France, and America* (Gainesville, FL: University Press of Florida, 2002).

Doody, M. A., *A Natural Passion: A Study of the Novels of Samuel Richardson* (Oxford: Clarendon Press, 1974).

—, 'Deserts, Ruins and Troubled Waters: Female Dreams in Fiction and the Development of the Gothic Novel', *Genre*, 10 (1977): 529–50.

—, 'The Gnostic *Clarissa*', in D. Blewett (ed.), *Passion and Virtue: Essays on the Novels of Samuel Richardson* (Toronto: University of Toronto Press, 2001), pp. 210–45.

Douglas, M., *Purity and Danger: An Analysis of Concepts of Pollution and Taboo* (New York: Praeger, 1966).

Doughty, O., 'The English Malady of the Eighteenth Century', *The Review of English Studies*, 2:7 (1926), pp. 257–69.

Dublin, L., *Suicide: A Sociological and Statistical Study* (New York: Ronald Press Co., 1963).

Duncan, B., *Goethe's* Werther *and the Critics* (Rochester, NY: Camden House, 2005).

During, S., *Cultural Studies: A Critical Introduction* (New York: Routledge, 2005).

—, 'Literature – Nationalism's Other? The Case for Revision', in H. K. Bhabha (ed.) *Nation and Narration* (London: Routledge, 1990), pp. 138–53.

Durkheim, E., *Suicide: A Study in Sociology*, trans. John A. Spaulding (New York: MacMillan Press, 1951).

Dussinger, J. A., '"*Ciceronian* Eloquence": The Politics of Virtue in Richardson's *Pamela*', in D. Blewett (ed.), *Passion and Virtue: Essays on the Novels of Samuel Richardson* (Toronto: University of Toronto Press, 2001), pp. 27–51.

—, 'Conscience and the Pattern of Christian Perfection in *Clarissa*', *PMLA*, 81:3 (1966): 243–44.

Eagles, R., *Francophilia in English Society, 1748–1815* (London: MacMillan Press, 2000).

Eagleton, T., *The Rapes of Clarissa* (Minneapolis, MN: University of Minnesota Press, 1982).

Eisenstein, Z., 'Writing Bodies on the Nation for the Globe', in S. Ranchod-Nilsson and M. A. Tetreault (eds), *Women, States, and Nationalism: At Home in the Nation?* (London: Routledge, 2000), pp. 35–53.

Ellis, M., *The Politics of Sensibility: Race, Gender and Commerce in the Sentimental Novel* (Cambridge: Cambridge University Press, 1996).

Ellman, M., *The Hunger Artists: Starving, Writing and Imprisonment* (Cambridge, MA: Harvard University Press, 1993).

Edensor, T., *National Identity, Popular Culture and Everyday Life* (Oxford and New York: Berg, 2002)

Englehardt, H. T., *The Foundations of Bioethics* (Oxford: Oxford University Press, 1996).

Epstein, J., *The Iron Pen: Frances Burney and the Politics of Women's Writing* (Madison, WI: University of Wisconsin Press, 1989).

Erickson, R. A., *Mother Midnight: Birth, Sex, and Fate in Eighteenth-Century Fiction* (New York: AMS Press, 1986).

—, '"Written in the Heart": *Clarissa* and Scripture', in D. Blewett (ed.), *Passion and Virtue: Essays on the Novels of Samuel Richardson* (Toronto: University of Toronto Press, 2001), pp. 170–209.

Faber, M. D., 'Shakespeare's Suicides: Some Historic, Dramatic and Psychological Reflections', in E. S. Schneidman (ed.), *Essays in Self-Destruction* (New York: Science House, 1967), pp. 30–58.

Fairbairn, G. 'Suicide, Language, and Clinical Practice', *Philosophy, Psychiatry, and Psychology*, 5:2 (1998), pp. 157–69.

Fairweather, M., *Madame de Staël* (New York: Carroll & Graf Press, 2005).

Fara, P., *An Entertainment for Angels: Electricity in the Enlightenment* (New York: Columbia University Press, 2002).

Fasick, L., *Vessels of Meaning: Women's Bodies, Gender Norms, and Class Bias from Richardson to Lawrence* (Dekalb, IL: Northern Illinois Press, 1997).

Fedden, H. R., *Suicide: A Social and Historical Study* (New York: Benjamin Blom, 1972).

Field, D., and J. Hockey and N. Small (eds), *Death, Gender and Ethnicity* (London: Routledge, 1997).

Finnis, J., *Natural Law and Natural Rights* (Oxford: Clarendon Press, 1979).

Fissell, M., *Vernacular Bodies: The Politics of Reproduction in Early Modern England* (Oxford: Oxford University Press, 2004).

Fliegelman, J., *Prodigals and Pilgrims: The American Revolution against Patriarchal Authority, 1750–1800* (Cambridge: Cambridge University Press, 1982).

Flint, C., *Family Fictions: Narrative and Domestic Relations in Britain, 1688–1798* (Palo Alto, CA: Stanford University Press, 1998).

Foster, J. R., 'Smollett's Pamphleteering Foe Shebbeare', *PMLA*, 57:4 (1942), pp. 1053–100.

Foucault, M., *The History of Sexuality: Volume One*, trans., R. Hurley (New York: Vintage, 1990).

—, *Discipline and Punish: The Birth of the Prison*, trans., A. Sheridan (New York: Vintage, 1995).

—, *The Birth of the Clinic: An Archaeology of Medical Perception*, trans. A. M. Sheridan (London and New York: Routledge, 2003).

Fournier, M., 'The Pathology of Reading: The Novel as an Agent of Contagion', in C. L. Carlin (ed.), *Imagining Contagion in Early Modern Europe* (New York: Palgrave, 2005), pp. 195–211.

Fox, C. (ed.), 'Defining Eighteenth-Century Psychology: Some Problems and Perspectives', in *Psychology and Literature in the Eighteenth Century* (New York: AMS Press, 1987), pp. 1–22.

Frege, D., *Speaking in Hunger: Gender, Discourse, and Consumption in* Clarissa (Columbia, SC: University of South Carolina Press, 1998).

Freud, S., 'Beyond the Pleasure Principle', in *On Metapsychology: The Theory of Psychoanalysis*, trans. J. Strachey (New York: Viking Penguin, 1984), pp. 269–338.

—, 'Mourning and Melancholia', in *On Metapsychology: The Theory of Psychoanalysis*, ed., J. Strachey (New York: Viking Penguin, 1984), pp. 245–68.

Fry, C. L., *Charlotte Smith* (New York: Twayne, 1996).

Fulhop-Miller, R., *The Triumph over Pain* (New York: Literary Guild of America, 1938).

Gallagher, C., *Nobody's Story: The Vanishing Acts of Women Writers in the Marketplace. 1670–1820* (Berkeley, CA: University of California Press, 1994).

Gardiner, M. *Critiques of Everyday Life* (London: Routledge, 2003).

Gellner, E., *Nations and Nationalism* (Oxford: Blackwell, 1983).

Gidal, E., 'Civic Melancholy: English Gloom and French Enlightenment', *ECS*, 37:1 (2003), pp. 23–45.

Giddens, A., *Modernity and Self-Identity* (Cambridge: Polity Press, 1991)

Gilroy, A., '"Candid Advice to the Fair Sex" or, The Politics of Maternity in Late Eighteenth-Century Britain', in A. Hornver and A. Keane (eds), *Body Matters: Feminism, Textuality, Corporeality* (Manchester: Manchester University Press, 2000), pp. 17–28.

Girard, R., *Violence and the Sacred*, trans. P. Gregory (Baltimore, MD: John Hopkins University Press, 1977).

—, *The Scapegoat* (Baltimore, MD: Johns Hopkins University Press, 1986).

Glenn, G. D., 'Inalienable Rights and Locke's Argument for Limited Government: Political Implications of a Right to Suicide', *Journal of Politics*, 46:1 (1984), pp. 80–105.

Goldberg, B., 'Romantic Professionalism in 1800: Robert Southey, Herbert Croft, and the Letters and Legacy of Thomas Chatterton', *ELH*, 63:3 (1996), pp. 681–706.

Goldberg, R., *Sex and the Enlightenment: Women in Richardson and Diderot* (Cambridge: Cambrige University Press, 1984).

Goldhammer, J., *The Headless Republic: Sacrificial Violence in Modern French Thought* (Ithaca, NY: Cornell University Press, 2005).

Goodden, A., *Madame de Staël: Dangerous Exile* (Oxford: Oxford University Press, 2008).

Gordon, A., *Ghostly Matters: Haunting and the Sociological Imagination* (Minneapolis, MN: University of Minnesota Press, 1997).

Gordon, S. P., *The Power of the Passive Self in English Literature, 1640–1770* (Cambridge: Cambridge University Press, 2002).

Gracia, D., 'Ownership of the Human Body: Some Historical Remarks', in A. M. J. Henk, T. Have, and J. V. M. Welie (eds), *Ownership of the Human Body: Philosophical Considerations on the Use of the Human Body and Its Parts in Healthcare* (Boston, MA: Kluwer Academic Publishers, 1998), pp. 67–80.

Greenblatt, S., *Renaissance Self-Fashioning: From More to Shakespeare* (Chicago, IL: University of Chicago Press, 1980).

Greenfeld, L., *Nationalism: Five Roads to Modernity* (Cambridge, MA: Harvard University Press, 1992).

Gregg, J., 'Blanchot's Suicidal Artist: Writing and the (Im)Possibility of Death', *Substance*, 55 (1988), pp. 49–70.

Gregg, S., '"A Truly Christian Hero": Religion, Effeminacy and Nation in the Writings of the Societies for Reformation of Manners', *Eighteenth-Century Life*, 25:1 (2001), pp. 17–28.

Grenby, M. O. *TheAnti-Jacobin Novel: British Conservatism and the French Revolution* (Cambridge: Cambridge University Press, 2001).

Grogan, C., 'The Politics of Seduction in British Fiction of the 1790s: The Female Reader and *Julie, ou La Nouvelle Héloïse*', *ECF*, 11:4 (1999), pp. 321–39.

Grosz, E., *Volatile Bodies: Toward a Corporeal Feminism* (Bloomington, IN: Indiana University Press, 1994).

—, *Space, Time, and Perversion: Essays on the Politics of the Bodies* (New York: Routledge, 1995).

—, 'Thinking the New: Of Futures yet Unthought', *Symploke*, 6:1 (1998): 38–55.

Grundy, I., 'Seduction Pursued by Other Means? The Rape in *Clarissa*', in C. Houlihan Flynn and E. Copeland (eds), *Clarissa and Her Readers* (New York: AMS Press, 1999), pp. 214–55.

Guerrini, A., *Obesity and Depression in the Enlightenment: The Life and Times of George Cheyne* (Norman, OK: University of Oklahoma Press, 2000).

Gwilliam, T., *Samuel Richardson's Fictions of Gender* (Palo Alto, CA: Stanford University Press, 1993).

Habermas, J., *The Structural Transformation of the Public Sphere: An Inquiry into a Category of Bourgeois Society*, trans. T. Burger (Cambridge, MA: MIT Press, 1996).

Hacking, I., *The Taming of Chance* (Cambridge: Cambridge University Press, 1990).

Haller, W., *The Elect Nation: The Meaning and Relevance of Foxe's Book of Martyrs* (New York: Harper & Row, 1963).

Hannaway, C. and A. La Berge, 'Introduction: Paris Medicine: Perspectives Past and Present', in *Constructing Paris Medicine* (Atlanta, GA: Rodopi, 1998), pp. 1–70.

Harris, J., *Samuel Richardson* (London: Cambridge University Press, 1987).

Harris, J. G., *Foreign Bodies and the Body Politic: Discourses of Social Pathology in Early Modern England* (Cambridge: Cambridge University Press, 1998).

Hawes, C., 'Cosmopolitan Nationalism', in P. Smallwood (ed.), *Johnson Revisioned: Looking Before and After* (Lewisberg, PA: Bucknell P, 2001), pp. 37–63.

Healy, M., *Fictions of Disease in Early Modern England: Bodies, Plagues and Politics* (New York: Palgrave, 2001).

Healy, R., 'Suicide in Early Modern and Modern Europe', *Historical Journal*, 49 (2006), pp. 903–19.

Hekman, S., 'Subjects and Agents: The Question for Feminism', in J. Kegan Gardiner (ed), *Provoking Agents: Gender and Agency in Theory and Practice* (Urbana, IL: University of Illinois Press, 1995), pp. 194–207.

Hemlow, J., *Fanny Burney: Selected Letters and Journals* (Oxford: Clarendon Press, 1986).

Heng, G. and J. Devan, 'State Fatherhood: The Politics of Nationalism, Sexuality, and Race in Singapore', in A. Parker (ed.), *Nationalisms and Sexualities* (New York: Routledge, 1992), pp. 328–51.

Hensley, D. C., 'Thomas Edwards and the Dialectics of Clarissa's Death Scene', *Eighteenth-Century Life*, 16 (1992), pp. 130–52.

Heyd, M., *Be Sober and Reasonable: The Critique of Enthusiasm in the Seventeenth and Early Eighteenth Centuries* (New York: E.J. Brill, 1995).

Higonnet, M., 'Suicide: Representations of the Feminine in the Nineteenth Century', *Poetics Today*, 6 (1985), pp., 103–18.

—, 'Speaking Silences: Women's Suicide', in S. R. Suleiman (ed.), *The Female Body in Western Culture: Contemporary Perspectives* (Cambridge, MA: Harvard University Press, 1986), pp., 68–83.

—, 'Frames of Female Suicide', *Studies in the Novel*, 32:2 (2000), pp. 229–42.

Higonnet, P., *Goodness beyond Virtue: Jacobins during the French Revolution* (Cambridge, MA.: Harvard University Press, 1998).

Hill, T., *Ambitiosa Mors: Suicide and Self in Roman Thought and Literature* (New York: Routledge, 2004).

Hinton, L., 'The Heroine's Subjection: Clarissa, Sadomasochism, and Natural Law', *Eighteenth-Century Studies*, 32:3 (1999), pp. 293–308.

Hobsbawm, E., 'Introduction: Inventing Tradition', in E. Hobsbawm and T. Ranger (eds), *The Invention of Tradition* (Oxford: Blackwell, 1983), pp. 1–15.

Hoeveler, D. Long, *Gothic Feminism: The Professionalization of Gender from Charlotte Smith to the Brontes* (University Park, PA: Pennsylvania State University Press, 1998).

Holland, N., 'The Death of the Other/Father: A Feminist Reading of Derrida's Hauntology', *Hypatia*, 16:1 (2001), pp. 64–71.

Hollis, K., 'Fasting Women: Bodily Claims and Narrative Crises in Eighteenth-Century Science', *Eighteenth-Century Studies*, 34:4 (2001), pp. 523–38.

Hooff, A. J. L. van., *From Autothanasia to Suicide: Self-killing in Classical Antiquity* (London: Routledge, 1990).

Houlbrooke, R., *Death, Religion, and the Family in England, 1480–1750* (Oxford: Clarendon Press, 1998).

Houston, R. 'The Medicalization of Suicide: Medicine and the Law in Scotland and England, circa 1750–1850', in J. Weaver and D. Wright (eds), *Histories of Suicide: International Perspectives on Self-Destruction in the Modern World* (Toronto: University of Toronto Press, 2009), pp. 91–118.

Hudson, N., *Samuel Johnson and the Making of Modern England* (Cambridge: Cambridge University Press, 2003).

Hundert, E. J., 'The European Enlightenment and the History of the Self', in R. Porter (ed.), *Rewriting the Self: Histories from the Renaissance to the Present* (London: Routledge, 1997), pp. 72–83.

Hunter, J. P., Before Novels: The Cultural Contexts of Eighteenth-Century English Fiction (New York, W.W. Norton & Co., 1990).

Huston, R., 'The Medicalization of Suicide: Medicine and the Law in Scotland and England, circa 1750–1850', in D. Wright and J. Weaver (eds), *Histories of Suicide: International Perspectives on Self-Destruction* (Toronto: University of Toronto Press, 2009), pp. 91–118.

Hutchinson, J., 'Moral Innovators and the Politics of Regeneration: The Distinctive Role of Cultural Nationalists in Nation-Building', *International Journal of Comparative Sociology*, 33 (1992), pp. 101–17.

Jameson, F., *Fables of Aggression: Wyndham Lewis, the Modernist as Fascist* (Berkeley, CA: University of California Press, 1979).

—, 'Marx's Purloined Letter', *Ghostly Demarcations: A Symposium on Jacques Derrida's Specters of Marx*. London: Verso, 1999. 26–67.

Jed, S. H., *Chaste Thinking: The Rape of Lucretia and the Birth of Humanism* (Bloomington, IN: Indiana University Press, 1989).

Jennings, B., 'Biopower and the Liberationist Romance', *The Hastings Report*, 40:4 (2010), pp. 16–20.

Jerinic, M., 'Challenging Englishness: Frances Burney's *The Wanderer*', in A. Craciun and K. E. Lokke (eds), *Rebellious Hearts: British Women Writers and the French Revolution* (Albany, NY: State University of New York Press, 2001), pp. 63–84.

Johnson, C. L., *Equivocal Beings: Politics, Gender, and Sentimentality in the 1790s: Wollstonecraft, Radcliffe, Burney, Austen* (Chicago, IL: University of Chicago Press, 1995).

Johnson, N. E., *The English Jacobin Novel on Rights, Property and the Law: Critiquing the Contract* (London: Palgrave, 2004).

Jones, D. 'Radical Ambivalence: Frances Burney, Jacobinism, and the Politics of Romantic Fiction', *Women's Writing*, 10:1 (2003), pp. 3–25.

Jones, V., *Women in the Eighteenth Century: Constructions of Femininity* (London and New York: Routledge, 1990).

Jones, W., *Consensual Fictions: Women, Liberalism, and the English Novel* (Toronto: University of Toronto Press, 2005).

Joy, M., 'Beyond the Given and the All-Giving: Reflections on Women and the Gift', *Australian Feminist Studies*, 14:30 (1999), pp. 315–32.

Kaplan, K. J. and M. Schwartz, 'To Be or Not to Be? The Question of Suicide', *Journal of Psychology and Judaism*, 24:1 (2000), pp. 17–25.

Kelley, M., 'Passive Suicide', *L'Esprit Créateur*, 40:1 (2000), pp. 69–78.

Keymer, T., 'Richardson's *Meditations:* Clarissa's *Clarissa*', in M. A. Doody and P. Sabor (eds), *Samuel Richardson: Tercentenary* (Cambridge, Mass.: Cambridge University Press, 1989), pp. 89–109.

—, *Richardson's* Clarissa *and the Eighteenth-Century Reader* (Cambridge: Cambridge University Press, 1992).

Kidd, C., *British Identities before Nationalism: Ethnicity and Nationhood in the Atlantic World, 1600–1800* (Cambridge: Cambridge University Press, 1999).

King, K., 'Spying on the Conjurer: Haywood, Curiosity and the Novel in the 1720s', *Studies in the Novel*, 30:2 (1998), pp. 178–93.

Kinkead-Weekes, M., *Samuel Richardson: Dramatic Novelist* (Ithaca, NY: Cornell University Press, 1972).

Kirwan, J., *Sublimity* (New York: Routledge, 1995).

Koehler, M., '"Faultless Monsters" and Monstrous Egos: The Disruption of Model Selves in Frances Burney's *Evelina*', *The Eighteenth Century: Theory and Interpretation* 4:1 (2002), pp. 22–8.

Kowaleski-Wallace, E., *Consuming Subjects: Consuming Subjects* (New York: Columbia University Press, 1997).

Krell, D. F., *Contagion: Sexuality, Disease, and Death in German Idealism and Romanticism* (Bloomington, IN: Indiana University Press, 1998).

Kristeva, J., *Nations without Nationalism* trans. L. S. Roudiez (New York: Columbia University Press, 1990).

—, *The Powers of Horror: An Essay on Abjection*, trans. L. S. Roudiez (New York: Columbia University Press, 1982).

Kumar, K., *The Making of English National Identity* (Cambridge: Cambridge University Press, 2003).

Kushner, H., 'Women and Suicidal Behaviour: Epidemiology, Gender and Lethality in Historical Perspective', in S. Canetto and D. Lester (eds), *Women and Suicidal Behaviour* (New York: Springer Press, 1995), pp. 11–35.

—, 'Suicide, Gender, and the Fear of Modernity', in J. Weaver and D. Wright (eds), *Histories of Suicide: International Perspectives on Self-Destruction in the Modern World* (Toronto: University of Toronto Press, 2009), pp. 19–52.

Labbe, J. M., *Charlotte Smith: Romanticism, Poetry and the Culture of Gender* (Manchester: Manchester University Press, 2003).

Lacan, J., *Le seminaire, Livre VIII, Le transfert, 1960–1961*, ed. Jacques-Allain Miller (Paris: Seul, 2000).

LaCapra, D., *History, Politics, and the Novel* (Ithaca, NY: Cornell University Press, 1987).

Laclau, E., 'On Imagined Communities', in P. Cheah and J. Culler (eds), *Grounds of Comparison: Around the Work of Benedict Anderson* (New York: Routledge, 2003), pp. 21–8.

Lamb, J., *The Rhetoric of Suffering: Reading the Book of Job in the Eighteenth Century* (Oxford: Clarendon Press, 1995).

Lampert, F. J., 'Goethe, Ossian and Werther', in F. Stafford and H. Gaskill (eds), *From Gaelic to Romantic: Ossianic Translation* (Amsterdam: Rodopi, 1998), pp. 97–106.

Landes, J., 'The Public and the Private Sphere: A Feminist Reconsideration', in J. B. Landes (ed.), *Feminism, the Public and the Private* (Oxford: Oxford University Press, 1998), pp. 135–62.

Lanser, S., 'Befriending the Body: Female Intimacies as Class Acts', *ECS*, 32:2 (1998–9), pp. 179–98.

Le Bon, G., *The Crowd a Study of the Popular Mind* (Whitefish, MT: Kessinger Publishing, 2003).

Leder, D., 'A Tale of Two Bodies: The Cartesian Corpse and the Lived Body', in D. Welton (ed.), *Body And Flesh: A Philosophical Reader* (Malden, MA: Blackwell Press, 1998), pp. 54–78.

Lederer, D. 'Honfibú', in J. Watt (ed.), *From Sin to Insanity: Suicide in Early Modern Europe* (New York: Cornell University Press, 2004), pp. 116–37.

Lefebvre, H. *The Critique of Everyday Life, Vol. One* (London: Verso, 1991).

Leenaars, A., 'Suicide Notes and Predictive Patterns', *Bulletin of the Menninger Clinic*, 55:1 (1991), pp. 123–4.

Lenz, J. M. R., 'Letters on the Morality of *The Sorrows of Young Werther*', in T. J. Chamberlain (ed.), *Eighteenth-Century German Criticism* (New York: Continuum, 1992), pp. 197–203.

Lind, V., 'The Suicidal Mind and Body: Examples from Northern Germany', in J. Watt (ed.), *From Sin to Insanity: Suicide in Early Modern Europe* (Ithaca, NY: Cornell University Press, 2004), pp. 64–80.

Loewenstein, D. and P. Stevens (eds), 'Introduction: Milton's Nationalism. Challenges and Questions', in *Early Modern Nationalism and Milton's England* (Toronto: The University of Toronto Press, 2008), pp. 3–25.

London, A., 'Avoiding the Subject: The Presence and Absence of Venereal Disease in the Eighteenth-Century Novel', in L. Merians (ed.), *The Secret Malady: Venereal Disease in Eighteenth Century Britain and France* (Lexington, KY: University Press of Kentucky, 1996), pp. 213–27.

Loraux, N., *Tragic Ways of Killing a Woman*, trans. A. Forster (Cambridge, MA: Harvard University Press, 1987).

Lowe, B., *Victorian Fiction and the Insights of Sympathy* (London and New York: Anthem Press, 2007).

Lynch, D. S., 'The (Dis)locations of Romantic Nationalism: Shelley, Staël, and the Home-Schooling of Monsters', in M. Cohen and C. Dever (eds) *The Literary Channel: The Inter-National Invention of the Novel* (Princeton, NJ: Princeton University Press, 2002), pp. 194–224.

—, *The Economy of Character: Novels, Market Culture, and the Business of Inner Meaning* (Chicago, IL: University of Chicago Press, 1998).

MacArthur, E. J., *Extravagant Narratives: Closure and Dynamics in the Epistolary Form* (Princeton, NJ: Princeton University Press, 1990).

MacCannell, J. F., *The Regime of the Brother: After the Patriarchy* (London: Routledge, 1991).

MacLeod, A. E., 'Hegemonic Relations and Gender Resistance: The New Veiling as Accommodating Protest in Cairo', *Signs*, 17:3 (1992): pp. 533–51.

MacDonald, M., 'Suicide and the Rise of the Popular Press in England', *Representations* 22 (1988), pp. 36–59.

—, 'Debate: The Secularization of Suicide in England 1660–1800', *Past and Present*, 119 (1988), pp. 165–70.

—, 'The Medicalization of Suicide in England: Laymen, Physicians, and Cultural Change, 1500–1870', in C. E. Rosenberg and J. Golden (eds), *Framing Disease: Studies in Cultural History* (New Brunswick, NJ: Rutgers University Press, 2000), pp. 85–103.

MacDonald, M., and T. R. Murphy, *Sleepless Souls: Suicide in Early Modern England* (Oxford: Clarendon Press, 1990).

Macpherson, Sandra. 'Lovelace, Ltd.' *ELH*, 65:1 (1998), pp. 99–121.

Maltsberger, J. and M. J. Goldblatt (eds), *Essential Papers on Suicide* (New York: New York University Press, 1996).

Mandeville, B., *The Fable of the Bees: Or, Private Vices, Publick Benefits*, ed. P. Harth (New York: Penguin, 1970).

Mann, B. A., *Native American Speakers Of The Eastern Woodlands: Selected Speeches And Critical Analyses* (Westport, CT: Greenwood Publishing, 2001).

Manzo, K. A., *Creating Boundaries: The Politics of Race and Nation* (Boulder, CO: Lynne Rienner Press, 1996).

Marsh, I., *Suicide: Foucault, History, and Truth* (Cambridge: Cambridge University Press, 2010).

Marshall, D., 'Fatal Letters: Clarissa and the Death of Julie', in C. Houlihan Flynn and E. Copeland (eds), Clarissa *and Her Readers: New Essays for the* Clarissa *Project* (New York: AMS Press, 1999), pp. 213–54.

Martin, N., 'Physician-Assisted Suicide and Euthanasia: Weighing Feminist Concerns', in R. N. Fiore and H. Lindemann Nelson (eds), *Recognition, Responsibility, and Rights: Feminist Ethics and Social Theory* (New York: Rowan and Littlefield, 2003), pp. 131–43.

Matthes, M., *The Rape of Lucretia and the Founding of Republics* (University Park, PA: Penn State University Press, 2000).

Matthews, E., 'Choosing Death: Philosophical Observations on Suicide and Euthanasia', *Philosophy, Psychiatry, and Psychology*, 5:2 (1998), pp. 107–11.

May, G., 'The Fascination of Suicide', in M. Gutwirth, A. Goldberger, and K. Szmurlo (eds), *Germaine de Staël: Crossing the Borders* (New Brunswick, NJ: Rutgers University Press, 1991), pp. 174–180.

McAllister, M. E., 'Stories of the Origin of Syphilis in Eighteenth-Century England: Science, Myth and Prejudice', *Eighteenth-Century Life*, 24:1 (2000), pp. 22–44.

McCann, A., *Cultural Politics in the 1790s: Literature, Radicalism, and the Public Sphere* (London: MacMillan Press, 1999).

McCrea, B., 'Clarissa's Pregnancy and the Fate of Patriarchal Power', *Eighteenth-Century Fiction*, 9:2 (1997), pp. 125–48.

McKenna, A., *Violence and Difference: Girard, Derrida, and Deconstruction* (Urbana, IL: University of Illinois Press, 1992).

McKeon, M. (ed.), *Theory of the Novel* (Baltimore, MD: Johns Hopkins Press, 2000).

—, *The Secret History of Domesticity* (Baltimore, MD: Johns Hopkins University Press, 2007).

McClintock, A., '"No Longer in a Future Heaven": Nationalism, Gender, and Race', in G. Eley and R. G. Suny (eds), *Becoming National: A Reader* (New York: Oxford University Press, 1996), pp. 260–83.

McManners, J., *Death and the Enlightenment: Changing Attitudes to Death among Christians and Unbelievers in Eighteenth-Century France* (New York: Oxford University Press, 1981).

McMaster, J., 'Reading the Body in *Clarissa*', in C. Houlihan Flynn and E. Copeland (eds), *Clarissa and her Readers: New Essays for the* Clarissa *Project* (New York: AMS Press, 1999), pp. 189–213.

McMurran, M. H., 'National or Transnational? The Eighteenth-Century Novel', in M. Cohen and C. Dever (eds), *The Literary Channel: The Inter-National Invention of the Novel* (Princeton, NJ: Princeton University Press, 2002), pp. 50–72.

Meltzer, F., *For Fear of the Fire: Joan of Arc and the Limits of Subjectivity* (Chicago, IL: University of Chicago Press, 2001).

Menninger, K., *Man against Himself* (New York: Harcourt Brace, 1938).

Merians, L. E. (ed.), 'Introduction', in *The Secret Malady: Venereal Disease in Eighteenth-Century Britain and* France (Lexington, KY: University Press of Kentucky, 1996), pp. 1–14.

Merrick, J., 'Suicide in Paris, 1775', *From Sin to Insanity: Suicide in Early Modern Europe* (Ithaca, NY: Cornell University Press, 2004), pp. 158–174.

Merritt, J., *Beyond Spectacle: Eliza Haywood's Female Spectators* (Toronto: University of Toronto Press, 2004).

Messenger, A., *His and Hers: Essays in Restoration and Eighteenth-Century Literature* (Lexington, KY: University Press of Kentucky, 1986).

Messer-Davidow, E., 'Acting Otherwise', in J. Kegan (ed.), *Provoking Agents: Gender and Agency in Theory and Practice* (Urbana, IL: University of Illinois Press, 1995), pp. 23–51.

Meyer, T., 'Gender Ironies of Nationalism. Setting the Stage', in T. Meyer (ed.), *Gender Ironies of Nationalism: Sexing the Nation* (London: Routledge, 2000), pp. 1–24.

Miller, D. A., _Jane Austen, or the Secret of Style_ (Princeton, NJ: Princeton University Press, 2003).

Miller, J. and E. Fuller Torrey, _Invisible Plague: The Rise of Mental Illness from 1750 to the Present_ (New Jersey: Rutgers University Press, 2002).

Miller, N., _The Heroine's Plot_ (New York: Columbia University Press, 1980).

Miller, P. N., _Defining the Common Good: Empire, Religion and Philosophy in Eighteenth-Century Britain_ (Cambridge: Cambridge University Press, 1994).

Minois, G., _History of Suicide: Voluntary Death in Western Culture_, trans. Lydia G. Cochrane (Baltimore, MD: Johns Hopkins Press, 1999).

Mizruchi, S., _The Science of Sacrifice_ (Princeton, NJ: Princeton University Press, 1998).

Moglen, H., _The Trauma of Gender: A Feminist Theory of the English Novel_ (Berkeley, CA: University of California Press, 2001).

Mohanty, C. T., 'Cartographies of Struggle: Third World Women and the Politics of Feminism', in C. T. Mohanty, L. Russo and A. Russo (eds), _Third World Women and the Politics of Feminism_ (Bloomington, IN: Indiana University Press, 1991), pp. 1–47.

Monta, S. B., _Martyrdom and Literature in Early Modern England_ (Cambridge: Cambridge University Press, 2005).

Moore, L. L., _Dangerous Intimacies: Toward a Sapphic History of the British Novel_ (Durham: Duke University Press, 1997).

Morrissey, S. 'Drinking to Death: Vodka, Suicide, and Religious Burial in Russia', _Past and Present_, 186 (2005), pp. 117–46.

Mortensen, P., _British Romanticism and Continental Influences: Writing in an Age of Europhobia_ (New York: Palgrave, 2004).

Mostov, J., 'Sexing the Nation/Desexing the Body', in T. Meyer (ed.), _Gender Ironies of Nationalism: Sexing the Nation_ (London: Routledge, 2000), pp. 89–112.

Mullan, J., 'Feelings and Novels', in R. Porter (ed.), _Rewriting the Self: Histories from the Renaissance to the Present_ (London: Routledge, 1997), pp. 119–34.

Murray, A., _Suicide in the Middle Ages_, 2 vols (Oxford: Oxford University Press, 1998).

Nairn, T., _Faces of Nationalism: Janus Revisited_ (London: Verso, 1997).

Nestor, D., 'Virtue Rarely Rewarded: Ideological Subversion and Narrative Form in Haywood's Later Fiction', _SEL_, 34 (1994), pp. 579–98.

Newman, G., _The Rise of English Nationalism: A Cultural History, 1740–1830_ (New York: St. Martin's Press, 1987).

Novak, M. E., 'Boundaries of the Self: Crises of Mind and Body' (Review), _Eighteenth-Century Studies_, 37:4 (2004), pp. 683–6.

Novak, M., 'The Sensibility of Sir Herbert Croft in _Love and Madness_ and the _Life of Edward Young_', in P. Korshin (ed.), _The Age of Johnson_ (New York: AMS Press, 1987), pp. 189–207.

Noys, B., _The Culture of Death_ (Oxford: Berg, 2005).

Nussbaum, F. A., *The Limits of the Human: Fictions of Anomaly, Race, and Gender in the Long Eighteenth Century* (Cambridge: Cambridge University Press, 2003).

—, 'Private Subjects in William Cowper's "Memoir"' in P. Korshin (ed.), *The Age of Johnson* (New York: AMS Press, 1987), pp. 307–26.

—, *Torrid Zones: Maternity, Sexuality, and Empire in Eighteenth-Century English Narratives* (Baltimore, MD: Johns Hopkins University Press, 1995).

Ober, W. B., 'Eighteenth-Century Spleen', *Psychology and Literature in the Eighteenth Century*, ed. C. Fox (New York: AMS Press, 1987), pp. 225–58.

O'Dea, M. and K. Whelan (eds), *Nations and Nationalisms: France, Britain, Ireland and the Eighteenth-Century Context* (Oxford: Voltaire Foundation, 1995).

Oliver, K., *Subjectivity without Subjects: From Abject Fathers to Desiring Mothers* (New York: Rowman & Littlefield Press, 1998).

Outram, D., *The Body and the French Revolution* (New Haven, CT: Yale University Press, 1989).

Packham, C., 'The Physiology of Political Economy: Vitalism and Adam Smith's *Wealth of Nations*', *Journal of the History of Ideas*, 63:3 (2002), pp. 465–81.

Palti, E., 'Romantic Philosophy and Natural Sciences: Blurred Boundaries and Terminological Problems', *Contributions*, 1:1 (2005), pp. 83–108.

Parker, A., 'Bogeyman: Benedict Anderson's "Derivative" Discourse', in P. Cheah and J. Culler (eds), *Grounds of Comparison: Around the Work of Benedict Anderson* (New York: Routledge, 2003), pp. 53–74.

Pasco, A. H., *Revolutionary Love in Eighteenth- and Early Nineteenth-Century France* (Burlington, VT: Ashgate, 2009).

Pateman, C., *The Sexual Contract* (Palo Alto, CA: Stanford University Press, 1988).

Pearson, J., *Women's Reading in Britain, 1750–1835* (Cambridge: Cambridge University Press, 1999).

Pettman, J. J., 'Boundary Politics: Women, Nationalism and Danger', in M. Maynard and J. Purvis (eds), *New Frontiers in Women's Studies: Knowledge, Identity, and Nationalism* (London: Taylor & Francis, 1996), pp. 187–202.

Phillips, D., 'The Influence of Suggestion on Suicide: Substantive and Theoretical Implications of the Werther Effect', *The American Sociological Review*, 39:3 (1974), pp. 340–54.

Pierson, R. R., 'Nations: Gendered, Racialized, Crossed with Empire', in I. Blom, K. Hagemann and C. Hall (eds), *Gendered Nations: Nationalisms and Gender Order in the Long Nineteenth Century* (Oxford: Berg, 2000), pp. 41–62.

Piven, J. S., *Death and Delusion: A Freudian Analysis of Mortal Terror* (Charlotte, NC: Information Age Press, 2004).

Pocock, J. G. A., *Virtue, Commerce, History: Essays on Political Thought and History, Chiefly in the Eighteenth Century* (Cambridge: Cambridge University Press, 1985).

Pollak, E., *Incest and the English Novel, 1684–1814* (Baltimore, MD: Johns Hopkins University Press, 2003).

—, *The Poetics of Sexual Myth: Gender and Ideology in the Verse of Swift and Pope* (Chicago, IL: University of Chicago Press, 1985).

Porter, R. *A Social History of Madness: Stories of the Insane* (London: Weidenfeld & Nicholson, 1987).

—, 'Introduction', in G. Cheyne, *The English Malady* (London: Tavistock/Routledge, 1991), pp. i–xl.

—, 'Introduction', in R. Porter (ed.), *Rewriting the Self: Histories from the Renaissance to the Present* (London: Routledge, 1997), pp. 1–16.

—, *Flesh in the Age of Reason* (London: Allen Lane, 2003).

Pratt, K. J., *War, Suicide, and the Death Drive in Classical Antiquity* (Los Angeles: California State University Press, 1984).

Pritchard, C., *Suicide – The Ultimate Rejection? A Psycho-Social Study* (Buckingham: Open University Press, 1995).

Probyn, E., 'Bloody Metaphors and Other Allegories of the Ordinary', in N. Alarcón, C. Kaplan and M. Moallem (eds), *Between Woman and Nation: Nationalisms, Transnational Feminisms, and the State* (Durham, NC: Duke University Press, 1999), pp. 47–62.

Prozerov, S., *Foucault, Freedom, and Sovereignty* (Burlington, VT: Ashgate, 2007).

Quill, T., 'Preface', in M. P. Battin (ed.), *Death Debate: Ethical Issues in Suicide* (Saddle River, NJ: Prentice-Hall, 1996), pp. i–vi.

Quinlan, S., 'Sensibility and Human Science in the Enlightenment', *Eighteenth-Century Studies* 37:2 (2004), pp. 296–301.

Radhakrishnan, R., *Diasporic Mediations: Between Home and Location* (Minneapolis, MN: University of Minnesota Press, 1996)

Ragland, E., *Essays on the Pleasures of Death: From Freud to Lacan* (New York: Routledge, 1995).

Raymond, D., '"Fatal Practices": A Feminist Analysis of Physician-Assisted Suicide and Euthanasia', *Hypatia*, 14:2 (1999), pp. 1–25.

Redfield, M., 'Imagi-Nation: The Imagined Community and the Aesthetics of Mourning', in P. Cheah and J. Culler (eds), *Grounds of Comparison: Around the Work of Benedict Anderson* (New York: Routledge, 2003), pp. 75–106.

—, *The Politics of Aesthetics: Nationalism, Gender, Romanticism* (Stanford, CA: Stanford University Press, 2003).

Reineke, M. J., *Sacrificed Lives: Kristeva on Women and Violence* (Bloomington, IN: University of Indiana Press, 1997).

Renan, E., 'What is a Nation?', in H. K. Bhabha (ed.), *Nation and Narration* (London: Routledge, 1990), pp. 8–22.

Retterstol, N., *Suicide: A European Perspective* (Cambridge: Cambridge University Press, 1993).

Rey, R., 'Vitalism, Medicine and Society', in R. Porter (ed.), *Medicine in the Enlightenment* (Amsterdam: Rodopi, 1995), pp. 274–88.

Richetti, J., *The English Novel in History, 1700–1799* (New York: Routledge, 1999).

—, 'Histories by Eliza Haywood and Henry Fielding: Imitation and Adaptation', in K. T. Saxton and R. P. Bocchicchio (eds), *The Passionate Fictions of Eliza Haywood: Essays on her Life and Work* (Lexington, KY: University Press of Kentucky, 2000), pp. 240–58.

Robert, M., *The Origins of The Novel* (Brighton: Harvester Press, 1980).

Rogers, K. M., *Feminism in Eighteenth-Century England* (Brighton: Harvester, 1982).

—, *Frances Burney: The World of 'Female Difficulties'* (New York: Harvester Wheatsheaf, 1990).

Romani, R., *National Character and Public Spirit in Britain and France, 1750–1914* (Cambridge: Cambridge University Press, 2002).

Roulston, C., *Virtue, Gender, and the Authentic Self in Eighteenth-Century Fiction: Richardson, Rousseau, and Laclos* (Jacksonville, FL: University Press of Florida, 1998).

Routledge, C. and J. Arndt, 'Self-Sacrifice as Self-Defence: Mortality Salience Increases Efforts to Affirm a Symbolic Immortal Self at the Expense of the Physical Self', *European Journal of Social Psychology*, 38:3 (2008), pp. 531–41.

Runte, R., 'Dying Words: The Vocabulary of Death in Three Eighteenth-Century English and French Novels', *Canadian Review of Comparative Literature*, 4 (1979), pp. 360–8.

Sawday, J., 'Self and Selfhood in the Seventeenth Century', in R. Porter (ed.), *Rewriting the Self: Histories from the Renaissance to the Present* (London: Routledge, 1997), pp. 29–48.

Saxton, K. T., 'Telling Tales: Eliza Haywood and the Crimes of Seduction in *The City Jilt, or, The Alderman turn'd Beau*', in K. T. Saxton and R. P. Bocchicchio (eds), *The Passionate Fictions of Eliza Haywood: Essays on her Life and Work* (Lexington, KY: University Press of Kentucky, 2000), pp. 115–42.

Scarry, E., *The Body in Pain: The Making and Unmaking of the World* (New York: Oxford University Press, 1985).

Schiffman, R., 'A Concert of Werthers', *Eighteenth-Century Studies* 43:2 (2010), pp. 207–22.

Schmitt, C., 'Techniques of Terror: Technologies of Nationality. Anne Radcliffe's *The Italian*', *ELH*, 61:4 (1994), pp. 853–76.

Schwyzer, P., *Literature, Nationalism, and Memory in Early Modern England and Wales* (Cambridge: Cambridge University Press, 2004).

Seale, C., *Constructing Death: The Sociology of Dying and Bereavement* (Cambridge: Cambridge University Press, 1998).

Seaver, P., 'History of Suicide: Voluntary Death in Western Culture' [review], *Perspectives in Biology and Medicine*, 45:2 (2002), pp. 311–15.

Sena, J., 'Melancholic Madness and the Puritans', *Harvard Theological Review*, 66: 3 (1973), pp. 293–309.

Shapin, S., 'Trusting George Cheyne: Scientific Expertise, Common Sense, and Moral Authority in Early Eighteenth-Century Dietetic Medicine', *Bulletin of the History of Medicine*, 77:2 (2003), pp. 263–97.

Shaw, J., 'Religious Experience and the Formation of the Early Enlightenment Self', in R. Porter (ed.), *Rewriting the Self: Histories from the Renaissance to the Present* (London: Routledge, 1997), pp. 61–71.

—, *Miracles in Enlightenment England* (New Haven, CT: Yale University Press, 2006).

Shildrick, M. and J. Price (eds), 'Openings on the Body: A Critical Introduction', in *Feminist Theory and the Body* (Edinburgh: Edinburgh University Press, 1999), pp. 1–15.

Shilling, C., *The Body and Social Theory* (London: Sage Publications, 1993), pp. 180–5.

Sibley, D., 'Survey 13: Purification of Space', *Environment and Planning D: Society and Space*, 6 (1988), pp. 409–21.

Siebers, T., 'The Werther Effect: The Esthetics of Suicide', *Mosaic*, 26:1 (1993), pp. 15–34.

Siena, K. 'Suicide as an Illness Strategy in the Long Eighteenth Century', in J. Weaver and D. Wright (eds), *Histories of Suicide: International Perspectives on Self-Destruction in the Modern World* (Toronto: University of Toronto Press, 2009), pp. 53–72.

Sill, G., 'Neurology and the Novel: Alexander Monro primus and secundus. Robinson Crusoe, and the Problem of Sensibility', *Literature and Medicine*, 16:2 (1997), pp. 250–65.

Siskin, C., *The Work of Writing: Literature and Social Change in Britain, 1700–1830* (Baltimore, MD: Johns Hopkins University Press, 1998).

Sjoholm, C., *The Antigone Complex: Ethics and the Invention of Feminine Desire* (Palo Alto, CA: Stanford University Press, 2004).

Slattery, D. P., *The Wounded Body: Remembering the Markings of Flesh* (Albany, NY: State University of New York Press, 2000).

Smith, A., *Gothic Radicalism: Literature, Philosophy and Psychoanalysis in the Nineteenth Century* (London: MacMillan Press, 2000).

—, *National Identity* (London: Penguin, 1991).

Smith, D., *The Conceptual Practices of Power: A Feminist Sociology of Knowledge* (Toronto: University of Toronto Press, 1990).

Sontag, S., *Illness as Metaphor* (New York: Farrar, Strauss and Giroux, 1978).

Spacks, P. M., 'The Grand Misleader: Self-Love and Self-Division in Clarissa', *Studies in the Literary Imagination*, 28:1 (1995), pp. 35–41.

—, *Privacy: Concealing the Eighteenth-Century Self* (Chicago, IL: University of Chicago Press, 2003).

Spearey, S., 'Substantiating Discourses of Emergence', in Angela Keane and Avril Horner (eds), *Body Matters: Feminism, Textuality, Corporeality* (New York: St Martin's Press, 2000), pp. 170–84.

Spinoza, B., *Ethics* (New York: Dover, 1955).

Spivak, G. C., 'Can the Subaltern Speak?', in C. Nelson and L. Grossberg (eds), *Marxism and the Interpretation of Culture* (Chicago, IL: University of Illinois Press, 1988).

Springborg, M., *Feminizing Venereal Disease: The Body of the Prostitute in Nineteenth-Century Medical Discourse* (London: MacMillan Press, 1997).

Sprott, S. E., *The English Debate on Suicide from Donne to Hume* (La Salle, IL: Open Court, 1961).

Stachniewski, J., The *Persecutory Imagination: English Puritanism and the Literature of Religious Despair* (Oxford: Clarendon Press, 1991).

Stafford, W., *English Feminists and Their Opponents in the 1790s: Unsex'd and Proper Females* (Manchester: Manchester University Press, 2002).

Starna, W. A., 'The Diplomatic Career of Canasatego', in W. A. Pencak and D. K. Richter (eds), *Friends and Enemies in Penn's Woods: Indians, Colonists, and the Racial Construction of Pennsylvania* (University Park, PA: Pennsylvania State University Press, 2004), pp. 144–63.

Starr, G. G., *Lyric Generations: Poetry and the Novel in the Long Eighteenth Century* (Baltimore, MD: Johns Hopkins University Press, 2004).

Stengel, E., 'The Social Effects of Attempted Suicide', *Canadian Medical Association Journal*, 74: 2 (1956), pp. 116–120.

Straub, K., *Divided Fictions, KY: Fanny Burney and Feminine Strategy* (Lexington: University Press of Kentucky, 1987).

—, 'The Guilty Pleasures of Female Theatrical Cross-Dressing and the Autobiography of Charlotte Charke', in J. Epstein and K. Straub (eds), *Body Guards: The Cultural Politics of Gender Ambiguity* (New York: Routledge, 1991).

Strenski, I., *Contesting Sacrifice: Religion, Nationalism, and Social Thought in France* (Chicago, IL: University of Chicago Press, 2002).

—, *Theology and the First Theory of Sacrifice* (Leiden: Brill, 2003).

Suglia, J., *Hölderlin and Blanchot on Self-Sacrifice* (**New York: Peter Lang, 2004**).

Sweet, R., 'Antiquaries and Antiquities in Eighteenth-Century England', *ECS*, 34:2 (2001), pp. 181–206.

Temple, K., *Scandal Nation: Law and Authorship in Britain, 1750–1832* (Ithaca, NY: Cornell University Press, 2003).

Thaddeus, J. F., *Frances Burney: A Literary Life* (London: MacMillan Press, 2000).

Thompson, E. P., *The Making of the English Working Class* (New York: Vintage, 1966).

Thompson, H., *Ingenuous Subjection: Compliance and Power in the Eighteenth-Century Domestic Novel* (Philadelphia, PA: University of Pennsylvania Press, 2005).

Thompson, J., *Models of Value: Eighteenth-Century Political Economy and the Novel* (Durham, NC: Duke University Press, 1996).

Thompson, M. G., *The Death of Desire: A Study in Psychopathology* (New York: New York University Press, 1985).

Thompson, P., 'Abuse and Atonement: The Passion of Clarissa Harlowe', in D. Blewett (ed.) *Passion and Virtue: Essays on the Novels of Samuel Richardson* (Toronto: University of Toronto Press, 2001), pp. 170–209.

Thorn, J., '"A Race of Angels": Castration and Exoticism in Three Exotic Tales by Eliza Haywood', in K. T. Saxton and R. P. Bocchicchio (eds), *The Passionate Fictions of Eliza*

Haywood: Essays on her Life and Work (Lexington, KY: University Press of Kentucky, 2000), pp. 168–93.

Timmons, J. R., 'A 'Fatal Remedy': Melancholy and Self-Murder in Eighteenth-Century England', in Paul Korshin (ed.), *The Age of Johnson Vol. 10* (New York: AMS Press, 1990), vol. 10, pp. 259–84.

Truman, J. C. W., 'John Foxe and the Desires of Reformation Martyrology', *ELH*, 70:1 (2003), pp. 35–66.

Trumpener, K., *Bardic Nationalism: The Romantic Novel and the British Empire* (Princeton, NJ: Princeton University Press, 1997).

Turner, B. S., *The Body and Society: Explorations in Social Theory* (London: Sage Press, 1996).

Vandekerckhove, L., *On Punishment: The Confrontation of Suicide in Old-Europe* (Leuven, Belgium: Leuven University Press, 2000)

Vasterling, V., 'Butler's Sophisticated Constructivism: A Critical Assessment', *Hypatia*, 14:3 (1999), pp. 17–38.

Vaughn, G., 'Mother, Co-muni-cation, and the Gifts of Language', in E. Wyschogrod (ed.), *The Enigma of Gift and Sacrifice* (New York: Fordham University Press, 2002), pp. 91–116.

Vila, A. C., *Enlightenment and Pathology: Sensibility in the Literature and Medicine of Eighteenth-Century France* (Baltimore, MD: Johns Hopkins Press, 1998).

Wahl, C. W., 'Suicide as a Magical Act', in E. S. Edwin, S. Schneidman and N. L. Farberow (eds), *Clues to Suicide* (New York: McGraw-Hill, 1957).

Walz, R., *Pulp Surrealism: Insolent Popular Culture in Early Twentieth-Century Paris* (Berkeley, CA: University of California Press, 2000).

Watson, N. J., *Revolution and the Form of the British Novel 1790–1825* (Oxford: Clarendon Press, 1994).

Watt, J. R., 'Introduction', in J. R. Watt (ed.), *From Sin to Insanity: Suicide in Early Modern Europe* (Ithaca, NY: Cornell University Press, 2004), pp. 1–9.

—, 'Suicide, Gender, and Religion: The Case of Geneva', in J. R. Watt (ed.), *From Sin to Insanity: Suicide in Early Modern Europe* (Ithaca, NY: Cornell University Press, 2004), pp. 138–57.

Weir, A., *Sacrificial Logics: Feminist theory and the critique of identity* (New York: Routledge, 1996).

Weisman, 'Self-Destruction and Sexual Perversion', in E. S. Schneidman (ed.), *Essays in Self-Destruction* (New York: Science House, 1967), pp. 265–99.

Weiss, G., 'The Body as a Narrative Horizon', in J. J. Cohen and G. Weiss (eds), *Thinking the Limits of the Body* (Albany, NY: State University of New York Press, 2003), pp. 25–38.

Wellbery, C., 'From Mirrors to Images: The Transformation of Sentimental Paradigms in Goethe's The Sorrows of Young Werther', *Studies in Romanticism*, 25:2 (1986), pp. 231–49.

Wellbery, D., 'Morphisms of the Phantasmatic Body: Goethe's *The Sorrows of Young Werther*' in V. Kelly and D. von Mucke (eds), *Body and Text in the Eighteenth Century* (Stanford, CA: Stanford University Prses, 1994), pp. 67–91.

Wenk, S., 'Gendered Representations of the Nation's Past and Future', in I. Blom, K. Hagemann and C. Hall (eds), *Gendered Nations: Nationalisms and Gender Order in the Long Nineteenth Century* (Oxford: Berg, 2000), pp. 63–77.

Werth, J. (ed.), *Contemporary Perspectives on Rational Suicide* (Ann Arbor, MI: Braun-Brumfield, 1999).

Wikborg, E., 'Political Discourse versus Sentimental Romance: Ideology and Genre in Charlotte Smith's *Desmond*', *English Studies: A Journal of English Language and Literature*, 78 (1997), pp. 522–31.

Williams, C., '"Inhumanly Brought Back to Life and Misery": Mary Wollstonecraft, *Frankenstein*, and the Royal Humane Society', *Women's Writing*, 8:2 (2001), pp. 212–34.

Williams, E., *The Physical and the Moral: Anthropology, Physiology and Philosophical Medicine in France* (Cambridge: Cambridge University Press, 1994).

—, 'Medicine in the Civic Life of Eighteenth-Century Montpellier', *Bulletin of the History of Medicine*, 70:2 (1996), pp. 205–32.

Williamson, M., *Raising Their Voices: British Women Writers, 1650–1750* (Detroit, MI: Wayne State University Press, 1990).

Wilson, E. A., 'Gut Feminism', *differences: A Journal of Feminist Cultural Studies*, 15:3 (2004), pp. 66–94.

Wilson, J. P., '*Clarissa*: The Nation Misrul'd', in A. J. Rivero, G. Justice and M. Collins (eds), *The Eighteenth-Century Novel* (AMS Press, 2003), vol. 3, pp. 65–96.

Wilson, K., 'Citizenship, Empire, and Modernity in the English Provinces, *c.*1720–1790', *ECS*, 29:1 (1996): 69–96.

—, *The Island Race: Englishness, Empire and Gender in the Eighteenth Century* (London: Routledge, 2003).

Wolf, J., *The Social Production of Art* (New York: New York University Press, 1993).

Wolf, S. M., 'Gender, Feminism, and Death: Physician-Assisted Suicide and Euthanasia', in S. M. Wolf (ed.), *Feminism and Bioethics: Beyond Reproduction* (Oxford: Oxford University Press, 1996), pp. 282–317.

Wolfe, A., *Suicidal Narrative in Modern Japan* (Princeton, NJ: Princeton University Press, 1990).

Wolff, C. G., *Samuel Richardson and the Eighteenth-Century Puritan Character* (Hamden, CT: Shoestring Press, 1972).

Woodstock, L., 'Hide and Seek: The Paradox of Documenting a Suicide', *Text and Performance Quarterly*, 21:4 (2001), pp. 247–60

Wymer, R., *Suicide and Despair in the Jacobean Drama* (Sussex: Harvester Press, 1986).

Yadav, A., *Before the empire of English: literature, provinciality, and nationalism in eighteenth-century Britain* (New York: Palgrave Macmillan, 2004).

Yolton, J., *Thinking Matter: Materialism in the Eighteenth Century* (Minneapolis, MN: University of Minnesota Press, 1983).

Zias, H., 'Who Can Believe? Sentiment versus Cynicism in Richardson's *Clarissa*', *Eighteenth-Century Life*, 27:3 (2003), pp. 99–122.

Zigarovich, J., 'Courting Death: Necrophilia in Samuel Richardson's *Clarissa*', *Studies in the Novel*, 32: 2 (2000), pp. 12–28.

Zizek, S., *The Plague of Fantasies* (London: Verso, 1997).

—, 'The Act and its Vicissitudes', *The Symptom*, 6 (2005), pp. 1–3.

Zomchick, J., *Family and the Law in Eighteenth-Century Fiction: The Public Conscience in the Private Sphere* (Cambridge: Cambridge University Press, 1993).

Zonitch, B., *Familiar Violence: Gender and Social Upheaval in the Novels of Frances Burney* (Newark: University of Delaware Press, 1997).

Zuckerman, A., 'Plague and Contagionism in Eighteenth-Century England: The Role of Richard Mead', *Bulletin of the History of Medicine*, 78:2 (2004), pp. 273–308.

Bibliography of Journals and Newspapers

Anon., 'England's New Religion', *Daily Gazetteer,* 17 November 1738, p. 1053.

Anon., 'A late accident', *The Ladies Magazine*, 19 February 1747, p. 62.

Anon., 'The Last Guinea Club', *Connoisseur*, 9 January 1755, p. 297

Anon., 'Letters on the English Nation', *Monthly Review* XII, April and May 1755, pp. 387–8.

Anon., 'To Mr. Fitz-Adam', *World*, 23 September 1756, p. 185.

Anon., 'Some Observations on the Causes of Suicide', *Gentleman's Magazine*, vol. 26, 1756, p. 28.

Anon., 'A Receptacle for Suicides', *The World*, 9 September 1756, p. 169.

Anon., 'To Mr. Fitz Adam', *The World*, 23 September 1756, pp. 190–200, on p. 192.

Anon., 'Reflections on Suicide', *London Magazine* March 1762, pp. 144–6, on p. 144.

Anon., 'Review: Herbert Croft's *Love and Madness' The London Magazine* 1780, vol. 50, p. 179.

Wendeborn, Mr, 'On the Character of the English', *Literary Magazine and British Review* (London: C. Forster, 1791), pp. 193–7, on p. 196.

INDEX

Sterne, Laurence
    Tristram Shandy, 91
stigma, xi, 8, 38, 73, 89–90, 95, 110, 115,
    126, 129, 165, 179
Strenski, Ivan, 18, 20
sublimity, 136, 139, 160, 169–72
suffering, 73–4, 81, 142, 161, 171, 190
    Christ, 68
    pain, 170–1, 180
    see also martyrdom
Suglia, Joseph, 41
'suicide', term, 1–2
Suicide, The, 94
suicide attempts, 29
suicide bombers, xi
suicide notes, x, 41
    in novels
        Haywood's, 35–6, 41
        Lydia, 99–100
        Richard and Bridget Smith, 107, 126
survivors, x–xi, 4, 19
Sweet, Rosemary, 112
Sym, John, 45
sympathy, 29, 120–2

Tate, Nahum
    Present to the Ladies, 36
Taylor, Martha, 62
Thompson, E. P., 147
Thompson, Peggy, 68
time, 1, 27, 73, 84–5
Timmons, Jeffrey, 15
Tissot, S. A. D., 122, 128, 148
transnationalism, xvi, xvii, 10, 19, 126, 127,
    149, 152, 175, 182, 189, 190
Truman, James C. W. 16, 74
Trumpener, Katie, 47

Vaughn, Genevieve, 14
venereal disease, 105, 109–11, 113
victimhood, ix, 14, 27, 32, 51, 54
violence, 28, 125, 149
virtue, 10, 48, 92–3, 105
    British, 8

female, 29, 30, 55, 69, 76, 77, 101, 173
vitalism, xvi–xvii, 151–3, 155–6, 161–2,
    167–9, 181–3
    organismic, 172–3

Walpole, Horace, 102
war, 171–2
Weaver, John, x
Welbery, Caroline, 121
'Werther effect', xiv, xvi, 19, 115–23,
    127–31, 132–43, 145, 146, 149, 188,
Westminster Abbey, 101–2, 103–4, 111
Wikborg, Eleanor, 140
will (determination), ix, 18, 38, 64, 123, 131,
    134, 143, 148, 149, 157
    free, 67, 87
    to live, 86, 87
    Lucretia, 69
    in novels
        Clarissa, 54, 55, 57–60, 61–3, 65,
            67–8, 73, 82
        Haywood's, 29, 30, 49
    see also agency; death wish
will (testamentary), 60–1, 79, 85
Williams, Helen Maria, 136
    Julia, 147
Wilson, Kathleen, xiv
Wolf, Susan M., 17
Wolfe, Alan, 44
Wolff, Cynthia, 63–4
Wollstonecraft, Mary, 32, 159–60
women, 23–5, 26–7, 76, 180–1, 185–7
    identity, 68
    see also female suicide; femininity;
        feminism
World, The, 1, 10, 76, 96

Young, Edward, 82
    Night Thoughts, 184, 185

Zias, Heather, 66
Zigarovich, Jolene, 84
Žižek, Slavoj, 41, 81
Zomchick, John, 67